Suffering
from
Realness

MASS MoCA

DelMonico Books • Prestel
Munich London New York

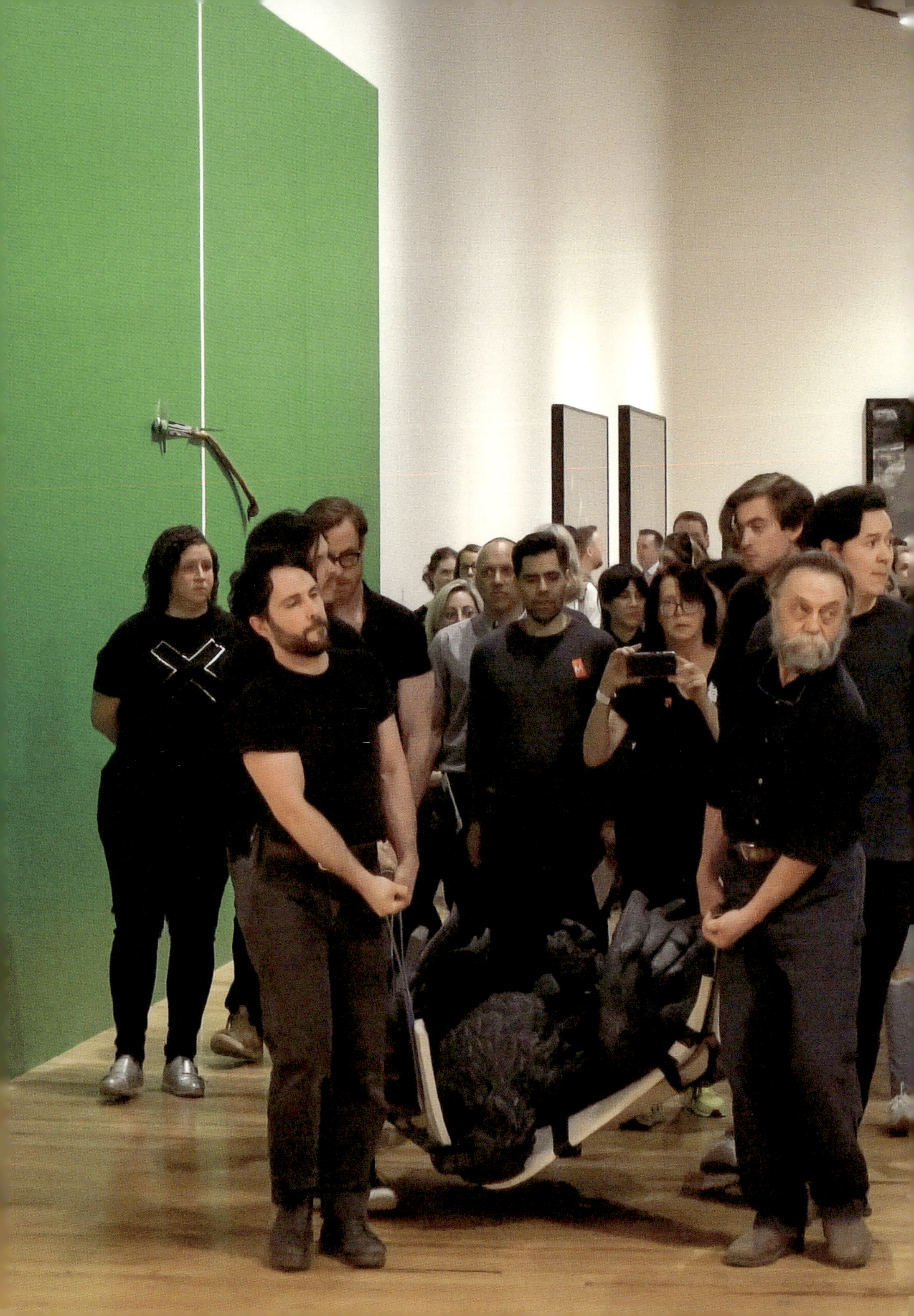

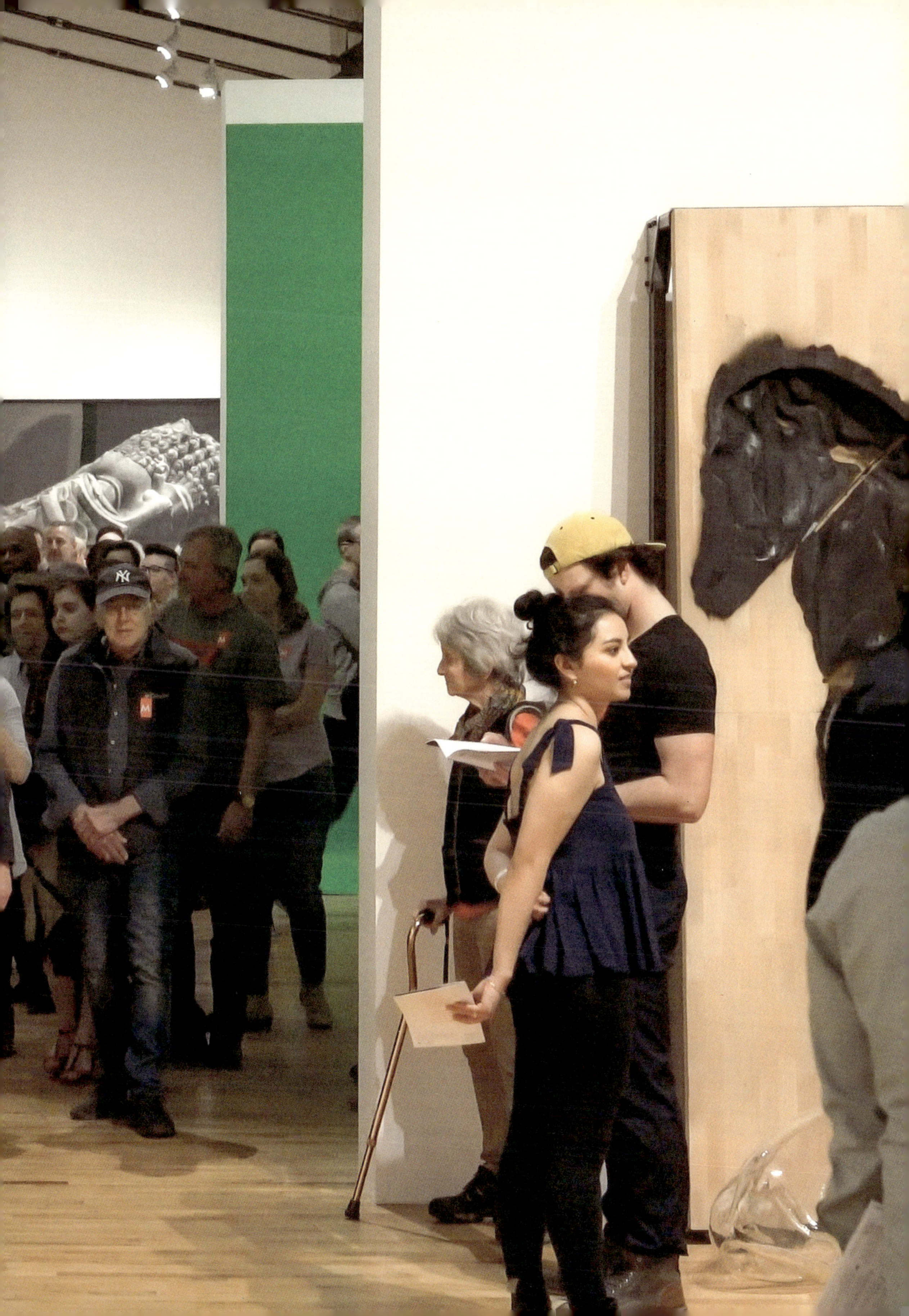

Section 2
The Body in Pain

Section 3
Finding Hope in the Dark

Foreword

—

The idea of truth has undergone a change of late. It used to be the liberal left who railed against the idea of a single, authoritative, objective reality, arguing instead for a multiplicity of points of view, a truth that came in many shades of gray. Currently, that's reversed, and the now-fact-checking left have suddenly become converts to the idea of one whole truth, while the right wing have come to the conclusion that a sort of parallel universe of alternative facts exists, sometimes by dint of proclamation and sheer audacity.

If it's bad in the United States, it's still a walk in the park compared to the utter breakdown of accepted norms of reality in Africa, where political leaders often have to defend their own identity, insisting that they are not clones of themselves, or mysterious body doubles. A recent *Wall Street Journal* headline read: "Nigerian President Attacked as Being Unreal." Even though Barack Obama has had to defend the location of his birth, and Donald Trump's claim on the legitimacy of his presidency seems to carry with it a permanent asterisk, at least no one seems to doubt the veracity of their very existence as human beings ... at least, not yet.

When the bonds of trust and our civil contract evaporate, life gets complicated. People once used the phrase "get real" when they wanted to say "you're being unrealistic," or "it's time to face reality here." But almost no one uses those phrases anymore: it's just too much to ask. The ground of truth has become fractured and contentious. However, all of this uncertainty makes a great backdrop for artists, whose job is to formulate and communicate their own reality. In a way, artists are now flying unopposed, as the realities and narratives of their art become every bit as solid as the world in which we walk and talk every day. The rules of engagement have changed, calling to mind a classic Gary Larson *Far Side* cartoon showing two fishermen in a small rowboat overflowing with fish, despite the posted limit of one keeper per person. In the background, we see an ominous mushroom cloud rising as one of the fishermen shrugs and says to the other, "All bets are off."

Suffering from Realness curator Denise Markonish writes about the sense of liberation that comes from making art during a time that can feel so precarious. If it's a slippery world out there, the artists of *Suffering from Realness* find a surprising number of ways to wrest hope, humor, and basic human empathy from a world in which the very meaning of words is under serious pressure. If the constant adjudication of facts is wearing us down, looking at art full of wit, sharp detail, and passion is restorative, stabilizing, and perhaps as real as it can get today.

I join Denise and the trustees in thanking the artists for their work, and also, everyone on the MASS MoCA staff whom help make these projects possible. Thank you to the lenders to the exhibition: the artists, Carol and David Kaplan, Dalal Ani and Zack Arnold, Alexandra and Ted Shor, Reginald and Aliya Brown, Ronald Feldman Gallery, David Shelton Gallery, Susanne Vielmetter Gallery, Metro Pictures Gallery, Carolina Nitsch+Elisabeth Ross Wingate, and Gladstone Gallery. And, of course, besides a lot of hard work and sweat equity, it also takes actual cash to gather and exhibit art, and for that we are kindly beholden to the Artist's Resource Trust, a fund of the Berkshire Taconic Community Foundation; lead support from Christopher and Alida Latham; contributing support from Bridget Rigas; and additional support from Caroline Cunningham and Donald Young. Generous funding for the exhibition catalog comes from the Elizabeth Firestone Graham Foundation. All programming at MASS MoCA is made possible in part by the Barr Foundation, Horace W. Goldsmith Foundation, and Mass Cultural Council.

—

Joseph C. Thompson
Director, MASS MoCA

What's Louis my killa?
What's drugs my deala?
What's that jacket, Margiela?

Doctors say I'm the illest
'Cause I'm suffering from realness

Introduction

These Days

—

And all things hushed.
Yet even in that silence a
new beginning, beckoning,
change appeared.

Rainer Maria Rilke,
Sonnets to Orpheus I (1922)

In 2009, we opened the exhibition *These Days: Elegies for Modern Times*, only my second show as a curator for MASS MoCA. The word hope was in the air. We were just exiting the Bush years and an exciting young candidate named Barack Obama was taking the world by storm. Artist Shepard Fairey made a poster of Obama with the word "hope" emblazoned across it. Would the United States elect its first African-American president? It sure would.

And soon Obama's hope became like a prophecy. I remember gathering with colleagues as we watched his inauguration with tears in our eyes and pride in our hearts. But I also remember thinking that this blind hope could be dangerous, because Obama had an awful lot of hard work ahead, taking office when the economic recovery from the Great Recession was still in its fragile beginnings. With that in mind I asked a group of six artists to respond to that moment—both the hope and the anxiety—with their own elegies. These artists—George Bolster, Chris Doyle, Micah Silver, Robert Taplin (who is also in *Suffering from Realness*), Sam Taylor-Wood, and Pawel Wojtasik—created poetic takes on things like the refugee crisis, the reckoning, apocalypse training, war, and Hurricane Katrina. The brochure for that show, named after chanteuse Nico's song of the same title, opened with the Rilke quote above. It seemed like the perfect encapsulation of what everyone was feeling—a quiet wait for change.

And while change did come, it was far more complicated than just fulfilling Obama's prophecy of hope. In the intervening years, a dark force started to rise in opposition to Obama's light: Donald Trump, a cartoonish reality star/real estate crook, was its most visible manifestation. As it became clear that Trump's bid for the presidency was real, and not a publicity stunt, I started to formulate the exhibition that would become *Suffering from Realness*. It began as a meditation on how artists utilize representation and imagery to infuse art and our shared lives with new and different voices, a more robust representation of race, a more fluid view of gender, and a wider array of lived experiences. Then in 2011, Jay-Z and Kanye West released the album *Watch the Throne*, which included the song "Ni**as in Paris." In the song, West raps: "Doctors say I'm the illest, 'cause I'm suffering from realness." I remember rewinding that song over and over, listening, trying to understand the phrase, and thinking: "That would be a great title for a show!"

This title hung around in the back of my mind as I started to compile lists of artists to visit and with whom to engage. It became clear that the idea of realness was slippery: what is real to one person may not seem real to someone else. It touched on the phrase "truthiness," coined by Stephen Colbert about the Bush administration, and its precarity became more apparent when phrases like "fake news" and "alternative facts" were bandied about. Were we entering an era where truth had died, and if so, did it take the whole idea of "realness" with it? It soon became clear that this was not the case, in fact, the truthier things became, the more real we felt them to be.

In 2016, Trump was elected. I was in Texas with an artist who said to me, with tears in her eyes, "How can I keep making art? How will it matter?" I was stunned but answered, "Because you have to, and it will."

I still believe that.

Over the years of working on this show and talking with the artists, it has become apparent that while there is great suffering in living within the real, there is also great reward. The reward comes when the community unites in times like these, to sustain one another, to fight for the basic human rights that matter to us most, and to laugh out loud at the absurdity of our political reality today. All of the artists in this show do just that, and I am proud to bring them together, creating a powerful vortex of all things real.

This book does that too. I am honored to include poems by Solmaz Sharif and Saul Williams, alongside essays by Andy Campbell and Rebecca Rickman, and a new short parable by Jesse Ball. Together, these texts address history, technology, empathy in the face of tyranny, and the (sometimes thin) margins of day-to-day life. Also included are the artists' voices, in the form of interviews, each answering a set of seven questions posed by some of today's most varied thinkers: Fred Moten, Adam Curtis, Aruna D'Souza, Gonzalo Casals, Michael Weber, Cat Gund, and Elaine Scarry. I asked each of these people what they might want to hear from artists about the state of the human condition today; the answers are full of both rage and tenderness.

I think, strange as it might seem, that the world is more hopeful today than when Obama's slogan first came to light. I say this not because of how policy is being made, or how some of those we trust to lead are behaving. I say this because people finally seem moved to act. Seeing the next generation coming together—young people like Emma González standing before a crowd of millions in silent fury at an anti-gun rally—caring and demanding a better future, gives me hope, at any rate.

I am reminded of that Nico song, "These Days," which served as the title for the exhibition ten years ago, particularly the line, "These days I seem to think about/ How all the changes came about my ways/ And I wonder if I'll see another highway."

It's not nostalgia to think this way, because it is important to take stock of the changes of the past to realize that, with concrete action, with realness, we will in fact see another highway.

—

Denise Markonish
Senior Curator,
Managing Director
of Exhibitions

following page:
Kanye West visiting with James Turrell in *Perfectly Clear* at MASS MoCA, December 27, 2018

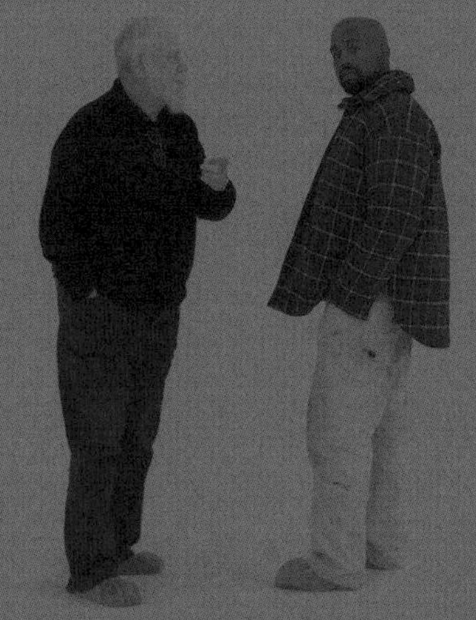

Rewriting the History of Our Future[1]

—

Denise Markonish

"Cadillacs, Coca-Cola and cocaine, presidents and psychopaths, Norman Rockwell and the mafia ... the dream of America endlessly unravels its codes, like the helix of some ideological DNA. But what would happen if we took the United States at its face value and constructed an alternative America?" —J. G. Ballard[2]

In the introduction to his 1981 book *Hello America*, J. G. Ballard asks for an alternative America. However, on November 8, 2016, Ballard seemed like a prophet. His book, from the Reagan years, tells the story of an expedition to America—a barren wasteland following a late-twentieth-century energy crisis. The characters land in New York City to see a sunken Statue of Liberty; they travel across the country vying for power, even arguing about who gets to squat in the now empty White House. When they reach Las Vegas, they find another human, a man calling himself "Charles Manson," who declares that he is the forty-fifth president of the United States. Manson surrounds himself with robots of past presidents, like a Disney World exhibit run amok. At one point in the book, Manson tells Wayne, one of the main characters, that he wants to "make America great again."[3]

Doctors Say I'm the Illest 'Cause I'm Suffering from Realness

Of course, "Make America Great Again" was a slogan used by Ronald Reagan in 1980, so Ballard is less of a seer and his words are more of a reminder that history is cyclical. On that fateful day in November 2016, it seemed nearly impossible, to liberal America, that Donald Trump had been elected. This xenophobic clown, with his long tie flapping in the wind and absurd frothy comb-over, was a corrupt real estate tycoon and reality show host, not a president. Ballard wasn't alone in his prescience, for in 1988 the band REM released the song "World Leader Pretend," with Michael Stipe singing eerily contemporary lyrics about knowing weapons and building walls, saying "I demand a rematch" and "This is my world and I am world leader pretend."[4] With these prophetic offerings, liberal America should not have been surprised that Trump got elected, for the signs have long been there. In his 2016 documentary for the BBC, *HyperNormalisation*, filmmaker Adam Curtis outlines the trajectory leading to Trump. The film begins with Curtis, in voice-over, stating that "we live in a strange time. Extraordinary events keep happening that undermine the stability of our world ... over the past forty years, politicians, financiers and technological utopians, rather than face up to the real complexities of the world, retreated. Instead, they constructed a simpler version of the world in order to hang on to power. And as this fake world grew, all of us went along with it because the simplicity was reassuring. Even those who thought they were attacking the system—the radicals, the artists, the musicians, and our whole counterculture—actually became part of the trickery, because they, too, had retreated into the make-believe world, which is why their opposition has no effect and nothing ever changes."[5]

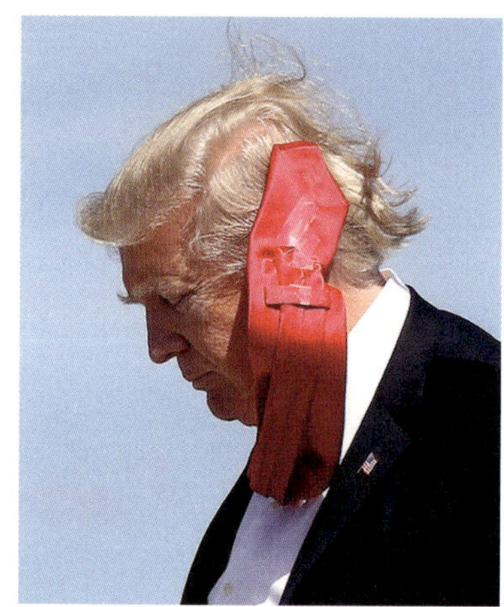

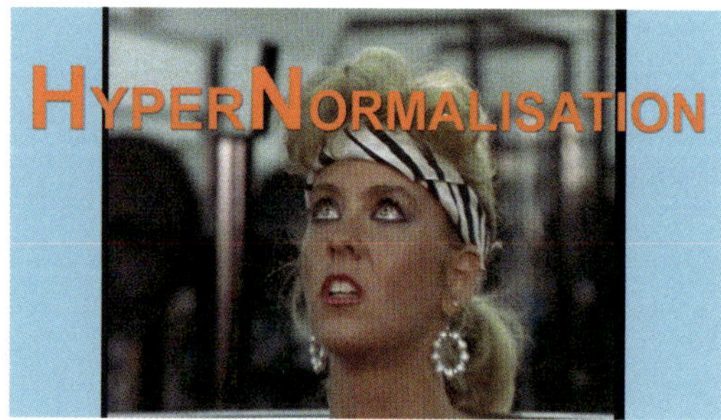

Curtis borrows the phrase "hypernormalisation" from Russian author Alexei Yurchak, who used it to describe the acceptance of false beliefs, fed to the citizens of Russia by its government in the period of late socialism (1960s–1970s), and the subsequent breakdown of trust, truth, and citizenship.[6] Curtis traces a similar path in America, particularly as it relates to foreign affairs with the Middle East. The film opens in Manhattan in 1975 as the city, on the brink of financial collapse, looks toward banks for bailouts. This leads young entrepreneurs like Donald Trump to begin buying up cheap real estate with government tax breaks, turning New York City into a home for the rich. Paralleling this, Curtis goes deep into the US relationship with the Middle East, including the Reagan administration's use of Muammar Gaddafi as a pawn to fracture countries in the region, most evident in the angering of Syria's then president Hafez al-Assad, leading to the use of suicide bombing as a deadly weapon. The film goes on to discuss the rise of the Internet as a space of retreat from reality and ends with a discussion of Russian president Vladimir Putin's relationship with Trump.

Curtis's film was released just before the 2016 presidential election, before perception management and truthiness turned into alternative facts and fake news, before we felt nostalgic for the buffoonery of George W. Bush, and before civil liberties were taken away as nonchalantly as lollipops before dinnertime. We are in an era where realness is under suspicion, but watching Curtis's film reminds us that it has been this way for a long time. In 2011, Jay-Z and Kanye West released the album *Watch the Throne*, including the song "Ni**as in Paris," on which West raps: "Doctors say I'm the illest / 'cause I'm suffering from realness." This lyric presaged the musician's over-the-top public behavior and mental-health issues.

left:
***HyperNormalisation*, 2016, directed by Adam Curtis for the BBC**

right:
Donald Trump (photo by Joe Burbank/Orlando Sentinel/TNS via Getty Images)

West addressed these struggles on 2018 albums like *Ye* and in collaboration with Kid Cudi on *Kids See Ghosts*. On the latter album's track "Reborn," West vulnerably states, "I was off the chain, I was often drained / I was off the meds, I was called insane / What an awesome thing, engulfed in shame."[7] Most recently, to the shock and awe of many, West was seen smiling next to Trump in his own reinterpretation of the "Make America Great Again" red baseball cap that had become so ubiquitous during the 2016 presidential campaign. Then,

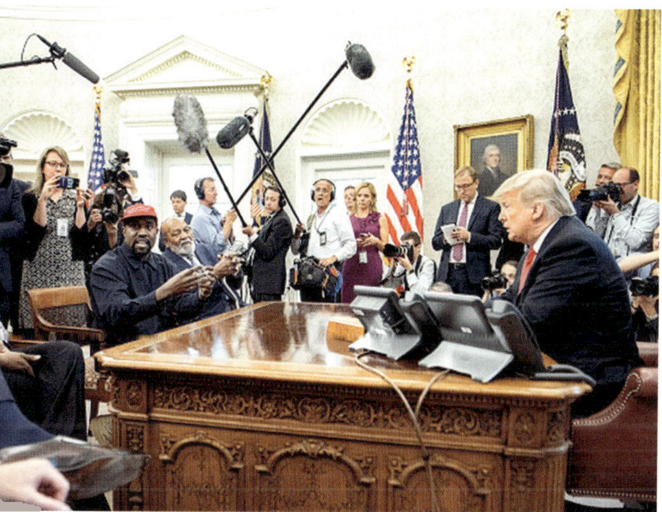

in the early days of 2019, West took to Twitter endorsing the President yet again.[8] Was this a publicity stunt? It's hard to know, but it gives increased weight to West's 2011 phrasing. Because "suffering from realness," both the phrase and this exhibition, begs the question, "what exactly is realness?" and asks artists working in America to answer this call.[9]

Perhaps realness is that jolt we felt when Trump was elected. However, while this radical shift from the compassion of Barack Obama to the inhumanity of Trump may have started with a retreat to the hypernormal, the apathy lasted only briefly. Instead, many Americans have woken up from the stupor of the last forty years. In her 2018 book, *Call Them By Their True Names*, Rebecca Solnit discusses this very awakening, stating, "I find great hope and encouragement in the anxiety, fury, and grief of my fellow residents of the United States. It's not that I'm eager to see people suffer but that I'm relieved that so many are so far from indifferent. I feared after the election that those of us who are not directly targeted would do what people have often done during despotic regimes: withdraw into private life, wait it out, take care of themselves and no one else. Something else happened instead."[10]

This "something else" that Solnit talks about came in the form of action: the Women's March gathering more than three million protesters on January 21, 2017, just one day after Trump's inauguration; #metoo calling out against sexual harassment; the February 14, 2018, fatal school shooting in Parkland, Florida, and the subsequent founding of Never Again MSD, a student-led political action committee for gun control; Emma González, survivor of the Parkland shooting, standing on stage for six minutes and twenty seconds, the duration of the shooting, at the March for Our Lives on March 24, 2018; the clearheaded testimony of Dr. Christine Blasey Ford against Brett Kavanaugh for sexual harassment charges; and the 2018 mid-term elections, which saw a number of firsts in electoral

Kanye West, Jim Brown, and Donald Trump in the White House (photo by Ron Sachs/Consolidated News Pictures/Getty Images)

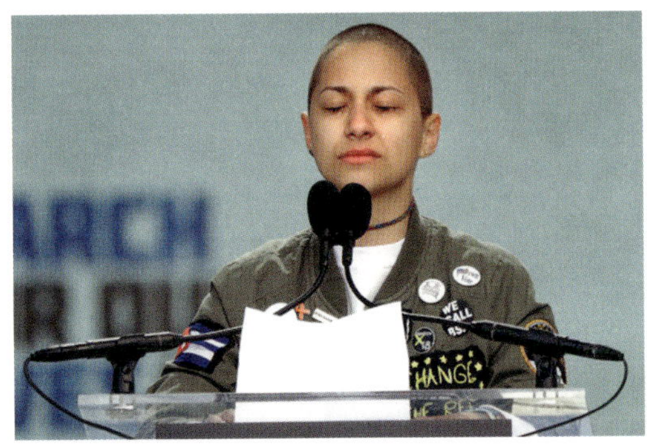

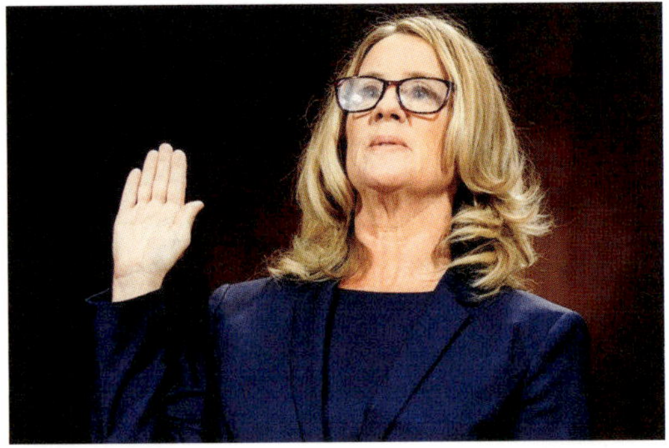

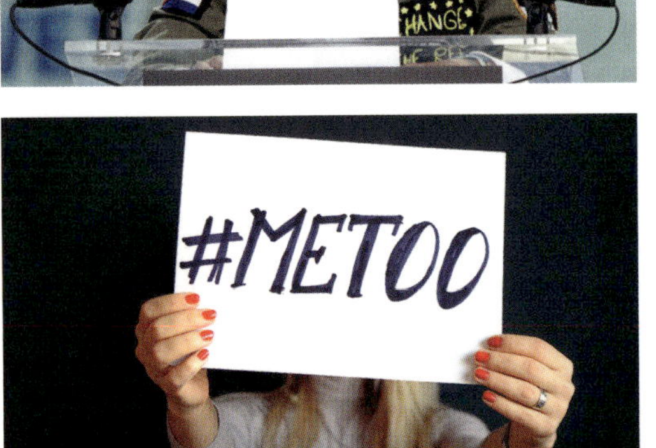

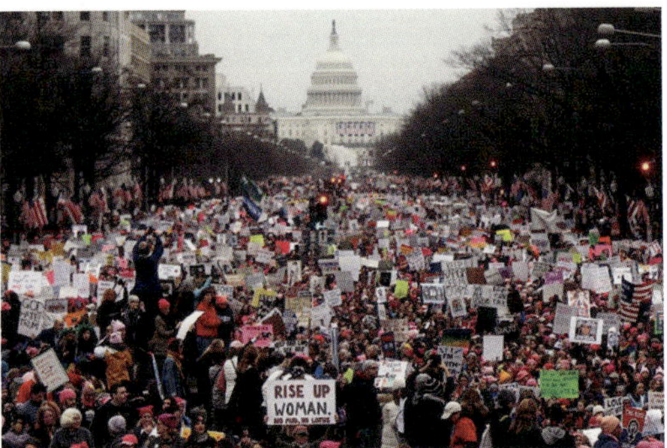

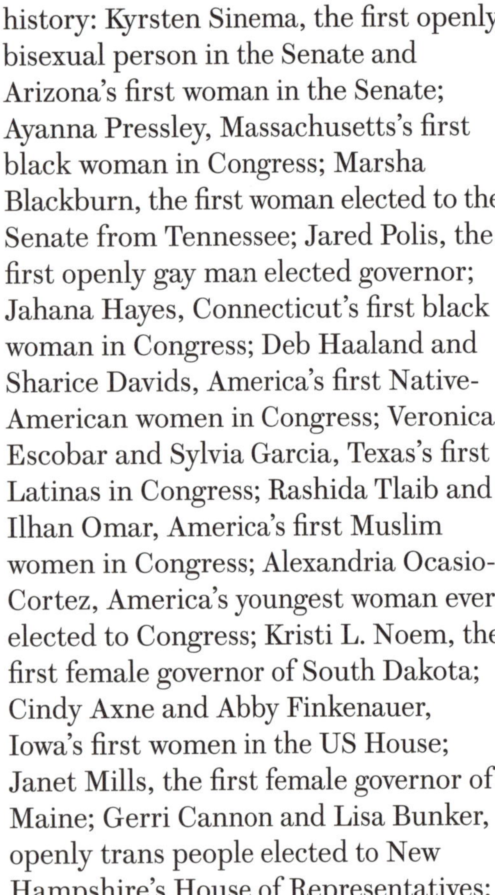

history: Kyrsten Sinema, the first openly bisexual person in the Senate and Arizona's first woman in the Senate; Ayanna Pressley, Massachusetts's first black woman in Congress; Marsha Blackburn, the first woman elected to the Senate from Tennessee; Jared Polis, the first openly gay man elected governor; Jahana Hayes, Connecticut's first black woman in Congress; Deb Haaland and Sharice Davids, America's first Native-American women in Congress; Veronica Escobar and Sylvia Garcia, Texas's first Latinas in Congress; Rashida Tlaib and Ilhan Omar, America's first Muslim women in Congress; Alexandria Ocasio-Cortez, America's youngest woman ever elected to Congress; Kristi L. Noem, the first female governor of South Dakota; Cindy Axne and Abby Finkenauer, Iowa's first women in the US House; Janet Mills, the first female governor of Maine; Gerri Cannon and Lisa Bunker, openly trans people elected to New Hampshire's House of Representatives; and more.[11] Despite these victories, it is important not to become complacent, or go hypernormal, thinking that these changes are the signal of a turnaround. Kavanaugh was still elected to the Supreme Court and the NRA still has a stranglehold over gun-control laws. But this is remarkable progress, which can and should not be discounted. It reminds us that, as Australian comedian Hannah Gadsby said in her 2018 Netflix

clockwise from top left:

Emma González address: hundreds of thousands attend March for Our Lives rally in Washington, DC, March 24, 2018 (photo by Chip Somodevilla/Getty Images)

Washington, DC — September 27, 2018: Christine Blasey Ford swears in at a Senate Judiciary Committee hearing on Capitol Hill (photo by Melina Mara/Pool/The Washington Post via Getty Images)

Thousands attend Women's March on Washington, with the US Capitol in the background, January 21, 2017, in Washington, DC (photo by Mario Tama/Getty Images)

Woman holding "#metoo" sign. (photo by Mihai Surdu/Unsplash)

special, *Nanette*, "Your resilience is your humanity." And through this resilience we have to continue to stand up and let our voices be heard.

Stop, Children, What's That Sound, Everybody Look What's Going Down

Throughout history, art has served as a platform, a mountain, a rooftop from which to shout about suffering from realness. From Francisco Goya (1746–1828) and Leon Golub (1922–2004) all the way to the present, artists recognize their responsibility to speak to their time. Goya's *The Disasters of War (Los desastres de la Guerra)* (1810–20), a suite of eighty-two prints chronicling the Spanish resistance to Napoleon's army during the Peninsular War (1808–14), is one example. These images show piles of bodies, violence, and futile attempts at perseverance. But what makes

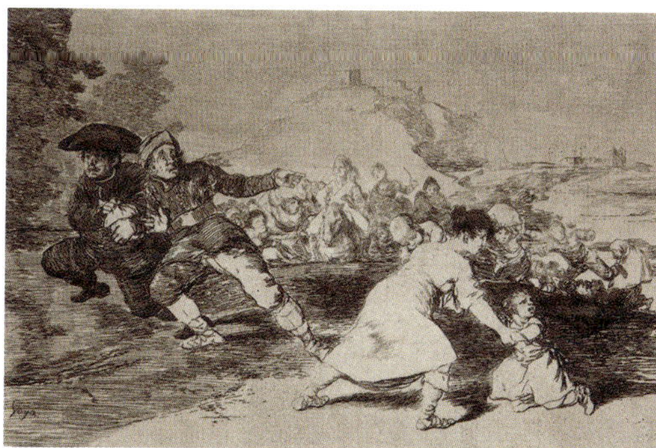

Francisco Goya, *The Disasters of War (Los desastres de la Guerra)*, plate No. 44 (1st edition, Madrid: Real Academia de Bellas Artes de San Fernando, 1863)

them unique is that rather than depict the heroes of war, as did many of his contemporaries, Goya chose to focus on dehumanizing destruction. Of this work, Susan Sontag writes: "The ghoulish cruelties in *The Disasters of War* are meant to awaken, shock, wound the viewer. Goya's art, like Dostoyevsky's, seems a turning point in the history of moral feelings and of sorrow—as deep, as original, as demanding. With Goya, a new standard for responsiveness to suffering enters art.... The account of war's cruelties is fashioned as an assault on the sensibility of the viewer."[12] In the face of such a wakeup call, art that valorizes nationalism seems almost saccharine. Just look at Norman Rockwell's (1894–1978) *Four Freedoms (Freedom of Speech, Freedom of Worship, Freedom From Want*, and *Freedom From Fear*; 1943)—at an abundant Thanksgiving table, the diners (all with Caucasian faces) smile at the American dream. A dream only available to some.

Counter to Rockwell's Americana are the European artists of the two World Wars, such as George Grosz (1893–1959), Otto Dix (1891–1969), Käthe Kollwitz (1867–1945), and Pablo Picasso (1881–1973). Both Grosz and Dix served in the German Army during WWI, volunteering to fight for their country. However, this did not result in patriotism; instead they chose to depict the harsh realities of war. Dix's *Stormtroopers Advancing Under Gas* (1924) depicts a terrifying mob of soldiers in gas masks, arms raised as they advance toward the picture plane, while Grosz's portfolio of prints from 1919 to 1920, *God With Us* (a phrase inscribed on the belt buckles of German soldiers), depicts the artist's deep disdain for the capitalist military, representing those in charge as absurdist caricatures. It is hard to not see Trump in these figures, posturing across the page like Ubu Roi, the absurdist king from Alfred Jarry's 1896 play of the same name, with his rotund belly and a pin-shaped head that resembles the hooded cloaks of the Ku Klux Klan.

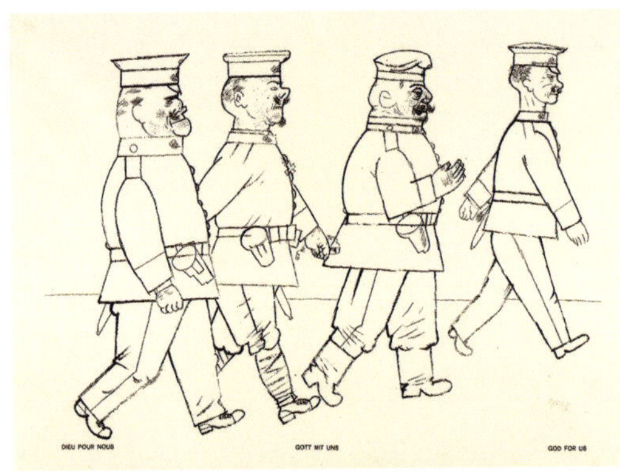

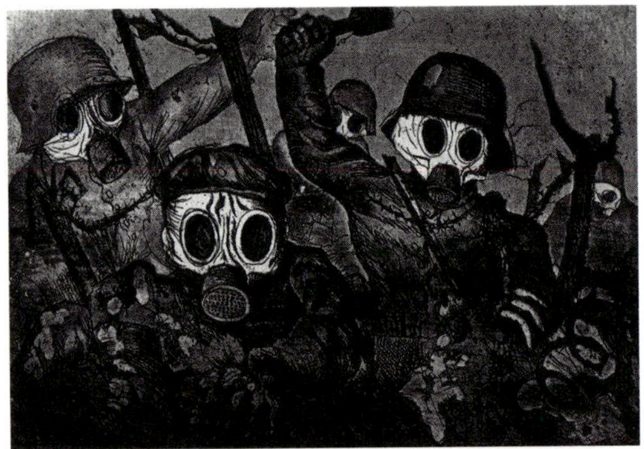

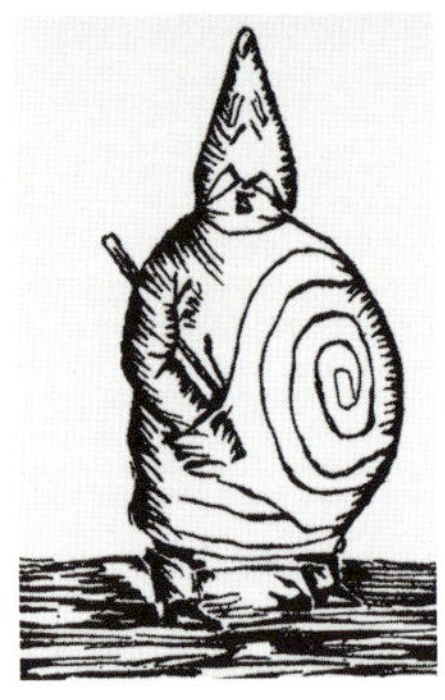

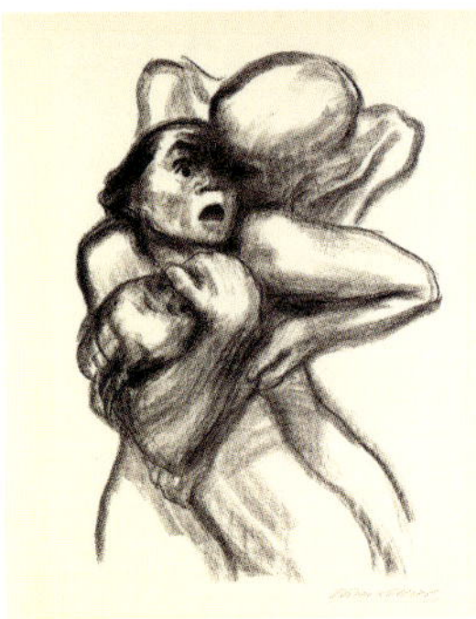

This use of caricature and farce exists alongside images of anguish similar to those seen in Goya's *The Disasters of War*. This suffering is evident in Kollwitz's *Death* (1934–7) prints, which depict the figure of death—a shadowy man—taking over the most vulnerable members of society: women and children. In *Death Seizes a Woman* (1934), we see a mother clutching a child, as death wraps its cold arms around them both. The anguish on the mother's face is palpable, not unlike Picasso's *Guernica* (1937), his response to the Nazis' bombing of the eponymous Basque town during the Spanish Civil War. The grisaille painting, stretching twenty-five feet long and eleven feet tall, depicts a trampling bull, a symbol of military power, and a braying horse that calls out against the onslaught of war. As with Kollwitz, perhaps the most poignant element of Picasso's painting is the depiction in the lower left corner of a wailing mother holding her dead child defiantly in the face of the bull—asking it, and us, to bear witness to brutality.

This aim to show the face of suffering also became a driving force for artists working in the United States. Abandoning Rockwell's nuclear family, artists such as Golub, his wife Nancy Spero (1926–2009), the collective Group Material (active, 1979–96), and Jenny Holzer instead showed us a new America, a real America, suffering and all. In the 1960s and 1970s, distraught over the Vietnam War, Golub and Spero made work in the tradition of Dix, Grosz, Kollwitz, and Picasso. Golub's *Vietnam II* (1973)—an unstretched canvas of over forty feet by nine feet—shows a group of American soldiers brandishing machine guns in front of an armored car. Their presence is beyond menacing. However, the focal point of the painting is a group of Vietnamese citizens, mouths agape in fear. A large

clockwise from top:

George Grosz, *God with us (Gott mit uns)*, from the portfolio *God with Us (Gott mit uns)*, 1919 (published 1920)

Otto Dix, *Stormtroopers Advancing Under Gas (Sturmtruppe geht unter Gas vor)* from *The War (Der Krieg)*, 1924

Käthe Kollwitz, *Death Seizes a Woman (Tod packt eine Frau)*, 1934

Alfred Jarry, Representation of Père Ubu, c. 1896

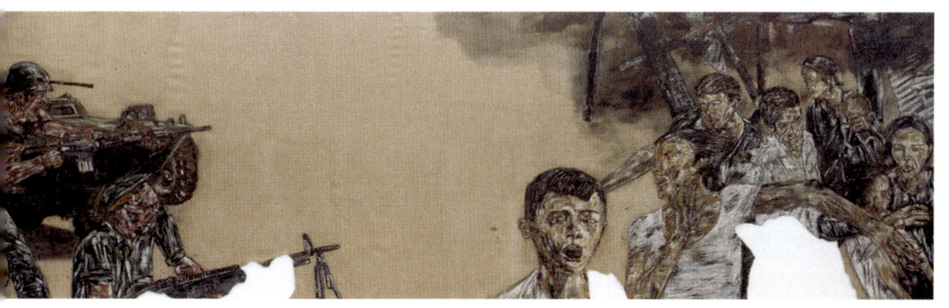

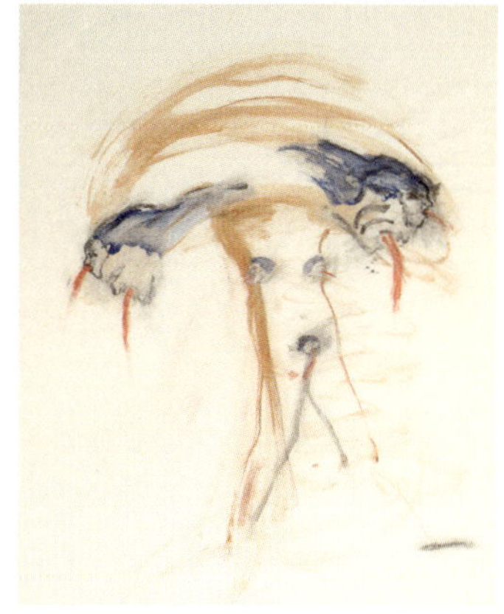

gap of neutral canvas divides the two groups, much like the gap between the warring government and citizens such as Golub, who protested the invasion. Tension in empty space is also evident in the work of Spero, whose *The War Series* (1966–70) was created as a result of the politics of Vietnam. Rendered in gouache on paper, the drawings show the rage of war and the dissonance of violence. Like those of Golub, Spero's works contain copious amounts of negative space, creating a vast tension between action, both ended and predicted, and aftermath.

In the 1980s, artists continued to address society's injustices, from Group Material's[13] 1989 mixed-media work reconstructing the history of the AIDS epidemic and the government's complicit ignorance of those suffering, to Holzer's chilling paintings rendered from available redacted documents of wars in Iraq and Afghanistan, including the handprints of civilians who died at Abu Ghraib (fingers curled in rigor mortis). So where does this history bring us? History is a continuum, leading the artists of today to grab the ring of realness from their predecessors in order to continue to show suffering head on, hoping for a future. In her book, *The Art of Cruelty*, Maggie Nelson writes: "The most interesting work—past, present, or future—is or will be that which dismantles, boycotts, ignores, destroys, takes liberties with, or at least pokes fun at the avant-garde's long commitment to the idea that the shocks produced by cruelty and violence—be it in art or in political action—might deliver us, through some never-proven miracle, to a more sensitive, insightful, enlivened, collaborative, and just way of inhabiting the earth, and of relating to our fellow human beings."[14] This dismantling may be ugly business, but cynicism will get us nowhere. Instead, we must regain control of reality, evacuating the hypernormal. This awakening is present in Curtis's strategic use of the 1979 anthem "Dream Baby Dream," by the band Suicide, in *HyperNormalisation*. Alan Vega's sonorous voice reminds us to "Dream Baby Dream / Keep those dreams burnin' / Those dreams keep you free / You gotta make them dreams come true / So keep holdin' on / Dream Baby Dream / Forever."[15]

What Condition My Condition Was In

In order to dream baby dream, it is imperative to understand what one is dreaming for—what is one's

left to right:
Leon Golub, *Vietnam II*, 1973

Nancy Spero, *Female Bomb*, 1966

understanding of the human condition. This complex state encompasses the personal and universal, and topics such as racism, violence, gender equality, the politicized body, the anxious body, the complexity of responsibility, and the future. It is impossible to consider the human condition without entertaining both sides of the coin: the hope and also the crisis. Elaine Scarry writes that "it will gradually become apparent that at particular moments when there is within a society a crisis of belief—that is, when some central idea or ideology or cultural construct has ceased to elicit a population's belief either because it is manifestly fictitious or because it has for some reason been divested of ordinary forms of substantiation—the sheer material factualness of the human body will be borrowed to lend that cultural construct the aura of 'realness' and 'certainty.'"[16] In 2016, we found ourselves in such a precarious situation, in a crisis of belief, where the auras of realness and certainty have come under threat. It is in such moments that we often turn to artists to reveal some truths—Goya and Picasso did just that, and the artists in *Suffering from Realness* take up this charge.

Robert Taplin's figurative works get to the heart of what it means to be human, and his *History of Punch* series (2005–18) is no exception. In these works, "Punch" is Punchinello, the sixteenth-century Neapolitan trickster character derived from the commedia dell'arte, and most popularly known from the children's puppet shows, "Punch and Judy." These skits often involve slapstick and violence, which Taplin found to be an ideal metaphor for how people treat each other in contemporary society. Punch is a character, but it's also an action that our gut feels in the midst of this crisis of uncertainty. Taplin says, "Punch is a figure of aggravated ambivalence. His comic vulgarity, lack of inhibitions, and his apparent absolution from the normal requirements of society make him a figure of abuse and fascination. He is both a pariah and a free spirit, an alien among us who demonstrates the power of shame and guilt by ignoring them completely." He goes on to say that Punch "also clearly wields considerable power, the power of the despised, the unknown, the exotic, the outsider. We would like to ignore him or just get rid of him, but we recognize him. We don't trust him, but, under the right circumstances, we might even follow him. We watch him with a queasy fascination and lingering self-reproach."[17] In Taplin's description, Punch doesn't seem far from the politicians we see posturing in the news: grotesque and power hungry.

The works in this series are rendered in all white, ghosts of sorts, with Punch in a commedia dell'arte clown costume.

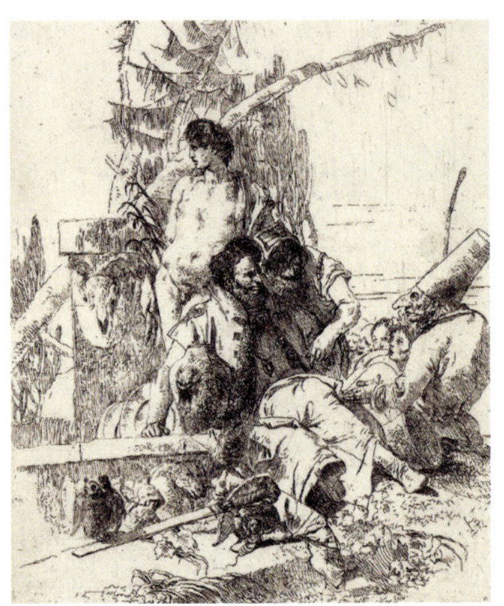

Giovanni Battista Tiepolo (1696–1770), Puchinello Gives Counsel from the series *Scherzi di Fantasia*, c. 1743–57

In *Punch Makes a Public Confession* (2014), Taplin created a larger-than-life-size version of the character at a podium, greeting visitors at the entrance to the exhibition. This unlikely mascot is silent, forever before speech. One hand rests across his heart and his head is slightly lowered in mock sincerity; Taplin arrests this moment, eternally keeping Punch from revealing anything to us, turning his secrets into power and reminding us that politics is performance. Other works balance absurdity with poignancy, such as *Punch Stopped at the Border* (2005), which depicts a border guard handcuffing Punch, whose bags are splayed open at his feet. Momentarily, we may feel bad, but then we notice a wicked grin on Punch's face. He looks right at us, defiant in the face of authority. In this moment, we know Punch has something to hide. Perhaps that something is revealed in *Punch Does a Magic Trick* (2018), in which our clown pulls a sheet off a table in one ta-da movement, only to reveal a small nuclear mushroom cloud exploding underneath. Punch looks pleased with his trick, reminding us that power is not to be trusted.

The absurdity of power endures in Aziz + Cucher's work, which often utilizes costuming, clown figures, patterns, and other tropes of corporate culture. Their new multi-channel video installation, *You're Welcome, and I'm Sorry* (2019), takes the form of a Dadaist romp through the global financial crisis, which began in 2008 and continues to be felt today. The videos, shot on an iPhone, follow two sets of costumed characters, some wearing masks made from shirts, neckties, and deconstructed power suits. One figure even has a series of cascading ties running all the way from neck to floor (making Trump's tie seem stumpy in comparison). Abruptly interspersed with these figures is another group of costumed characters that imply the specter of white supremacy, dressed in white overalls and masks printed with photographs of people pulled from the Internet. Together, these characters inhabit an installation that is kaleidoscopic and carnivalesque, with screens of various sizes, a pulsating soundtrack intercut with multilingual ranting, and walls conjuring the circus with stripes of colors derived from bank logos. For Aziz + Cucher, this work addresses the economic inequalities that polarize our country, and aims to create a "visceral space that reflects on the irrational forces that mold our political and economic systems and where the characters embody wildly divergent emotions: from menace to absurdity to despair to despondency."[18]

This work breaks from reality, as Aziz + Cucher film their characters in front of green screens, a cinematic device used to place different backdrops behind filmed action. This technique reminds us that reality is often constructed. Aziz + Cucher then drop their chimerical characters, dancing, stomping, and gesticulating, into various scenes, from hi-tech rooms with scrolling data screens to the site of the World Economic Forum in Davos, an Alpine resort in Switzerland. This annual meeting is a breeding ground for an elite mix of international business owners, politicians, and celebrities, with the aim to "improve the state of the world."[19] Davos, as the meeting is called colloquially, is seen by some as a liberal haven to discuss open borders, free trade, and globalization; others criticize it as a place where "the world's luminaries come together ... for the sake of coming together; it's a networking event dressed up as a mega-seminar on policy."[20] So, it is fitting that part of Aziz + Cucher's video was filmed in this location. Their characters are like aliens, but somehow they seem to fit right in at Davos, evoking the shamanistic qualities and mystifying belief structures inherent to financial and political power. This chaotic farce reminds us of the absurdity of power, and, in the end, recalls poet Wisława Szymborska's *Children of Our Age*, in which she writes, "Whether you like it or not, / your genes have a political past, / your skin, a political cast, your eyes, a political slant ... To acquire a political meaning / you don't even have to be human. / Raw material will do, / or protein feed, or crude oil."[21] Power and absurdity rolled into one.

MPA's installation *1, 2, 3, For* (2019) also pulls back the veil to expose the reality beneath. Her work grapples with the notion of what is real in a society where loose facts and reinforced binaries run to wild proliferation. MPA starts with transgender activist, science fiction author, and feminist tarot expert Rachel Grace Pollack. Pollack is not simply interested in divination and fortune telling; rather, she states that Tarot is a work of "spiritual imagination ... a teaching on cleansing ourselves of our fears and guilt so that we may open the heart to divine mystery."[22] For MPA, this cleansing is an essential part of recapturing what is real. MPA aims to get closer to realness by exploring numerology, in particular numbers 0 to 4. This serves as the basis for delving into binaries such as the cardinal directions, alpha and omega, and the Tarot suits (swords, cups, wands, and coins or disks) to illuminate the behavior of socially dominant binary distinctions such as gender, class, race, etc. MPA reveals that binaries are constructed realities, and that in these constructed sites there exists a place of suffering, a place where we are forced into "either/or" boxes. To break these confines, MPA looks toward Pollack's "spiritual imagination" and encourages magic as a means to dismantle the boxes.

As visitors approach MPA's installation, they are confronted by four walls painted with green-screen paint. This device sets up the work as a site of theater, where binaries and their disempowerment are on display. This is where the numerology is enacted. The walls of the installation make up the 4; 3 is a sword being split in two by a wand (giving us 3 pieces). The Tarot suits, swords and wands, signify power/authority and the action of the will, respectively. Here the sword becomes the violence of society, and the only power strong enough to defeat it, to cleave it, is the wand of human will, of magic. Next, 2 appears on facing walls in the form of a pair of ultramarine circles, signifying alpha and omega—the beginning and the end. But rather than being level or equal to one another they are off center, immediately breaking the binary power of the pair. On the last wall is 1—a crack breaking the plane of the wall and spreading from 0, which is a hole in the wall, allowing us to peer behind its reality. At the center of the installation an ammonite fossil is embedded in the floor. This fossil originally came from a prehistoric sea creature believed to have lived 65 million years ago, and has a distinctively inwardly spiral shape, much like a Fibonacci spiral, which mathematicians consider an infinite equation. The ammonite, due to its age and distinct geometry, is believed to have great healing power. Here, it serves as the center of energy, above which a pendulum swings in the four cardinal directions—north, south, east, and west. Together, these elements point to the complexity and beauty of relationships that organize our species, representing them as an ever-expanding spiral. Within this vortex, we might consider the strictures, seductions, and illusions of binaries. One last look at the green walls, and we notice that the façade is sliding and peeling away to reveal the inner guts of the wall, reminding us of the reality beneath the theater.

MPA's peeling walls enhance the slippage of reality, which is further explored in Keith Sklar's paintings and installation. As a painter, Sklar builds up surfaces, layering image upon image and casting kitsch objects in paint, before attaching the deflated skins to the surfaces of his already dense compositions. In *Swell* (2019), from afar we see garish colors and patterns over the surface; there is a tangle of nude bodies—part art history, part pornography. At this distance, the painting reads flat; however, upon close inspection it is evident that there are two canvases attached to one another, with the deflated cast paint bubbling across their surfaces like recently burst pustules. Up close, the work becomes all texture and the bodies are more felt than seen. Works like this sit next to paintings such as *Declaration* (2019), an anxious canvas with text scrawled across the surface: Im Mobilized; Im Paled; Im Mortal; Im Proper. Sklar attempts to eradicate the words, smearing their surfaces, obscuring their visibility, but never erasing them. This impotent gesture reminds us that the words always bleed back to the surface. In Sklar's hand these words—immobilized, impaled, immortal, improper—become a concrete poem, revealing the dichotomy, anger, and guilt of struggling with the human condition as a middle-class white male.

These paintings are the Greek chorus to *Sitting Down for a Drink with My Shadow* (2019) an installation in which the world is a-tilt and the human condition melts directly into the floor. This composition contains paintings and installation elements, beginning with a tilted wall that leans dangerously into the gallery space, propped up by a marching row of small toys, hardly able to bear its weight. On this wall hangs Sklar's painting *Core Value*, with a large hole bored through it and into the wall (a drilling bore, not a boring bore—or is it?). Through this hole we see *The Hoard*, a cacophony of materials that becomes more visible as one views the composition from the side. *The Hoard* is a junk drawer of nightmares, with objects bursting at the seams. But there is no drawer to close; instead we are forced to confront the mess, which is exactly how Sklar feels about our current political climate. The materials in *The Hoard* function as puns and homophones—steal/steel; stud (human)/stud (building material); felt (material)/felt (action); knots/nots; lead (material)/lead (action); stained glass and window panes/pains. Nestled in the pile are reproductions of historic white-hetero-male artworks, all done on colored acetate, rendering them semi-transparent, devaluing amidst the junk and their own sexist politics. Across *The Hoard* is a sharp raking shadow, which passes through the material, and covers a bar at the end of the wall that is sinking into the floor, as if it were made of quicksand. Punctuating the dark shadow are shards of color from the art historic reproductions, showing that optimism can break through the despair in the form of light. On the counter of the bar sits a broken water feature, a 3D printed model of Frank Lloyd Wright's Fallingwater, lying feeble and small on its side. In Sklar's world nothing is as it seems and everything is as it seems, reminding us that "things fall apart; the centre cannot hold; / Mere anarchy is loosed upon the world."[23]

Your Eyes Signal Pain

In her book *On Regarding the Pain of Others*, Susan Sontag writes about the power of war photography, stating: "Let the atrocious images haunt us. Even if they are only tokens, we cannot possibly encompass most of the reality to which they refer, they still perform a vital function. The images say: This is what human beings are capable of doing—may volunteer to do, enthusiastically, self-righteously. Don't forget."[24]

Jennifer Karady subverts the power of the wartime image. Rather than focus on the battle, Karady turns her lens to the lasting effects of war upon soldiers, revealing what haunts them, what they don't forget. For the past ten years, Karady has worked on *Soldiers' Stories from Iraq and Afghanistan*, a series in which she collaborates with veterans returning from the wars in these countries, focusing on the difficulties of adjusting to civilian life. She works over time, building trust so that the veterans feel comfortable opening up to her about not just their wartime experiences, but also their home lives afterwards. Karady works with each veteran to choose one story, which is recreated as a theatrical photograph, merging their two realities: war and home. Karady also records each soldier's story and exhibits it alongside the photograph. By giving voice to their experiences, Karady allows the veterans to regain power over their memories, opening up pathways for them to talk to their loved ones and begin to heal.

What sets Karady's photographs apart from other wartime images is that they are not actually portraits, instead they rely on film tropes, becoming like stills from longer narratives. This allows her to explore the surreality of wartime. For example, in *Former Staff Sergeant Andrew Davis, 75th Ranger Regiment, U.S. Army, veteran of Operation Iraqi Freedom and Operation Enduring Freedom, with wife, Jodie, and Iraq war veterans and friends Tom and Andy; Saratoga Springs, NY, October 2009*, three soldiers smile as they wash blood from their clothes. Two men wear novelty glasses with eyes dangling out on springs. In Davis's story, we learn that while in combat one of his fellow squad members was hit by an explosive, pushing his eye out of its socket. After that happened, Davis says, they "started joking about it, making eyesight jokes, which sounds morbid to your average person, but it's the only way to get through it." Adjacent to the cohort of men is Davis's wife, sitting outside of this experience, but still present as a symbol of support. *Former Specialist Brittny Gillespie, 139th Military Police*

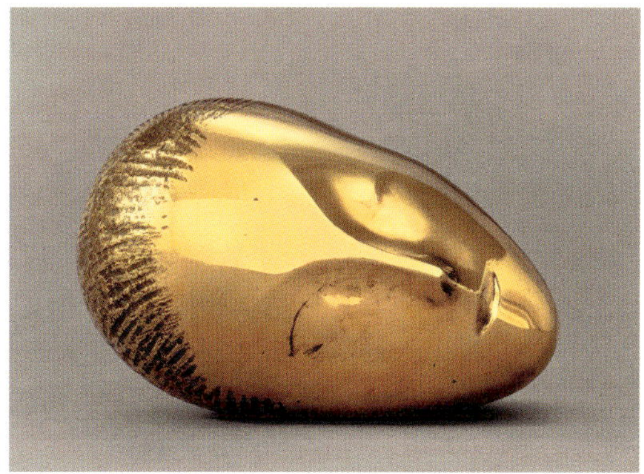

Company, 16th MP Brigade, U.S. Army, veteran of Operation Iraqi Freedom, with Volunteers of America Los Angeles Battle Buddy Elizabeth Saucedo and friend Corey; Los Angeles, CA, February 2014, shows a less-discussed side of the army: sexual assault. Gillespie lies in bed; one arm is hurling a pillow, which hovers in mid-air, revealing her anguished face. There is a man leaving the room, and after reading Gillespie's story we understand that she was raped by a fellow unit member before being deployed to Iraq. Gillespie tried to tell senior officers, but was ignored, or worse, told it was consensual. Here, in Karady's photograph, we are reminded that suffering doesn't just take place on the battlefield.

Wangechi Mutu is known predominantly for her paintings and collages depicting hybrid-dystopic female figures—part animal, part human, part cyborg. Mutu has reintroduced sculpture into her practice, using materials such as petrified tree roots, crystals, bones, cow horns and mirrored glass. Across all media, she is dedicated to showing formidable female figures regaining power. Challenging mainstream notions of idealized beauty, upsetting the representation of Africana figures in the canon of Western art history. For example, *Mwotaji The Dreamer* (2016),

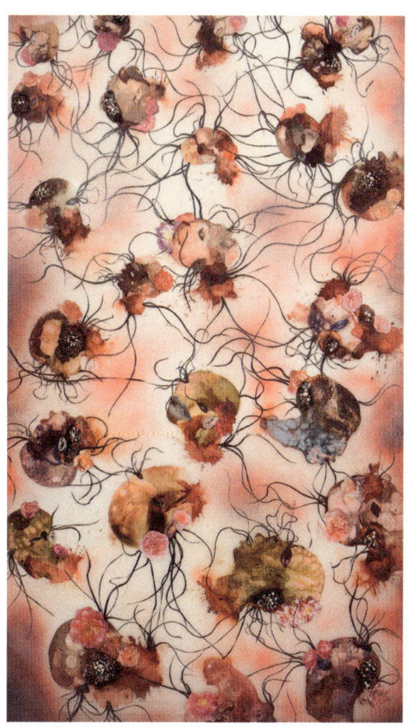

immediately recalls the resting African Punu or Dan mask that inspired the artist Constantin Brancusi's (1876–1957) *Sleeping Muse* (1910). Brancusi's sculpture depicts an abstracted bronze shaped head with slight features and plaited hair, peacefully resting atop a pedestal. Mutu's self-portrait, *Mwotaji The Dreamer*, consists of a polished bronze head and neck with an elaborate hair-do of braided knots. *Mwotaji*'s neck seems strained, and despite her serene closed eyes, there is tension in her lips as she rests her head on a cold marble pillow. The head of *Mwotaji*, which means "dreamer" in *Kiswahili*, seems decapitated, or freed from her body, as is also evident in Mutu's drawing *Fallen Heads* (2010), in which a cascade of heads float across a fleshy pink ground. For *Mwotaji*, it is in the state of death

left to right:
Constantin Brancusi, *Sleeping Muse*, 1910

Wangechi Mutu, *Fallen Heads*, 2010

that she has separated from the real world and remains in an eternal dream state. Paired with this sculpture is *One Cut* (2018), a startling work showing a hand severed at the forearm that retains a tight grip on a giant "panga" (machete). Despite the violence of this image, the long, carefully painted, blood-red fingernails are the first thing one notices. It is hard to know if this weapon did the cutting or if the mere threat of a woman in power, a woman brandishing a knife, resulted in the severing. What is remarkable is that, despite its dismemberment, the hand holds the machete resolutely—the veins and tendons flexed—as if it still has one cut left in it, like Judith severing the head of Holofernes.

In Mutu's *Mary and Magda* (2018) we see two crossed legs without feet lying on a table. The legs are soft and pliable, voluptuous objects. The surface of these objects is tanned, stained leather. But there is a Frankenstein quality to the legs, as Mutu reveals the stitches holding them together, nearly bursting at the seams. For Mutu, this work references the hypocrisy of globalization and the morphing of beauty standards—the wealthy over-fed world praising an emaciated physique and the poor economies across the planet preferring curves as a symbol of wealth and fertility, authority and womanhood. Mutu made her first version of this work in 1998 from used pillows collected from friends. The pillows carried within them oils, sweat, saliva and skin that would leech forth, staining the surface of the sculpture. In her new version, she instead uses pigskin, which is the closest to human skin and a cruelly over-farmed animal. As a result, the sculpture exists between comfort and objectification, like a maternal lap on which to sit or a trophy atop its steel table. Additionally, the title of the work conjures Mary Magdalene, referencing the often-oppositional female icon from The Bible, alternately hailed as Jesus Christ's confidant and mourner, and possibly a repentant prostitute. In the end, all of Mutu's depictions, like Mary Magdalene, will never tell their full story; instead we are left to dream, to hope that these figures have moved past the violence enacted upon them and are newly empowered.

In *The Body in Pain*, Elaine Scarry writes, "Whatever pain achieves, it achieves in part through its unshareability, and it ensures this unshareability through its resistance to language."[25] Cassils's work *Inextinguishable Fire* (2007–15) shares the unshareable. The performance and video work borrows its title from Harun Farocki's (1944–2014) 1969 film of the same name. Farocki's film begins with him reading a statement by Vietnamese citizen Thai Binh Danh about napalm attacks, after which Farocki states: "If we show you a picture of napalm burns, you'll close your eyes. First, you'll close your eyes to the pictures, then you'll close your eyes to the memory. Then, you'll close your eyes to the facts."[26] The filmmaker then extinguishes a cigarette on his own arm. This inability to understand the suffering of others is key in Cassils's work, who uses their[27] body in extreme ways to speak about issues of pain and the transformation of the transgender body. Trained as a stunt person and bodybuilder, Cassils goes to extremes for their art. Borrowing from Hollywood stunt techniques, *Inextinguishable Fire* presents Cassils

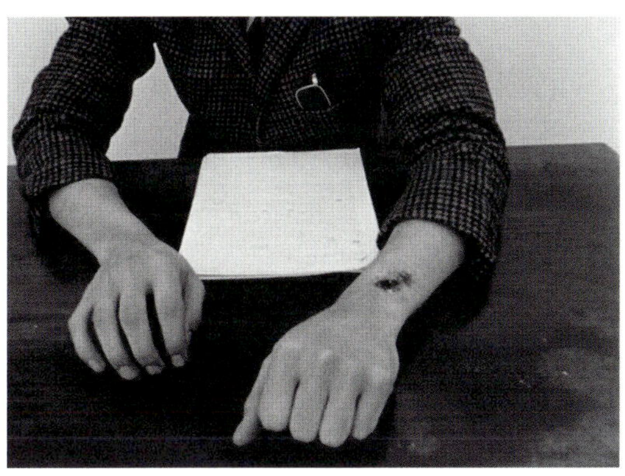

in a full-body burn, a self-immolation that was performed live at the National Theatre in London on April 2, 2015. As the audience entered the theater, Cassils stood on stage, stoically meeting their gaze. After the people were seated, stunt specialists coated Cassils's body in layers of fire-retardant long underwear, and slathered on a freezing solution. This allows the body to reach a hypothermic state, because the danger of a fire stunt is that if the body perspires, the moisture will literally boil the skin. After this process, Cassils was set ablaze, burning for fourteen seconds before falling to their knees to be extinguished.

Upon exiting the theater, the stupefied patrons were greeted with the video version of *Inextinguishable Fire*, previously recorded on a Hollywood soundstage, playing on screens outside. In the video, the performance is slowed down,[28] turning fourteen seconds into fourteen minutes, forcing viewers to contemplate the violence through the mediated lens of the camera. When exhibited, this slowing down allows the viewer to spend time with both image and action. We see a close-up of Cassils's eyes, with flames surrounding their face. This eye contact immediately creates empathy, connecting the audience to Cassils as a fellow human. In this moment, it becomes evident that while this is a simulation, the performance of a full-body burn is still a dangerous act. We see in Cassils's eyes a mixture of emotions, from fierce resistance to empathy and fear. As the flames surround Cassils's face, the camera slowly zooms out, revealing the artist's entire body, the soundstage, and the stunt coordinators, rendering the performative aspect of this violence transparent as the soundtrack of the flames metaphorically licks our ears. The final element of the installation is a series of glass sculptures, like ampules, that hang in the gallery. Each vessel was handbown by the artist, capturing a single breath. There are fourteen sculptures, one for each second that Cassils burned.

In 1992, Hayv Kahraman and her family were forced to flee their home in Iraq shortly after the government of Baghdad threatened to drop chemical weapons across the region, leading to the Kurdish refugee crisis just one year earlier. It took eleven days for Kahraman and her family to reach safety. In that same year, a charity concert called "The Simple Truth: A Concert for Kurdish Refugees," was organized. This televised fundraising campaign was based on the 1985 Live Aid concert, staged to raise money for the Ethiopian famine. Kahraman was ten years old and remembers her favorite musicians—Whitney Houston, Sting, and others—performing "in solidarity," while images of distraught Kurdish refugees appeared on the stadium jumbotrons. Kahraman felt the disconnect between her lived reality and the way in which that experience

Harun Farocki, *The Inextinguishable Fire*, 1969

was turned into a spectacle of suffering. In her book, *The Ironic Spectator*, Lilie Chouliaraki breaks down this complicated notion, writing, "On the other hand, by virtue of the gap between zones of suffering and western publics, these spectacles of suffering simultaneously separate those who watch at a distance from those who act on the spot."[29]

Kahraman embodies the marginality between spectator and subject, for just as she identifies with the refugee, she also finds kinship with the celebrity, the person/artist in the public eye, being watched. Her series *Silence is Golden* (2018) synthesizes this back and forth between spectator and subject. Kahraman began by inventing her own fictitious humanitarian campaign (a take-off of Bono's (RED) organization[30]). Instead of red, Kahraman uses gold, referencing an Arabic saying, "If speaking is silver then silence is gold."[31] All of her works begin with the figure, a stylized version of herself, painted on raw linen or wood that turns skin tone eerily pale, a nod to art historic depictions of idealized (i.e., European) female nudes. In *Three Celebrities* (2018), three women in resplendent robes stand before us—two of them pointing at a pile of gold while the third raises her arms to the sky, as if to claim the prize. The story Kahraman constructs is of three celebrities sitting around wondering what to do with the money they collected for a charity. Kahraman writes: "The first says: 'I have an idea. Let's draw a circle, throw all the money up in the air, and what falls *inside* the circle, we give to the poor.' The second says: 'I have a better idea. Let's draw a circle, throw all the money up in the air, and what falls *outside* the circle, we give to the poor.' Then the third says: 'I have an even better idea. Let's draw a circle, throw all the money up in the air, and what falls to the ground we keep!'"[32] Since all of Kahraman's figures are based on herself, in these works we see both the artist and the artist as charity-minded celebrity, collapsing lived experience and spectatorship. In another work, *Pussy Gold* (2018), she takes this to the next step, painting a figure on wood, legs spread, with a donation slot between her labia, forcing us to witness the commodification and sexualization of the figure of the suffering Other.

Bye, Bye Miss American Pie

Writer James Baldwin often talked about the traps of history, writing in one essay that "American history is longer, larger, more various, more beautiful, and more terrible than anything anyone has ever said about it,"[33] and in another, "To accept one's past—one's history—is not the same thing as drowning in it; it is learning how to use it. An invented past can never be used; it cracks and crumbles under the pressures of life like clay in a season of drought."[34] These sentiments illustrate the malleable nature of history, the fact that not all stories are written, and that, as a result, we must be conscious of the history we do write and rewrite. This corrective act of righting history's wrongs is evident in the work of Titus Kaphar. After taking his first art-history class in college, Kaphar realized that endless lessons were spent on European art, yet little if any time was spent on African and African-American art. Kaphar didn't see himself represented as artist or subject, unless it was as a subservient background figure. This inequity stuck with him, so when he began painting, he decided to shift the focus. Kaphar utilizes historic images, repainting them to either cut out the Caucasian figures or whitewash them, so that the African Americans can take center stage. The amending of history is apparent in *Seeing Through Time 2* (2018), in which Kaphar collages together two images—the first depicting a contemporary portrait of an African-American woman, the other of a wealthy aristocratic European woman being offered flowers by a black child that she has enslaved. These images are layered on top of one another, after which Kaphar excises the white woman, cutting away her head, torso, and arms, to reveal the contemporary figure beneath. The result is that the slave boy in the historic painting appears to be offering his flowers to the contemporary African-American figure, shifting the focus of the narrative and creating new connections throughout history.

Kaphar uses similar tactics in sculptures that question the power dynamics of American representation. In *Monumental Inversions: George Washington* (2016), Kaphar investigates commemoration and monument making—getting to the heart of who gets represented. In this work, we see a life-size impression of George Washington seated on horseback and carved inversely into wood. The carving is covered in scorch marks. From the sooty black cavity, we see pieces of glass, some still stuck in the horse's haunches, while others have tumbled out onto the ground. The burnt wood is the result of the hot glass hitting the wood carving, which serves as a mold, literally scorching history into its surface and allowing it to fall to pieces. The burnt figure reminds us that national heroes are fleeting. *A Pillow for Fragile Fictions* (2016) is a companion to *Monumental Inversions* and also depicts George Washington in glass. However, this time Kaphar presents a glass bust of the first president resting on a pillow of smooth marble. It immediately conjures Brancusi's *Sleeping Muse* and Mutu's *Mwotaji The Dreamer*—three heads lying in front of us, each dreaming their own secret dream. Kaphar's dreamer reveals elements of Washington's history, for inside his head is a brown liquid made of rum, tamarind, lime, and molasses. In researching Washington, Kaphar found an account of him bartering with traders in the West Indies, giving them a man whom he had enslaved in exchange for quantities of the above-listed ingredients. Kaphar's new monuments do not valorize; instead, through their translucency, they reveal the histories behind the figures on horseback in our town squares.

Like Kaphar, Robert Longo asks us to remember. Creating monumental charcoal drawings that freeze moments in time, Longo allows us to stare and come face to face with how images are mediated in our current age. Throughout his career, Longo has scoured sources from television, film, newspapers, and now the Internet. In the early 1980s he became known for his series *Men in the Cities*—larger-than-life drawings of men in business suits and women in dresses, all in contorted poses. These became iconic images of the era, but were also eerily pertinent after images of suited figures falling from the World Trade Center towers during the horrifying events of 9/11 graced our television screens. Of his process, Longo says, "Drawing is a very

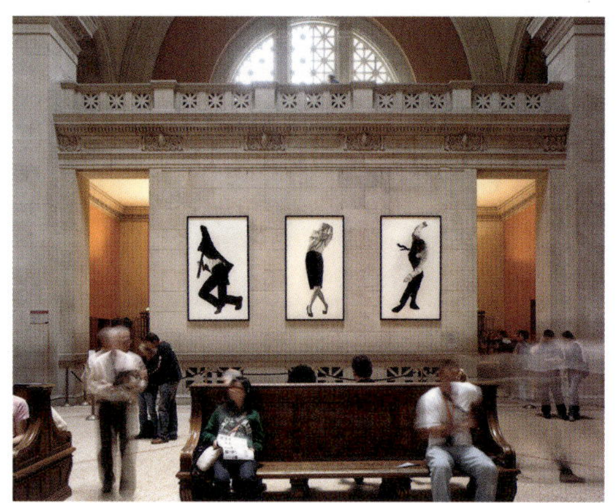

specific way of analyzing something. You digest the image on a molecular level, which I find extraordinary. A photograph is recorded in an instant. A drawing takes months to make. That reference to time is important, as is the fact that my works are often composites. They are abstractions, in a way."[35] So, while his images come from the inescapable barrage of media information, the hyper-real drawings themselves slow us down, asking us to notice the details, and, ultimately, question the truth. Longo challenges these images to be held accountable, rather than forgotten in the next news cycle.

Longo's most recent work pictures the troubled history of our times—a bullet hole in the window at Charlie Hebdo; a shrouded statue of Robert E. Lee; a fragment from the Head of Lamassu, destroyed by Isis in Iraq; etc. Two works in particular address the various protests we have seen in the news in the last five years. *Untitled (St. Louis Rams / Hands Up)* (2016) shows a football player Kenny Britt in the "hands up, don't shoot posture." This is a detail from a larger image dated November 30, 2014, when five players from the St. Louis Rams—Britt (who organized the protest), Tavon Austin, Stedman Bailey, Jared Cook, and Chris Givens—entered the field with arms raised, protesting in solidarity with the events in Ferguson, Missouri, following the shooting by police officer Darren Wilson of Michael Brown, an unarmed black man. The local police officers' association denounced the Rams' actions, leading to other sports-centered protests relating to the unfair treatment of African Americans, most famously carried out by football star Colin Kaepernick "taking a knee" rather than standing for the national anthem.[36] In Longo's drawing a single athlete, helmet on, hands in the air, stands in what looks like a cloud of smoke that seems less like a sports arena and more like the streets of protest. In this frozen moment, we become witness to both the protest, but also, eerily, to the shooting. *Untitled (Nathan Bedford Forrest Statue Removal; Memphis, 2017)* (2018) also stands in pause, as two cranes are poised to remove a statue of a man on horseback; the tableau evoking the disturbing optics of lynching. The figure is Nathan Bedford Forrest, a cotton farmer, slave owner, Confederate Army general, and the first leader of the Ku Klux Klan. A monument to Bedford was erected in Memphis, Tennessee, in 1904, when Jim Crow was alive and well. In 2017, the city council of Memphis voted to sell the park to a nonprofit after which the statue could finally be removed. Longo reminds us, with the drawing's cranes on the brink of effecting the removal, that toppling monuments doesn't erase history, it merely readjusts the focus.

Robert Longo, *Men in the Cities, Triptych*; "The Pictures Generation, 1974–1984"; Great Hall, The Metropolitan Museum of Art, New York, 2009

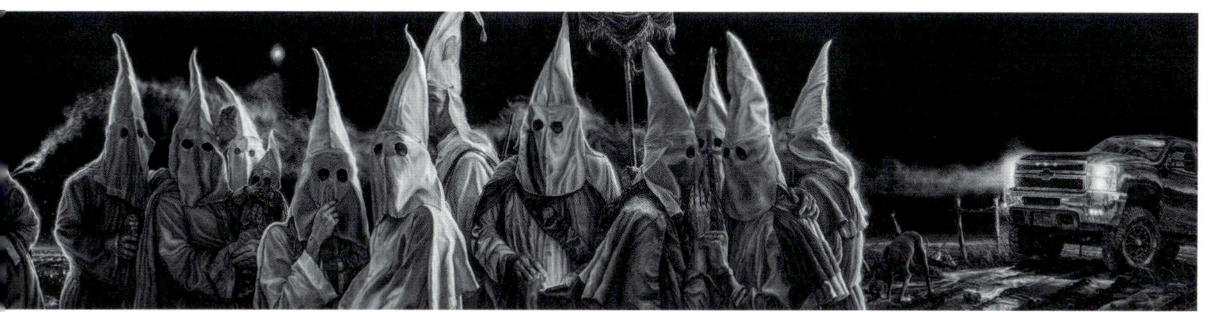

Vincent Valdez is deeply engaged in American history, particularly in relation to Mexican-American communities. His series *The Strangest Fruit* (2013) depicts contemporary Latinos in ecstatic poses, reminiscent of ascensions. However, the postures for these paintings are based on images of the lynching of Mexicans along the Texas-Mexico border, a near-forgotten history. Most recently, Valdez has undertaken a long-term series entitled *The Beginning is Near*, comprised of three sections: *The City*, *Dream Baby Dream*, and *The New Americans*.[37] For *The City* (2015–16), Valdez tackled one of the darkest sides of America—the Ku Klux Klan—painting a thirty-foot-long frieze of hooded figures. This is not a historic image, instead we see a person looking at an iPhone, drinking from a can of Budweiser, and even a hooded baby wearing Nike shoes. Their eyes meet ours, and we immediately realize that this violent chapter in American history is far from over. Just as the artist was finishing *The City*, boxer Muhammad Ali died, and Valdez, who had previously painted images of boxers, was astounded by the eulogists for the funeral, seeing it as a rare critical moment when various races and denominations came together to celebrate a man who fought for underrepresented Americans. *Dream Baby Dream* (2017–18) is a series of twelve paintings that focus on the podium, wreaths of flowers, and eulogists,[38] who are silent, hesitant, and even uncertain about their willingness to speak. This potential muteness serves as an apt metaphor for our troubled times. Rendered in black, white, and grey, there are touches of red around the eyes, noses, and hands of the mourners, reminding us of our resistance to remain numb even after all we have lost and continue to lose. The ten portraits are accompanied by two panels, one of the empty podium—the reconciliatory speeches yet to be given—and the other, a vertical panel, displaying a funeral wreath. The cascading ribbon is emblazoned with the lyrics from punk band Suicide's "Dream Baby Dream," the song so effectively used in Curtis's *HyperNormalisation*, reminding us to "keep those dreams burnin'."

Adriana Corral unearths histories that have been obscured, especially as they relate to the plight of Mexicans and Mexican Americans. In her book *Hope in the Dark*, Rebecca Solnit writes: "Amnesia leads to despair in many ways. The status quo would like you to believe it is immutable, inevitable, and invulnerable, and lack of memory of a dynamically changing world reinforces

Vincent Valdez, *The City I*, 2015–16

this view. In other words, when you don't know how much things have changed, you don't see that they are changing or that they can change."[39] Corral attempts to right this amnesia by creating minimalist counter monuments to forgotten stories. In *Voces de la Perdidas (Voices of the Lost)* (2010), Corral focused on the history of femicide in Juarez, Mexico. Since the 1990s, women have been disappearing in Juarez, with little law enforcement action. To give form to this tragedy, Corral started with the names of eight women who were raped, tortured, and murdered on November 6, 2001, at Campo Algodonero, an open cotton field in Juarez: Esmeralda Herrera Monreal, Laura Berenice Ramos Monárrez, Claudia Ivette González, María de los Ángeles Acosta Ramírez, Mayra Juliana Reyes Solís, Merlín Elizabeth Rodríguez Sáenz, and María Rocina Galicia. She then used soil from the site to create ceramic body tags that hung from the gallery ceiling, serving as objects of commemoration and reminders of violence. Most recently, Corral executed her largest work to date, *Unearthed: Desenterrado* (2018), an installation

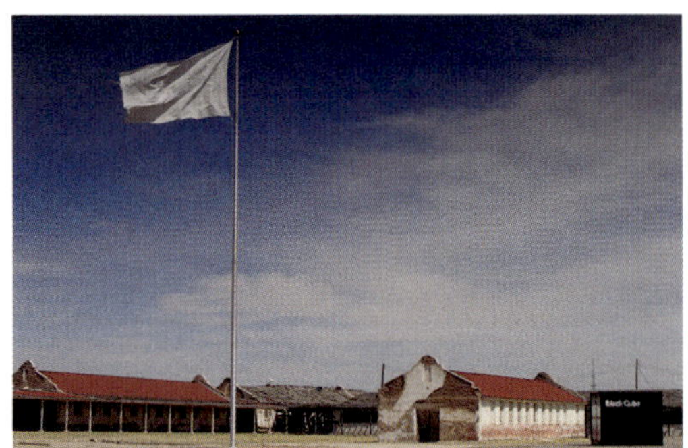

at the historic Rio Vista Farm near El Paso, Texas. On this site, from 1942 to 1964, the US federal government, in partnership with Mexico, oversaw one of the last foreign-worker programs in the country: the Bracero Program. Bracero, meaning manual labor in Spanish, accepted over 80,000 Mexican workers per year into the United States, where in order to gain entry at the border they underwent medical and psychological examinations, and were fumigated with DDT. At Rio Vista Farm there is no memorial of what happened on that soil, so Corral made her own—a sixty-foot flagpole with an 18 x 12 foot white-cotton flag. One side of the flag is embroidered with an American Bald Eagle, the symbol of the United States, while on the other is the Golden Eagle, representing Mexico.[40] Both birds are rendered white on white, making their ghostly talons, ensnared mid-air, a poignant symbol for the ongoing struggles between the US and Mexico. Over time, the flag unraveled, disappearing just like the original story.

Corral and Valdez have teamed up for *Suffering from Realness* to present *Requiem* (2016–19), a multi-part work consisting of a sculpture of an American Bald Eagle, a series of dates incised directly into the wall, and the *Dream Baby Dream* paintings. A requiem is a mass for the souls of the dead, and here Corral and Valdez have used this form to take stock of American history. They began by asking 243 Americans, marking the age of the American Republic in 2019, to submit dates of historical significance, such as: "September 1987—I was 27 years old. Left NYC for San Francisco. I stood staring at the 'for lease' signs that lined the sidewalks of the Castro District while apartment hunting.

Adriana Corral, *Unearthed: Desenterrado*, 2018

I realized the vacancies were the result of AIDS." Or "July 1916—Mayor Tom Lee writes a telegram to Surgeon General in Washington requesting funding to build a delousing facility for hundreds of dirty, destitute Mexican laborers arriving in El Paso, TX."[41] This collection of history of the people by the people was burned by Corral, who frequently utilizes ash in her work. These ashes of America were used by Valdez to patinate a bronze sculpture of an eagle, lying on its back in self-distress, a startling image of the exhaustion of our country. Corral then laboriously cut each date directly into the gallery wall, literally scarring the museum with American history. Corral and Valdez write that "Requiem is an urn. It embodies a people's truth about the complex historic and present realities of living in America. Binding these truths together is an act of reconciliation, it is a way of offering a platform for 243 citizens and non-citizens to testify to what they have witnessed, discovered, and/or endured in their American experience."[42] To this end, Corral and Valdez staged a New Orleans-style Second Line funeral parade for the opening of *Suffering from Realness*; carrying the eagle into its resting place for the next year, they reminded us to mourn, but also to celebrate the fact that collective action can signal change and lead to rewriting the history of the future. As Eli Wiesel declared as he accepted the Nobel Peace Prize in 1986, "Just as man cannot live without dreams, he cannot live without hope. If dreams reflect the past, hope summons the future."[43] Corral and Valdez provide hope, and dreams baby dreams.

Sweet Dreams Are Made of This

Dreams seem hard to come by lately, especially when the nightmare of everyday life is so pressing. In 2004, Howard Zinn wrote "The Optimism of Uncertainty" in the wake of 9/11. What would Zinn, who died in 2010, make of our current political climate? Would he still believe, hope, and dream? Would he still stand behind writing: "I am totally confident not that the world will get better, but that we should not give up the game before all the cards have been played. The metaphor is deliberate; life is a gamble. Not to play is to foreclose any chance of winning. To play, to act, is to create at least a possibility of changing the world."[44] Despite dark times, then and now, to give up hope is to just let the darkness win. Zinn didn't want that then, and he likely would not want it now. He would have encouraged us to continue playing the game, for if we stop dreaming there is no chance for the future.

Christopher Mir's paintings describe a deep personal mythology, tied to his own consciousness and manifested in a stream of free-association images. The artist writes, "I want to make a pictorial expression of the electric hum of the nervous system—and the sublime poetry of atmospheric space."[45] This allows Mir's paintings to exist in a liminal space—between the collective and singular; between anxiety and hope. There is a dreamlike quality to his work, particularly in his floating quotidian objects made strange against scratchy backgrounds of color. For example, in *Teeth* (2018) a stack of pearly whites is delicately balanced as a wobbly pyramid against a blue ground. This is the stuff of nightmares. But what shifts Mir's work from mere

Freudian analysis is the pyramid itself, the reorganization of teeth. Have they done this themselves, or has another being arranged them for us? Either way, the orderly nature of the stack, against the jumpy backdrop of paint, turns this composition into something simultaneously terrifying and absurd. The same can be said for *Broken Model* (2018), in which Mir paints a silhouette of a plane—one wing, and the tail floating in space, broken off from its body. The central image is painted over a white background, which is scraped away to reveal darkness underneath. In this cloudy sky the plane hovers, still seemingly flying despite the impotency of its construction. The title then reminds us that this is a model airplane, and the image is no longer a threat but a toy to play with, assuaging our fears.

The juxtaposition of Mir's images next to one another allows the mind to wander surrealistically in a free-associative dream state, hovering between flowers, teeth, candles, airplanes, and boxers. In *Disco Grid* and *Flowers* (both 2018), Mir gives us seemingly innocuous images. The first depicts a trio of figures atop a red hill. These shadowy bodies could be the enemy, but they could also be dancing in the glittery reflections of a disco ball, as the red ground is covered in its telltale square white bits of light. In *Flowers* we see a bouquet, both alive and dying, with wild leaves reaching out toward the edge of the canvas. Like *Broken Model*, *Flowers* is mostly monochromatic, with the blooms themselves rendered in dark-blueish black and the background mostly white, with a dark ground underneath. It gives the effect, especially where ground and flowers meet and their colors blend, that the flowers are somehow asserting dominance over their own space. Mir's grid of paintings in *Suffering from Realness* is reminiscent of a game and the playing cards that Zinn references. This work reminds us that no matter how difficult the fight may be—as seen in a painting of two sparring boxers—we must keep playing the game, whether it gives us dreams, nightmares, or a combination of the two.

Joey Fauerso's work also exists in between things: between painting and sculpture; between film and performance; between humor and tragedy. This vacillation comes from her dedication to blending life with art. Like many artists, Fauerso used to keep her studio practice separate from her home life. That all changed when, at thirty-eight years of age, she was diagnosed with breast cancer. While undergoing treatment, Fauerso witnessed her two young sons playing a game of pretend they called "Dog Hospital." She overheard phrases like, "These are the operators" and "These are the rescue persons," realizing that her boys were processing what was happening to their mother. In this moment, Fauerso understood that she could no longer silo the relationship of herself to her body, to her children/family, and to her work. As a result, she started to blend these worlds together, turning her children's game of pretend into the artist book *Dog Hospital* (2015), in which we see the "operators"—tuxedoed men with surgical masks—and the "rescue persons"—tender portraits of her sons.

When the political landscape turned topsy-turvy in 2016, Fauerso wanted to address her own "visceral response to living in the United States during a time of total political and moral collapse."[46]

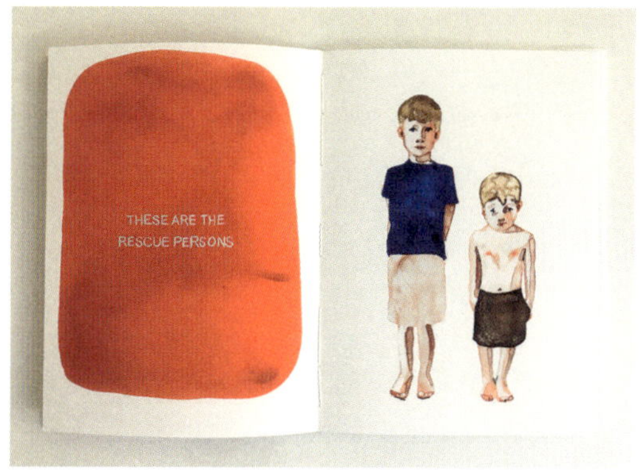

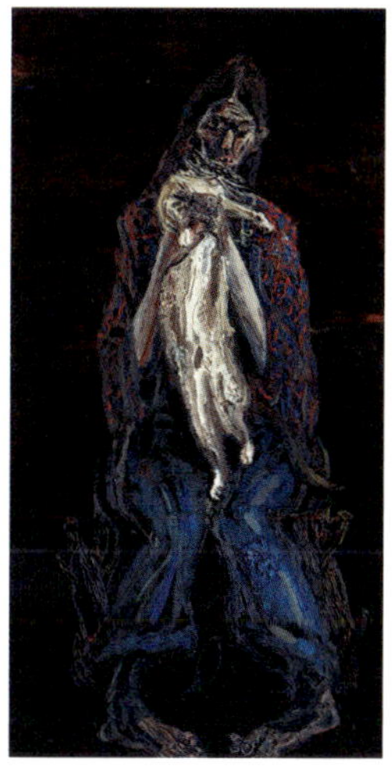

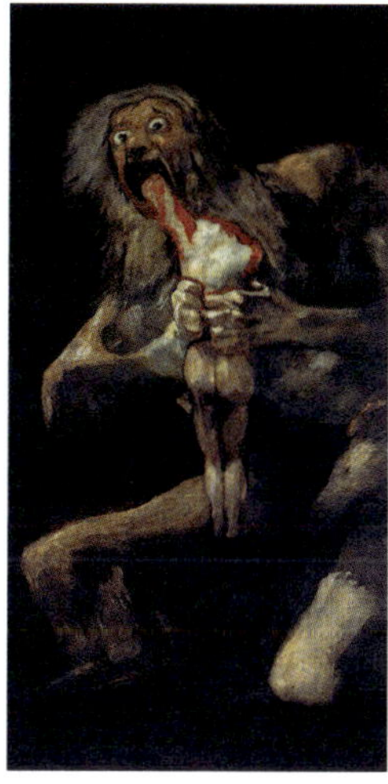

To do this, she turned to her sons once again, overhearing her younger say to her elder, "You destroy every special thing I make," turning a sibling conflict into an achingly accurate description of how the artist felt after Trump was elected. This phrase became the title of a mixed-media installation. The other thing to change in Fauerso's studio was her desire to cease using carcinogenic painting materials, leading to a technique akin to mono-printing. Covering canvas with a thin field of non-toxic paints, Fauerso uses spatulas, squeegees, cloth, and other tools to create quick, gestural images. It is a reductive technique, where she takes away paint, allowing the image to emerge. She uses this tactic in *You Destroy Every Special Thing I Make* (2017–19), where a series of monochromatic drawings casually spill across the wall: a funeral ceremony on the Ganges River in India; Joan of Arc at a pyre looking longingly upwards; a vertical pile of women's bodies neatly nestled into one another. These images come from a place of anxiety—for women's bodies, for war, for the human condition. Amongst the images are blocks of wood, small arrangements of built environments, layering the work with complexity. Adjacent to this tableau is a series of videos in which Fauerso worked with her sons and her friends to build and knock down various constructions. The soundtrack is thundering, and the act of toppling is satisfying, playful, aggressive, and cathartic. The building and rebuilding plays in a continuous loop, much like the cycle of politics and life. This work also conjures the Jewish concept of Tikkun Olam, meaning "fixing up," and referring to deeds of kindness performed to repair the world. Despite the political and moral collapse from which Fauerso started, it is clear that, through this work, she and her family are performing acts of Tikkum Olam.

Allison Schulnik's work is also concerned with the cyclical nature of our universe. Schulnik is best known for her works in paint and stop-motion animation, through which she explores materiality, pathos, and fantasy; the paintings are so densely layered one gets lost in their crevasses; the Claymation films are lyrical and fluid. In *Lady with*

left to right:
Joey Fauerso, *Dog Hospital*, (detail), 2015

Allison Schulnik, *Lady With Cat*, 2015

Francisco Goya, *Saturn Devouring his Son*, from the series *Black Paintings*, c. 1819–1823

a Cat and *Centaurette in a Forest* (both 2015), she presents two heavily impasto surfaces. The first is a self-portrait, depicting Schulnik holding a stretched-out cat to her face in an attempt to show it love, while the cat seems to alternately resist and acquiesce. The faces of both human and animal are painted in thick layers, to the point of seemingly merging into each other. In the image, which is reminiscent of Goya's painting *Saturn Devouring His Son* (c. 1819–23), it is unclear if we are witnessing an act of love or destruction. The darkness of this painting melts away in the saccharine pastel tones of *Centaurette in a Forest*. Here we see a centaurette, a female centaur inspired by the Disney film *Fantasia* (1940), where these mythological creatures were seen in The Pastoral Symphony. Schulnik's centaurette brazenly displays her bare-breasted torso, putting both arms coquettishly behind her head. Standing amidst a camouflage of flora and fauna, the centaurette's face is more Brothers Grimm than Disney.

Alongside her paintings, Schulnik has made a number of stop-motion animation films. In *Eager* (2014), Schulnik creates a new version of *Fantasia*'s symphony, this one starring a slinky figure writhing on the ground. Her long hair, rendered in clay, is both stringy and fluid, and she appears to have no face and a body that bends as if boneless. A hybrid, she is not quite human, not quite animal. The figure multiplies and three of them dance in unison, their bodies blending into a lush thicket of forest. Schulnik's newest work, *Moth* (2019), stems from this thinking. Shifting from clay to gouache on paper, this film is light and airy, as compared to the fleshiness of the Claymation works; it makes sense, as a moth is a light and airy insect. The artist draws and animates the creature as though it is flying and fluttering before our eyes. The concept for the film came when a moth hit the window of her studio, continuing to develop through her pregnancy with and the birth of her first child. The film is about this cycle, about how emotion, motherhood, and nature can come together. The film also illuminates the need to take care of the things around us in order to leave space for the dance of nature to exist. It is no coincidence that Schulnik was trained as a dancer; it is evident in *Eager*, where the figures are actually choreographed, but even more so in *Moth*, where this tiny, vulnerable creature isn't just hitting a window, but is soaring across the screen. Perhaps hope, as Emily Dickinson wrote, is not just a thing with feathers. Remember, feathers alone can't fly, but the wings they coalesce into can. Taking the moth into consideration, hope is a thing with wings "that perches in the soul / And sings the tune without the words / And never stops—at all."[47]

Dance Like the Streets Are Paved with Gold

In *Hope in the Dark*, Solnit writes: "Your opponents would love you to believe that it's hopeless, that you have no power, that there's no reason to act, that you can't win. Hope is a gift you don't have to surrender, a power you don't have to throw away."[48] For Jeffrey Gibson, this gift comes from the realization of what art can do. For years, Gibson resisted referencing his Native-American identity in his work—fearing that it would marginalize him in the art world—until he realized that he need not dampen a single part of himself. So, over the last ten years he has referenced and celebrated traditional native materials and crafts, utilizing tipi poles, beads, and metal jingles used in powwow regalia. Gibson deftly merges these materials with references to politics, literature, and music, alongside nods to art world tropes such as Minimalism and Afrofuturism. The result is an empowered body of work that fiercely holds onto the gifts of hope and love, as seen in his elaborately encrusted punching bags. By taking an object associated with both aggression and strength, and transforming it into a beaded message board for equality, Gibson reminds us that history, identity, love, and fear can have power over us unless we imbue them with our own truth and render them fabulous. Gibson's punching bags are emblazoned with phrases like *Love is the Drug* (2017)—turning Grace Jones's version of a song originally written and recorded by Roxy Music into beads and adorning the rest of the bag with heart charms—or *Power Power Power* (2017), which reads "black power, yellow power, pink power, blue power." With this work, we no longer need to punch our way through life, for it gives us all the fight we need.

Gibson has recently turned his attention to making garments—like versions of the punching bags that can be worn. These garments contain kaleidoscopic patterns made from Gibson's paintings and sculptures, and are strung with beads, jingles, and decorative shoe laces. In these works, hiding is not an option, as they proudly display their hearts on their sleeves. *SPEAK TO ME SO I CAN UNDERSTAND* (2018) incorporates a vintage Iroquois patchwork and a warrior figure made by Gibson, turned into a fabric where the images are doubled and mirrored and accompanied by the phrase "PEOPLE LIKE US" over and over again. This phrase also appears in *PEOPLE LIKE US* (2018), where it forms a background across which cascade shredded ribbons, iridescent futuristic fabric, and bruised emojis, collaged together with Trump's tweets about transgender bans in the military. And lastly, *Clown Witness* (2018) references a modified version of a *New York Times* headline "Tribes File Suit Over Bears Ears," which details Trump's decision to reduce the size of the Bears Ears National Monument, a protected public land long held as sacred to a number of Native-American tribes. This series spells out the struggles of various communities (native, queer, artists, etc.) in our current political climate. The garments are aspirational, hanging

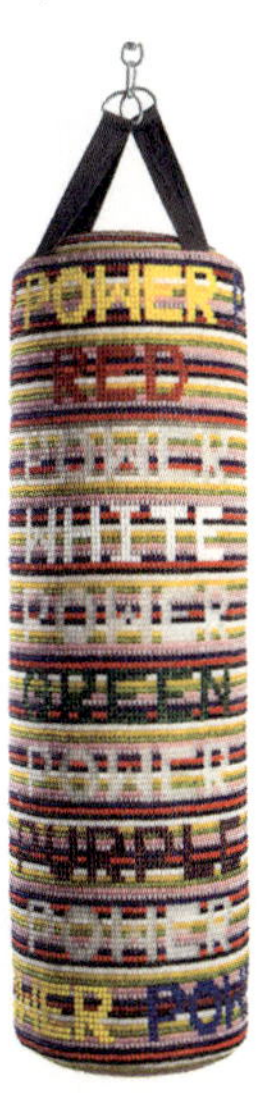

left to right:
Jeffrey Gibson, *Love is the Drug*, 2017;
***Power Power Power* , 2017**

from the ceiling on tipi poles and also existing in a series of photographs, staged by Gibson, of people of color proudly wearing the garments like warriors for hope, equality, and change. These works, which are based on the regalia used in faith-based ceremonies including traditional Lakota garments worn by members of the Ghost Dance—a pacifist movement that culminated in the 1890 Wounded Knee massacre, yet remains active today—are ultimately objects that pay homage to the past while signaling the future. But most of all, Gibson's works come as much from the museum as from the dance floor, harnessing early drag culture and figures, such as Leigh Bowery, who exuberantly displayed their identity for all to see. Gibson reminds us to dance and to embrace power, the truest form of hope we can find.

In his essay *Nothing Personal*, James Baldwin writes that "nothing is fixed, forever and forever and forever, it is not fixed; the earth is always shifting, the light is always changing, the sea does not cease to grind down rock. Generations do not cease to be born, and we are responsible to them because we are the only witnesses they have. The sea rises, the light fails, lovers cling to each other, the children cling to us. The moment we cease to hold each other, the moment we break faith with one another, the sea engulfs us and the light goes out."[49]

If hope is a thing with feathers, we must also remember that while we must hold on to hope—hold on to the things that matter—we must also let it fly, let the seas rise, the light fall, the lovers cling, and the children sing. In the face of so much despair, it is the lack of hope that will extinguish the light. The artists in *Suffering from Realness* keep this light burning, keep dream baby dreaming; providing a sliver of optimism, they show how tenderness and collective action can lead to a new form of realness, one tied less to uncertainty and more to liberation. No longer bound, we can "resist or move on, be mad, be rash, smoke, and explode,"[50] and, ultimately, find hope in something lasting and real.

—

1 The essay title comes from reality show participant Angela Deem on the TLC show *Before the 90 Days*. The subtitles for this essay come from various music references: Kanye West and Jay-Z's "Ni**as in Paris" (K. West, S. Carter, C. Hollis, M. Dean, W. A. Donaldson, 2011); Buffalo Springfield's "For What It's Worth" (Stephen Stills, 1966); Kenny Rogers's "Just Dropped In" (Mickey Newbury, 1978); Morrissey's "The Harsh Truth of the Camera Eye" (Steven Morrissey/Mark Edward Cascian Nevin, 1991); Don McLean's "American Pie" (1971); Eurythmic's "Sweet Dreams (Are Made of This)" (Annie Lennox/David A. Stewart, 1983); and Saul Williams's "Dance" (2011).

2 J. G. Ballard, *Hello America* (London: W.W. Norton & Co, 1981), p. 10.

3 Ibid., p. 172.

4 From the album *Green*, released by Warner Bros., 1988

5 Adam Curtis, *HyperNormalisation*, released October 16, 2016, by the BBC.

6 Alexei Yurchak, *Everything Was Forever, Until it was No More: The Last Soviet Generation* (Princeton: Princeton University Press, 2005).

7 Published by G.O.O.D. Music and Def Jam Recording.
8 West removed the "Again," so the hat read "Make America Great."
9 On December 27, 2018, West visited MASS MoCA with rapper Tyler, the Creator and artist James Turrell. Upon being asked about his visit to Trump's White House, West said that he believed Trump was like comedian Andy Kaufman and was creating brilliant theater, and that he had liked being in the Oval Office because he could feel the ghosts there.
10 Rebecca Solnit, "Hope in Grief," in *Call Them By Their True Names: American Crises* (Chicago: Haymarket Books, 2018), p. 167.
11 Kayla Epstein and Eugene Scott, "Historic Firsts of the 2018 Midterms," *The Washington Post*, November 7, 2018, and Christina Caron, "In 'Rainbow Wave' L.G.B.T Candidates are Elected in Record Numbers," *The New York Times*, November 7, 2018.
12 Susan Sontag, *Regarding the Pain of Others* (London: Picador, 2004), pp. 44–45.
13 Group Material formed in 1979; members included Doug Ashford, Julie Ault, Tim Rollins, and Felix Gonzales-Torres.
14 Maggie Nelson, *The Art of Cruelty* (New York: W.W. Norton & Company, 2012), p. 264.
15 Suicide, "Dream Baby Dream" (Martin Reverby/Boruch Bernowitz; 1979, Island Records).
16 Elaine Scarry, *The Body in Pain: The Making and Unmaking of the World* (Oxford: Oxford University Press, 1987), p. 14.
17 Robert Taplin, "A Reminiscence," in *Two Sculpture Series 2006–2016*, self-published catalogue.
18 In a note to the author, May 31, 2018.
19 The slogan of World Economic Forum is "Committed to Improving the State of the World." weforum.org/events/world-economic-forum-annual-meeting-2018
20 Alex Shephard, "Donald Trump, Davos Man," *The New Republic*, January 10, 2018. The ineffectualness of such an elite gathering came under further scrutiny when, in 2018, Trump became the first president to attend in nearly twenty years (Clinton was the last in 2000).
21 Wisława Szymborska, *Poems New and Collected, 1957–1997*, trans. Stanisław Baranczak and Clare Cavanagh (New York: Harcourt, Inc., 1988), pp. 200–201.
22 rachelpollack.com/writing/notes.html#forestofsouls
23 William Butler Yeats, *The Second Coming*, 1919.poetryfoundation.org/poems/43290/the-second-coming
24 Sontag, *Regarding the Pain of Others*, p. 115.
25 Scarry, *The Body in Pain*, p. 4.
26 Jessica Lynn Posner, "Artist as Alchemist: A Review of Cassils's "Monumental," *QED: A Journal in GLBTQ Worldmaking*, Vol. 5, No. 1 (Spring 2018), p. 130.
27 Cassils uses the gender-neutral pronouns they/them/their.
28 The film was shot on a Phantom high speed camera at 14,000 frames per second. Standard definition cameras shoot 30 frames per second, therefore the high-speed camera reveals more detail when slowed down.
29 Lilie Chouliaraki, *The Ironic Spectator: Solidarity in the Age of Post-Humanitarianism* (Oxford: Polity, 2004), pp. 27–28.
30 (RED) is a licensed brand founded by musician Bono and Bobby Shriver, with the aim of raising awareness and funds for the elimination of HIV/AIDS in African countries. It was initiated in 2006 at the World Economic Forum in Davos.
31 From an email to the author, June 14, 2018.
32 Ibid. This story relates to Jeffrey Archer, the British politician who staged "The Simple Truth" concert; he was photographed with a check he said represented over 50 million pounds raised, none of which was received by the Red Cross.
33 James Baldwin, "A Talk to Teachers," in *The Price of the Ticket: Collected Nonfiction, 1948–1985* (New York: St. Martin's Press), p. 332.
34 James Baldwin, "Down at the Cross: Letter from a Region in My Mind," in *The Fire Next Time* (New York: Vintage Reissue edition, 1992), p. 81.
35 Kate Fowle, "Time Traveling: Robert Longo in Conversation with Kate Fowle," in *Proof: Francisco Goya, Sergei Eisenstein, Robert Longo* (Moscow: Garage Museum of Contemporary Art), p. 103.
36 The first high-profile athletic protest took place when Tommie Smith, Gold Medal winner for the 200-meter sprint at the 1968 Summer Olympics in Mexico City, and John Carlos, the Bronze Medal winner, each raised a fist and bowed their heads as they stood on the podium as the US anthem played at the medal ceremony.
37 The first two parts of the series are complete, while the third, which focuses on contemporary portraits, is in progress.
38 Valdez purposely does not reveal the identities of his selected portraits, instead he chooses them for their symbolic representation of a wide range of Americans. Age, ethnicity, dress, posture, and expression were factors in his choices.
39 Rebecca Solnit, *Hope in the Dark: Untold Histories Wild Possibilities* (Chicago: Haymarket Books, Second edition, 2016), p. xix.
40 The drawing for the eagles is by Vincent Valdez.
41 Here is an edited version of the dates submitted by the author: January 28, 1986, the Challenger Space Shuttle explodes—an eerie precursor to the media society we live in today, where everything is broadcast and we have all become collective witnesses; LA Riots; O. J. Simpson; 9/11.
42 In an email to the author, January 7, 2019.
43 nobelprize.org/prizes/peace/1986/wiesel/26054-elie-wiesel-acceptance-speech-1986/
44 Howard Zinn, "The Optimism of Uncertainty," in *The Nation*, September 2, 2004.
45 In an email to the author, October 26, 2018.
46 In an email to the author, September 18, 2017.
47 Emily Dickinson, "'Hope' is the Thing with Feathers," from *The Complete Poems of Emily Dickinson*, ed. Thomas H. Johnson (Cambridge: The Belknap Press of Harvard University press, 1951).
48 Solnit, *Hope in the Dark*, p xi.
49 Richard Avedon and James Baldwin, *Nothing Personal* (Cologne: Taschen, reprint edition, 2017), p. 121.
50 Morrissey, "Hold On to Your Friends" (Alain Whyte/Steven Morrissey), from *Vauxhall and I* (1994, Parlophone and Sire/Reprise).

Section 1

What Condition My Condition Was In

Letter to My Students the Day After the Election

—

Andy Campbell

On Tuesday, November 8, 2016, I took a group of graduate students out to see Judy Baca's The Great Wall of Los Angeles *(1978–). We lazily walked along the Tujunga Wash, looking at the mural from above, talking all along the way. Baca's history of Los Angeles begins not with the forty-four* pobladores, *but with the Chumash, a people who were present long before settler colonialists expanded their empire. Using this centering of indigenous life as a base, Baca and her hundreds of collaborators detail across hundreds of yards those indelible moments that change history—both for good (Thomas Alva Edison's invention of the lightbulb) and for ill (the Zoot Suit Riots of 1943). We also talked as a class, in a more informal way, about the presidential election happening that day (almost everyone in the group had already voted). The students and I were hopeful that in a race between Hillary Clinton (a Democratic stalwart) and Donald Trump (a Republican upstart and the bloviating id of American exceptionalism), Clinton would carry the day. We were wrong, of course. It pained me to think that the day we just lived through would be one of those terrible turning points on Baca's wall—my imagined subtitle: civility substituted by cruelty.*

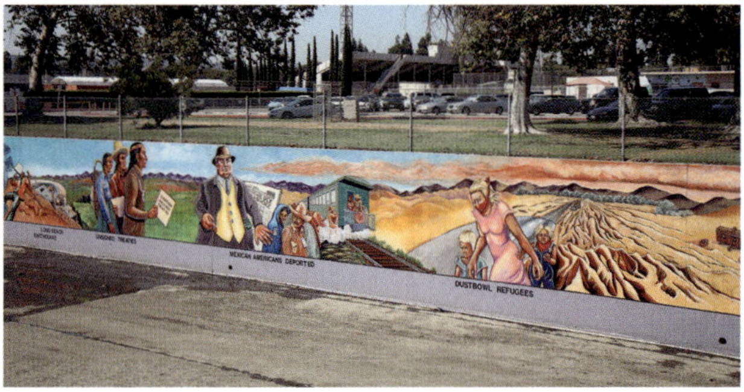

Judith Baca detail from the 1930s section of the *Great Wall of Los Angeles*, 1976

The morning after the election, I was slated to teach a large undergraduate class dedicated to the histories of art, design, and visual culture. The class had well over one hundred students, and I didn't know, when I awoke early in the morning, whether I was up for teaching. We were meant to cover the Bauhaus, and I had given the students readings and a brief assignment. In addition to Walter Gropius's well-known manifesto and program of study, and a text on Herbert Bayer's Universal type, I assigned a text by art historian Saloni Mathur that discussed a 1922 exhibition of Bauhaus works in Calcutta, to suggest the transit of Bauhaus principles. This particular class is always this way: I teach canon while also subverting, or turning, its revelations back onto a more expanded world. I also had the students complete Wassily Kandinsky's color-form association exercise, in which the artist proposed "empirical" relations between the colors red, blue, and yellow, and the shapes of a square, circle, and triangle (respectively).

I thought hard about canceling class—maybe, like me, my students needed mental space more than they needed to be in class. I sat down at my kitchen table at a loss—and wept. I obviously couldn't just "teach the Bauhaus" as was the plan; but I also couldn't be derelict in my duties as an instructor. I decided, instead, to write a letter to my students, one that would bring the lessons I hoped to transmit in class discussion to bear on the present moment. I opened up my laptop and began to write. Before I read it to the class, I had them anonymously write down what they were feeling about the election onto notecards—these were collected and then distributed back to the students at random. The following letter is only lightly edited from the original, so as to give the reader more context.

My Dear Students,

I must begin with a confession. It will probably not be all that surprising: today I found it difficult to get out of bed. Sleep was difficult, too, but once I had found its solace, it was nearly impossible to give it up.

I thought about canceling class today. It certainly would have been a relief for me, because as of seven this morning, I didn't know what I was going to do. To continue on with the day's plan—a discussion of Bauhaus design both in Germany and India—seemed to be a willful glossing over of the important events of last night. On the other hand, to resituate the class as a processing session seemed too unfocused. This is not to doubt that there are a lot of strong feelings and thoughts in this room; ones that beg to be heard, absorbed, and synthesized. There is elation and also despair—about many things, not just who won the presidential election.

Perhaps these words would be more effective if I spoke them extemporaneously, "from the heart," as it were. This is certainly how I usually conduct class. I do my homework to internalize the content for the day, and prepare for the barrage of questions and thoughts you have about the day's topic. I always leave class—with few exceptions—feeling buoyant in the wake of your presence. Because I derive a lot of joy and pleasure from this style of teaching, it might be odd now that I speak words that are pre-written, sentiments sealed in the editing process (even if it was only hours ago now). Well, today is a very different day than yesterday, and the strategies of yesterday might not make sense today.

I write because it is what I do when I can't make sense of the world. I realize that this is a way to enact some control in a moment where I don't particularly feel in control. Because this represents a break from how things are normally run in class, I hope you don't feel I'm being too dramatic in my tactics (although I've certainly been accused of it many times before). I write to you because it is the best I can do today.

There are many ways to view, review, dissect, and disavow (or avow) the election results from last night. I spent the better part of the morning scrolling through these. There will be more to come. More when Donald Trump takes office. More after his first one hundred days. And when the next election cycle begins again in earnest. I have my own thoughts about Trump, informed by my experiences as a queer person in this world, with many friends and family who are also queer, who are also people of color, who are also, or have been, disabled, mentally ill, and/or poor. You can probably tell from that list—a "basket of deplorables" if there ever was one—that I'm not the biggest Trump fan; not the biggest Mike Pence fan. It is the purpose of this letter to tell you why I believe the way I do and why I do what I do, in the hopes that you might find solidarity in it or a foil for your own ideas. This is certainly how I work: in fact, it is what a good life in teaching is all about.

In that spirit I want to share the words and works of a few artists and thinkers. Along the way, I'll address our readings and the topics that we were supposed to cover today. It won't be a full class worth of me talking, we'll probably end early. For today, when I stop talking class will be over.

I want to begin with a sentiment written by the French philosopher Jean-Luc Nancy, from his book of collected essays called *Being Singular Plural*: "What I have in common with another Frenchman is the fact of *not* being the same Frenchman as him, and the fact that our 'Frenchness' is never, nowhere, in no essence, in no figure, brought to completion."[1]

This acknowledgment of an unshared sense of Frenchness, of difference in identity, is a difficult, but I would argue necessary, pill to swallow. Nancy expresses this sentiment in an essay about the Bosnian War—a war that raged in Bosnia and Herzegovina for over three years (1992–1995). It was a gruesome civil war that resulted in the ethnic cleansing (a polite phrase for genocide) of Muslim Bosniaks and Catholic Croats by the Bosnian Orthodox Serbs. Because of this charged context, Nancy's words take on a somewhat ominous cast—if we can't all agree to be French together, Bosnian together, American together, then what have we got, really? It would appear to be a bleak picture. Nancy's work, which is sometimes difficult for me to get through, has consistently provided me with an opportunity to rethink the terms of social engagement, both interpersonal and intranational. In the popular imagination, we are all bonded by a sense of being and belonging *within* a certain nationality; in this formulation, what unites us is always stronger than what separates us. Nancy tells us that one's "Frenchness" is not like another's—or that one's "Americanness" is not like another's, which is in stark contrast to the imaginative work that "nation" purports to do. But this is a fantasy. There are many times in US history where a person or class of person is rendered un-American. In the 1950s it was communists and homosexuals; it was brown and black folks seeking civil rights.

Our diverse polity is probably somewhat represented in this class: some are citizens with full voting rights, others have come from US territories (Puerto Rico; Guam) where they might have been able to vote in a primary, but had no vote and no electoral college representation on election night. Some do not have IDs, and thus could not vote. Some do not have a home, or a reliable way to get to and from the polls. Others in this class are naturalized citizens elsewhere, holding different passports, perhaps watching this event unfold in horror or amusement, or some admixture of both. Some have already drawn connections to leaders in their home countries; to Rodrigo Duterte in the Philippines, or perhaps Marine Le Pen in France. Both, it should be noted, are happy with last night's election results.

The we/us of this class is not defined by what brings us together, but the spacing between us.

How we consider ourselves in relation to one another is of vital importance to this moment, and to all others that proceed from it. You hold in your hand [via the distributed notecards] the anonymous thoughts or feelings of someone who is not you; someone who is not sanctioned to be on your Facebook wall, or Snapchat, and thus not a pre-selected member of your circle. You might find yourself in accord or in alliance with the words you hold; you may find yourself in striking opposition to them; or perhaps, even, unmoved and apathetic in their wake. Through anonymity the burden of being responsible for this person's feelings and thoughts should be somewhat lifted. You confront another person, whose life experiences in no way identically match your own. Such differences are profound and meaningful ... you are surrounded at all times by this difference. I hope you take comfort in this, because it has the capacity to be liberating ...

My Dear Students,
This is why we spent the first four weeks in this class learning the canon and then augmenting, building, and deeply questioning its foundations. It is also why for the rest of the semester we imagine together what another history—or perhaps more accurately histories—might look like. Difference can be an engine, and not simply an over-determination.

I have been thinking and re-reading this work by Zoe Leonard, much shared during this campaign cycle. My favorite version is a performative video reading by Mykki Blanco—a video I encourage all of you to watch. Leonard wrote this text in 1992, for a gay magazine that folded before it was ever published. Her text circulated amongst friends and colleagues for years, before being reproduced in the fifth issue of the queer art zine, *LTTR*. Most recently, Leonard's text was enlarged and wheat-pasted on the side of a building adjacent to the High Line in New York City. I had the opportunity to visit this place a couple of weeks ago with a friend, and to talk with his students about what they understood from it. Their insights were valuable and life-affirming; and I'm hoping you will have your own piece to say in relation to this text. I want to read it for you now. [2]

I want a dyke for president. I want a person with aids for president and I want a fag for vice president and I want someone with no health insurance and I want someone who grew up in a place where the earth is so saturated with toxic waste that they didn't have a choice about getting leukemia. I want a president that had an abortion at sixteen and I want a candidate who isn't the lesser of two evils and I want a president who lost their last lover to aids, who still sees that in their eyes every time they lay down torest, who held their lover in their arms and knew they were dying. I want a president with no airconditioning, a president who has stood on line at the clinic, at the dmv, at the welfare office and has been unemployed and layed off and sexually harrassed and gaybashed and deported. I want someone who has spent the night in the tombs and had a cross burned on their lawn and survived rape. I want someone who has been in love and been hurt, who respects sex, who has made mistakes and learned from them. I want a Black woman for president. I want someone with bad teeth ~~and an attitude~~, someone who has eaten ~~that nasty~~ hospital food, someone who crossdresses and has done drugs and been in therapy. I want someone who has committed civil disobedience. And I want to know why this isn't possible. I want to know why we started learning somewhere down the line that a president is always a clown: always a john and never a hooker. Always a boss and never a worker, always a liar, always a thief and never caught.

Zoe Leonard
***I Want a President*, 1992**
Typewritten text on paper; 11 x 8.5 inches

Perhaps the thing that most strikes me about Leonard's text is that it seems like it could have been written only yesterday, even though it was written nearly twenty-five years ago. Leonard's call for people whose lives have been deprived of rights (a condition that philosopher Giorgio Agamben calls "bare life") to take up the mantle of the presidency is inspiring. But many of the people Leonard writes about—sex workers, people with AIDS, people of color—are far, far away from the presidency, or even more localized halls of power. This could lead one to believe that Leonard's text is hopelessly naive; but that's only true if you read it as a ballot cast, rather than as a communal exercise in calling forth and collective destigmatization; an acknowledgment of the things that mark our daily lives, and the lives of our families and friends.

"And I want to know why this isn't possible," seems to me to be the turning point of Leonard's text. A demand for accountability, followed by an excoriation of power relationships in American politics.

If we believe the fiction of American exceptionalism, carefully countered by Zoe Leonard in her text, we might end up with something close to Herbert Bayer's Universal type. Its story is interesting, and reflects the ideologies that undergirded much of the Bauhaus's production after 1922. It is a typeface composed of sans-serif letter forms (none of that decorative or ornamental stuff), with an entirely lowercase alphabet. As you learned in your reading, this was because Bayer noted that we don't speak in capital letters.[3] Using an exclusively lowercase alphabet also had the advantage of saving time for the industrious worker. As Mills also relays, this Universal type, with its ostensible claims to universality, was eventually picked up and used for corporate identity brands such as the American Broadcasting Corporation and Bloomingdale's, even though, ironically, it was never produced as cast type. Once it became aligned with these corporate identities, its claim to universality, however flawed in its inception, became a needle too impossible to thread.

It is a blemishless type—vaunted for its clean, sleek, and forward-looking design. It was a failure in pragmatic as well as conceptual terms, and therefore highly instructive. Its creation was informed by an abhorrence of difference. It perpetuates a notion that there can be, or should be, one type for all. But it is not an evil thing, this typeface, it is just a product of the man in the time that he created it; his blindspots are its blindspots, uncoincidentally. Even within the Bauhaus things were not equitable in the way that an ideology of Universalism purports: women, for example, were usually segregated into the textile and weaving program, with a few exceptions. One of these was Marianne Brandt, whom we mentioned in class last time, and who created this collage [right] in 1930.[4] In it, a woman is dropped to her knees, arms raised up in praise or surrender, head thrown back. From each of her fingers is drawn a line that leads to the fist of a suited man, who holds out his arm. The implication is clear, and a devastating realization for anyone who wants to make of the Bauhaus an uncomplicated utopia. Women, Brandt argues visually, were controlled by the whims of men, like simple marionettes.

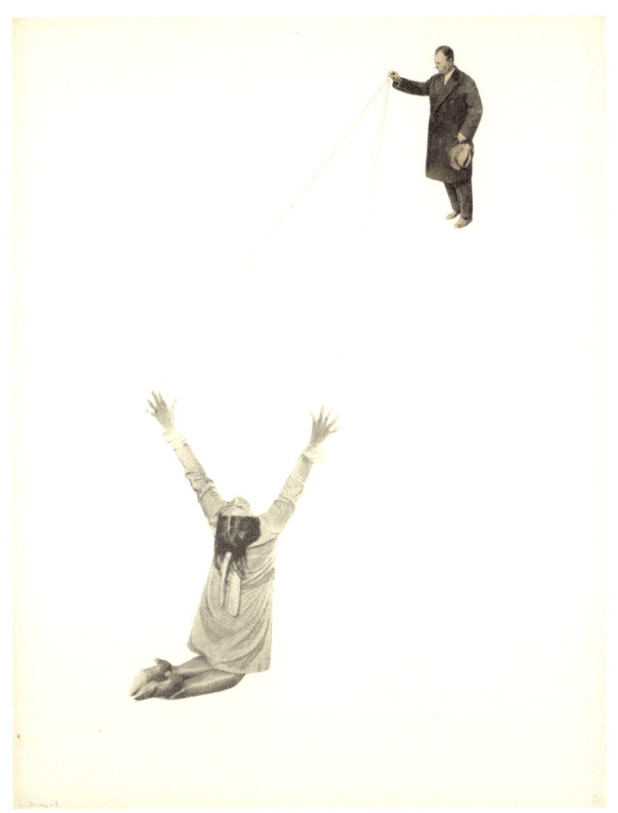

Marianne Brandt
***With All Ten Fingers (Mit allen zehn Fingern)*, 1930**
Photocollage of newspaper cuttings and graphite pencil on card

The exercise you completed for class today is another example of the flawed logic of universalism—Kandinsky believed that there was only one way to complete the test—a yellow triangle, a red square, a blue circle. Look at your own sheet, and now perhaps steal a peek at your neighbor's. A few of you may have magically aligned with Kandinsky's exercise, but most of you did not. The question then becomes what to do with all those outliers. Do we teach them to color in these shapes with the right colors, ensuring that they know exactly *why* the triangle is yellow, the square is red, and the circle blue ... as we do. Or are they hopeless? Should they just be sent away? There are some right now in our polity who take such a view toward others.

We repeat these exercises and rehearse these historical moments in this class because, as Saloni Mathur writes, "the real contribution [of revisiting the past] lies in what any self-conscious act of reinscription has the potential to make possible—the new ideas and communities it can activate, the nature of the discussion it can galvanize, and the new frameworks it can help construct for viewership and debate in the present."[5] Looking at the Kala Bhavan and the Bauhaus in equal measure (on the occasion of a re-staging of a 1922 exhibition of Bauhaus and Kala Bhavan works in Bengal), she insists that no simple equation can be drawn between the two... although both come from and respond to the rise of Nationalism in their respective countries. In Germany, this was ended by the Nationalist Socialist ethnic cleansing, which took many students of the Bauhaus with it, and in India it ended with the civil disobedience and de-colonialization independence movements. Mathur teases out how 1922 was a time of transition for Kala Bhavan and for the Bauhaus—how the descriptor of "Indian-ness" pervaded the dissatisfaction of Walter Gropius with the spiritual tendencies of Johannes Itten, a previous leader of the Bauhaus.

These exhibitions, these nations, these identities, these schools were "historical constellations that do not stand still for a viewer."[6] Today, I take lessons from Mathur's research, but also from her incredible gift for conveying her work through words. Because I do not have Mathur's facility I address you not once, or twice, but three times.

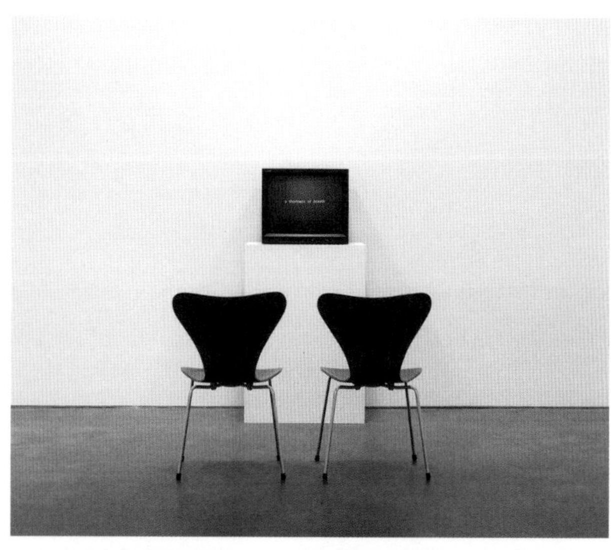

Felix Gonzalez-Torres
"Untitled" (A Portrait), 1991/1995
Video, monitor, pedestal and chairs
Overall dimensions vary with installation; Video: 5 minutes
Installation View: Felix Gonzalez-Torres. David Zwirner Gallery, New York, NY. April 27–July 14, 2017.

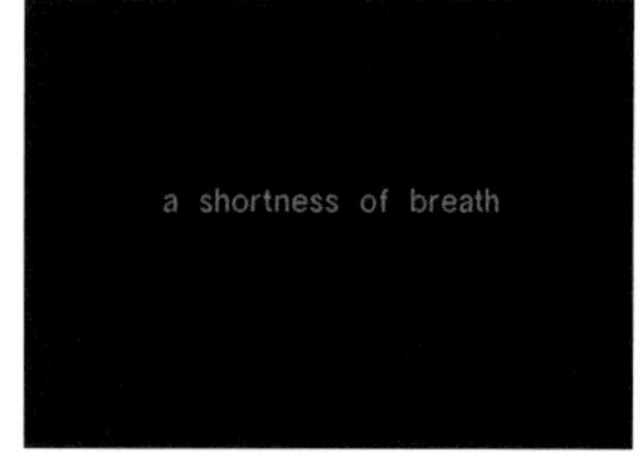

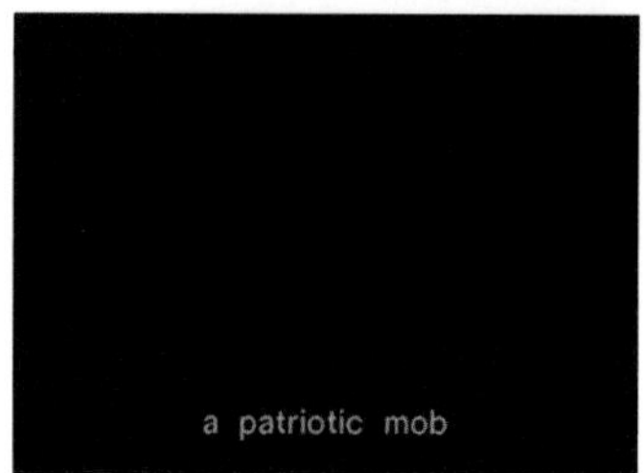

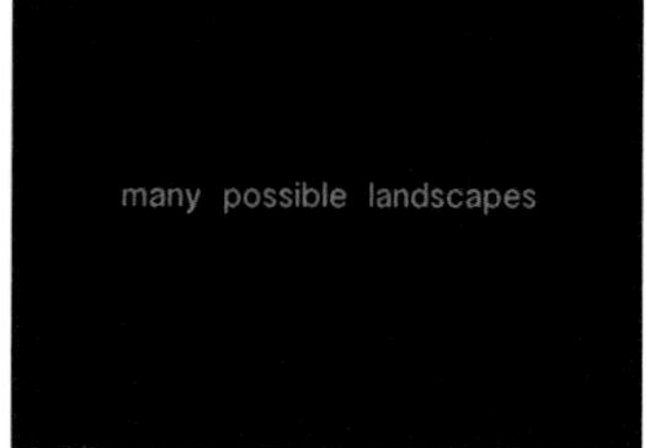

My Dear Students,
There is one other artwork I've been thinking about. It is a video work by the artist Felix Gonzalez-Torres—who I should mention, in light of our current moment, was an immigrant from Cuba, who then lived in Spain and Puerto Rico before migrating to New York and also spending time living in California. At some point during his life as an artist and a lover he seroconverted and became a person living with HIV/AIDS. He eventually died from AIDS, in the way that everyone who dies from AIDS dies, not from the virus itself, but from opportunistic infections decimating a vulnerable body. I wonder if he is one of the people Leonard imagined as a president, and now I imagine what a Gonzalez-Torres presidency would have been like....

Anyway, he's not an artist best known for his video work—in fact, I think this may be his only one. So it's an outlier of sorts. He's better known for piles of candy and stacks of paper—strings of light bulbs and paired forms: mirrors, rings, clocks. His aesthetic is both postminimalist and populist, beloved by many. This video is most closely related to his portraits, lists of events and dates from the sitter's life interspersed with larger socio-cultural milestones. However, in "Untitled" (A Portrait), the title renders the connotation to a specific person open and untethered. These lists were typically rendered in small photostats, or as text painted directly onto a wall, running around the perimeter of a room. The listed events appear out of order—so they're not teleologically biographical in the sense that most people think of a portrait or biography.

In this video, events are either displayed left justified at the top of the screen or centered at the bottom. Each one is held on the screen for a few seconds before the next replaces it. The events are banal and quixotic: "a rise in unemployment" could be any rise, from any year. "A temporary truce" could describe an international agreement just as well as an interpersonal one—tenuous, unsure. "A new lesion"—pretty sure what that one is, but which lesion, where? How long had it been there before s/he noticed? But this video, with its evocative phrases, is also about the amnesia that spaces history into cognitive chunks. Simultaneity is forsaken in favor of a toggling between backwards and forwards. The whole thing plays like a poem ... its meaning aleatory and constellated. Never standing still.

I feel today that I am somewhere between "a silver sea" and "civil disobedience" (two events in Gonzalez-Torres's work). I awoke with new and old worries for my friends and chosen family—and now I also secretly worry for you (although I almost took that part out because I think it sounds paternalistic and gross). But I do.

Telling you where I am today is one thing I *can* do. Another is to acknowledge my gratitude for you and for our work together, and for your willingness to engage. Curiosity, vigilance, empathy.

Please, enjoy the rest of the day and make it useful, because it is neither lost nor won for you.

With love,
Andy

—

1 Jean-Luc Nancy, *Being Singular Plural*, trans. Robert D. Richardson and Anne E. O'Byrne (Stanford, CA: Stanford University Press, 2000), p. 155.

2 Leonard's full text is available free and can be read here: iwantapresident.files.wordpress.com/2011/12/i_want_a_president_original.pdf.

3 Mike Mills, "Herbert Bayer's Universal Type in its Historical Contexts," in Ellen Lupton and J. Abbott Miller (eds.), *The ABCs of the Bauhaus: The Bauhaus and Design Theory* (Princeton, NJ: Princeton Architectural Press, 2000).

4 This collage can be found in *Tempo Tempo: The Bauhaus Photomontages of Marianne Brandt*, ed. Elizabeth Otto (Jovis, 2005).

5 Saloni Mathur, "The Exhibition as 'Re-Job': Reconstructing the Bauhaus in Bengal," in Regina Bittner and Kathrin Rhomberg (eds.), *The Bauhaus in Calcutta: An Encounter of Cosmopolitan Avant-Gardes* (Ostfildern: Hatje Cantz, 2013), p. 192.

6 Mathur, p. 199.

Rammellzee at the Battle of the Republic

—

Saul Williams

President of Archeological Indifference
Vice-President of Truth
Secretary of Statistics
Minister of Celebrity Injustice
Chief of Staff & Serpent
Blessed Page-Turner of The Great Book
of Misdeeds and Over-Estimations
Bishop of the Great Climate War
Minister of the Deteriorating Sky
Baron of Epic Boredom and Self-Indulgence
ALL GATHERED NOTABLES
I greet you on behalf of The Great Almighty
who was unable to pull himself from
what many are calling the greatest un-scripted reality show of all-time
the very conducting of your lives and attitudes.
We are very proud of the success of our show and network.
Not only have we successfully created
"racists" "bigots" "arrogant country-men"
"patriots" "heart-less capitalists"
but we have also maintained our position as
The Misbegotten, The Pure of Heart
The Heavenly Dove, The Docile Lamb
and The Forgiving Wife.

If Our Great Almighty
could be with us this evening
He would surely want each and every one of you
to know that He graciously accepts your inability to pay your rent
and that He is willing to allow you to do some of His work
so that we might lesson the gaps between the employed and unemployed.

It's not easy to sit back and allow
countless genocides, watch innocence murdered
see trickery and deceit over-ride common-sense and human compassion
and keep one's thumb held, steadily

on the remote control.

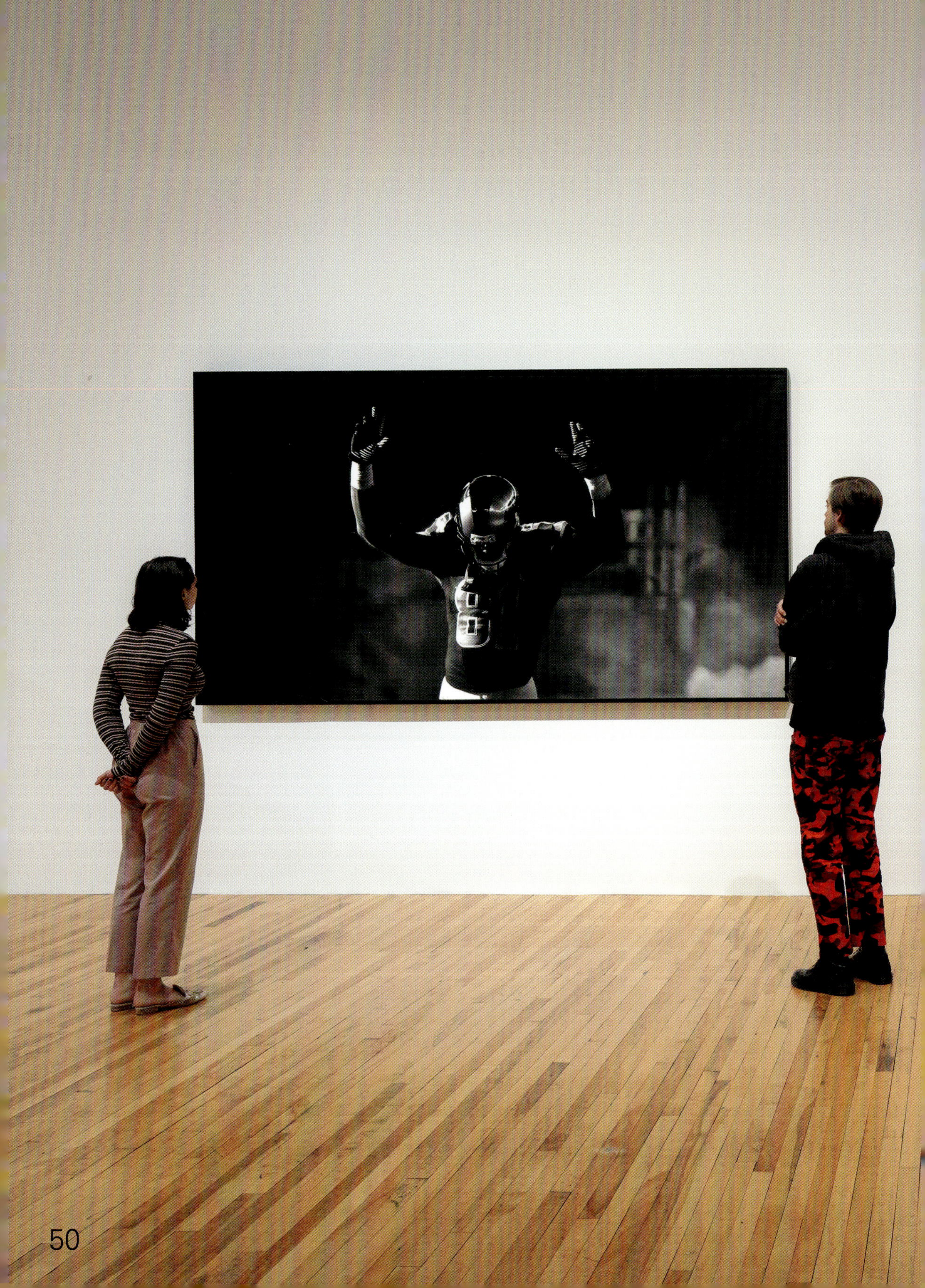

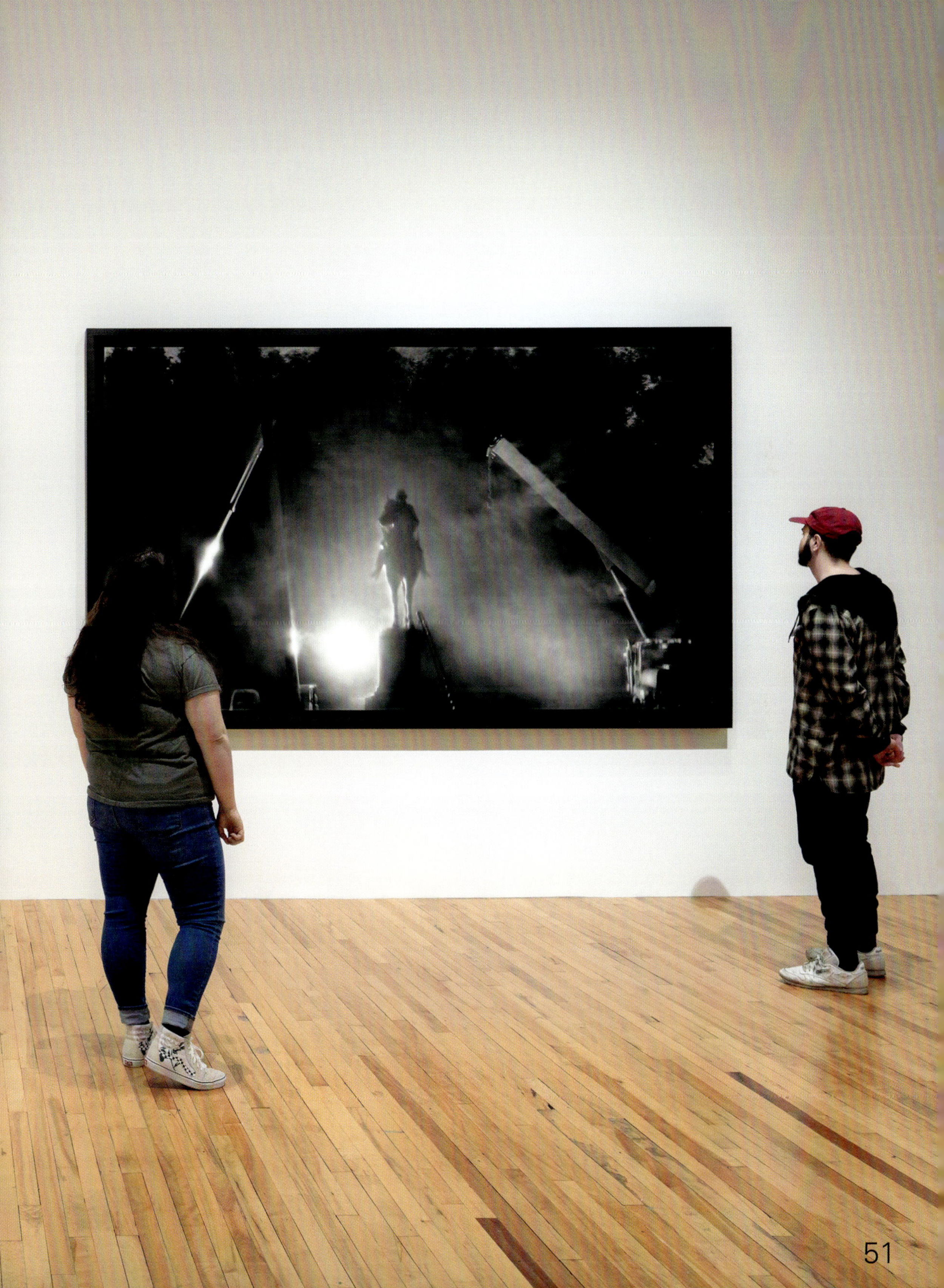

Fred Moten *(poet and scholar)*: When did the climate change? When did "this moment" become this moment?

Adam Curtis (*documentary filmmaker*): In an age where consumer capitalism constantly promotes the dream of expressing yourself, hasn't art become central to supporting and maintaining that power structure? However radical its messages are on the surface—isn't art underneath really constantly promoting the idea of self-expression and so promoting consumer capitalism? So maybe it's part of the problem?

Aruna D'Souza (*writer*): What is "real" in your practice—your way of working, your medium, your social, professional, material, cultural, political relationships, your proximity to institutions? And what is sustainable? Do the two categories (real and sustainable) overlap, and to what extent?

Gonzalo Casals (*executive director, Leslie-Lohman Museum of Gay and Lesbian Art*): Museums and cultural organizations once perceived as "pure" white boxes free of bias, are now being pushed to reckon with their own privilege and political baggage. As artists increasingly explore the meaning of "realness" in their work, I wonder how you negotiate the political context in which your work is inserted when it enters the museum.

Michael Weber (*magician, mentalist, and inventor*): The magician Karl Germain said that "conjuring is the only honest profession: a magician promises to deceive and does."[1] And Picasso said, "We all know that Art is not truth. Art is a lie that makes us realize truth."[2] In our current state, where there is no "truth," and "facts" have become a matter of opinion, how can artists wake us up from this unpleasant dream? How can you help us see the world and each other through a lens of hope, trust, and humanity?

Cat Gund (*producer, director, writer, and activist*): How do you hold on to something so no one can take it away? Your beliefs? Your body? Your love? What tethers us here?

Elaine Scarry (*writer*): Public health physicians distinguish between narrative compassion (where one or two or three people are at risk) and statistical compassion (where thousands or millions are at risk). We're fairly good at the first, and have many occasions to strengthen our capacity through daily acts of friendship and from reading literature. We're terrible at the second, and have almost no training in strengthening our feeble abilities in this region. To what extent can the medium you work in invite, or carry out, acts of narrative compassion and statistical compassion?

—

1 geniimagazine.com/wiki/index.php?title=Magicpedia:Quote_of_the_day/20
2 *Past Masters: Picasso Speaks*, 1923, ed. Scot Borofsky, editor, from *Picasso: Fifty Years of His Art* by Alfred H. Barr Jr., published for The Museum of Modern Art by Arno Press, New York, 1980.

Cassils

—

FM: When did the climate change? When did "this moment" become this moment?

Cassils: This moment demands we burst the bubble-basking, short-circuit self-righteous polarization, and jam the pendulum. We have to undo systems of white supremacy, sociopathic capitalism, free market lust, misogyny, sexism, transphobia, and homophobia, and can no longer ignore the finite resources and impending onslaught of climate disaster. The world's leading climate scientists have warned there are only a dozen years before global warming will significantly worsen the risks of drought, floods, extreme heat, and poverty for hundreds of millions of people. The species is running out of time to right our wrongs.

AC: In an age where consumer capitalism constantly promotes the dream of expressing yourself, hasn't art become central to supporting and maintaining that power structure? However radical its messages are on the surface—isn't art underneath really constantly promoting the idea of self-expression and so promoting consumer capitalism? So maybe it's part of the problem?

Cassils: I am a transgender artist making art in a time where the current administration wants to erase the existence of trans people and asserts that gender is defined by genitals at birth. I grew up before the Internet in the devastating shadow cast by the AIDS epidemic. Many queer artists were left to rot due to the negligence of the Reagan administration. Growing up there were no trans artists whose work I could access. Having such work available would not have "maintained the power structure," it would have given me a glimpse of a possible future, a chance to learn from the traditions and history of the oppressed. This question supposes a certain level of privilege where one's cultural contribution would be deemed worthy of sublimation into the nexus of the white, cis patriarchy.

AD: What is "real" in your practice—your way of working, your medium, your social, professional, material, cultural, political relationships, your proximity to institutions? And what is sustainable? Do the two categories (real and sustainable) overlap, and to what extent?

Cassils: Emory Douglas, Minister of Propaganda and designer for the Black Panther Party, stated that the purpose of visual art is to inspire a culture of resistance, resilience, and change. Each and every one of us has the capacity to be an oppressor. In order to be real and sustainable I must interrogate how I might be an oppressor and how I might be able to become a liberator for myself and for others. Upholding this ethos is real work. I attempt this way of operating across my formal and material choices, every public speaking engagement I give, how I contract labor and by advocating for artist fees. This pushes the work beyond the metaphoric and symbolic to enact real sustainable change.

GC: Museums and cultural organizations once perceived as "pure" white boxes free of bias, are now being pushed to reckon with their own privilege and political baggage. As artists increasingly explore the meaning of "realness" in their work, I wonder how you negotiate the political context in which your work is inserted when it enters the museum.

Cassils: If you can be seen, then you are real. Visibility is a trap. The increasing representation of trans identity throughout art and popular culture in recent years has been nothing if not paradoxical. Trans visibility is touted as a sign of a liberal society, but it has coincided with a political moment marked both by heightened violence against trans people (especially trans women of color) and by the suppression of trans rights under civil law.

All of us must work together to undo systems of sexism, homophobia, transphobia, misogyny, and white supremacy. As a white artist, my goal is to be self aware of my position of privilege and to leverage it to demand inclusion and fair wages for women, queers, and artists of color. If I see a lack of diversity amongst the selected artists in a group show, I suggest the curator expand their search. I see my work as a Trojan horse, I slip in visual representation of trans bodies into the canon of art history. By taking up space in the ivory towers of museums, my work inserts that "I too deserve to be here and so do you."

MW: The magician Karl Germain said that "conjuring is the only honest profession: a magician promises to deceive and does." And Picasso said, "We all know that Art is not truth. Art is a lie that makes us realize truth." In our current state, where there is no "truth," and "facts" have become a matter of opinion, how can artists wake us up from this unpleasant dream? How can you help us see the world and each other through a lens of hope, trust, and humanity?

Cassils: I have been experimenting with the concept of *Queer Darkness*: an employment of abstraction as a tactic of refusal to enter into the politics of inclusion. I have moved away from representation by obscuring my body through ice, concealing it the curling lick of flame, etching material with imprints of fists, knees, sweat, and struggle. By juxtaposing live performance and technology, I can force the audience to critically engage mediated images and to dissect the documentarian "truth" factor of images. I work with the properties of absence to problematize truth; from blinding the audience and searing an unstable after-image into their retinas, to the purposeful dropping frames in the timeline of a video, I point to all the lived experience that exists outside the periphery of the lens.

CG: How do you hold on to something so no one can take it away? Your beliefs? Your body? Your love? What tethers us here?

Cassils: In the wake of climate disaster, when violence against trans people was at an unprecedented high in 2018, I chose to give thanks for every day my community is alive. The sheer physicality of my live performances keeps me anchored in the present moment, where one false step would result in broken bones, hypothermia, or severe burns. I feel deeply alive, filled with power and light.

ES: Public health physicians distinguish between narrative compassion (where one or two or three people are at risk) and statistical compassion (where thousands or millions are at risk). We're fairly good at the first, and have many occasions to strengthen our capacity through daily acts of friendship and from reading literature. We're terrible at the second, and have almost no training in strengthening our feeble abilities in this region. To what extent can the medium you work in invite, or carry out, acts of narrative compassion and statistical compassion?

Cassils: Laverne Cox asserts that "it is revolutionary for any trans person to choose to be seen and visible in a world that tells us we should not exist." Contrary to popular hysteria, which considers the presence of trans people to be a threat, gender-nonconforming people, especially those of color, are extremely vulnerable to becoming the victims of attacks.

My work challenges us to examine our various modes of participation in repeated scenes of violence, as victims or instigators, as bystanders, as witnesses, as consumers of mass media. As an artist, I create a rupture in these routine processes of identification, objectification, and abjection, putting pressure on empathy and its failures.

***Inextinguishable Fire*, 2015**
pp. 56–7

***Fourteen Encapsulated Breaths*, 2017**
pp. 58–61

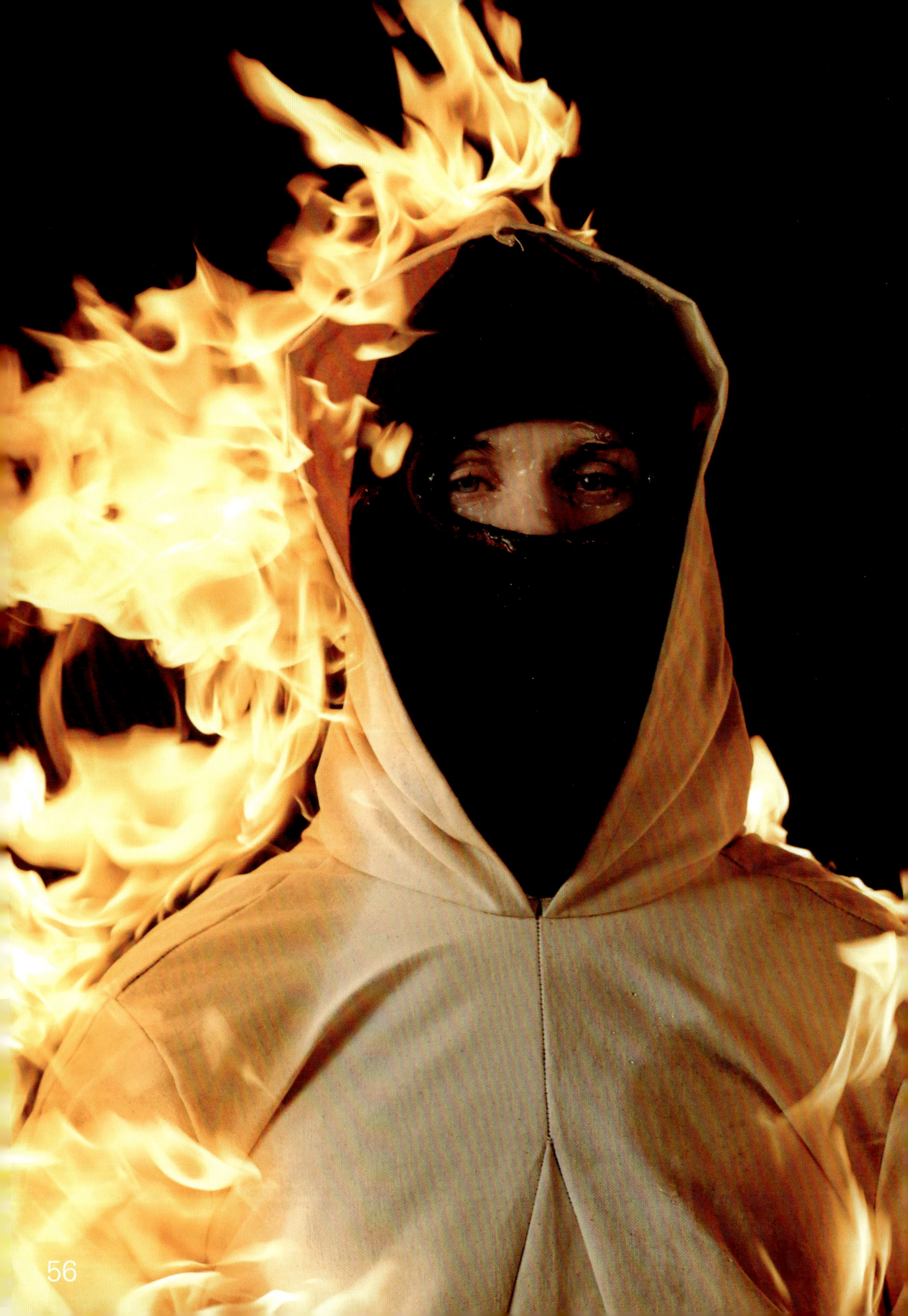

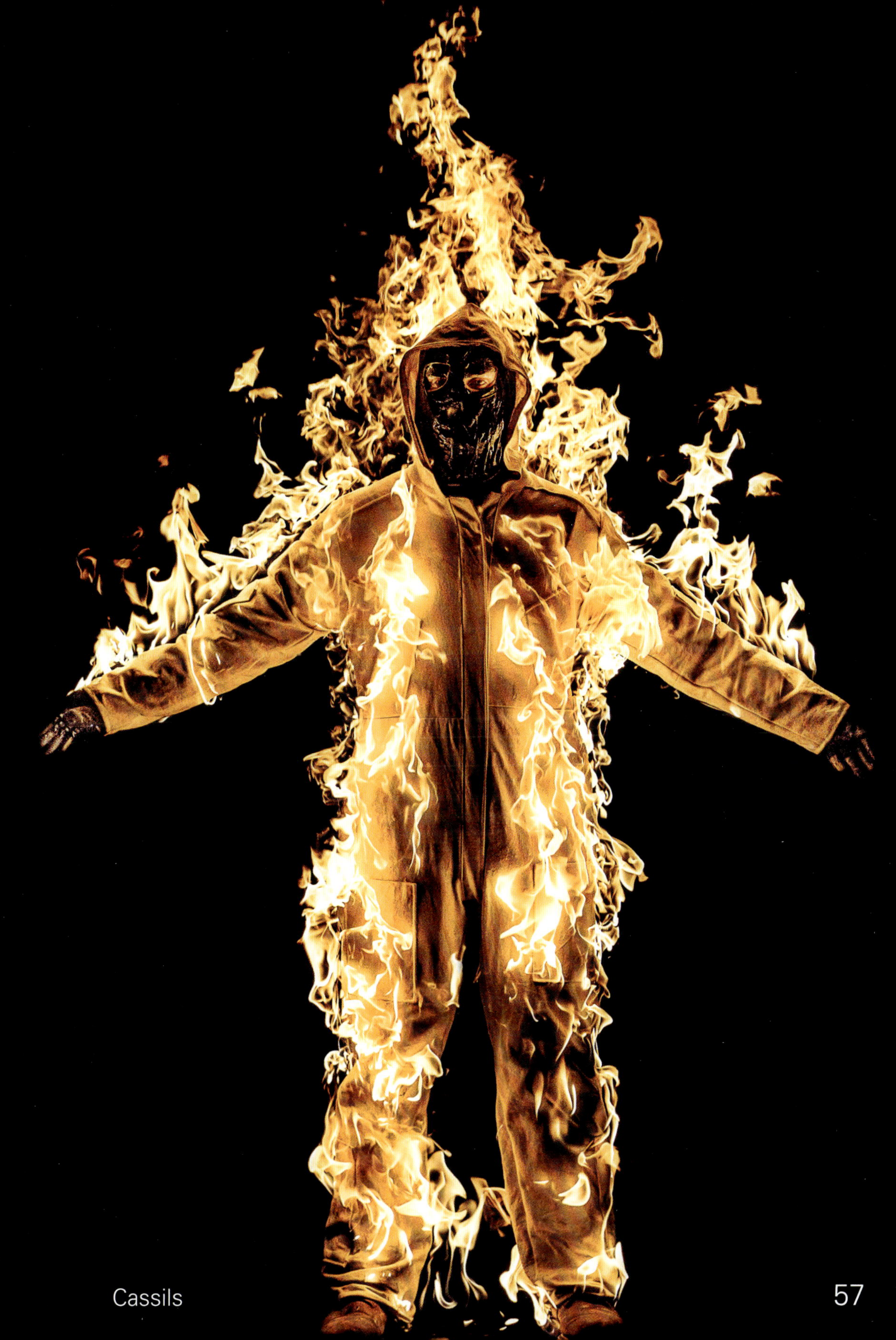

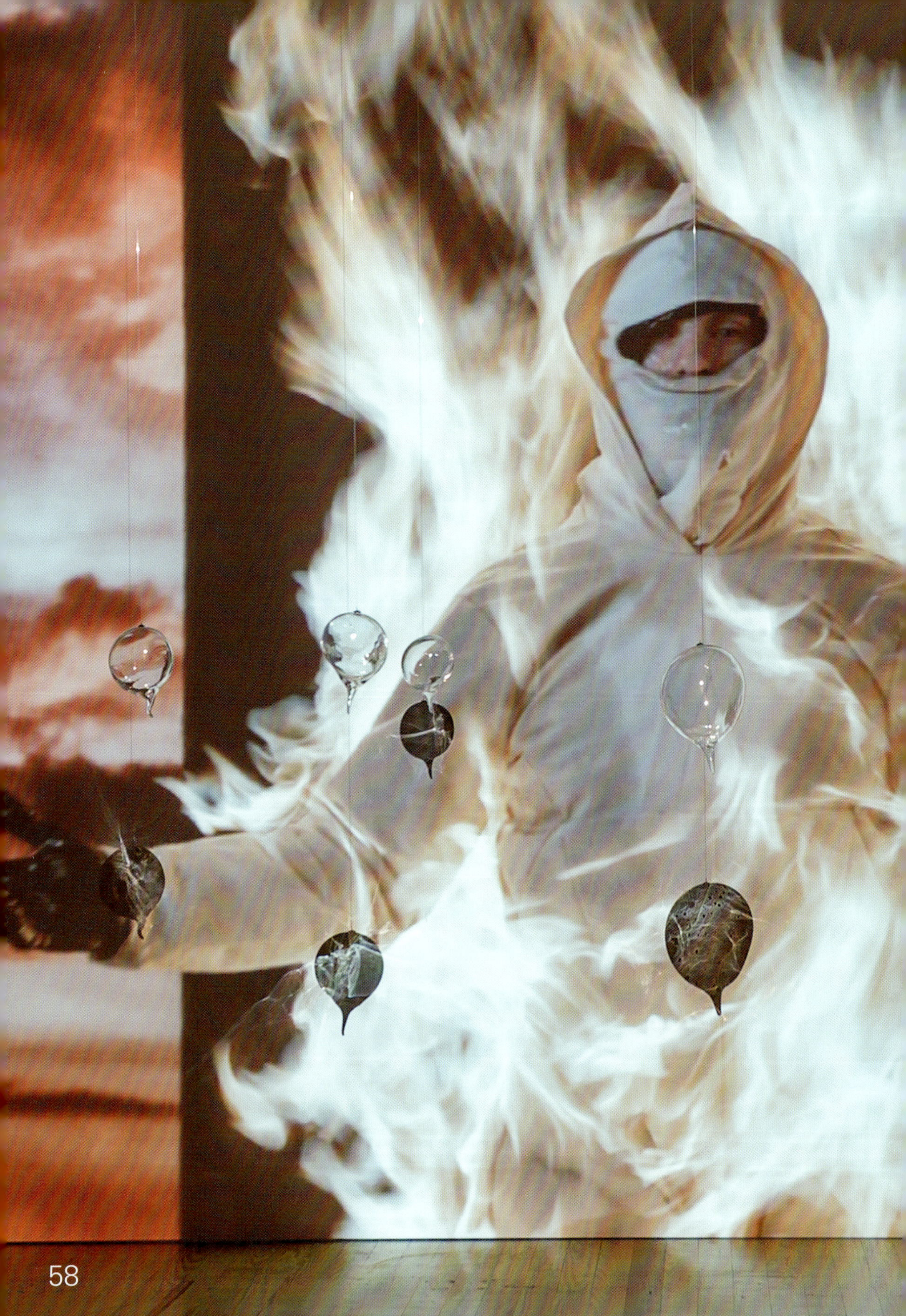

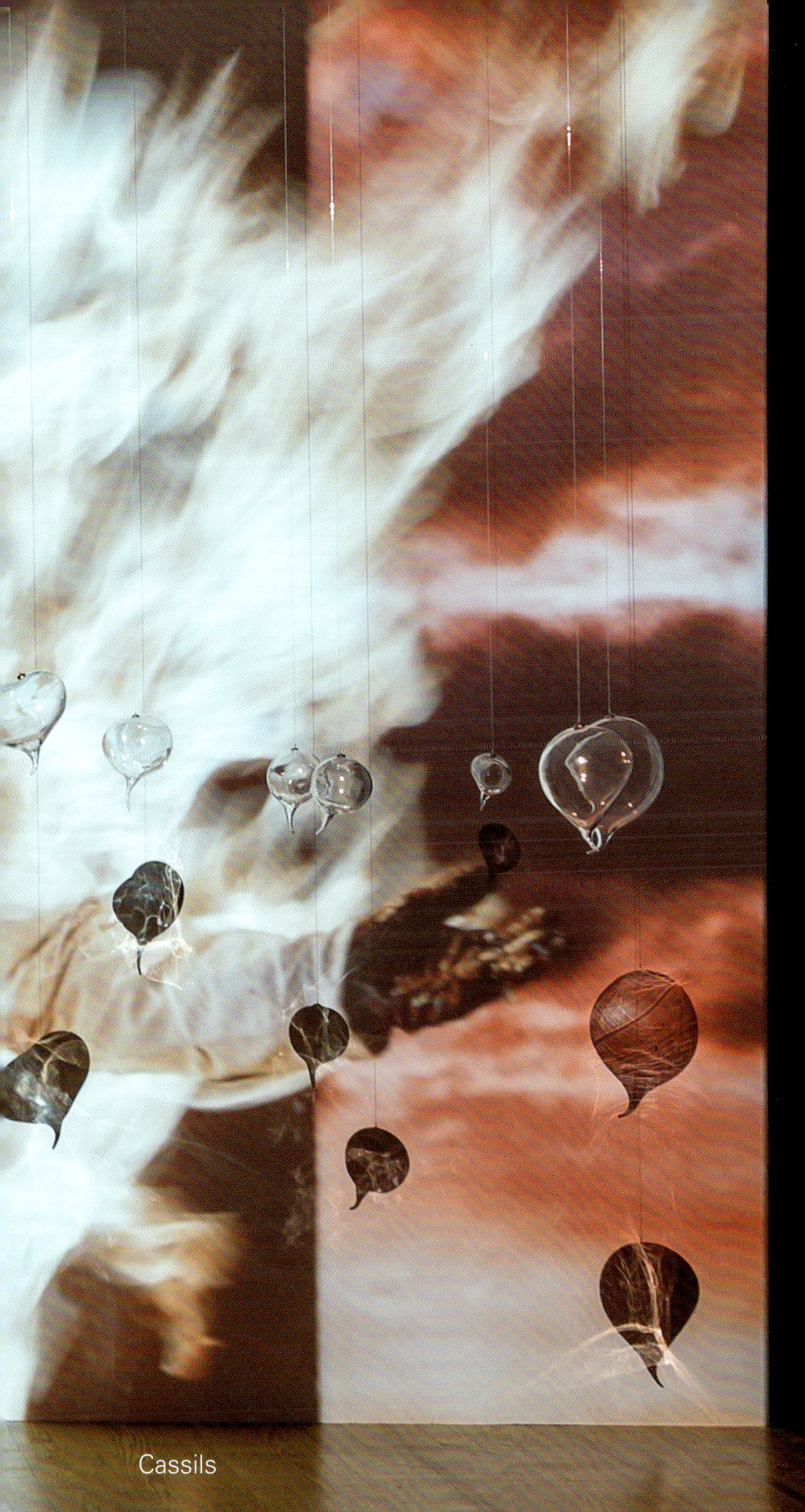

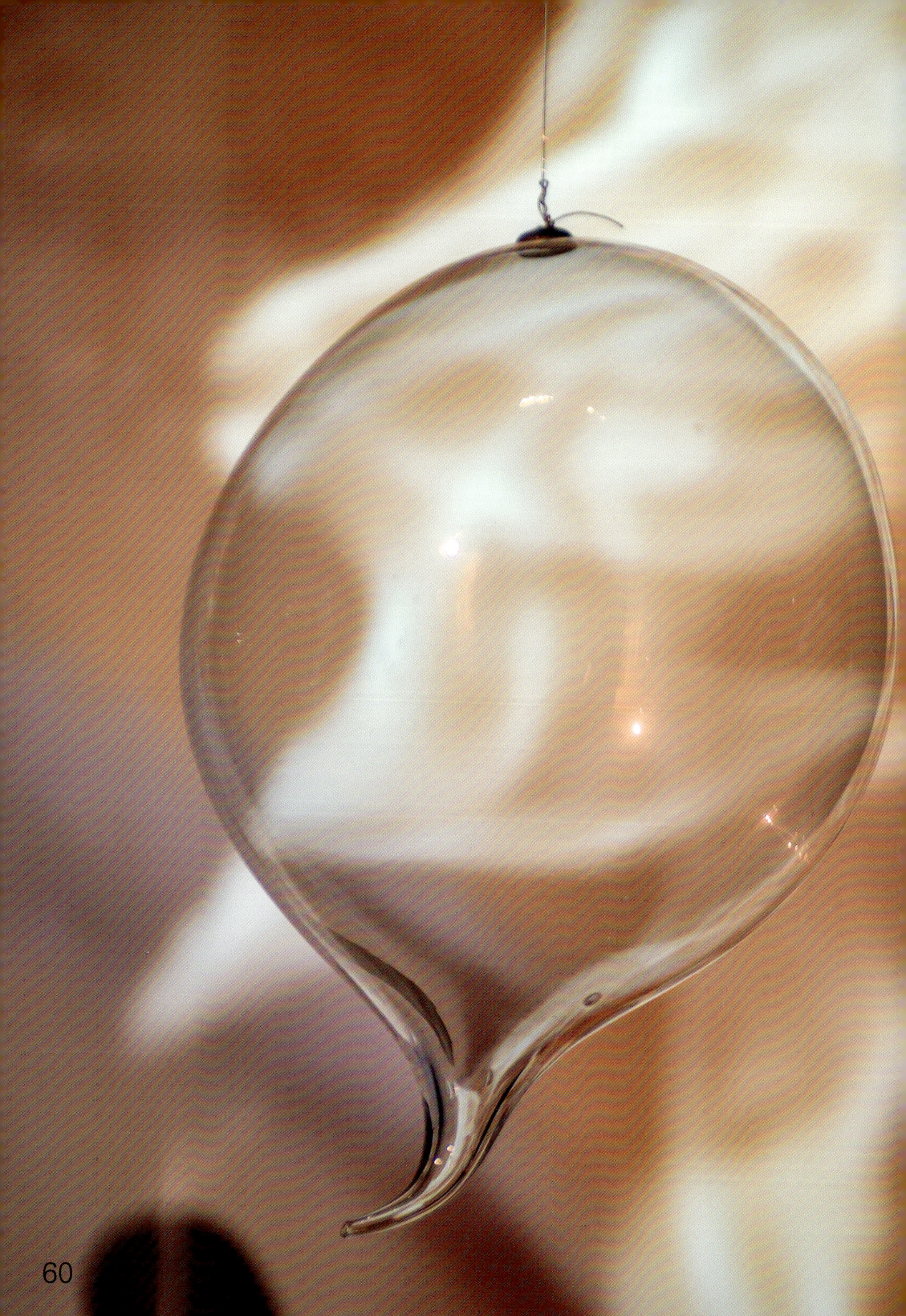

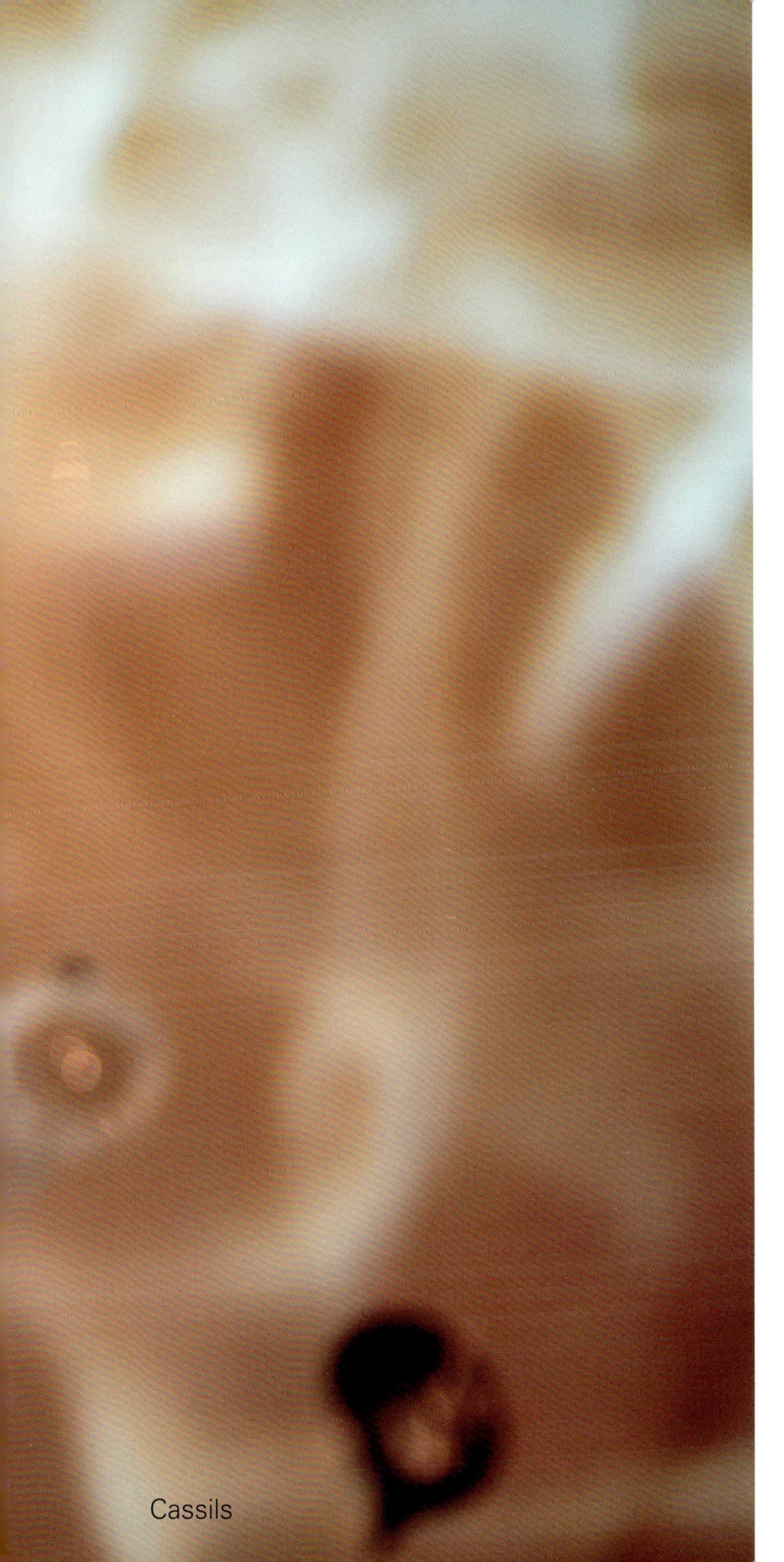

Cassils

Wangechi Mutu

—

FM: When did the climate change? When did "this moment" become this moment?

Mutu: The very definition of climate is the measurement of changes and the recording of the variation in the weather over periods of time. This moment that is causing deep upheaval, is a culmination of many decades of human neglect and arrogance. This moment has been a long time coming, and is a moment because those of us who are paying attention are frightened and have awoken to the fact that we are creating climate change and that we have a role to play in determining the future of this planet; that amidst this family of organisms, ecologies, landscapes, and natural phenomena, we are the only ones who can reverse the travesties we've released onto ourselves and our planet.

AC: In an age where consumer capitalism constantly promotes the dream of expressing yourself, hasn't art become central to supporting and maintaining that power structure? However radical its messages are on the surface—isn't art underneath really constantly promoting the idea of self-expression and so promoting consumer capitalism? So maybe it's part of the problem?

Mutu: Art is part of supporting and maintaining the power structure and is also part of the solution to dismantling this power. Art is part of the culture it exists in, and therefore is synchronized with the good things and with the problems.

AD: What is "real" in your practice—your way of working, your medium, your social, professional, material, cultural, political relationships, your proximity to institutions? And what is sustainable? Do the two categories (real and sustainable) overlap, and to what extent?

Mutu: I am most true to myself when I am actively making my work; turning raw materials and thoughts into ideas and objects that become things of their own, that carry the message and the meaning of what I stand for. In that space, I can hear and see and feel the sting and sensation of my existence. In the space of art making, I am most comfortable, I can think, understand myself, to gain and retain my dignity in this world. Through making I can reach out to others and commiserate and collaborate in changing the world as we know it. I also feel very much myself when I am in the presence of art that I love. When I am reading and witnessing and watching others reaching out and getting in-touch through their work, I feel such deep connection and love and realness.

GC: Museums and cultural organizations once perceived as "pure" white boxes free of bias, are now being pushed to reckon with their own privilege and political baggage. As artists increasingly explore the meaning of "realness" in their work, I wonder how you negotiate the political context in which your work is inserted when it enters the museum.

Mutu: Museums and institutions with a history and legacy carry old unpacked baggage. In some cases, they are thorough about refreshing and critiquing themselves, but often times, they need artists to hold mirrors up to them. When asked to include my work in esteemed institutions, I accept the challenge to speak about the things that are most pressing and painful to me and my society, through my Art. I feel most powerful inside my work, which is my platform, my weapon, my wand and barometer. To celebrate and subvert from within, utilizing materials and formal aggregates in the same way I employ interdisciplinary methods and pan-cultural Art Histories. Anything, that so strongly claims its purity ... is probably not so pure after all.

MW: The magician Karl Germain said that "conjuring is the only honest profession: a magician promises to deceive and does." And Picasso said, "We all know that Art is not truth. Art is a lie that makes us realize truth." In our current state, where there is no "truth," and "facts" have become a matter of opinion, how can artists wake us up from this unpleasant dream? How can you help us see the world and each other through a lens of hope, trust, and humanity?

Mutu: The very fact that it hurts and aggravates us (who believe in provable truths) when Truth is attacked and demeaned and abused is a sign that it is deeply valuable. There have always been some who work to hide the truth and who are afraid that the truth will undo their power and awaken the sleeping masses. I do not agree with Picasso; from my experience Art is a truth presented in ways that look unbelievable or untrue. For me Art is the truth presented as if it is fiction, or too good to be true.

CG: How do you hold on to something so no one can take it away? Your beliefs? Your body? Your love? What tethers us here?

Mutu: I hold onto what I value by becoming it. I work every day to live the things that I preach and I dream of. I work to be the best artist, mother, activist, spouse, friend, and feminist, that I can. I AM active day by day, bit by bit, in manifesting and growing and working, so it IS me.

ES: Public health physicians distinguish between narrative compassion (where one or two or three people are at risk) and statistical compassion (where thousands or millions are at risk). We're fairly good at the first, and have many occasions to strengthen our capacity through daily acts of friendship and from reading literature. We're terrible at the second, and have almost no training in strengthening our feeble abilities in this region. To what extent can the medium you work in invite, or carry out, acts of narrative compassion and statistical compassion?

Mutu: As children, our brains needed to develop the ability to see through the eyes and experiences of other people and living creatures through play acting or role playing, it's a way of learning compassion. But this "playing" goes away as we grow older, and as we stop pretending we no longer enjoy being other people or things. As we grow older, we are discouraged from seeing ourselves as something or someone who doesn't look like or seem like our people or our family. We are taught that it is safer to associate with people who look like us. But I think humor, comedy, performance, drama, literature, art, film, and music all have the power to pull ourselves closer to one another, and not see other humans as a big mass of problems. That way, we feel as if we are aware of one another's and each other's experiences.

***Mwotaji The Dreamer*, 2016**
pp. 64–5

***Mary & Magda*, 2018**
pp. 66–7

***One Cut*, 2018**
pp. 68–9

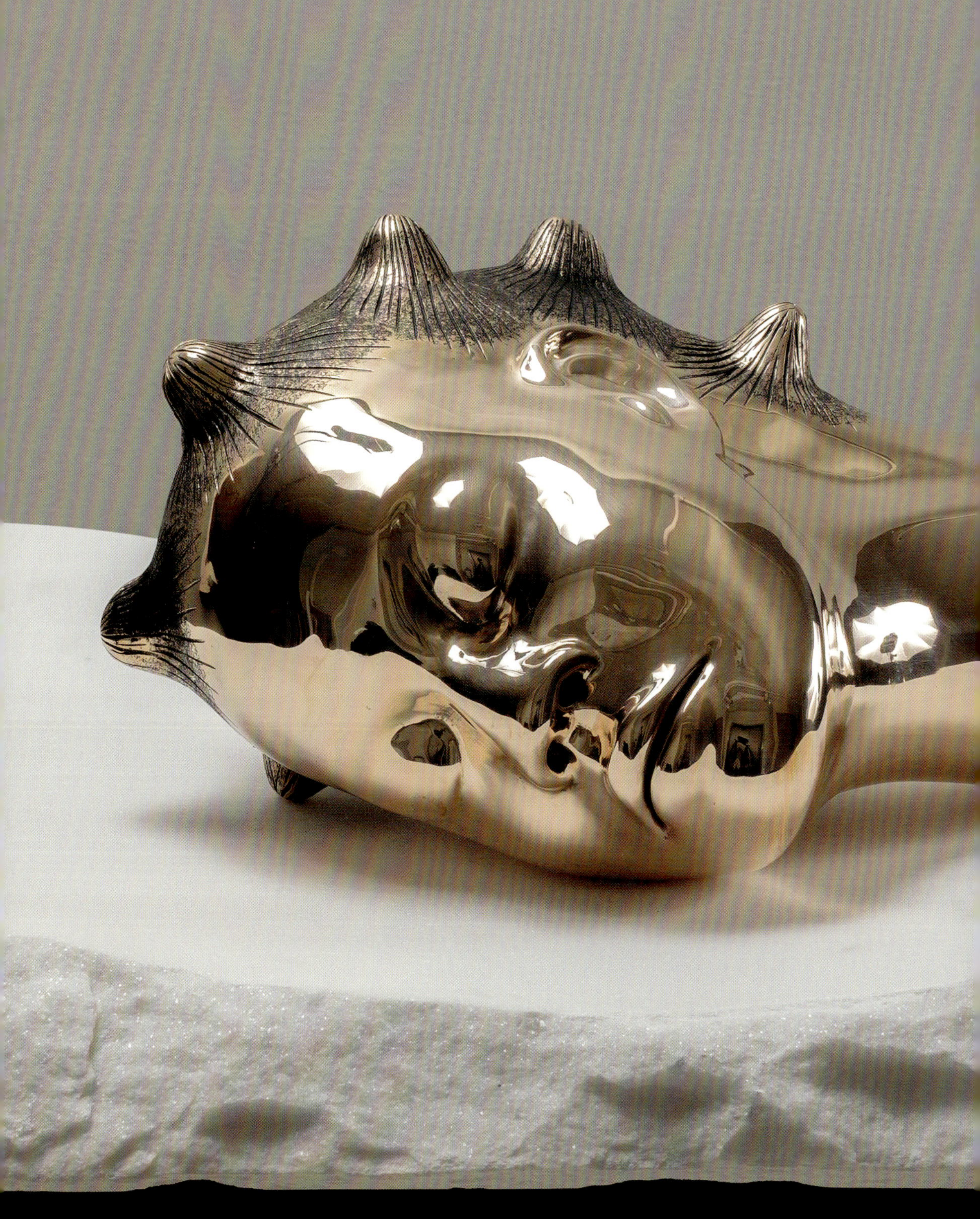

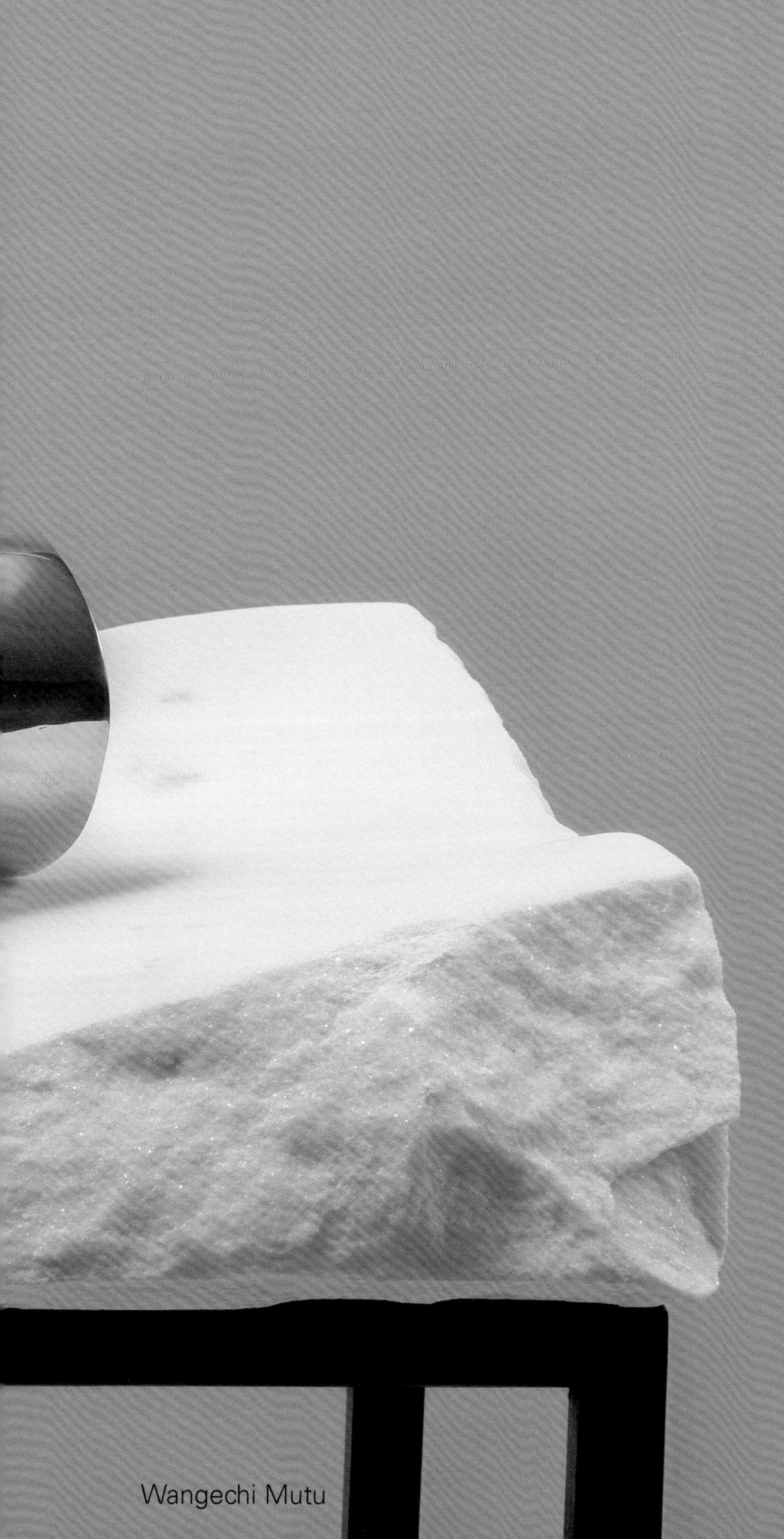

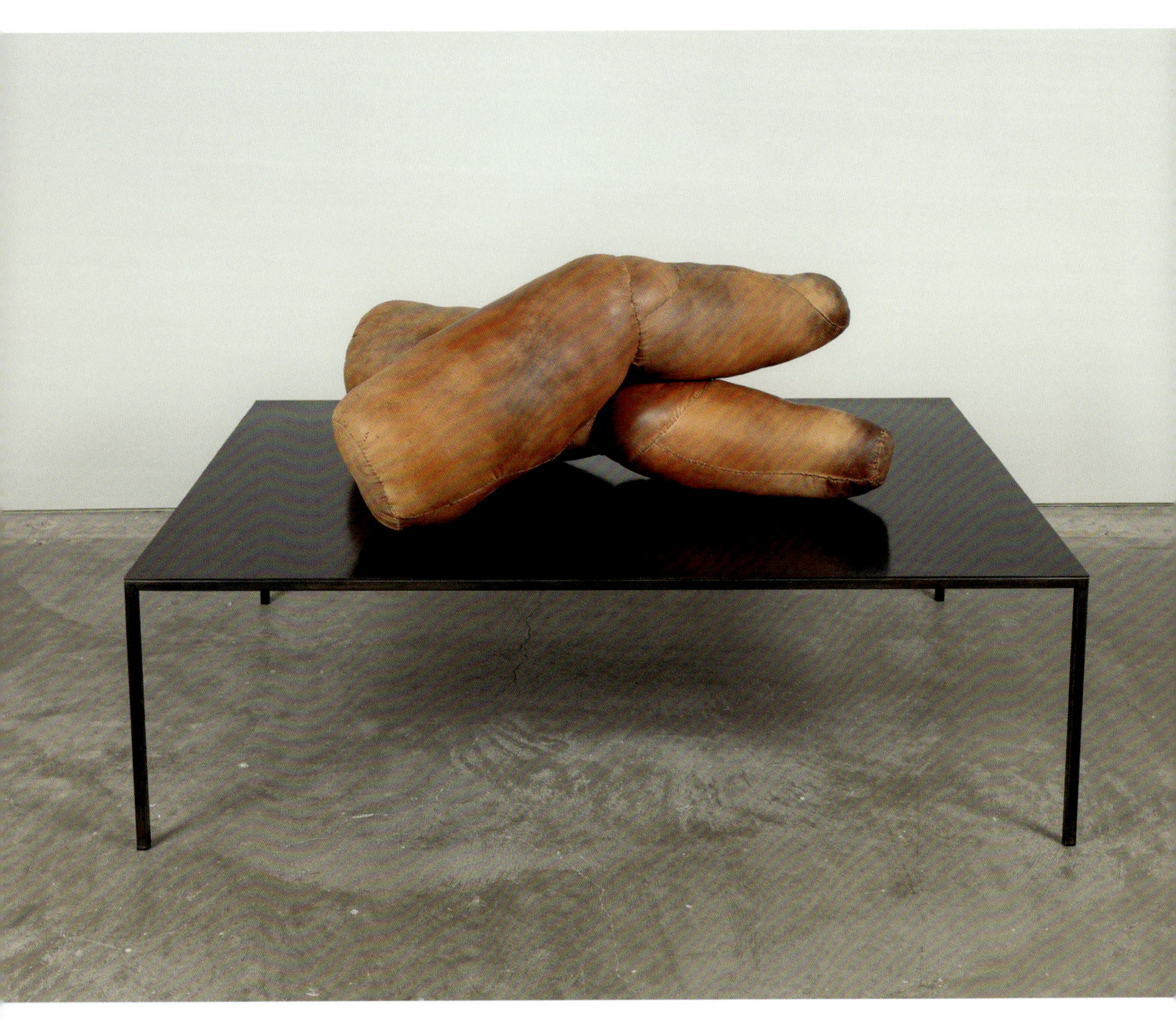

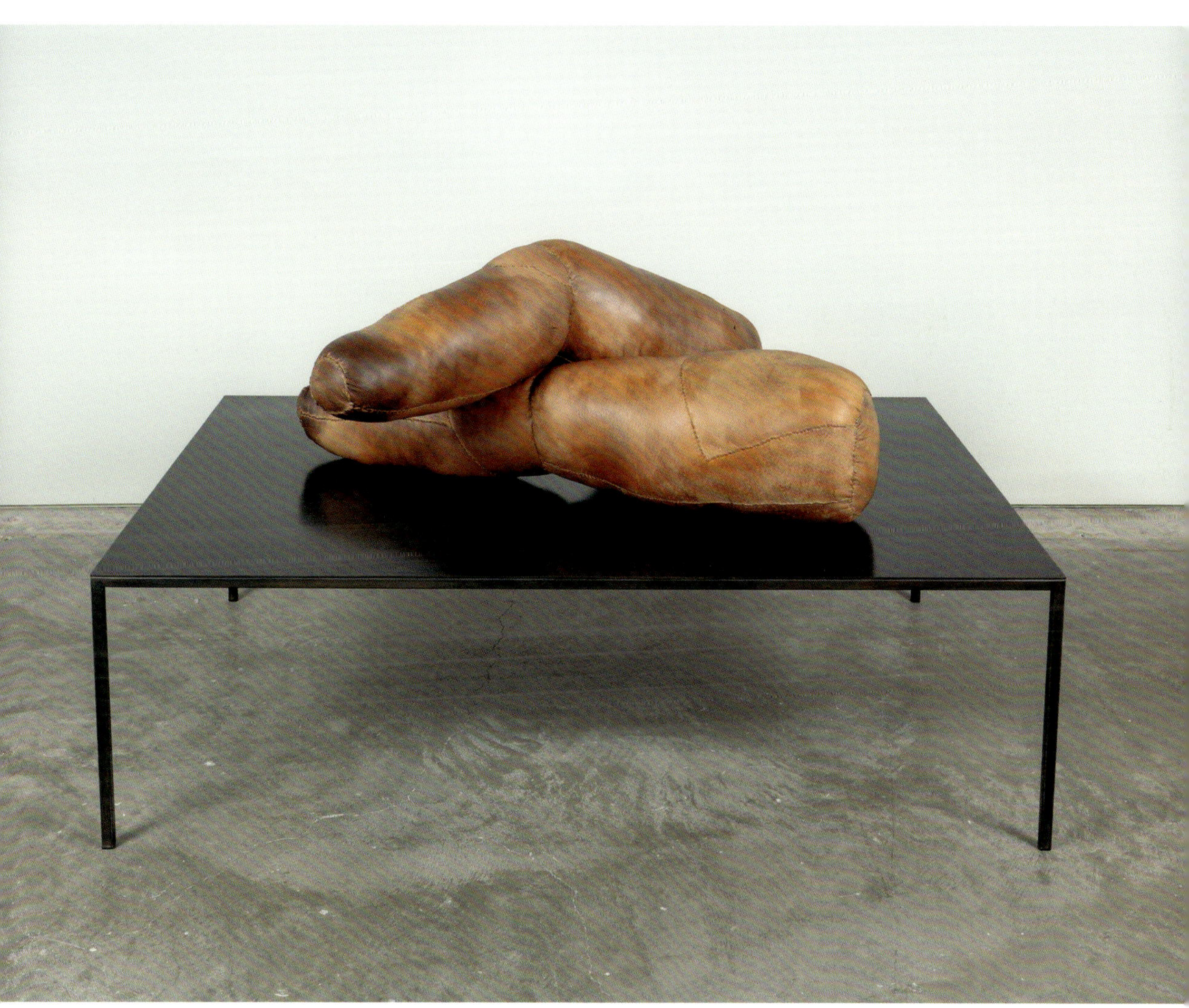

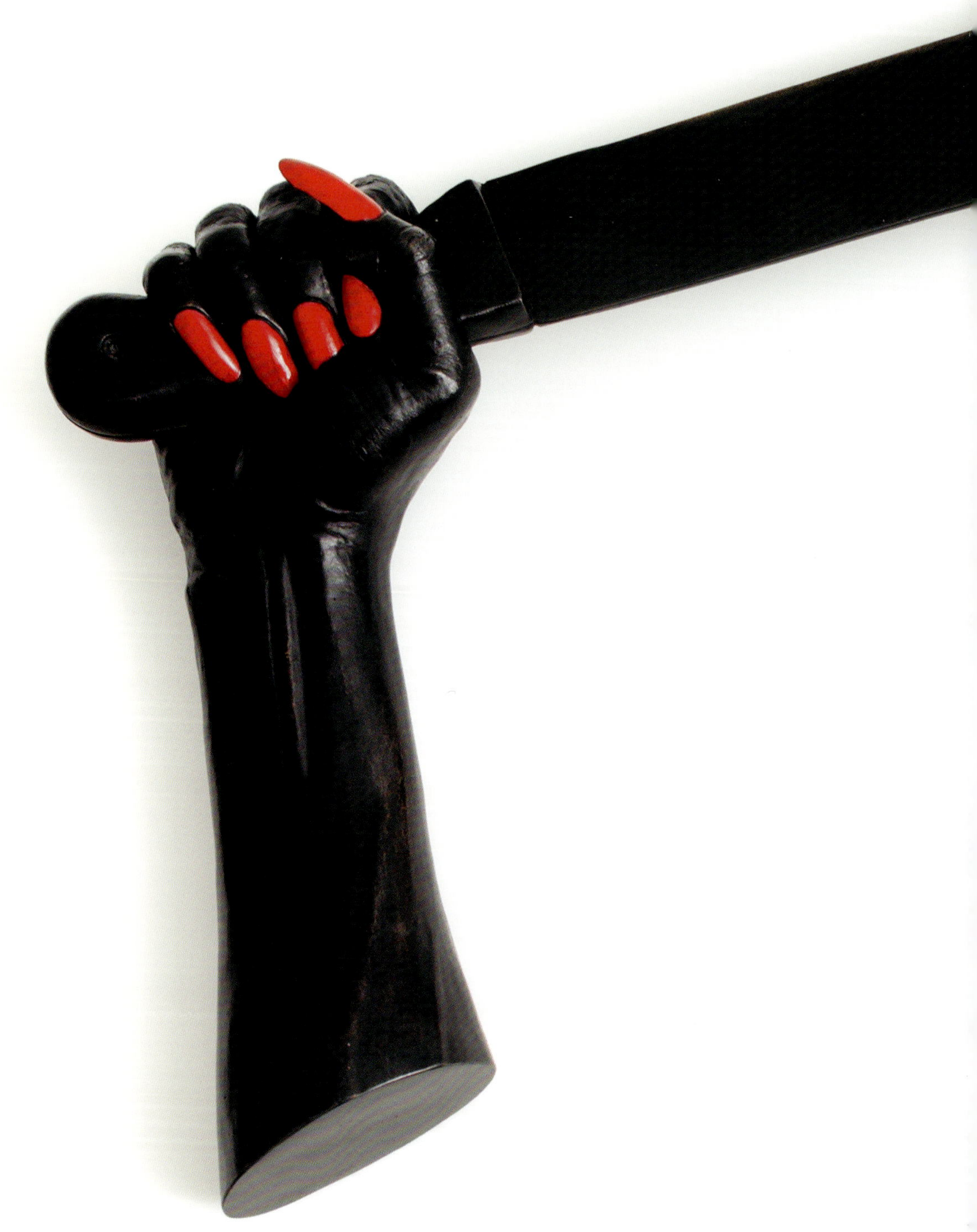

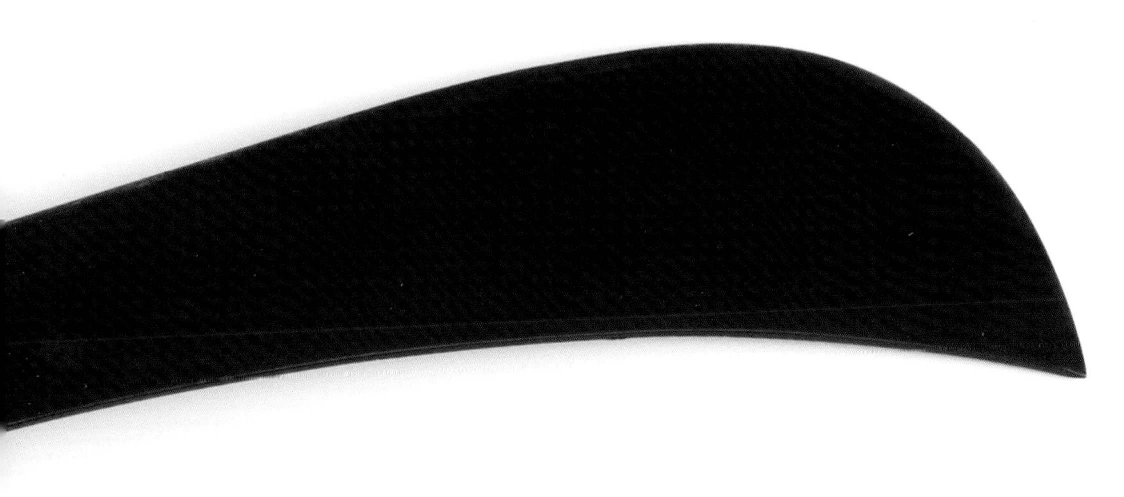

MPA

—

FM: When did the climate change? When did "this moment" become this moment?

MPA:

This question takes me to outerspace.

it seems our species, amongst the many earth species and planet Earth itself, are the result of cosmic eruptions, clamor, explosion … that humans are the particle evolution of light splitting billions of years ago … duality feels rooted in the weather of this event. whether this fragmentation is a permanent and fixed separation, or if the atom evolution of this universal explosion is magnetically one, in dependence with spiraling polarity?

AC: In an age where consumer capitalism constantly promotes the dream of expressing yourself, hasn't art become central to supporting and maintaining that power structure? However radical its messages are on the surface—isn't art underneath really constantly promoting the idea of self-expression and so promoting consumer capitalism? So maybe it's part of the problem?

MPA: self-expression, from what i understand, is inherent to our human species. art feels as long in time to me as self-expression in homo saps, existing in the instantaneous motion of our physical bodies to one another, and drawing in the sand communicating with sign and symbol to each other about experiences immaterial and material. Does your question anticipate that self-expression should or can in some manner impede in our species?

your question inspires in me a question of heads and tails.

heads and tails are encircled around a fire (that spectacle that warms, gathers, burns)

and head throws fire at tail, "stop expressing yourself". and tail has put out a lot of fires, and thrown fire itself. but what if the fire burns tail and spreads to the middle of the body connecting head and tail, and what if the fire burns through to the head. is this the beginning or end of this question and questions like this?

shit is always being taken. (like we are born, re-invent, die from non-consensual capitalist compost)

back at the fire, heads and tails are gathered and tail is dancing, expressing itself in fire's light and head watches tail in awe and expresses it's awe in sounds and the dance moves to the middle and then to the head and the whole body is moving gathered around the fire and this movement it feels like chaos but it feels like a stream of love because the dreams of the body were to love tail's movement and head's awe and were not dreams for head to fear tail's movement and for tail to be in de fence of head's awe. and is this movement the beginning or the end?

of this question and questions like it?

AD: What is "real" in your practice—your way of working, your medium, your social, professional, material, cultural, political relationships, your proximity to institutions? And what is sustainable? Do the two categories (real and sustainable) overlap, and to what extent?

MPA: my emotions are real.

but real emotions kill.

i was speaking to a friend recently about her intentions to merge somatic massage with her sex escort work to treat PTSD. this got us to talking about prostitutes in war depicted as the pleasure of the soldier, rather than a healer. and that … real emotions and real emotional work have not been sustainable in capitalism, but robbed, murdered, and re-formatted to perform on the pixel screens of distribution. capitalism married to white supremacy married to patriarchy has directed wars to kill the healing channels connecting our species with the elements of this planet and cosmos. whole systems have been perforated by and for economies of war. the somatic sex healer that tames the warrior, bringing he/she/they back into the fold—literally flesh folds that hold space for grief of battle, that bridge pleasure from pain that can reconnect balances in torn imbalances; has been diluted as an accessory of war rather than its counter-balance. the loving action potent in these eros-tic sex acts, is eclipsed by limited frame commodification. the body is present, but the art of sex magic, of healing erected egos drunk on displaced battle has been nearly completely lost.

sustainability cannot happen with war as the dominant economy of the planet because war implements us in extracting and extinguishing relation to one another and with the elements of the planet. BUT—can models of sustaining emotional abilities curb the economies of war?

GC: Museums and cultural organizations once perceived as "pure" white boxes free of bias, are now being pushed to reckon with their own privilege and political baggage. As artists increasingly explore the meaning of "realness" in their work, I wonder how you negotiate the political context in which your work is inserted when it enters the museum.

MPA: Dear white wall beast,

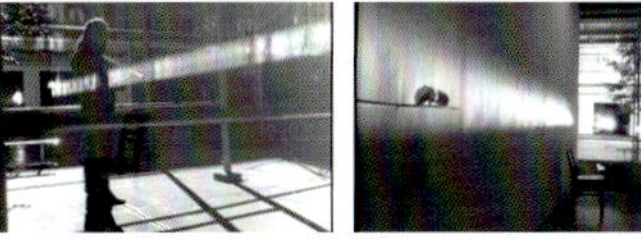

MW: The magician Karl Germain said that "conjuring is the only honest profession: a magician promises to deceive and does." And Picasso said, "We all know that Art is not truth. Art is a lie that makes us realize truth." In our current state, where there is no "truth," and "facts" have become a matter of opinion, how can artists wake us up from this unpleasant dream? How can you help us see the world and each other through a lens of hope, trust, and humanity?

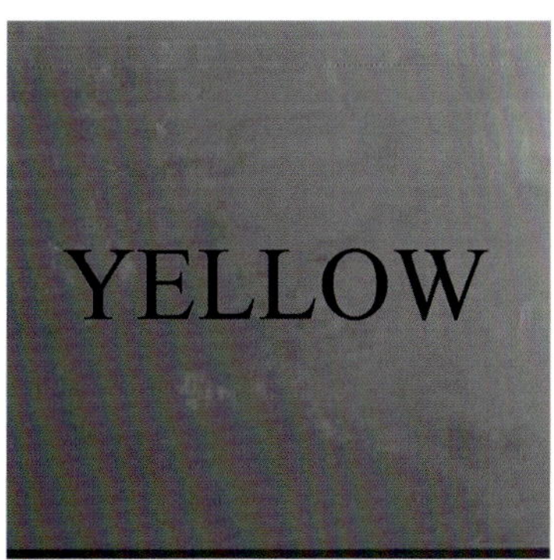

MPA: "lie"

CG: How do you hold on to something so no one can take it away? Your beliefs? Your body? Your love? What tethers us here?

MPA: great question. still answering. voice mail is full. is this defense i feel at the site of this question? do i want a border here where there should have been one, but there was none. cuz this body vessel i am host to has not been clearly mine.

ES: Public health physicians distinguish between narrative compassion (where one or two or three people are at risk) and statistical compassion (where thousands or millions are at risk). We're fairly good at the first, and have many occasions to strengthen our capacity through daily acts of friendship and from reading literature. We're terrible at the second, and have almost no training in strengthening our feeble abilities in this region. To what extent can the medium you work in invite, or carry out, acts of narrative compassion and statistical compassion?

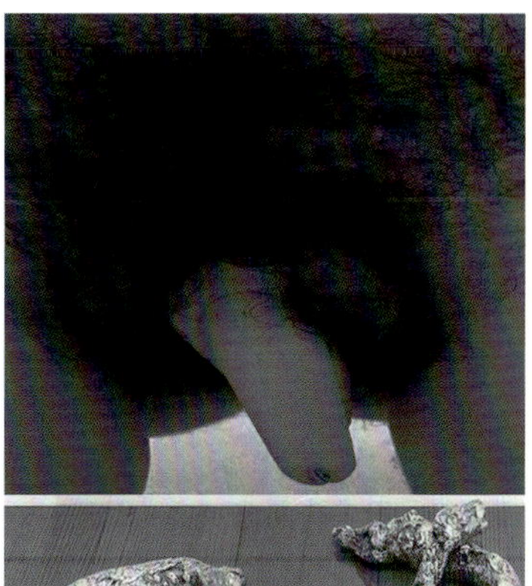

***1, 2, 3, For*, 2019**
(including *1, Copper Conductor*, and *Alpha and Omega*)
pp. 72–3

***3. Meeting of Sword and Wand*, 2019**
pp. 74; 76–7

***Center*, 2019**
p. 75

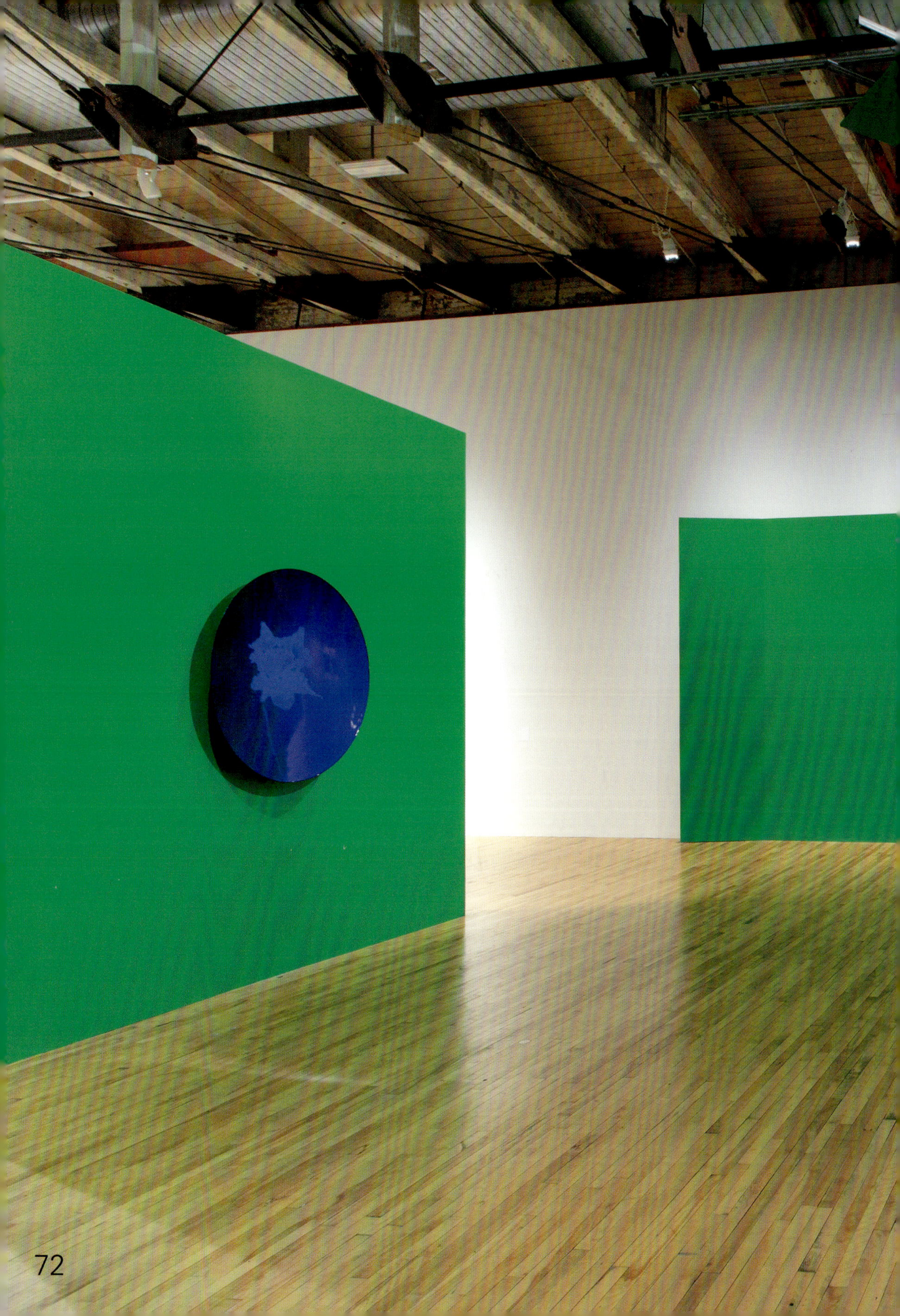

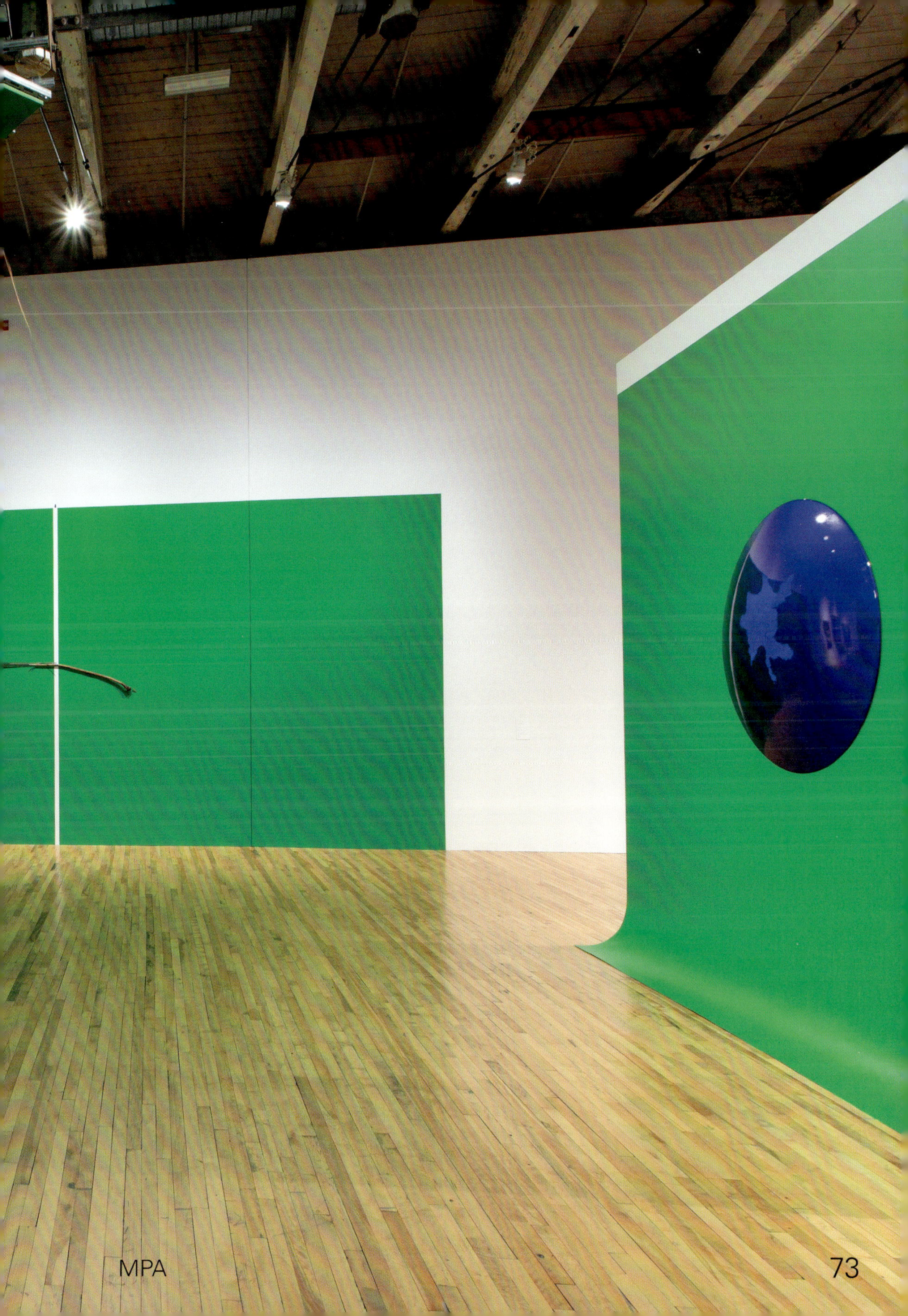

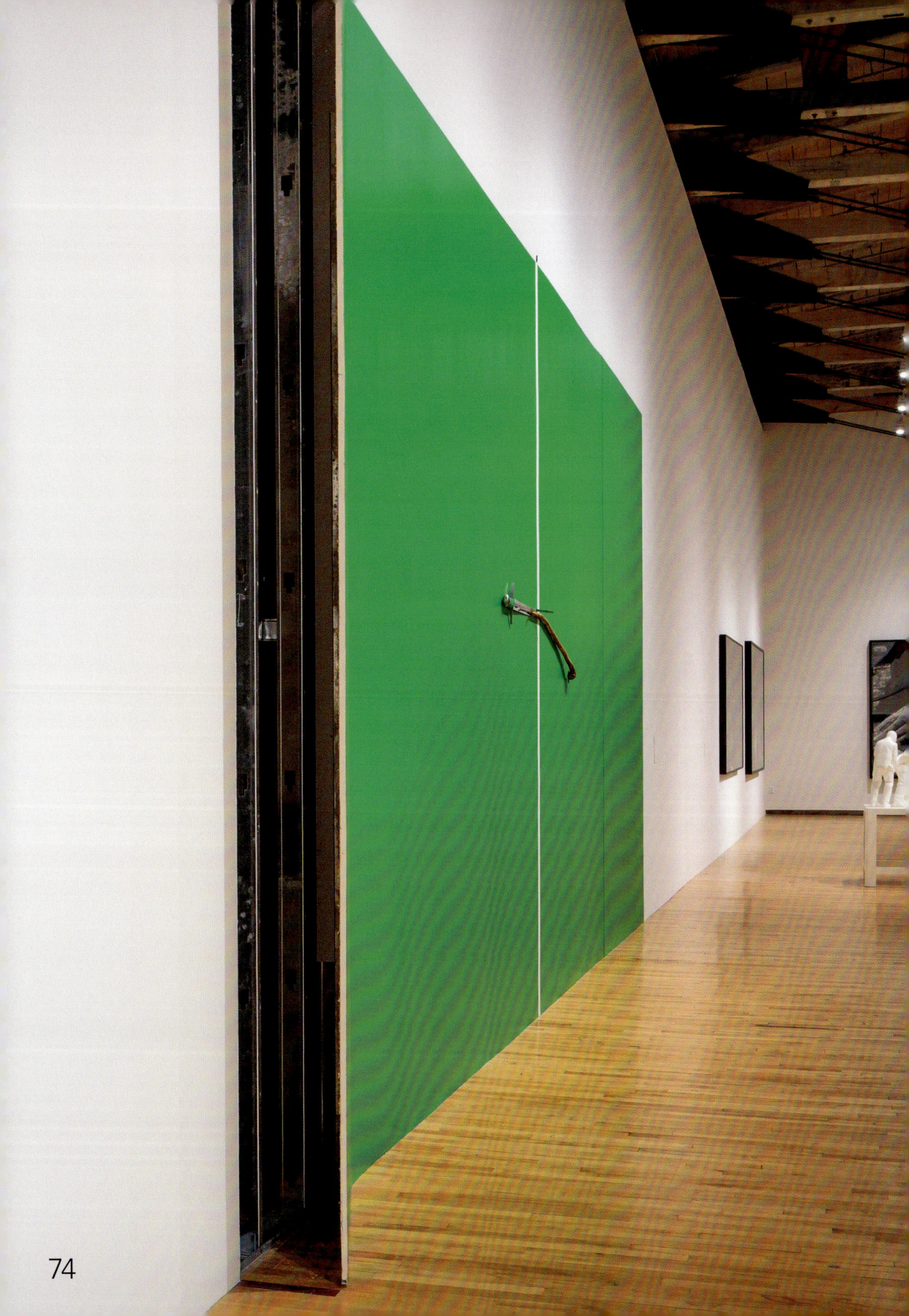

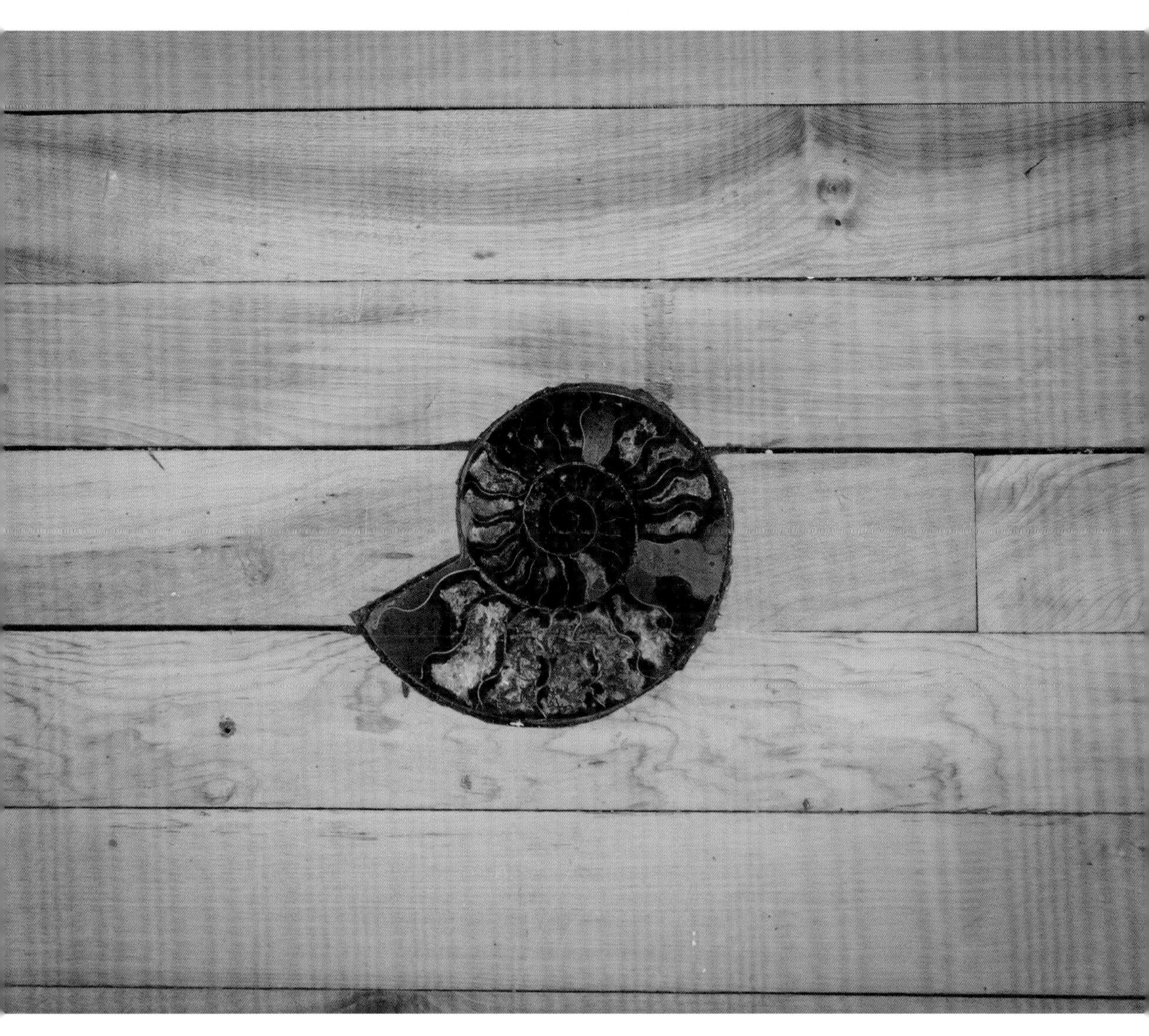

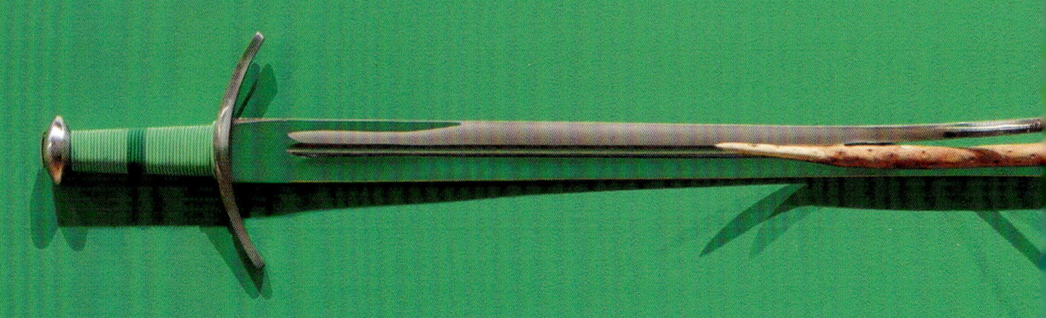

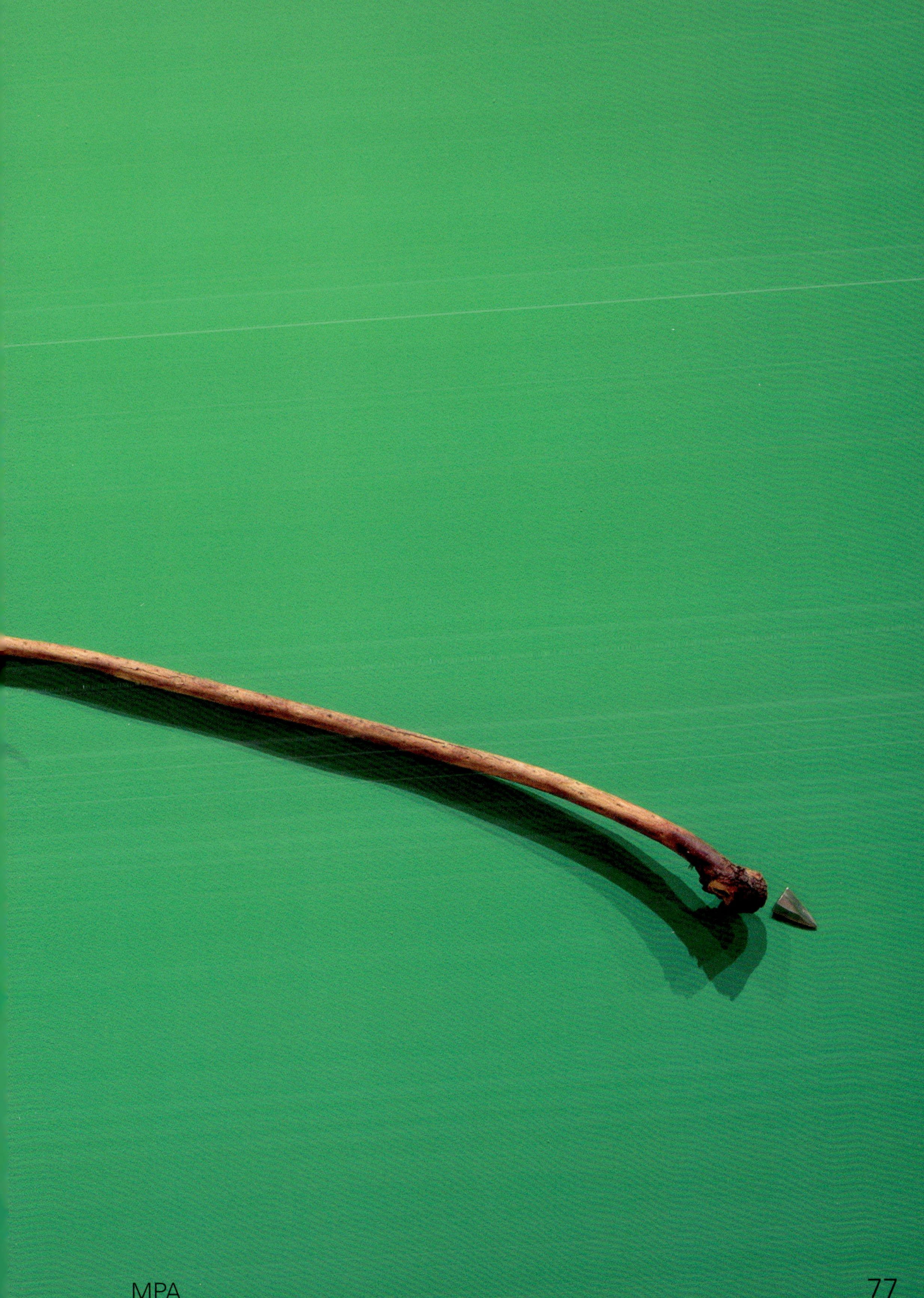

Robert Taplin

—

FM: When did the climate change? When did "this moment" become this moment?

Taplin: The climate is always changing—it's just faster right now. As E. O. Wilson has pointed out, we've just recently arrived at a somewhat realistic understanding of where we came from and what our place in the natural order really is. This awareness of how we fit in and the effect we are having on the biome and the atmosphere may have arrived too late for us to collectively alter our behavior. Our children and grandchildren will find out.

AC: In an age where consumer capitalism constantly promotes the dream of expressing yourself, hasn't art become central to supporting and maintaining that power structure? However radical its messages are on the surface—isn't art underneath really constantly promoting the idea of self-expression and so promoting consumer capitalism? So maybe it's part of the problem?

Taplin: Consumer capitalism, with its relentless—though patently absurd—exhortations to "follow your dream" and "be whatever you want to be," could be construed as a manipulation of the desire for self-expression. I don't see my art as aiding that effort. First, although advertising attempts to promote the fantasy that by buying a given product the consumer becomes more of an individual, it is glaringly clear that the opposite is true. The consumer is joining a tribe with each purchase, either a large tribe or an exclusive one depending on her means and social orientation. The art I make requires each person to examine it on her own initiative, in real space and time. The issue of allegiance or belonging is called into question by both the imagery and the presentation. Second, consumer capitalism is inherently wedded to a progressive idea of society. Advertising pushes everyone to accept the notion that their lives will be improved by each purchase and that the trajectory of consumer society is forward. Fine arts are under an obligation to address the tragic paradoxes of human existence, a subject that consumer capitalism has no time for whatsoever. Finally, I would say that the enemy of self-expression is not consumer capitalism, but rather forces within the art and literary world itself.

AD: What is "real" in your practice—your way of working, your medium, your social, professional, material, cultural, political relationships, your proximity to institutions? And what is sustainable? Do the two categories (real and sustainable) overlap, and to what extent?

Taplin: My interest in making art has always been about answering questions I have posed for myself. That has proved sustainable over forty years. It has not necessarily proved to be a realistic approach for sustaining social, political, or institutional relationships.

GC: Museums and cultural organizations once perceived as "pure" white boxes free of bias, are now being pushed to reckon with their own privilege and political baggage. As artists increasingly explore the meaning of "realness" in their work, I wonder how you negotiate the political context in which your work is inserted when it enters the museum.

Taplin: The world of the museum and fine art has always been built on inequality. The upper bourgeoisie has been the main support for the arts since the church left the field. The current trends toward creating a museum of entertainment and "viewer participation" are democratizing, but the look of the art begins to merge with the look of advertising. So, the question of how to address a non-museum audience with the vocabulary of fine art remains. I try and make art that is broadly legible but still challenging.

MW: The magician Karl Germain said that "conjuring is the only honest profession: a magician promises to deceive and does." And Picasso said, "We all know that Art is not truth. Art is a lie that makes us realize truth." In our current state, where there is no "truth," and "facts" have become a matter of opinion, how can artists wake us up from this unpleasant dream? How can you help us see the world and each other through a lens of hope, trust, and humanity?

Taplin: The intellectual and aesthetic milieu of the past thirty or forty years has insisted that truth is socially constructed, mediated by forces outside the individual and inaccessible except through a distorting screen of perceptual, political, and cultural bias. Working with these assumptions, the role of the artist has been to expose the lie, reveal the hidden agenda, and break the dominant image. This iconoclastic fury has turned back to bite us. As the likes of Steve Bannon have taken up the banner of deconstruction, we are forced to admit that cultural evolution has moved in directions that Michel Foucault and Jacques Derrida failed to anticipate. Fake news and the death of the author are related concepts.

I see our current dilemma in the context of the ongoing struggle between the rationalist (enlightenment) and the romantic (anti-enlightenment) forces of Modernism, that have been in contention since the eighteenth century. Postmodernism, poststructuralism, and postcolonialism are all fervently anti-enlightenment lines of thought that decry any claim to universal principles and assert that everything is political, contextual, and provisional—all nurture, no nature. While this has been a much-needed corrective to the bogus universalist claims of imperialism, colonialism, racism, and sexism, it has become a revolution that is eating its children. In our current catastrophe, the idealistic aspirations of the enlightenment, "We hold these truths to be self-evident ...," begin to look important again.

One way to repair this situation is to look to artists who have successfully found a détente between the opposing, yet entangled, forces of modernity—the rational and the irrational, the universal and the local, the progressive and the traditional, the classical and the vernacular, the quotidian and the mythic, the political and the personal: Francisco de Goya, George Eliot, Paul Cézanne, Charles Ives, Bertolt Brecht, Elie Nadelman, David Smith, Edward Hopper, Thelonious Monk, Leon Golub, Phillip Guston, William Tucker, Elizabeth Murray, William Kentridge, and Kerry James Marshal, among many others, have reached for this equilibrium.

CG: How do you hold on to something so no one can take it away? Your beliefs? Your body? Your love? What tethers us here?

Taplin: There is nothing that can't be taken away and, of course, eventually it all will be.

ES: Public health physicians distinguish between narrative compassion (where one or two or three people are at risk) and statistical compassion (where thousands or millions are at risk). We're fairly good at the first, and have many occasions to strengthen our capacity through daily acts of friendship and from reading literature. We're terrible at the second, and have almost no training in strengthening our feeble abilities in this region. To what extent can the medium you work in invite, or carry out, acts of narrative compassion and statistical compassion?

Taplin: Narrative compassion could be a rough description of my goals and interests over the last forty years. I have had scattered successes. Statistical compassion is altogether outside the reach of art as I practice it.

***Punch Makes a Public Confession,* 2012 (enlarged 2014)**
pp. 80–1

***Punch Stopped at the Border,* 2005 (enlarged 2019)**
pp. 82–3

***Young Punch Scratches His Burro's Ears,* 2007 (enlarged 2018)**
p. 84

***Punch Does a Magic Trick,* 2010 (enlarged 2018)**
p. 85

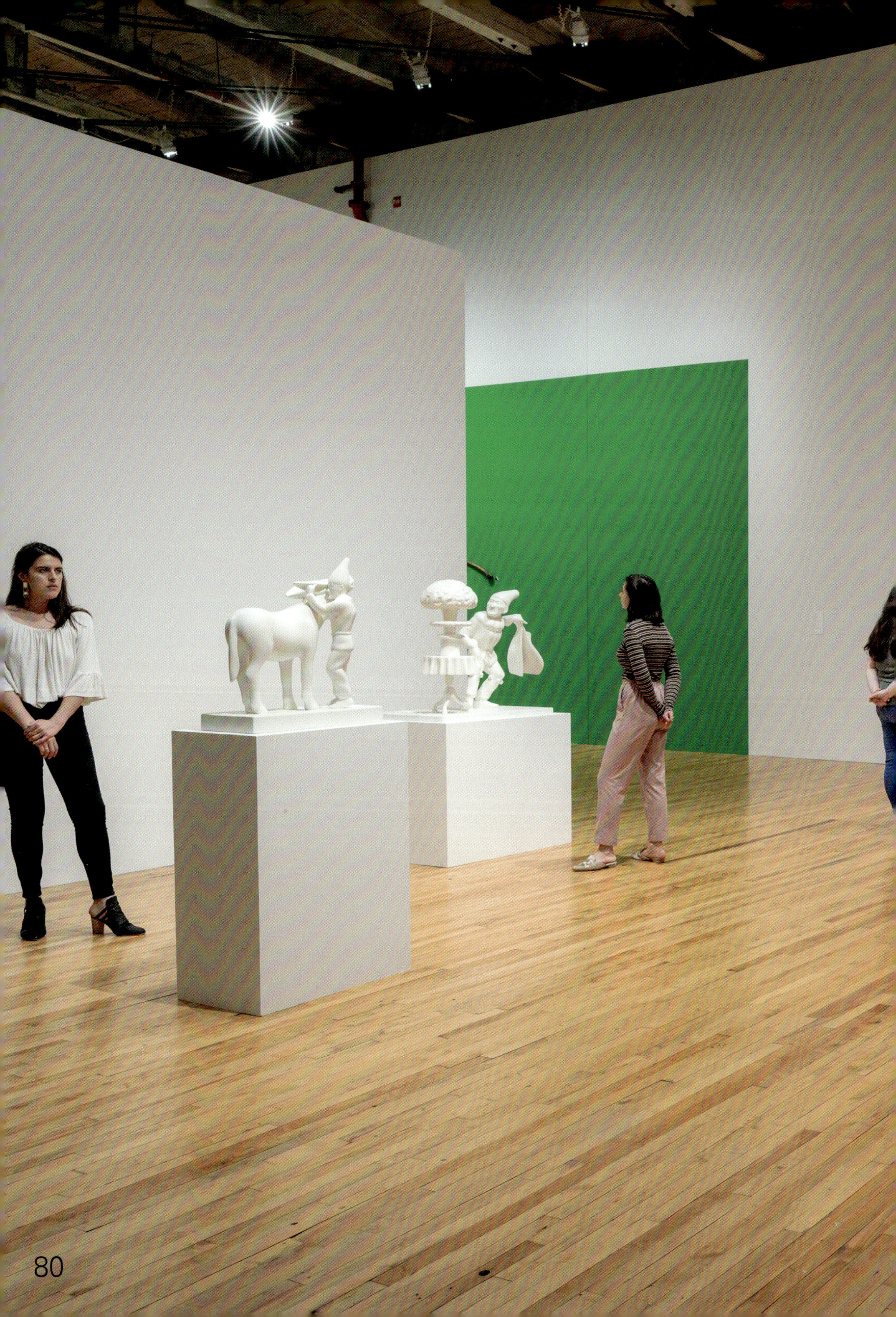

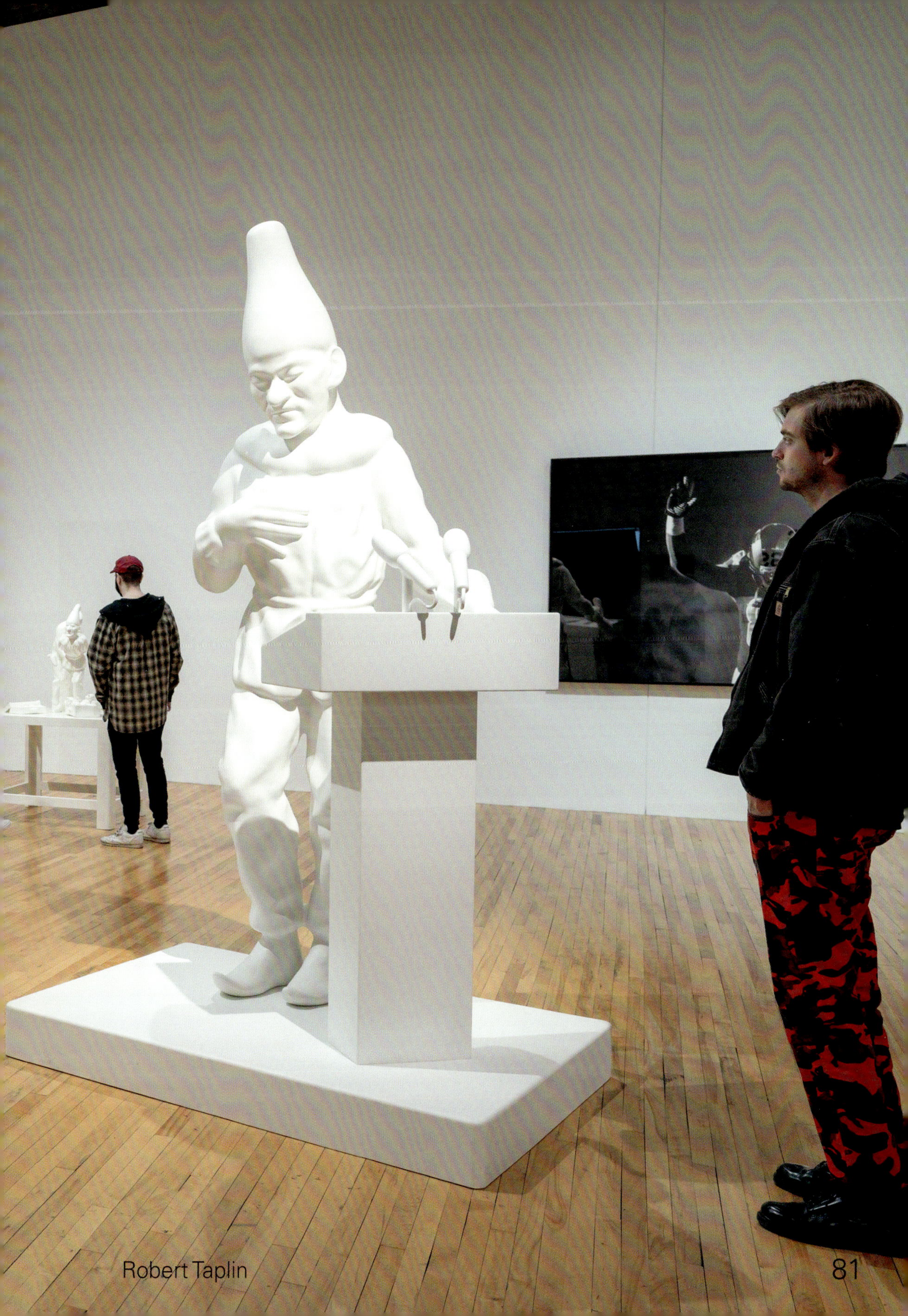

Robert Taplin

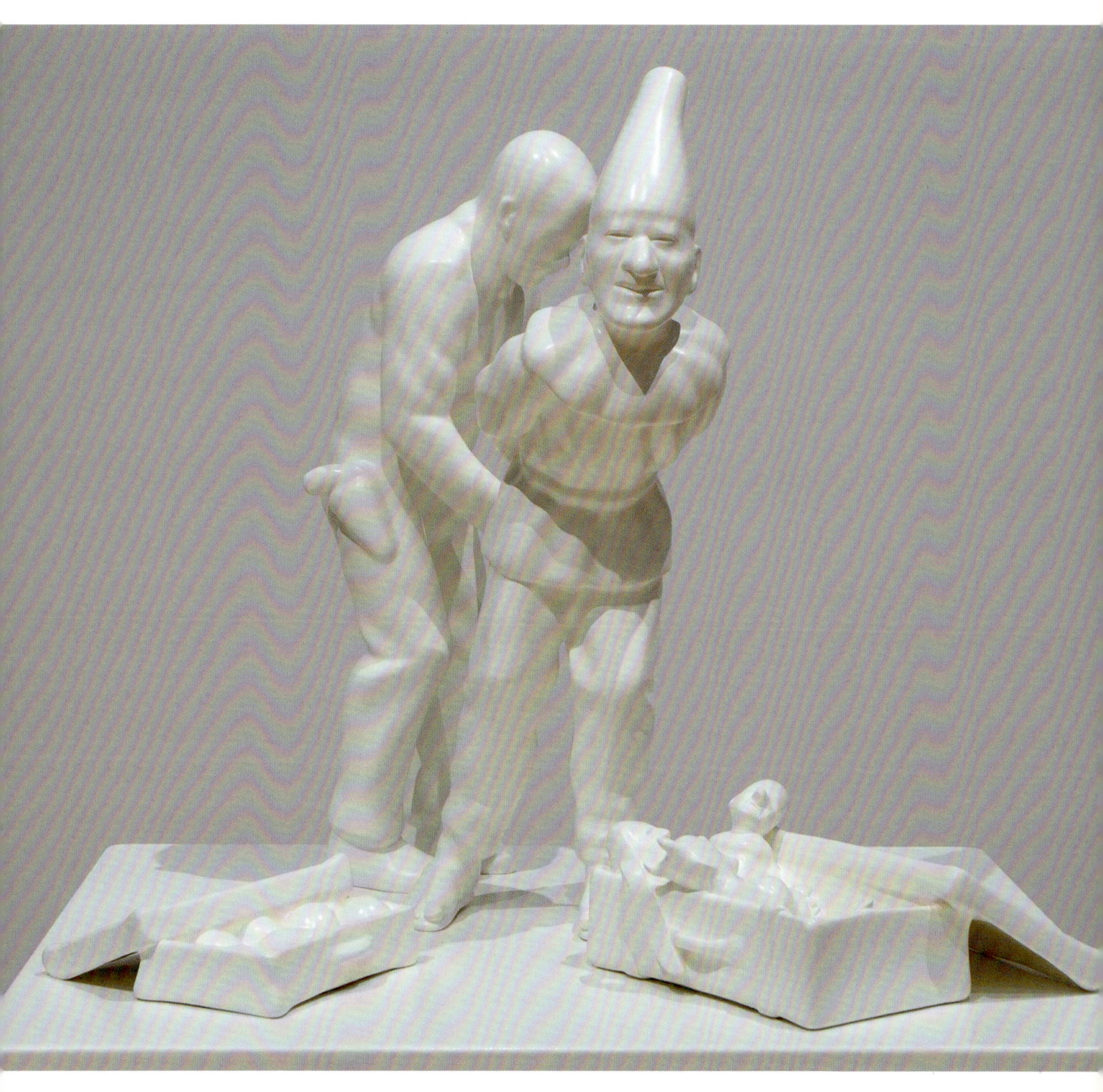

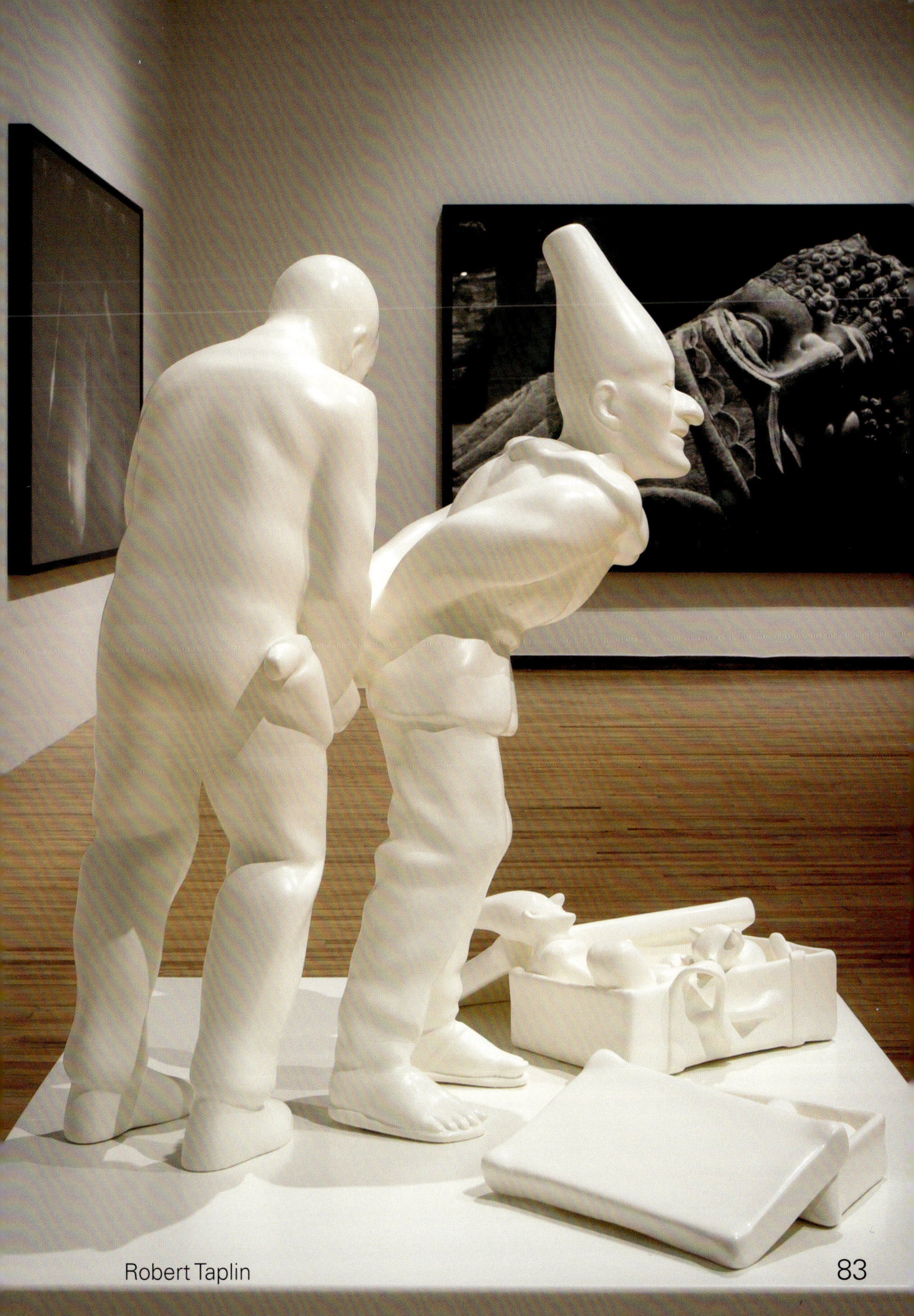

Robert Taplin

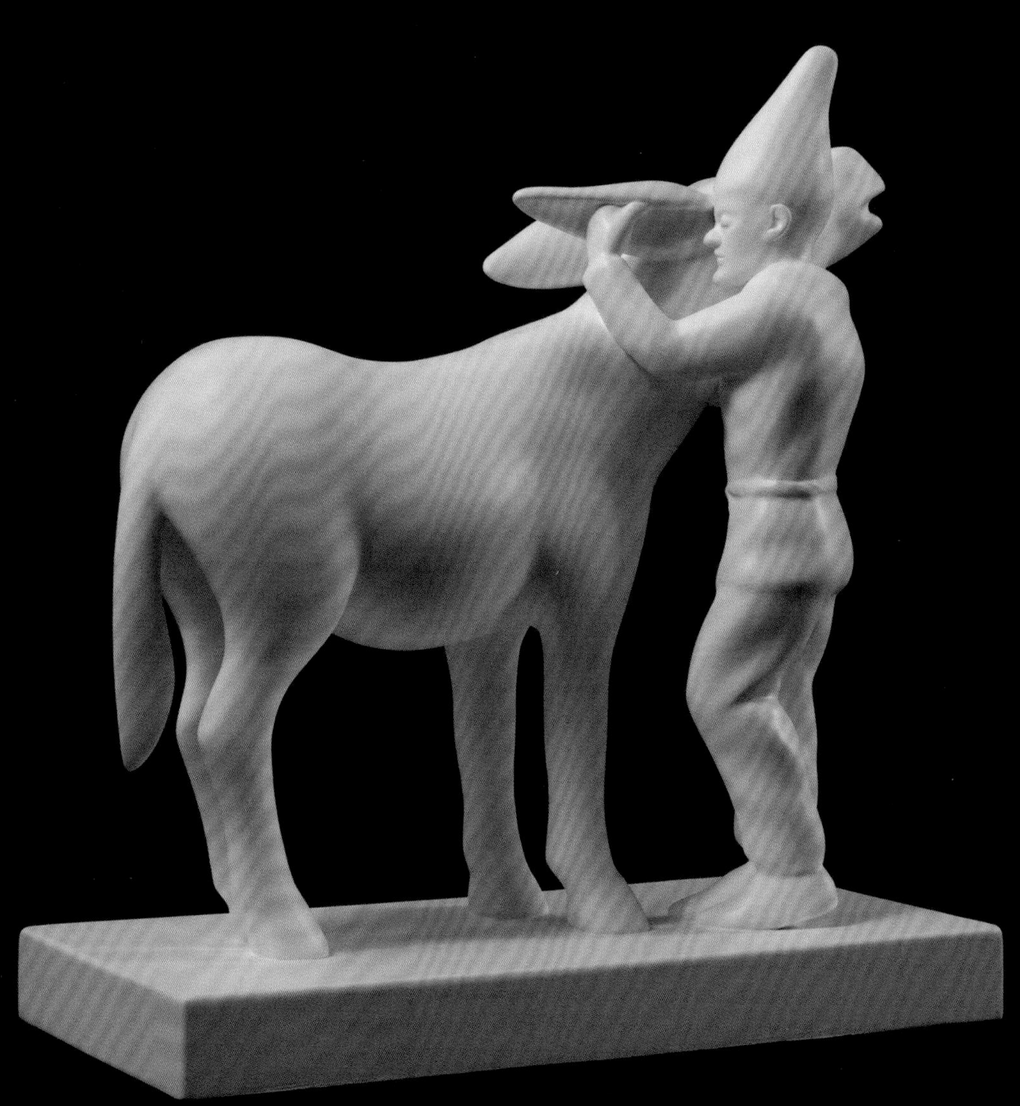

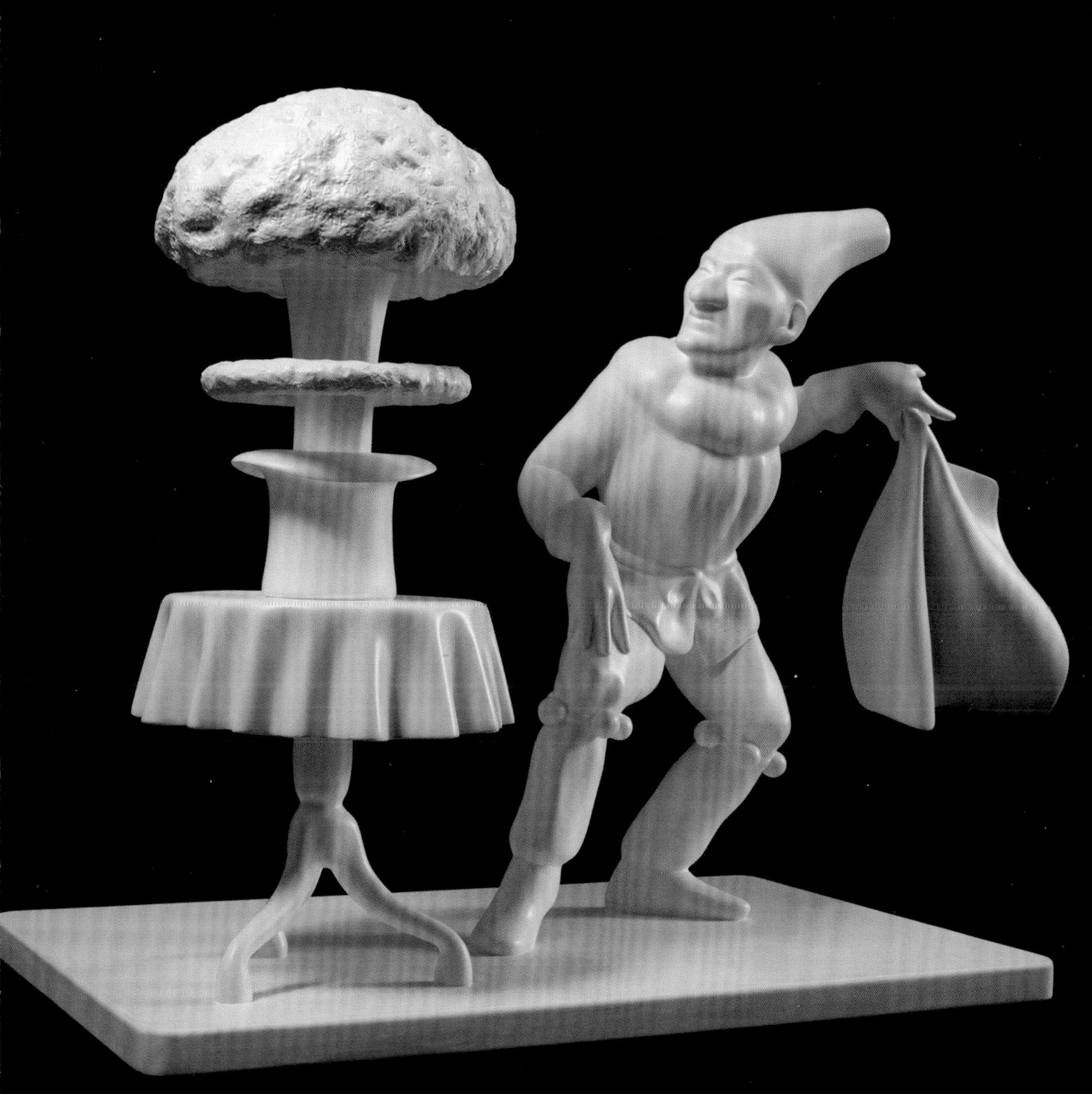

Aziz + Cucher

—

FM: When did the climate change? When did "this moment" become this moment?

Aziz + Cucher: There wasn't a definitive turn that brought us to this moment, but rather a gradual accumulation of events, which shaped recent history. The introduction of slavery in the US created racial divisions that are still felt today. Likewise, widespread industrialization and its reliance on fossil fuels has led to climate change. More recently, the deregulation of the banking system that was put in place in the Reagan/Thatcher years led to the financial crisis in 2008, the effects of which have not abated. And in the early 1990s, the World Wide Web superseded all other forms of mass communication and leading to a gross mistrust of information and the debasing of truth. Lastly, the sequence of wars in the wake of 9/11 is a significant factor in the formation of this moment.

AC: In an age where consumer capitalism constantly promotes the dream of expressing yourself, hasn't art become central to supporting and maintaining that power structure? However radical its messages are on the surface—isn't art underneath really constantly promoting the idea of self-expression and so promoting consumer capitalism? So maybe it's part of the problem?

Aziz + Cucher: Art as self-expression is really a fallacy promoted by capitalism to create the illusion of agency in a social space completely dominated by consumption. Art is a form of expression, but to us it does not necessarily involve the self as a central conceit or point of origin. We chose to work exclusively as collaborators almost twenty-eight years ago precisely to undermine the idea of an ego-driven art practice. Rather than ourselves, the reality around us is the driving factor from which our work emerges, filtered through a single, idiosyncratic point of view.

AD: What is "real" in your practice—your way of working, your medium, your social, professional, material, cultural, political relationships, your proximity to institutions? And what is sustainable? Do the two categories (real and sustainable) overlap, and to what extent?

Aziz + Cucher: The most real aspect of our practice is our commitment to the practice itself—to being moved by certain aspects of life so that we are compelled to make art about them; to taking risks with mediums, materials and ideas, to try to sustain our creative energy, despite the challenges that come with the pursuit of opportunities and recognition from a system known for its fickleness and ultimately conservative outlook. We think that if this is real, then it is sustainable because it is intrinsically tied to our nature.

GC: Museums and cultural organizations once perceived as "pure" white boxes free of bias, are now being pushed to reckon with their own privilege and political baggage. As artists increasingly explore the meaning of "realness" in their work, I wonder how you negotiate the political context in which your work is inserted when it enters the museum.

Aziz + Cucher: Artists must always consider the political framework where they exhibit, the communities in which those venues are based, and the diversity of the audiences that might be impacted by our work. We will not necessarily conform to those specific situations and demographics, but we will be mindful when making certain choices along the way. What's important is what we can contribute to the overall discourse that is initiated by the curator and the other artists in the show. Collectively, we can hopefully provide a platform for viewers to consider their own realness in new and more nuanced ways.

MW: The magician Karl Germain said that "conjuring is the only honest profession: a magician promises to deceive and does." And Picasso said, "We all know that Art is not truth. Art is a lie that makes us realize truth." In our current state, where there is no "truth," and "facts" have become a matter of opinion, how can artists wake us up from this unpleasant dream? How can you help us see the world and each other through a lens of hope, trust, and humanity?

Aziz + Cucher: When regarding the issue of "truth" or "facts" or the national nightmare we are living through, it is either naive or exceedingly demanding to expect artists not to be just as powerless as anyone else when it comes to battling the enormous forces that have made it possible for our society to reach such levels of irrationality and the weakening of our political institutions. The paradox is that we are living through the most honest of moments: our president is expected to deceive and he does, and his supporters revel in that. In this instance we just have to be citizens and advocate for political change through activism—art can become an activist tool, but in our appreciation such art can be effective in the moment yet can date very quickly.

CG: How do you hold on to something so no one can take it away? Your beliefs? Your body? Your love? What tethers us here?

Aziz + Cucher: We are tethered by our relationship: twenty-eight years of living and working together. And loving and respecting each other. This sounds impossibly romantic, but we have been lucky to be granted this opportunity to take care of each other and take care of our art together. Outside of the ravages of age and illness, it should not take great effort to hold on to the lived experience of one's life, where one comes from, and the various allegiances of family and culture forged through the years. Memories play a strong role in that. The same goes for friends, and communities, which can vary throughout time but always provide a web that reinforces our identity and sense of belonging.

ES: Public health physicians distinguish between narrative compassion (where one or two or three people are at risk) and statistical compassion (where thousands or millions are at risk). We're fairly good at the first, and have many occasions to strengthen our capacity through daily acts of friendship and from reading literature. We're terrible at the second, and have almost no training in strengthening our feeble abilities in this region. To what extent can the medium you work in invite, or carry out, acts of narrative compassion and statistical compassion?

Aziz + Cucher: This question of compassion, whether narrative or statistical, is very tied in our minds to realistic representations of the human form—and we have been committed to making figurative artwork since the beginning of our career—but even then, we might not be seeking such empathetic identification in every case. We don't think compassion is the most immediate reaction we are seeking in *You're Welcome, and I'm Sorry*, it is perhaps rather a sense of horror or discomfort, or a feeling of the uncanny or the absurd. All these feelings have the potential to generate a compassionate glance, but in this specific piece it is hard to want to elicit compassion of any kind for these ridiculously monstrous figures that we are using to represent dark, irrational forces in our society.

***You're Welcome, and I'm Sorry*, 2019**

pp. 88–93

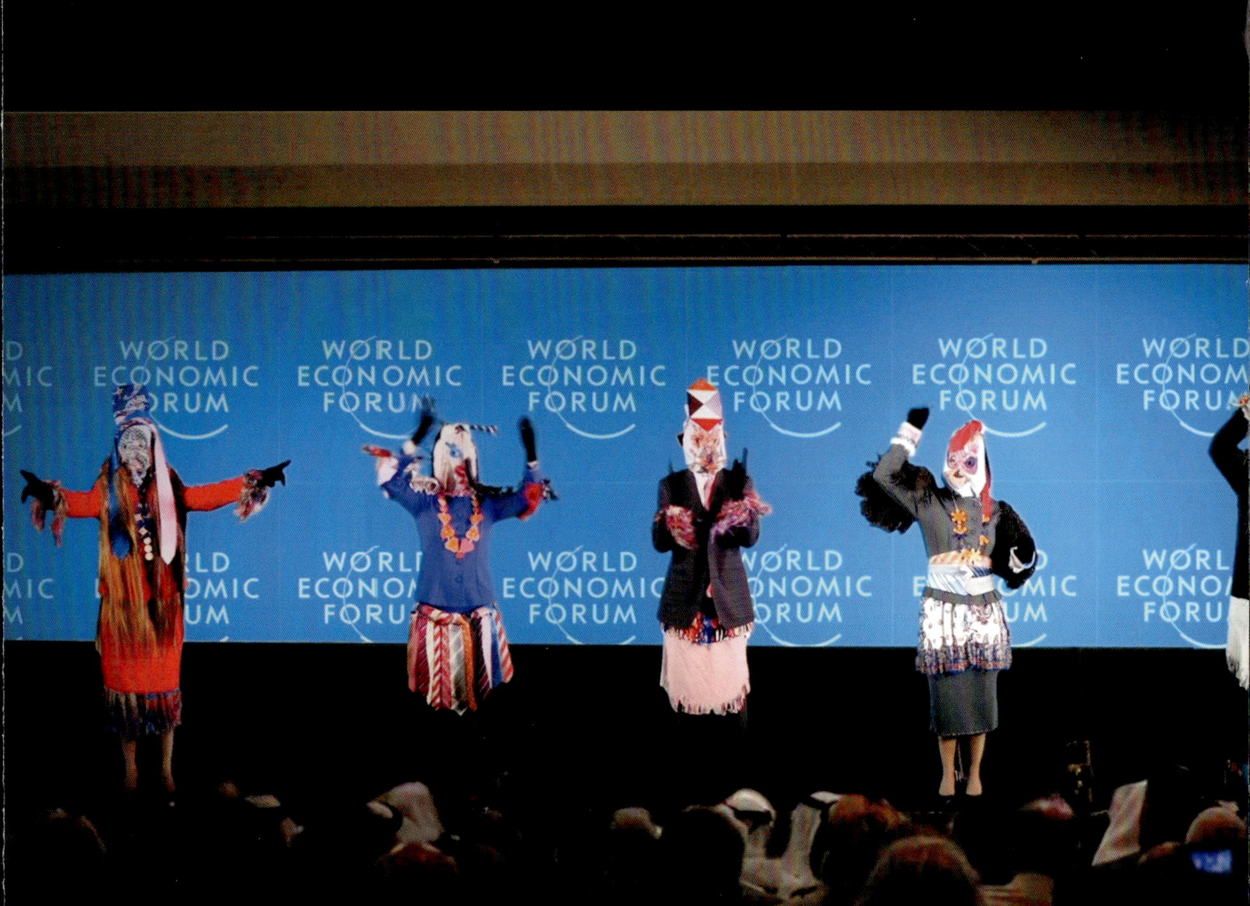
WORLD
ECONOMIC
FORUM

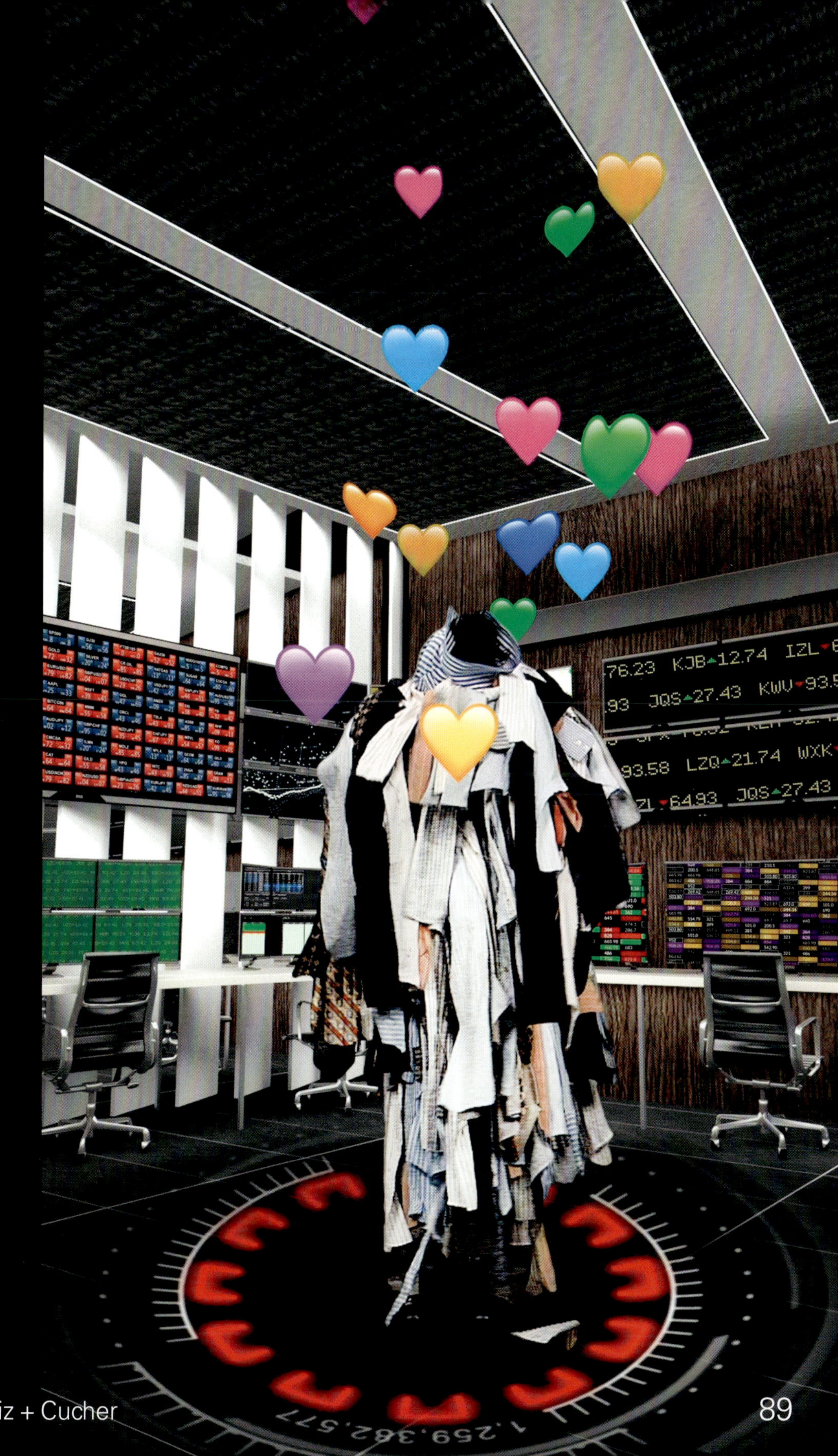
76.23 KJB▲12.74 IZL▼
93 JQS▲27.43 KWV▼93.5
93.58 LZQ▲21.74 WXK
64.93 JQS▲27.43
1,259,382,577

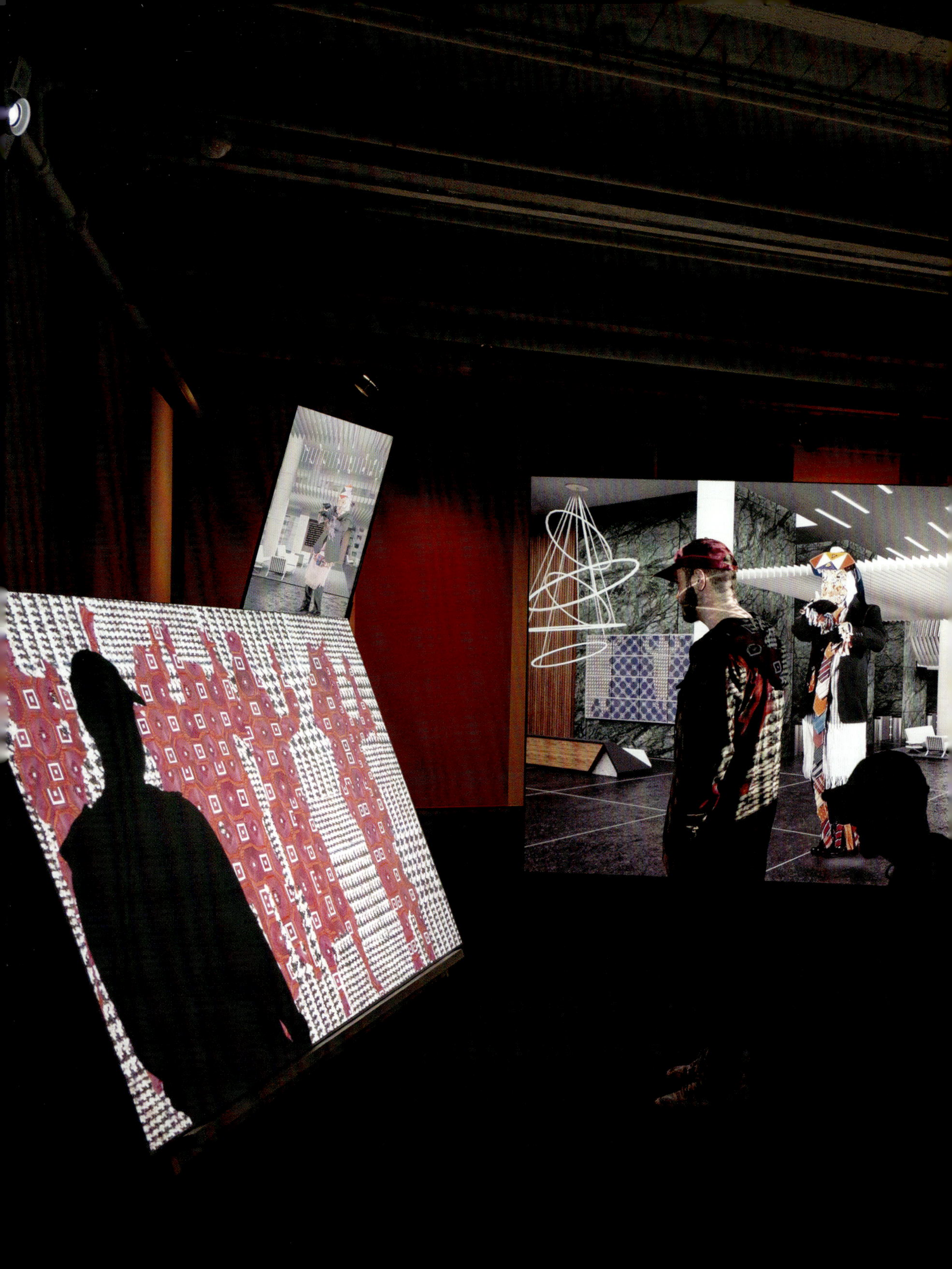

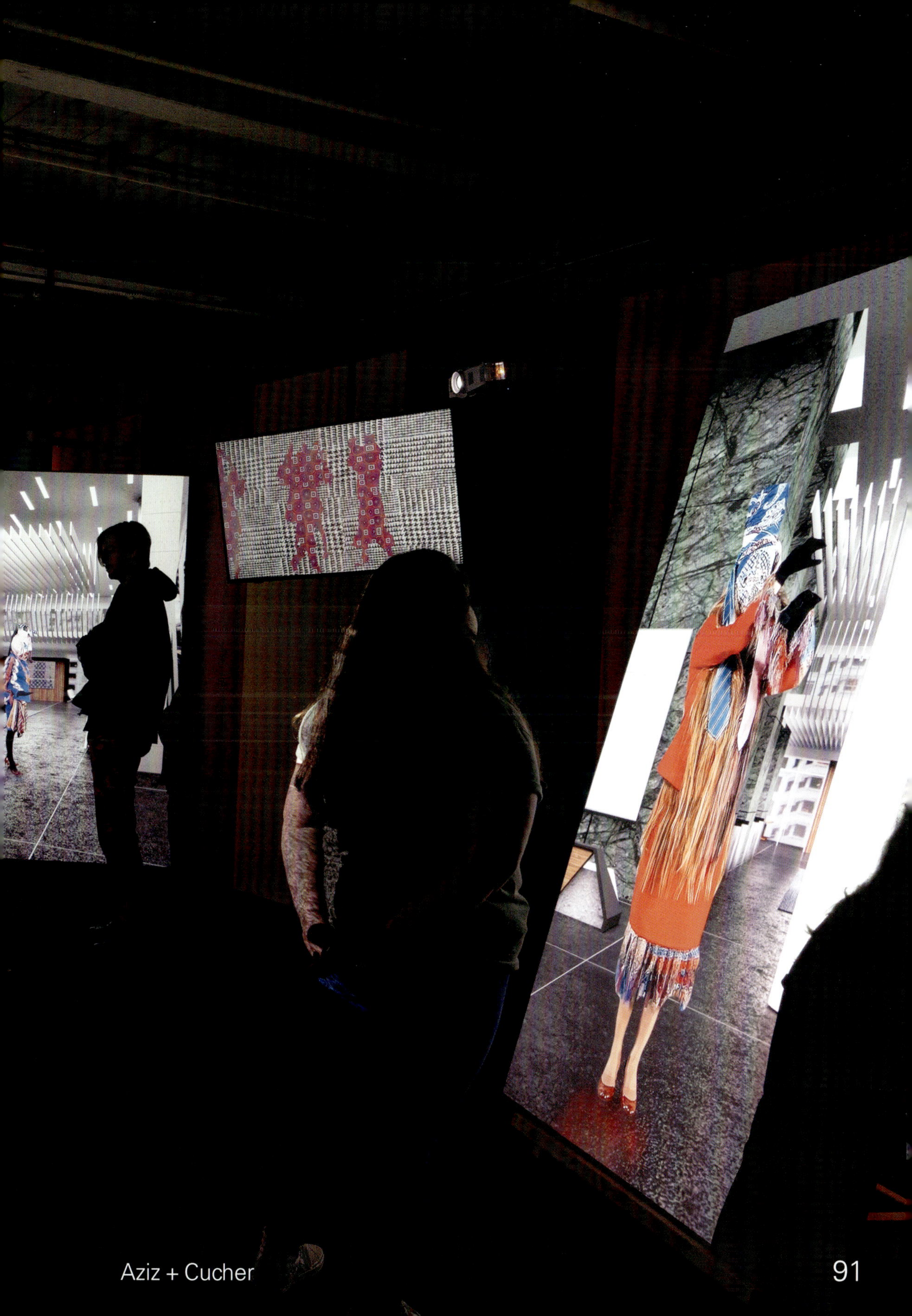

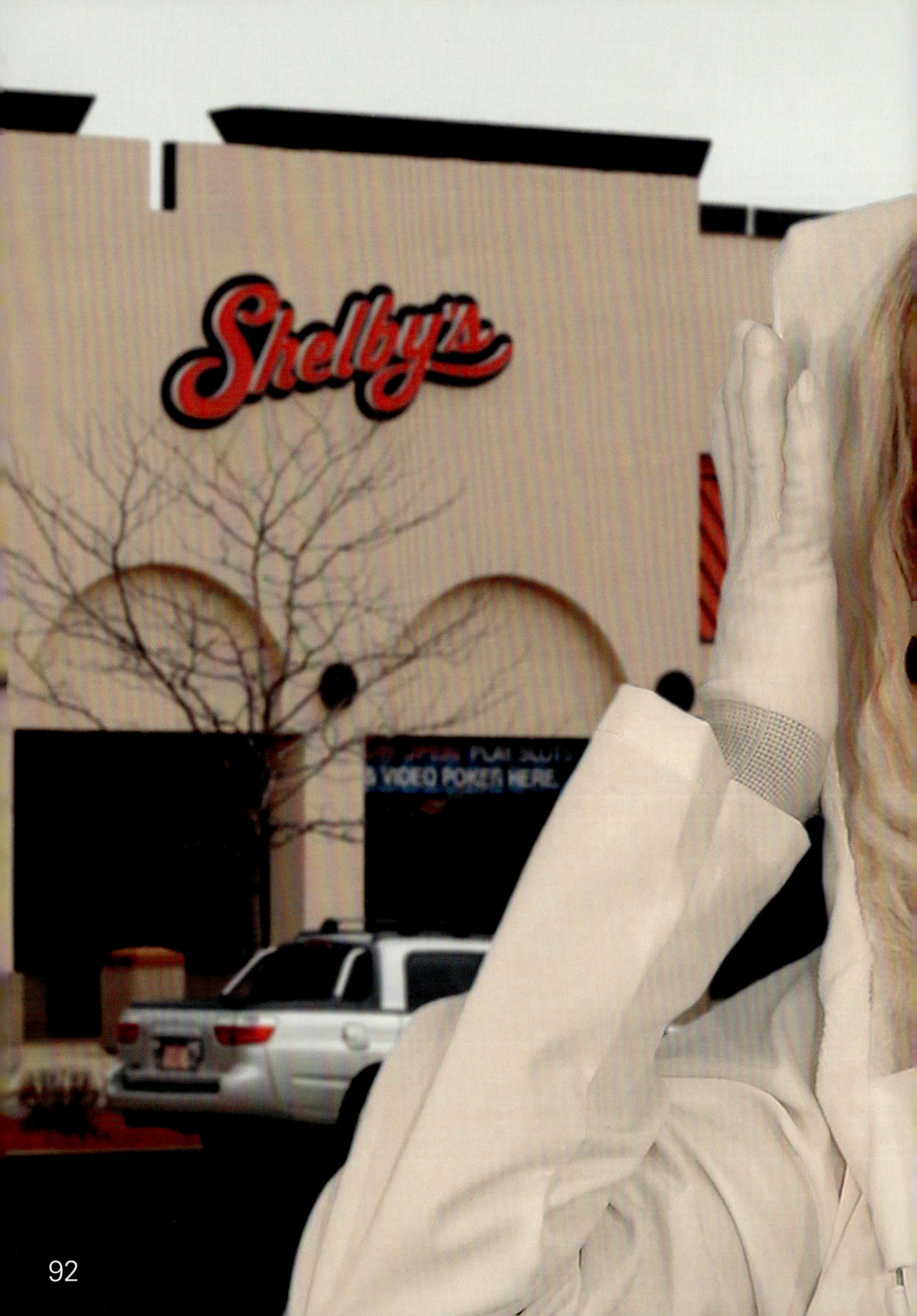
Shelby's

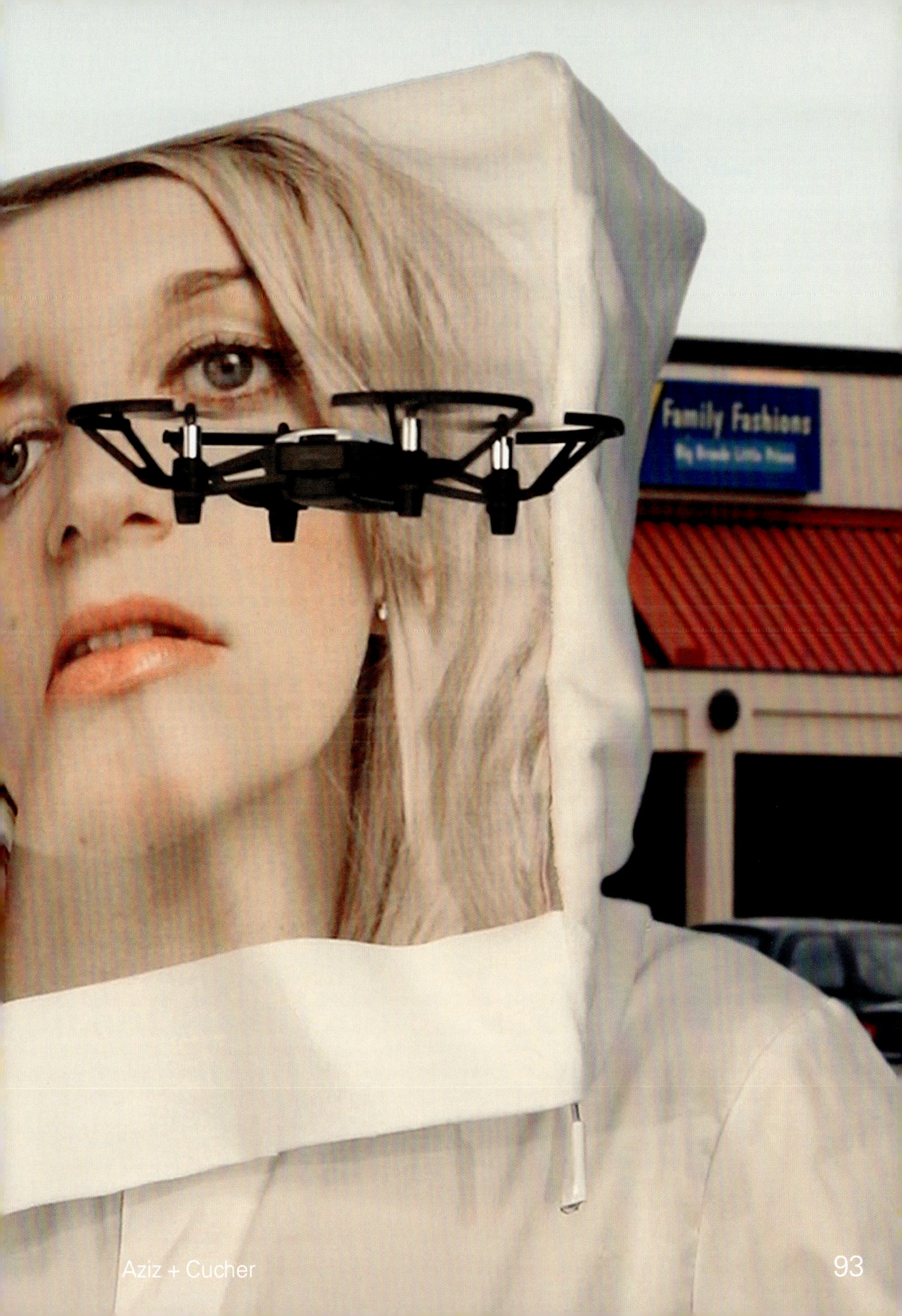
Family Fashions

Look

—

Solmaz Sharif

It matters what you call a thing: *Exquisite* a lover called me.
Exquisite.

Whereas *Well, if I were from your culture, living in this country,*
said the man outside the 2004 Republican National
Convention, *I would put up with that for this country;*

Whereas I felt the need to clarify: *You would put up with*
TORTURE, *you mean* and he proclaimed: *Yes;*

Whereas what is your life;

Whereas years after they LOOK down from their jets
and declare my mother's Abadan block PROBABLY
DESTROYED, we walked by the villas, the faces
of buildings torn off into dioramas, and recorded it
on a handheld camcorder;

Whereas it could take as long as 16 seconds between
the trigger pulled in Las Vegas and the Hellfire missile
landing in Mazar-e-Sharif, after which they will ask
Did we hit a child? No. A dog. they will answer themselves;

Whereas the federal judge at the sentencing hearing said
I want to make sure I pronounce the defendant's name
correctly;

Whereas this lover would pronounce my name and call me
Exquisite and lay the floor lamp across the floor,
softening even the light;

Whereas the lover made my heat rise, rise so that if heat
sensors were trained on me, they could read
my THERMAL SHADOW through the roof and through
the wardrobe;

Whereas *you know we ran into like groups like mass executions.*
w/ hands tied behind their backs. and everybody shot
in the head side by side. its not like seeing a dead body walking
to the grocery store here. its not like that. its iraq you know
its iraq. its kinda like acceptable to see that there and not—it
was kinda like seeing a dead dog or a dead cat lying—;

Whereas I thought if he would LOOK at my exquisite face
or my father's, he would reconsider;

Whereas *You mean I should be disappeared because of my family*
name? and he answered *Yes. That's exactly what I mean,*
adding that his wife helped draft the PATRIOT Act;

Whereas the federal judge wanted to be sure he was
pronouncing the defendant's name correctly and said he
had read all the exhibits, which included the letter I
wrote to cast the defendant in a loving light;

Whereas today we celebrate things like his transfer to a
detention center closer to home;

Whereas his son has moved across the country;

Whereas I made nothing happen;

Whereas *ye know not what shall be on the morrow. For what is
your life?* It is even a THERMAL SHADOW, it appears
so little, and then vanishes from the screen;

Whereas I cannot control my own heat and it can take
as long as 16 seconds between the trigger, the Hellfire
missile, and *A dog.* they will answer themselves;

Whereas *A dog.* they will say: Now, therefore,

Let it matter what we call a thing.

Let it be the exquisite face for at least 16 seconds.

Let me LOOK at you.

Let me LOOK at you in a light that takes years to get here.

Section 2

The Body in Pain

Houston: We have a problem!

Rebecca Rickman

A radical transformation of human behavior is underway as we embed technology into every aspect of our daily lives. It is a subject that requires our urgent attention. But our attention is not to be had, because it has been shattered and dispersed by the same technology that the revolution is delivering to us. The liberation of human attention has been described by philosopher James Williams as "the defining moral and political struggle of our time. Its success is the prerequisite for the success of virtually all other struggles."[1]

Yes, we are in the mother of all struggles, not only to keep up with our digital communication, but with the changes technology has wrought upon our selves, our lives, and the world around us. The speed of this transformation is unparalleled and some of us are having difficulty keeping pace. But should we even be trying? There are signs everywhere that if we don't slow down to gain perspective, mistakes will be made of a magnitude so consequential that we may not have the luxury of a second chance.

To place our Darwinian adaptation on hold and weigh its costs and benefits should not be interpreted as a Luddite resistance to progress and innovation. It is, in fact, our civic duty now that we can see how the use of technology is shaping patterns of human behavior that threaten to undermine our autonomy.

Technology (by which I generally mean digital devices and their content) is not, in itself, at the heart of the problem. It has delivered life-saving, cost-effective benefits and an infinite variety of experiences and opportunities that make the world an undeniably better place in which to live. For its ability to connect people around the globe and for its many future innovations, we can only be thankful. But we should not assume that technology alone will be the solution to every challenge we now face. Our future will be determined by the human intention—good or bad—that we program into our computers.

In light of recent revelations about the use of technology for darker purposes, it is hard to remember that the dawn of the Digital Age began with unparalleled optimism. It offered a new kind of Utopia that would unleash our human potential to solve the world's problems without ever leaving our desks. Those with the means to purchase this bright and shining dream rushed forth to drink the Kool-Aid, quickly leaving behind the doubters, the unaware, and those without the necessary financial resources.

It was the beginning of the digital gold rush; fortunes were made, then lost, and made again. It was indeed transformative, in ways both predictable and profoundly unexpected. The benefits were self-evident by their quick adoption as the new normal, but the hidden price tag was slow to reveal its true nature.

It turned out to be a Faustian bargain. Had we seen the fine print of this social contract, would we have agreed to its terms and conditions? We acquiesced to the surveillance, the tracking, and the trolling as an undesirable but inevitable price to be paid for convenience, information, and security. To whom, in any case, might we have addressed our concerns? No single entity could be held accountable and some of these problems resulted from the laws of unintended consequence.

However, the Cambridge Analytica scandal revealed irrefutable evidence of opaque transactions resulting in the trading of personal data for financial gain that caused a spectacular rupture in public trust. With our blinders removed, we find ourselves at a crossroads just as the speed and scale of change makes resistance and renegotiation appear beyond our individual grasp.

What was once a matter of choice to participate is now obligatory. What was once a great experiment is now our dominant way of life. There is a digital divide, and those that find themselves caught in it due to age, preference, or lack of opportunity are being marginalized for their failure to adapt to our new data-driven society.

Much of this pressure is created by the Disrupters: the tech innovators and venture capitalists who seem to believe we should feel unquestioning gratitude for the new market potentials they create, even as they cause profound social change for which they appear unwilling to accept responsibility.

Sean Parker, the first president of Facebook, remarked in November 2017, "God only knows what it's doing to our children's brains." Several days later, according to Evan Osnos of the *New Yorker*, Parker's former colleague Chamath Palihapitiya told an audience at Stanford, "The short-term, dopamine-driven feedback loops that we have created are destroying how society works—no civil discourse, no cooperation, misinformation, mistruth." His children, apparently, "are not allowed to use this shit."[2]

I would submit that if these products are not good enough for the children of Silicon Valley royalty, they are also not good enough for the rest of us.

It is therefore in our mutual interest to realign the creation and use of technology within a transparent and ethical framework. It should not, for example, be exploiting our attention with addictive design that feeds us chemical rewards as it mines us for data. The Stanford Persuasive Tech Lab was a pioneer in the study of computers as persuasive technologies with a view to changing people's beliefs or behavior. In the hands of ethical designers, this appears to be a perfectly benign idea; however, used as a tool for political change or economic gain, it quickly becomes a menace. With the genie now unleashed, we are left wondering how to get it back in the bottle.

Some matters should not be left to market forces for correction, and for those entities that fail the ethical stress test, there should be consequences. To achieve this objective, it is necessary for us to assume a shared sense of responsibility for the future not only on our own behalf, but also on behalf of the children growing up in this data-driven world. We must find ways to hold accountable the technologists, the investors that enable bad business plans and bad practices, and the politicians who fail to provide the legislative teeth to punish the offenders.

Before all else, however, we need to understand how our daily interaction with technology is transforming our inner architecture. This includes our bodies, our brains and the worldview we construct from our daily encounters with our surroundings.

These changes begin with the allocation of our attention. It is what we select as the focus of our attention that shapes who we become over time. If memory serves as an archive for our past experience and a resource for future thought and action, then we need to consider how the gravitational pull of digital devices has weakened our innate capacity to remember.

Because creating memory requires our attention, we find it increasingly difficult to form memory, given our digital habits. This is because it takes time to process information into memory and, increasingly, our attention has already been spirited away. We therefore depend upon our devices when we might previously have called upon what poet Gerard Manley Hopkins called the "Inscape": the distinctive inner landscape that constitutes our individual identity.

In 1992, the artist Thomas Bayrle wrote that "the great mistake of the future would be that as everything became digital, we would confuse memory with storage."[3] This prophecy has now become fact and its effects are clear. We have both forgotten how to remember, and, courtesy of the vast capabilities of digital storage, how to forget. Both functions are distinguishing hallmarks of the human brain.

The benefits of expanding our internal knowledge include the strengthening of conceptual understanding, independent critical thinking, and better navigational skills. It also strengthens the neural circuitry in the brain. Above all, it results in a greater feeling of autonomy. This is not to say there are not many positive benefits from the use of digital tools. But the failure to utilize one's memory eventually leads to attrition. Without memory, information cannot transmute into knowledge; without shared memory, societies fall apart.

Somewhere along the road to progress, and in small incremental steps, we have shifted from a position of cognitive self-reliance to one of radical dependence upon externalities over which we have no personal control. Let us not revisit the skepticism that greeted the adoption of writing and the invention of the printing press as arguments to normalize the moment. "We're being hypnotized little by little by technicians we can't see, for purposes we don't know," writes computer scientist Jaron Lanier. "We're all lab animals now."[4]

Our online digital habits are also being tracked and used to structure a custom-built reality in the form of algorithmic loops that feed back to us a world shaped by our own previously expressed preferences. Since no two people share the same preferences, they also cannot share the same reality, which undermines the very idea of common experience, common meaning or larger common purpose. As writer Anaïs Nin stated presciently, "We don't see things as they are. We see them as we are."[5]

These self-oriented worlds recall the research of German biologist Jakob von Uexküll who, in the early twentieth century, developed a set of theories about how living organisms perceive and respond to their environment or *Umwelt*. Each *Umwelt* represents an organism's unique life experience, which is created through a feedback loop of sense and response to its surroundings. Even organisms that share an identical environment shape their own subjective worldview. These ideas would, in due course, become influential in the field of computer science.

It is possible that this moment marks the beginning of a transition from the Age of Information to another age. Might this in fact be the beginning of the Post-Information Age? We are certainly in a state of informational paralysis. The ubiquity of access to all the world's information has led to a particular kind of fatigue, if not narcosis. And since not all the information is factually correct, we are obliged to dig deeper into the source material, if it is provided. However, there is no end to the digging. The general rabbit-holing and the unfinishability of the Internet increases the appeal of the image as a compressed form of communication, but this in turn has led to a flash-flood of visual information. What we need is guidance through this limitless cache of material. Unfortunately, many entities in which we place our trust for reliable curation have revealed their own fallibilities. We are therefore left to fall back on our own resources, buried up to our necks in the primordial ooze of data.

Paradoxically, knowledge is also disappearing in the midst of this informational glut. Indeed, entire ways of being-in-the-world are experiencing tectonic shifts. By this I mean the eco-system of culture as expressed through its particularities: its values, traditions, rituals, skills, architecture, food, language, and sense of place. When critical aspects of a culture, such as land, language, or even a profession come under threat, there is a systemic wobble along the line.

Such is the case in the Marshall Islands, where the future of ancient navigational techniques rests in the hands of Alson Kelen, potentially the world's final apprentice in the art of wave-piloting. Although "wayfinding" might appear to be an arcane subject in the Age of GPS, scientists have been working against the clock to understand the underpinning of the Islanders' navigational skills while it can still be measured. Meanwhile, the United States Military has become so concerned about its reliance on satellite technology that midshipmen are once again being trained at the US Naval Academy to use a sextant and navigate by the stars.[6]

The undermining of traditional forms of knowledge is illustrated by the threat to London taxi drivers through the arrival of Uber and other ride-sharing apps. Certification of a London taxi driver requires an investment of time, money, and supreme effort to commit to memory a map of the entire city, street by street and house by house. These drivers are, in effect, cultural historians. They are keepers of "The Knowledge" and part of a tradition that makes the fabric of London distinctive. The human toll and cost to culture of the system's potential demise is a regrettable yet familiar feature of our market-driven world.

How can we judge in the present moment what will be of interest or importance to future generations?

Increasing amounts of the world's knowledge and culture rely on digital platforms. As a result, we have a growing problem with regard to legacy. We should not assume that the Internet will be a reliable vehicle to carry forward our worldwide archive for future generations. It is not designed or organized for such a task. In a worst-case scenario, information could vanish by means of malicious hacking, incremental changes in technology, or through extreme forms of censorship. We cannot know what tools of disruption will be available in the future, but relying on YouTube video tutorials to carry culture forward is not a plan. Nor is it a substitute for the passing down of knowledge from one person to another.

The understanding we gain through the haptic experience of our three-dimensional world is fast giving way to streams of data that bypass these multisensory informational pleasures. The solution is not more sophisticated software that simulates our three-dimensional experience on a screen. We also need the tactile experience of objects, the thing-ness of culture, to ensure our survival and quality of life.

This idea is well understood in Japan, where the knowledge required to construct Shinto Shrines is kept alive by a tradition called *Shikinen Sengu* that mandates the rebuilding of particular shrines every twenty years. Not only does this ritual represent the Shinto belief in the death and renewal of nature and the impermanence of things, but it also ensures the continuity of craftsmanship from one generation to the next. If the material structure changes, the essence of the building continues, as demonstrated by the famous Ise Grand Shrine which is scheduled for its sixty-third recreation in 2033. The question is whether there would be a continuity of essence if the building were to be reconstituted by means of a 3D printer?

What would it be like to live in a world where the unquantifiable, metaphysical aspects of our existence were not taken into account as an integral part of our human value? The eye-popping statistics about drug and alcohol abuse, loneliness, anxiety disorders, depression and suicide suggest that society may already be tilting in that direction, and that many people's hopes and expectations for their lives are not being met.

We are also living in the shadow of the "Singularity": the potential future moment when computer generated super-intelligence might overtake the cognitive abilities of human beings. Before we become the architects of our own redundancy, I want to plead a case for human ingenuity and wisdom. When good intention is harnessed to technology, there is potentially no upper limit to what can be achieved. But technology that is beyond human oversight seems to me a frightening prospect.

In a modest but hopeful sign of change, the human hand has made a return in art, architecture, craft, design, and the slow-food movement. These and many other markers suggest the desire, by some people, for a way of life that is textured with our imperfections, requires intentional effort, allows for delayed gratification, and unfolds in real, unedited time. These small shifts should not be mistaken for mere exercises in nostalgia. Instead, they could be understood as an affirmation of singular human expression in the face of the increasing, algorithmically-generated conformity of screen culture.

However, it is important to note that many analog activities are surviving and flourishing because they are working in tandem with all forms of technology to expand human capabilities, control costs, and reach their potential audience.

This model should persuade us that technology is not, in itself, the enemy to be dispatched, but rather something that we can harness strategically with due consideration. But the extent of our engagement should always be a matter of choice. As writer Bill McKibben has noted, our "unique gift is our ability to restrain ourselves—to decide not to do something we're capable of doing. To set limits on our desires. To say 'enough.'"[7]

This is the moment to speak out and express our desire for restraint. There are many forks in the road ahead and we need, at each turn, to put ethics before profit, humanity before data, and education before exploitation. This is a tall order, but without these guiding principles we may find ourselves, in the not too distant future, posing for selfies with Mephistopheles.

—

1 James Williams, *Stand out of Our Light: Freedom and Resistance in the Attention Economy* (Cambridge, United Kingdom: Cambridge University Press, 2018).
2 Evan Osnos, "Can Mark Zuckerberg Fix Facebook Before It Breaks Democracy?," *The New Yorker*, September 2018.
3 Kevin Slavin, "2009: WHAT WILL CHANGE EVERYTHING?" Edge.org. Accessed November 27, 2018. edge.org/response-detail/11986
4 Jaron Lanier, *Ten Arguments for Deleting Your Social Media Accounts Right Now* (New York: Henry Holt and Company, 2018).
5 Anaïs Nin, *Seduction of the Minotaur* (Athens, OH: Swallow Press/Ohio University Press, 1961).
6 Kim Tingley, "The Secrets of the Wave Pilots," *New York Times Magazine*, March 2016.
7 Bill McKibben, "Being Good Enough," *Dark Mountain*, no. 8 (2015): p. 65.

Coltan as Cotton

—

Saul Williams

Hack into
dietary sustenance—
tradition vs. health.

Hack into
comfort/compliance.

Hack into the
rebellious gene.

Hack into doctrine.

Capitalism
in relation
to free labor
and slavery.

Hack into
the history of bank.

Is beating the odds
a mere act of joining
the winning team?

Hack into
desperation
and loneliness.

The history of
community
and the marketplace.

Hack into land rights
and ownership.

Hack into business law
proprietorship.

Hack into ambition
and greed.

Hack into forms
of government.
The history of revolutions

Their relation to suffering
and sufferance.

Hack into
faith and morality

the treatment of one
faith towards another.

Hack into masculinity
femininity/sexuality

what is taught
what is felt
what is learned
what is shared?

Hack into God

stories of creation
serpents and eggs.

Hack into nature

bio-dynamics
biodiversity
cycles and seasons.

Hack into time

calendars
Descartes
its relationship to doubt
is it wired to fear
the notion of control
the space/time
continuum

the force of gravity
whether
the opposite
of gravity
is freedom?

Hack into freedom
power
responsibility
justice
the Bill of Rights.

Hack into coincidence

the summer of '68
the 27 Club
the number of people
with Facebook profiles

people who
choose to share
people who
share too much
people who
seem lonely
people who
want to connect
people who

want to uplift
people who
need uplifting.

Hack into self-help
self-sufficiency and
self indulgence.

Hack into crazy.

Hack into lunatic.

Hack into star.
Hack into
infamous/notorious.

Hack into narcissism

the effects
of poverty
on the psyche

the effects of race
the effects of cruelty

the victims
that survived.

*There is a panel
marked* Survival.

*Three simple
copper wires
coiled 'round an orb.*

Hack into orbit

equatorial
land mines

useful and
precious metals

COLTAN AS COTTON.

Hack into hazardous

nuclear clue clear
cloud form and fish farm
cow farts and pig shit.

Hack into horse
industrial—digital.

Hack into code.

Use your instrument
as metaphor.
Harness your craft.

Hack into the mainframe.

Dismantle
definition
dogma
and duty.

Hack into destiny.

Hack into dreams

subtext and
subconscious

Hack into heart

cardio-Congo
blood rich in oil.

Hack into
suffering and despair.

Hack into the unfair
advantage of those
lucky enough to be born
into one family or
another
into one condition or
another.

Hack into the
circumstantial
evidence that proves the
obvious and wakes the
oblivious.

Hack into birthright

bloodlines:

royal and tainted.

Hack into superstition

old wives tales

the rituals of
the shaman.

Hack into chemistry

the pharmaceutical
Industry

the modern rape
of the forest.

Hack into DNA

the coiling serpents

the time it takes
for modern man
to determine whether
ancient men were foolish
or not.

Hack into
the database.

Hack into the
subconscious

the panel marked

survival.

Hack into celebrity.

Hack into the cultural
development of taste.

Hack into violence
fear and ignorance.

How are they linked?

Adriana Corral

—

FM: When did the climate change? When did "this moment" become this moment?

Corral: In 1916, Tom Lea, the Mayor of El Paso, sent this telegram to the Surgeon General, Rupert Blue in Washington, DC:

"HUNDREDS DIRTY LOUSEY DESTITUE MEXICANS ARRIVING AT EL PASO DAILY/ WILL UNDOUBTEDLY BRING AND SPREAD TYPHUS UNLESS A QUARANTINE IS PLACED AT ONCE/ THE CITY OF EL PASO BACKED BY ITS MEDICAL BOARD AND STATE FEDERAL AND MILITIA OFFICIALS HERE FEEL THAT THE GOVERNMENT SHOULD PUT ON A QUARANTINE/ PLEASE INVESTIGATE AND ADVISE ME THIS IS NECESSARY TO AVOID TYPHUS EPIDEMIC"[1]

One hundred and two years later, the President of the United States echoes Lea's words:

"The US has become a dumping ground for everybody else's problems.... When Mexico sends its people, they're not sending their best. They're not sending you.... They're sending people that have lots of problems, and they're bringing those problems with us. They're bringing drugs. They're bringing crime. They're rapists. And some, I assume, are good people.... These aren't people. These are animals."[2]

AC: In an age where consumer capitalism constantly promotes the dream of expressing yourself, hasn't art become central to supporting and maintaining that power structure? However radical its messages are on the surface—isn't art underneath really constantly promoting the idea of self-expression and so promoting consumer capitalism? So maybe it's part of the problem?

Corral: We all play a role in existing societal power structures. Some of us construct and maintain the system while others confront discriminatory structures to provide alternative views of a reality that is difficult to envision. My works serve as a catalyst for reflection and instigates shifts in power by creating a space for civic participation. My process depends on collaboration with human-rights activists who assist with development and, often, installation. Partnering with institutions that have strong ties to affected communities takes my work beyond the realm of self-expression. My work functions in the existing power structure to emphasize the voices of individuals who are strategically silenced and to point out systemic human rights violations in need of opposition. My work breaks a convenient silence.

AD: What is "real" in your practice—your way of working, your medium, your social, professional, material, cultural, political relationships, your proximity to institutions? And what is sustainable? Do the two categories (real and sustainable) overlap, and to what extent?

Corral: My work derives from real histories, narratives, individuals, victims, and the real sites where human rights violations have occurred or where the memories of these events have been removed and erased. The site, material from mass graves, architectural remains, and documents are the remnants of histories and narratives that motivate my work. Enlisting the help and collaboration of experts in different fields—anthropologists, writers, journalists, gender scholars, human rights attorneys, and the victims' families—provides me with the key data and infrastructure for the formation of my works.

GC: Museums and cultural organizations once perceived as "pure" white boxes free of bias, are now being pushed to reckon with their own privilege and political baggage. As artists increasingly explore the meaning of "realness" in their work, I wonder how you negotiate the political context in which your work is inserted when it enters the museum.

Corral: Time capsules, hidden texts embedded into walls, ash and soil residue, are a few of the methods that I employ to document marginalized histories that are normally removed from or ignored by mainstream institutions and museums. I consistently find ways to leave behind a presence of my work within exhibition/ institutional spaces. Inserting traces of my work into the "pure" cube of the art world is my way of activating and embedding a historic and contemporary memory into regulated and sometimes sterile environments.

MW: The magician Karl Germain said that "conjuring is the only honest profession: a magician promises to deceive and does." And Picasso said, "We all know that Art is not truth. Art is a lie that makes us realize truth." In our current state, where there is no "truth," and "facts" have become a matter of opinion, how can artists wake us up from this unpleasant dream? How can you help us see the world and each other through a lens of hope, trust, and humanity?

Corral: I resist the notion that there are singular truths to be revealed in art. My intention is to create work that poses more questions than provides answers. I use texts, both historic and contemporary, to etch multiple layers on a surface until they build up so densely that they blur and dissolve each other. This palimpsest is a metaphor for the erasure of facts and history. In the same vein I try to reveal subjects that are hidden and often forgotten. It brings me a sense of hope knowing that I can bring visibility to the invisible.

CG: How do you hold on to something so no one can take it away? Your beliefs? Your body? Your love? What tethers us here?

Corral: The costs are too high if we don't hold onto our beliefs, our bodies, our rights, and love. I believe strongly in the idea that the artist has an important social role and responsibility—historically and in our own time. My art tethers certain histories and narratives to the present day by illuminating ideas that have slipped from our collective consciousness, or were never imagined there to begin with. If there was ever a time to be vigilant, it is now.

ES: Public health physicians distinguish between narrative compassion (where one or two or three people are at risk) and statistical compassion (where thousands or millions are at risk). We're fairly good at the first, and have many occasions to strengthen our capacity through daily acts of friendship and from reading literature. We're terrible at the second, and have almost no training in strengthening our feeble abilities in this region. To what extent can the medium you work in invite, or carry out, acts of narrative compassion and statistical compassion?

Corral: I face this challenge when I'm researching or in the studio creating work. How can the unique and individual experience of one [abused and murdered woman, silenced student, mistreated worker] move us toward addressing systemic and egregious human rights violations? I try to illustrate both forms of compassion within my work by including one of our most precious senses, touch. Touch allows the body to feel, understand, connect to the outside world and promote healing.

—

1 National Archives, Washington, DC. RG 90 NC-34 10 Central Files, 1897-1923. Boxes 117–118 (Files 1248 to 1265).

2 Gregory Korte and Alan Gomez, "Trump ramps up rhetoric on undocumented immigrants: 'These aren't people. These are animals.'" *USA Today*, May 16, 2018.

***Requiem,* 2016–19**
pp. 108–11

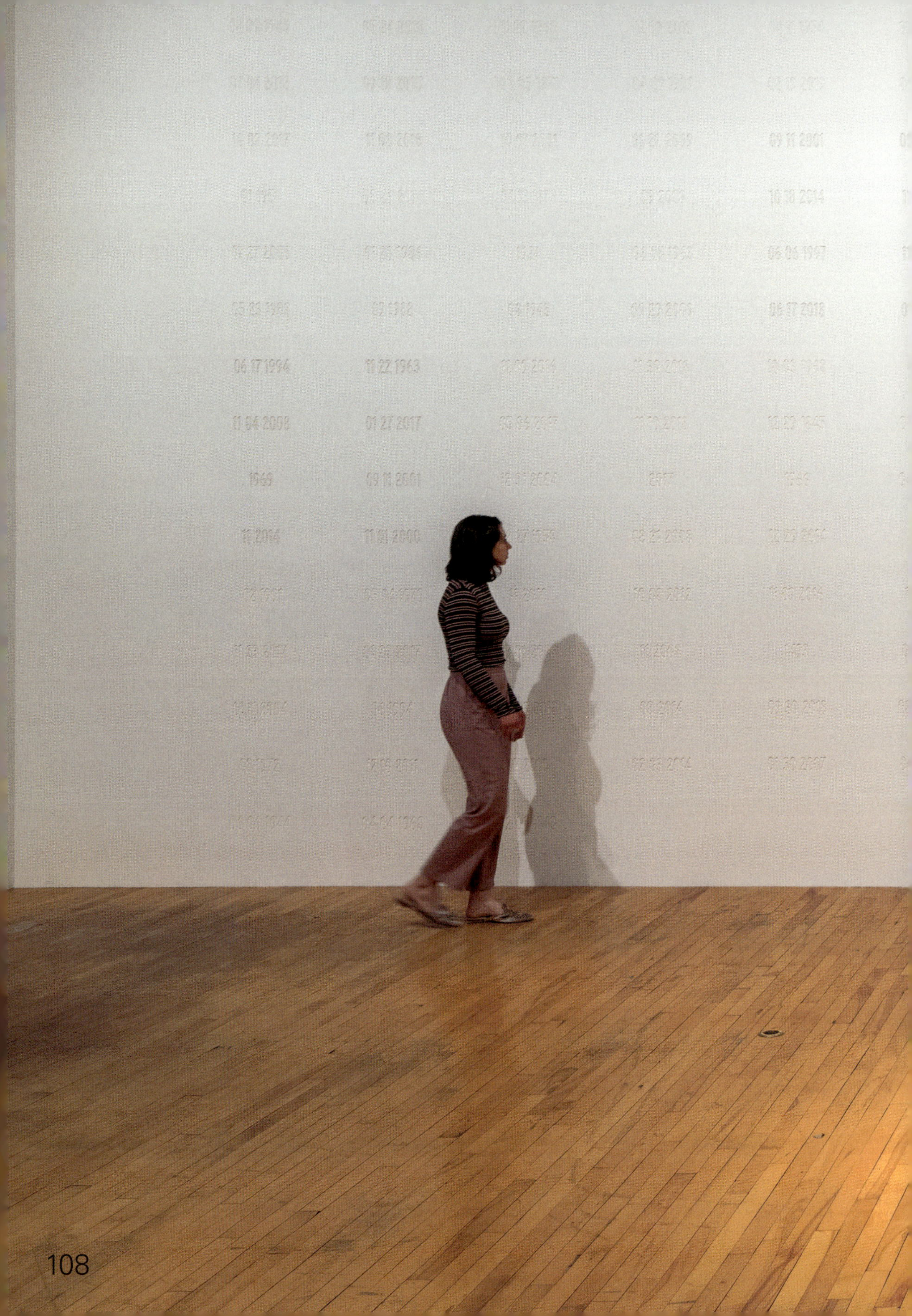
09 11 2001
10 18 2014
06 06 1997
06 17 2018
06 17 1994
11 22 1963
11 04 2008
01 27 2017
1969
09 11 2001
11 2014
11 01 2000

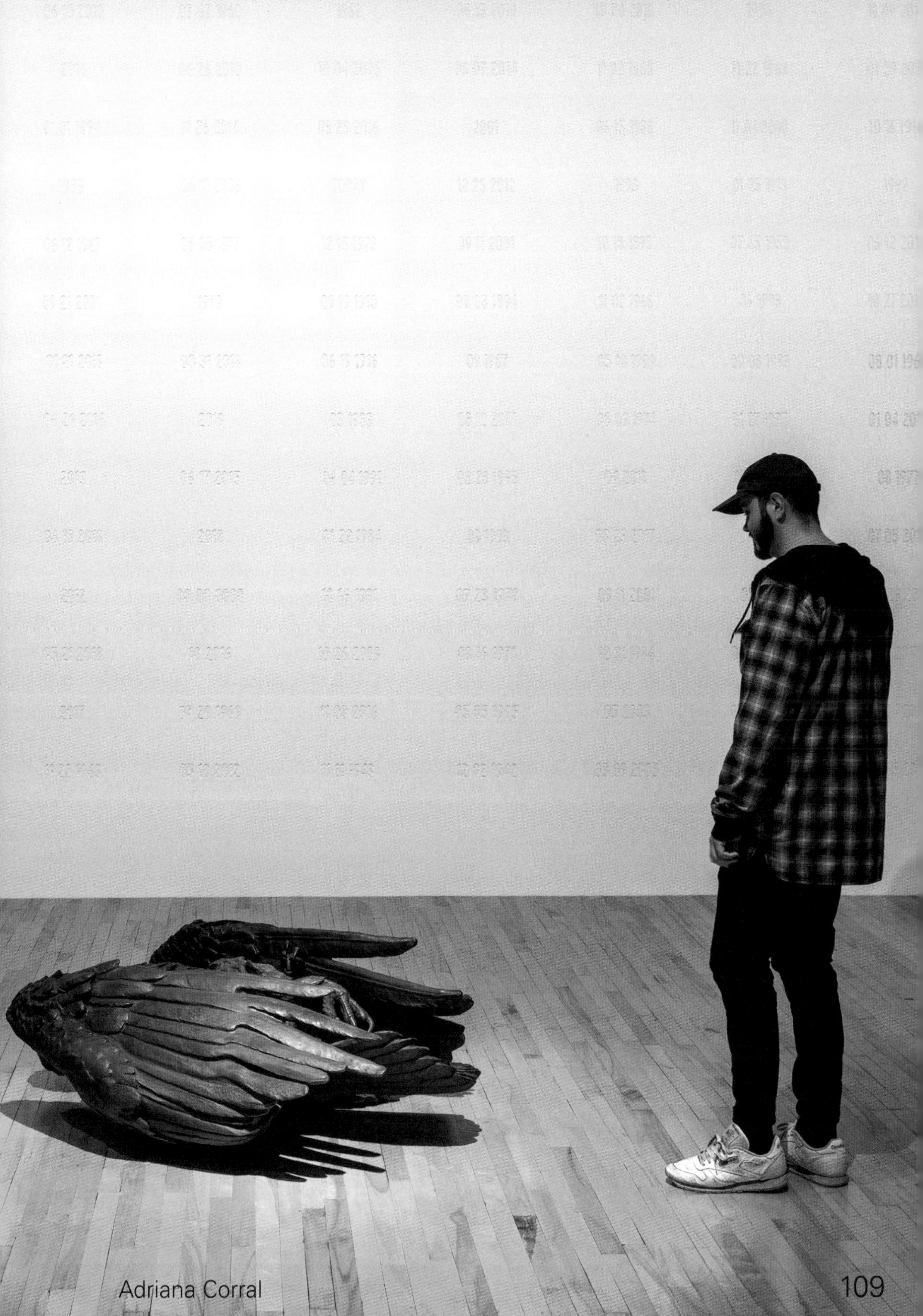

19.
January 1951: My great-grandmother submitted her master's thesis to the education department at the University of Texas at Austin in January of 1951. While working as a school principal in Edinburg in the 1940s, she saw increasing numbers of immigrant children in schools as a direct result of the Bracero Program. She examined their treatment, relations between them and other students, and the effect that deportation raids had in classrooms along the US-Mexico border from El Paso to Brownsville. In many instances, she writes of the sudden absence of these children from school and the effect it had on their classmates. Reading her thesis today, it is not dissimilar to the horrific accounts of family separations that were brought to national media attention in the summer of 2018. Under the Trump administration, the number of ICE workplace raids skyrocketed, leaving communities torn and schoolteachers left with the responsibility of comforting students whose parents or classmates were suddenly gone. However, what's horrific is not the novelty of President Trump's policy, but the familiarity of it (Native American, African American and Japanese American narratives come to mind). Although social media concern has waned, stories of immigrant family separation tragically continue—nor are they new, only forgotten.

20.
July 25, 1952: Constitution Day in Puerto Rico, which in any other country would be called Independence Day, but given that Puerto Rico is a colony of the United States, it cannot claim that celebration. Instead on July 25th islanders celebrate the creation of the island's constitution and of the Commonwealth of Puerto Rico. July 25, 1952, seemed to usher in a new era of US-Puerto Rico relations, based on consent of the governed and mutual understanding. Today in 2019 with Puerto Rico living under the power of a Fiscal Control Board that can effectively exercise power over nearly every facet of island life, the Commonwealth and the island's Constitution seem like empty promises.

21.
Summer of 1953: The first time my father crossed without papers into the U.S. through the Tijuana border was in 1953, when he was 14 years old. A border patrol agent caught him and handcuffed him to a telephone pole so that he could chase after another unauthorized immigrant. Before handcuffing my father to the pole, the migra, who was pissed off at my father for running, threw my father's sack lunch at his face. There was a bottle inside the sack that broke and gashed my father's forehead. "The wound wasn't too serious," my father tells me. Decades later my father took a pilgrimage of sorts, which led him to the spot where he was handcuffed to a pole. There's a fancy restaurant near that spot where he and my mother sat down to eat the most expensive meal they could order. That was all the revenge he needed.

22.
April 11, 1954: The most uneventful and boring day of the 20th century. Every day something of significance occurs, but nothing remarkable had happened on the said day in 1954, according to experts who inserted over 300 million important events of the century into a computer search program to calculate.

23.
1957: An image that is very vivid in mind even today was traveling on the train from Cd. Juarez, Chihuahua, Mexico to Cuauhtémoc, Chihuahua, Mexico with my grandmother Petra.
I was around 7 years old and remember seeing the different people that boarded the train as I set next to my grandmother.
The most interesting people to me where the Tarahumara Indians that boarded the train.
I remember the color of their clothes and the sandal type shoes they wore.
When we reached Cuauhtémoc my grandfather Raymundo was waiting for us at the train station to take us to the village where they lived and where I would spend my summers as a young boy.
As we left the train station on my grandfather's horse drawn buggy all I could see at a distance where the Tarahumara Indians walking toward the mountains.

24.
December 27, 1958: That Date is very important to me, because that is the day my Uncle was born but sadly he has died. That date is very important because my uncle and I were very close and he motivated me on a lot of stuff and if it weren't for him I don't think I would have gotten this far in life.

25.
1960: Sabidura 4 by the artist Gego
Line as human
the relation to express
the relation between
points, something that is entirely
abstract in the sense: of not
existing materially in nature.
Line as medium
indicates materially
the relation between
points in space, expressing visually
human descriptive thought.
Line as object to play with.

26.
7 de Julio de 1960. By this date I had turned 12 years old just a month earlier. It was Summer, school was out, and in the space of 24 hrs. I departed Cuba with my older brother and landed in the United States. I had visited the U.S. before but knew no home but Cuba. There were no goodbyes and, as it happened, many others were also leaving Cuba and our lives were tearing, fragmenting and leaving us with no country beneath us. I would soon realize that my experience of home was becoming a memory, never to be regained. I would also eventually realize that despite the searing pain of separation from all I held dear I was fortunate to have my family and together we would start anew. The hope for a restart or beginning is what the United States has symbolized since its founding... until now.

27.
1962: Woke up. Randomly picked up a book from shelf on my way to bathroom. "The Selling of the President 1968. Opened it up and landed by coincidence on this Appendix quote—"Nowadays everybody tells us that what we need is more belief, a stronger and deeper and more encompassing faith. A faith in America and in what we are doing. That may be true in the long run. What we need first and now is to disillusion ourselves. What ails us most is not what we have done with America, but what we have substituted for America. We suffer primarily not from our vices or our weaknesses, but from our illusions. We are haunted, not by reality, but by those images we have put in place of reality. " Daniel Borrstin/ The Image 1962

28.
June 5, 1963: When I was thirteen years old I remember feeling the excitement as I walked with my family to capture president John F. Kennedy parade down Montana St in El Paso, Texas. He was were there campaigning. This was the first time I remember feeling excited to be an American. However, it was a few months later that we were morning the untimely death of John F. Kennedy. I was stricken with sadness and kept recalling that moment when I saw him parade in the convertible just two blocks away from where we lived.

29.
November 21, 1963: My mother Josephine O. Guerra meets President John F. Kennedy upon his visit to Brooks Aerospace Medicine, where research for space travel and centrifugal forces is going on. She is in line to see the president and he stops shakes her hand and asks about the important work she is doing. My mom is ecstatic, proud and hopeful for the nations future. Does not want to wash her hand again.

30.
November 22, 1963: I was a senior in high school in San Antonio, Texas. I remember being called to an unscheduled assembly by the school principal that day and hearing from him that President John F. Kennedy had been shot and killed in Dallas. Most of us broke down in tears. One girl cheered. I felt afraid.

31.
November 22, 1963: The day I became an American was not the day I swore allegiance to the USA when I became a Naturalized citizen at age 18. I still longed for Brazil where I was born and my dreams were of there and the Portuguese language I so loved.The day I became an American was November 22nd, 1963 when John F. Kennedy was assassinated. By then I was a young mother with two very young sons, living in Metairie, Louisiana just outside of New Orleans. I watched television for hours in total shock as crowds on the streets of New Orleans cheered at his death, and the solemn transfer of power took place on Airforce 1. It was that shock and disbelief that such a senseless and brutal thing could happen in America that galvanized me into true citizenship.

32.
November 22, 1963: I was on my way from the motor pool in Fort Lewis, to the company area getting all our baggage back and package cuz we were heading out, somewhere, we didn't know where but we wound up on our way to Vietnam. I heard that President Kennedy was assassinated. That gave something to look forward to going. To see what we can do for our country. Not what our country can do for us. I will always remember that." what you can do for your country not what your country can do for you"

33.
November 22, 1963: As an 11 year old, sitting in a classroom in a small, remote west Texas community, I recall a teacher, with a smile on her face, stepping into the classroom stating that President Kennedy had been shot. My first reaction was sorrow, then confusion. During the days following, I stayed glued to the television, which was not generally allowed in our household, watching and listening to try and determine why anyone would have a smile on their face when announcing such a tragic event?

34.
November 22, 1963: One of the saddest and most memorable days of my life was November 22, 1963, the day that the 35th President of the United States, John F. Kennedy, was assassinated. President Kennedy only served 1,037 days. I was in my mid-twenties during his Presidency and to me and other dreamers, he represented our hopes for the future of the country. His courage, leadership, values, charisma and optimism sparked the idealism of my generation, one founded on peace and social justice and the equality of all people. In his words "the New Frontier is here, whether we seek it or not. Beyond that frontier are the uncharted areas of science and space, unsolved problems of peace and war, unconquered pockets of ignorance and prejudice, unanswered questions of poverty and surplus." He advocated better working conditions, more public housing, higher wages, lower prices, cheaper rents and more Social Security benefits for the aged.
In his inaugural address, he inspired all of us to see the importance of civic action and public service by his historic words by the challenge to "Ask not what your country can do for you—ask what you can do for your country."
The hopes and dreams of this "Camelot" period ended on this fateful day and we have not seen its likes, sadly, since then.

35.
November 22, 1963: I was an eleven-year-old 6th Grader at St, Henry's Catholic School President Kennedy was our first elected Catholic Leader. During class Sister Christina turns on the television and the excruciatingly painful news of the President's assassination is in full view, being replayed over and over. We are instructed to go home and be with our loved ones for the enormity of this horrific act is sinking in. The nation's hopes and dreams are dealt a huge blow. My interest in politics and human nature is heightened forever. We can only dream of what could have been. My mother cries, I am sad for America. A pall over our country. Innocence lost.

36.
November 22, 1963: I was born four years later to the day. Every year, as I celebrate my birthday, I think about this fateful day in American history. A single shot changed everything for one man, one family, one city, one nation, and one world. President John F. Kennedy's assassination marked the beginning of a dark era in our country's history that shifted from seeming innocence to one of violence, fear, and mistrust. We've recently entered another period of darkness. It's essential that good people stand up to represent the qualities of light and reason in the face of this darkness.

37.
1966: I'm a senior. My school counselor met with me for what I believed was to guide me through the college application process. She asked me why I was in her office and I told her I wanted to go to college. She told me that I wasn't college material and I should consider taking shop classes. To her, I was just the son of poor people who didn't graduate from high school. To my parents I was a son who could accomplish anything I set out to do. The same attitude was shown by them to my younger siblings. I am forever grateful to have had wonderful parents who believed in me.

38.
March, 1966, My father, then a Catholic priest, marched with Cesar Chavez in California. I happened across a PBS documentary about the Delano to Sacramento march years ago and saw my Dad marching in B&W video. It was something he was very proud of, as am I.

39.
March 15,1966: Was the day I met my now Husband of 53 years Guadalupe S. Olguin. He was walking down Rivas, en el mero hueso del westside, Lost, looking for his mother's new home. The smell of homemade tamales filling the air. He asked for directions and we haven't stopped guiding each other since.

40.
August 1, 1966: My mom would tell the story of how she had morning sickness, pregnant with my older sister, on August 1, 1966, so she didn't go to campus on that day when the gunman went to the top of the UT tower and started shooting, killing 16 people (including one unborn child). She would have passed the tower at that time, on her way to class. A chilling story, but always mythical to me, until as a young adult, I heard about Columbine and the reality sunk in. And now, almost weekly, young white men in America commit similar acts of terrorism.

41.
June 12, 1967: This is the date of the decision of the Loving vs. Virginia case that tore down anti-miscegenation laws in the United States. I am the product of an interracial marriage, my father is black and my mother is white. I am married to a person of a different race. Without the Lovings, I wouldn't be who I am today; I am eternally grateful for their bravery and their will to fight for the right to marry who you love, no matter the color of their skin.

42.
April 4, 1968: My dad, a Jewish guy from Brooklyn and my mom, a Creek and Sioux Indian (the nomenclature of the day) from South Dakota had settled in a small town in southern Oklahoma where my dad worked for Halliburton. It was and still is a hateful little place. It was early spring. I had just turned fourteen. A week and a few days later Martin Luther King was murdered, assassinated. I was walking to the grocery store and heard it in my transistor radio.
And that was the day I realized it. That was the day I realized that all the effort and chances my parents were taking in our town- working to desegregate the public pool, supporting the only nursing home that was run by a Baptist black pastor and was available to black citizens, providing lifeguards and swimming lessons on the 'east side' of town, supporting civil rights on that micro level as best they could-they were doing it for my siblings and me. They had by example after example wanted to shape us into true 'persons'. (A word used back then by a Jewish individual as a compliment.)
That was the date I took a deep breath and realized that the world was not just my existence in that town. But even if it was, it was time for me to start figure to out what it was I was going to stand for, regardless of consequences.

43.
April 4, 1968: I was a senior in college and remember walking into the lobby of my dorm and seeing a large group of other students all gathered around the television and then hearing from one of them that Dr. Martin Luther King, Jr. had been shot and killed in Memphis. There were tears again. How can this be!? I felt dismayed.

44.
May 1968: My father was working in the lettuce fields of Oregon, along with a group of men from our home town in the state of Durango, in Mexico. One of those men, who was also my uncle, receives a letter from home where his wife tells him, among other things, that I had been born. I am my dad's fourth child, but the first baby girl, the one he'd been waiting for. He immediately begins to secretly wish to be caught and deported so he can go home and meet me. His wish comes true. I learned this story years later, as an adult, when I call my parents from a work trip to Eugene, Oregon and I tell them that I just had the best salad ever that consisted of the freshest lettuce. Still on the phone, my father begins to narrate the story of working in the fields of Oregon and his desire to meet me. The after taste of the delicious salad turns bitter in my mouth. Far from being an activist, my father simply recounts (sometimes even funny) anecdotes about his experience as a migrant laborer in this country and the importance of their role. He does wish more people would "listen."

45.
May 6, 1968: El Paso, Texas. I am attending Texas Western College, which is now University of Texas at El Paso, and I get my military draft number of 89 which means I will be drafted to serve in the Vietnam War.

The U.S. is fiercely fighting communism. Luckily the war started winding down and I was never drafted to go to serve, but many of my friends did serve and some were killed in combat, I often think about them, they were great friends and the life that could of been with them! It was a sad time for the U.S. and the war came to an end as the TET offensive began the defeat of communism in 1975 as declared by president Nixon. Communism was seen as a great threat to the U.S. and the rest of the world.

46.
October 3, 1968: In a bloodless military coup, left-wing Peruvian General Juan Velasco seized power, deposing the democratically elected administration of Fernando Belaúnde, under which he served as Commander of the Armed Forces. Through a military revolution, General Velasco became Peru's 58th president. Three years later, in 1971, Velasco's then oppressive military dictatorship spurred my family into voluntary exile in the US. I was a little over a year old—my brother a few months old—and we would grow up in Miami, Florida, living in between worlds and in between cultures (US and Hispanic). When you're an immigrant, you're never truly home, anywhere. But as a direct result of our upbringing—operating in between worlds—we developed an expansive and inclusive worldview and are committed in our work to making sure everyone feels welcome, included, and meant to be here.

47.
November 2, 1968: Students at San Francisco State College began the "Third World Strike" to demand the immediate creation of an Ethnic Studies Department, the substantive hiring of nonwhite faculty, and the expansive recruitment of nonwhite students, Inspired by the international student movements and civil rights organizing, the five-month strike helped spur other strikes across the country, including at UC Berkeley, Columbia, and Cornell. Their pervasive demands to reimagine who belonged in a university and what constituted knowledge triggered significant institutional change, but also launched repressive and even violent responses. I remain grateful to those students for making my life as a student, researcher, writer, and professor possible. They give me faith in collective action.

48.
November 2, 1968: I am 10 years old. I entered our home in Floresville and heard the telephone ring. I answered the call and the person on the other side stated they wanted to speak to my mother. I looked at my mother and told her "someone wants to talk to you and they sound like someone died." My mother gets the phone. We look into each other's eyes. I start crying and screamed "Daddy's dead, Daddy's dead!" My father was dead, he died in a motor vehicle accident. His vehicle stalled

hijo quién solo acababa de cumplir su primer año.

115.
September 11, 2001: San Antonio, Tx, I was sitting in American History class, first period, an announcement was made that a plane had struck the world trade center in New York City, but class would not be cancelled. We jeered at the teacher, requesting to see the images on the TV in the corner of class, he declined and then refused. Over the course of the day, the images of the event and the eventual fall of the two towers were painted for me by peers who had been allowed to view the catastrophe in this or that teacher's class. I was obsessed with what was happening on the east coast...another plane hit the pentagon? This was not an accident, the repetition indicated intention, a plot, not an accident. I left school listening to the reports on the local radio news, lusting for the image, the images that were not available in the timely nature of now. I went to Yvette's house, she was watching the same news on every channel, the first collision, the second collision, views from the sky and the ground and the veils of smoke. For some the image stays fixed with its iconic, symbolic veil of tragedy, mystery, and complexity. I was so moved, watching the event over and over again, feeling myself loosing feeling with every angle, every pass, but more and more curious. Who made this thing? Who made this image? How did it all work. The images, more permanent than the event, became a catalyst for many of my future inquiries as an artist and educator. I keep excavating this deep wound for meaning, for light.

116.
September 21, 2001: My father died on 9/11/2001. Not in New York, but in Florida. With our country in turmoil and confusion, the days following my father's death delayed me in uniting with my mother, now a widow. It took me 10 days to secure a flight, from San Antonio to New York, which is where Papi wanted to be buried. You see, New York breathed new life into my Cuban father. New York was a rebirth into our American Dream. My father made a choice to flee Cuba and to denounce the tyranny of his homeland. When I was ten years old, and with only what we could carry, we left Cuba. As my flight into La Guardia was descending, it flew over the fresh site of what was the World Trade Center. I could see from my window the gray smoke still rising from the ashes and hovering over lower Manhattan. At that moment, I found myself reflecting on Papi's solemn gospel that America's freedom and strength were the envy of many nations. Yes, the Towers and many lives were pointlessly lost. And had Papi been alive to witness the tragedy he would have said that America is still the land of opportunity, and we will overcome.

117.
Oct 7, 2001: Even at a moment of supreme vulnerability, American colonial dominance seeps in everywhere. Following the events of 9/11, a photo of a pro Osama bin Laden demonstration in Bangladesh dominates the New York Times front page. In the forefront, a protester holds a poster featuring a large photo of bin Laden. A second glance however reveals the Muppet Bert from Sesame Street peering over bin Laden's right shoulder.

The protester got the poster from a printer in Dhaka. The printer, Mostafa Kamal, had scoured the internet for a powerful image of bin Laden to use in his photo collage design. Completely unfamiliar with Sesame Street, he unwittingly found what he was looking for on Bert is Evil, a parody website created by artist Dino Ignacio, featuring the character alongside infamous people and events. Kamal printed 2000 posters with this image and the AP and Reuters distributed the Bangladesh protest photo globally. Kamal later printed a new pro bin Laden poster with the image of Bert removed.

118.
November 1, 2001: The first time I heard about a political election in my life. I was very confused at the willful arguments on the radio.

119.
May 2003: I was on a trip cross country from Florida to LA and was spending the night in Houston. Earlier in the day I was pulled over by a cop who said I was criminally speeding. Meanwhile, I knew that the over packed car couldn't even reach the speed limit. When I argued he said to me: "In Texas, they trust cops more than the people." I checked into a motel late that night and at about 3am there was a booming pounding on the door. Terrified, I yelled out asking who it was—only to hear a whispered "we are going to have to break the door down." I realized I had to open the door and was met with a gun in my face. My companion and I were pulled onto the open-air walkway in our underwear while we were held at gunpoint while another man searched our room and belongings. It turned out they were undercover DEA agents that had a bad tip. What is freedom if the people who claim to hand it to you can take it at any time for any reason or none at all.

120.
1/11/2004: Driving from El Paso to Lubbock:
First stop, the body of 20 year old Christopher Maldonado is laid to rest in a cemetery on the edge of town. Six hours to go. Back on the road as the Franklin Mountains disappear in the rear view mirror, so does my naive sense of security. Value systems are permanently altered. Approaching the hypnotic West Texas plains, my paradigm has shifted.

121.
12.31.2004: The day that I lost my mother when I was only 3 years old.

122.
February 6, 2005: An ATF agent whispered to me that he had noticed a lot of "un-patriotic artwork" in our apartment.

123.
March 9, 2005: Who would have thought that being a border kid from the El Paso/Juarez region would shape me into a international carbon Ph.D. scientist with a mission to improve human livelihoods worldwide? Raised on the border allowed me to have a mix of US-Mexico cultures and also enjoy the benefits of the U.S. education system. While pursuing my environmental science degree at the University of Texas at El Paso, I had opportunities to succeed in the STEM field. During the fall of 2004, I was invited by one of my mentors, Dr. Aaron Velasco, to participate in a national SACNAS conference in Albuquerque NM. SACNAS is an inclusive national organization dedicated to fostering the success of Chicanos/Hispanics and Native Americans, from college students to professionals, in attaining advanced degrees, careers, and positions of leadership in STEM.

During the 2014 SACNAS conference I was introduced to a new community of scientists, a new familia. It was during this big conference of 3000+ scientists that I noticed that there were many scientists in the US that were bilingual like me, that when speaking English had an accent like me, that we all shared stories of those times when we felt like we didn't belong in the STEM field, and also had "pachangas" like me! Science finally felt like home! This inspiration drove me to bring the SACNAS feeling back to my other STEM friends at UTEP. So on March 9, 2005 (see attachment), along with my colleague Milka Montes, we co-founded the SACNAS Student Chapter at the University of Texas at El Paso (SACNAS @ UTEP).

Since then, the chapter has won numerous awards and mentored hundreds of minority students in STEM! The chapter has helped graduate many more diverse STEM minds and achieved great achievements in the STEM field worldwide! We have helped UTEP, a US funded institution, build a stronger and more diverse science! Being raised in the border allowed me to see that sometimes depending on where we come from, we sometimes might not feel welcomed in a space or time. This is true in 2018. However, the border also taught me that having two backgrounds meant having two advantages! The key is to turn these advantages into opportunities and most importantly, make sure to invite, include, and retain others with you! I believe I have done this and clearly, there is still have much more to do in the future. We need to embrace our differences, recognize our strengths, and empower those who are oppressed. We all, just like me, need help not just to achieve our dreams and to also help others achieve their own dreams.

124.
July 23, 2005: I had committed a number of felonious crimes by this time, but the crime that lead to my first arrest wasn't committed by me at all. I was taken in for questioning and even after a polygraph "proved" my innocence, the police still weren't happy with my negative attitude and the fact that they hadn't found the culprit. After a few hours of grown men trying to break me, a 14-year-old boy, my mother barged in demanding they let me go. So they did.

This incident instilled a deep mistrust in the very institution I thought was meant to keep me safe. This incident made me realize I can't trust the police, and now 13 years later I'm still constantly looking over my shoulder, I can't imagine the mistrust my friends and family who aren't straight, white, and male, must feel. My heart wrenches every time I hear of another person of color getting killed by the police. And every time I read news headlines of racist cops killing out of ignorance and fear in order to uphold a racist system, I remember how lucky I was that day, and every day, to be white because innocence doesn't matter in American society.

125.
April 10, 2006 Jersey City: My wife, Nanette Hernandez, and I go to Liberty State Park to hear our son, Mateo Cartagena, speak at an immigrants' rights rally on a day that 102 cities held simultaneous protests in support of our country's immigrants—all led by Latinos and Latinas. That spring saw millions of immigrants hit the streets to demand dignity. My son led an unauthorized high school walkout, marched through Jersey City without permits then spoke to hundreds of sympathizers. Like his sister and our immediate family, dissent runs through our veins.

126.
April 11, 2006: House of Blues, the Wailers lyrically preached to emancipate ourselves from mental slavery none but ourselves can free our minds improvising the anger, fear and all emotions marinated in the Bayou post the slaughter of communities and habitats by man made hurricanes. Jazz raging on Frenchmen Street. Looting by NOPD. Our city became a radioactive laboratory. Outsiders saw financial potential. The revolution of grassroots was sparked per the people of New Orleans had awoken from the euphemisms of the greatest Nation. The deception of help and support from Earth's 'most ethically perfect government'. Bush Jr & Cheney Inc., shielded with their squad of mercenaries, Black Water. Federal, State and Local would impose power upon or door to door not with help but to take inventory of each structure on the Anarchist voodoo ridden streets of New Orleans and take each citizens gun. We would become stronger by uniting and standing together. I had awoken to see the requiem of a city. I found my calling, as a critical thinker I became an activist. I stood for those whom couldn't voice themselves, they had no representation per they had remained cogs as products of the system by the system per our systematic slavery's demand. I would call upon the spirit of Fred Hampton. "I am a revolutionary." Make levees not war. Only those of color, of lower class and status were affected most and as we began to use the Master's tools, the Master became alarmed in time to avoid its demise. The Danzinger Bridge killings would be the norm to dismantle the grassroots movements. I was broken by the overwhelming power and excessive force so ran and drowned in bourbon, whiskey and sorrows. "Amigo, no te aguites." Un mestizo como yo? He would be one of many migrants from Latin America we would bring over contracted by the company whom received the

and thought, "I know racism is not dead, but this shows that it doesn't have all the power."

140.
January 20, 2009: Saratoga Springs, NY. I was at Yaddo, an artist's colony, watching President Obama's first inauguration with about a dozen other folks. It was in the teens that day, and the heat was out in the one room that had a TV, so we were all in parkas and gloves, our breath steaming in the air. The TV was a old-school model, maybe 16." There was no cable—only rabbit ears wrapped in aluminum foil. Fuzzy picture, freezing conditions, everyone bitching about both—until the ceremony started. And then we all watched, in awe, as the first Black president was sworn in and addressed the nation. My heart was so full. It seemed, that day, that we had finally started to rectify some of the terrible racial injustice on which our country was founded. Even now, knowing the ugly backlash that came after, that remains one of the most beautiful memories of my life. And a bright spark of hope, in a very bleak time, for America's future.

141.
Jan 20 2009: Crammed into our office lunch room me and my colleagues are watching President Obama's first inauguration take place. I am working in London and we are all full of excitement that during this protracted period of global strife and recession the first black President has been elected. There is a buoyant sense of hope and expectation for change. Will this mark the moment when America steps forward to lead the rest of the world towards a more peaceful and just future? Only time will tell...

142.
January 22, 2009: It seemed like every night my mom was asking me to translate a list of questions for an important test. I felt proud that I knew some of the answers. I had just learned some of the material in history class. In Spanish I explained to her some of the things I knew, like what the 13 stripes on the U.S. flag mean, what the branches of government are, and what an amendment was. One morning ride to drop me off at my middle school she was all dressed up and I could sense she was nervous. When I came back home that day she seemed much more relieved and happy. I did not realize the importance of it back then but I was happy she passed her test and she was happy that it was her first day as a U.S. citizen.

143.
September 29, 2009: My grandfather, a veteran of the Korean War, laying his veterans hospital bed naming the end of his battle with cancer. He said to me "I'm not good enough to live." My grandfather, who served our country, not good enough to live how is that fair?

144.
10.2009: This was the first day I was allowed to legally drive alone. I remember getting into my 2004 Ford Ranger pick up truck and driving my self to high school. Being able to play my own music and drive alone for the first time was such a liberating experience. It was one of the first times I felt fully free and autonomous.

145.
October 26, 2009: San Diego, California.
We stayed in the kitchen because it was the brightest room in the house and you could still see parts of the sky from the windows. All of the other rooms took on a gray pallor, and the windows were darkened with a thick coat of ash. We were restless, because we hadn't gone outside in two days—we couldn't breathe.

146.
November 2nd, 2009:

Lost in translation.... lol

Hi Mijo,
Here's the translation of the song I wanted to help you to pronounce the words.

Love You!
Grandma

The Supremes- No puedes dar prisa al amor
No puedes dar prisa al amor
No, te necesitas esperar
Ella dijo que el amor no biene facil
Es un juego de dar y aceptar

147.
June 10th, 2010: I am a 22 year old young woman away from my border hometown in Texas for the first time, attending a friend's wedding in Ohio. My mom calls me on the phone to check on me and I respond to her in Spanish like I always do. I hear in a disgusted tone a remark: "Is that girl speaking Spanish?" and it's the first time I realize and feel like a minority. It opened my eyes to the reality that I am part of a culture in my own country that is widely misunderstood and looked down upon.

148.
June 26, 2010: When I was 10 years old I always loved to go outside and play with my neighbors. The thought of my father always came to mind. I always remember the day he left when I was just two years old. I always hoped that someday he would come back and tell me he loved me. While I was playing with my neighbors, my mom called me inside and she handed me her phone and it was my father. He was sobbing over the phone saying that he loved me and hoped to see me again. Ever since that day I would always remember the day he called me. I still remember the exact words he told me when we were talking over the phone. Hopefully one day I will get the chance to meet him one more...

149.
July 2010: I was in my Dads car while he was inside my Moms house they had a guy down the street that had a Pontiac GTO. I think he was testing his speed so he came down the street doing 110 I think and he lost control and hit the back of my dads truck while I was in the back seat and My dads car swung around and the man who owned the GTO totaled it.

150.
11-2010: November of 2010 is significant to because it was the first time my parents took me to Puerto Rico to meet my Dad's side of the family. With this trip I got to meet my distant cousins and learn more about my other race.

151.
December 10, 2011: Life can't be real. Growing up in a small East Texas town where racism thrived and the motto was always "us vs them" can't be life. The past is where the pain lies, but the future is what you make of it. Your perception of life doesn't have to be the same as the majority which can be challenging for the minority. Her teachings always revolved around making your own decisions and that I say her, I am referring to my grandmother, the person who raised me. When others spoke ill of my father, she remained silent, allowed me to form my own thoughts of what I believed versus what I heard.

However, this day will always begin with a moment of silence because this is the date when she passed away. This also happens to be my father's birthday. I thank her for the lessons she taught me about this life. If I would've allowed the opinions of others to influence my decisions, I wouldn't have the relationship that I have with him now. When I say him, I am referring to my father who experienced heartache at an early age with the passing of his father. I didn't know how to process the death of someone as close to me as my grandmother, but received support from him based on his past.

This is the future. Life is real and was never so apparent than this date itself.

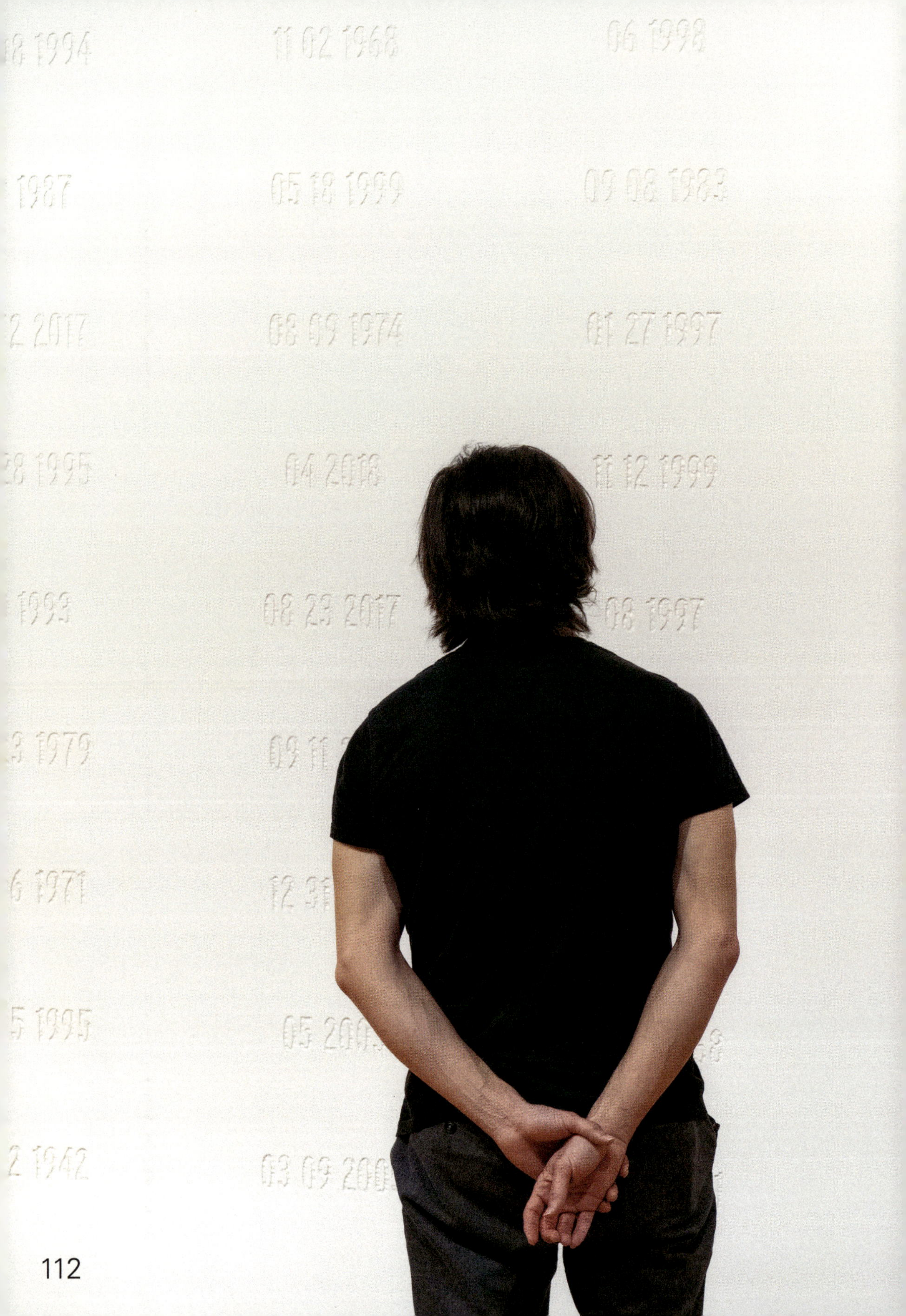
11 02 1968
06 1998
05 18 1999
09 08 1983
08 09 1974
01 27 1997
04 2018
11 12 1999
08 23 2017

1966
03 04 2018
2015
08 11 2017
03 1966
09 13 2007
01 09 1996
2016
10 2009
05 13 1985
2017
01 2016
04 04 1968
08 14 2017
04 11 2006
2012
04 2018
05 1968
2015
07 22 2018
11 22 1963

Vincent Valdez

—

FM: When did the climate change? When did "this moment" become this moment?

Valdez: The voices of the dead are still speaking. Waiting to be heard. "We are the United States of Amnesia. We learn nothing because we remember nothing."[1]

AC: In an age where consumer capitalism constantly promotes the dream of expressing yourself, hasn't art become central to supporting and maintaining that power structure? However radical its messages are on the surface—isn't art underneath really constantly promoting the idea of self-expression and so promoting consumer capitalism? So maybe it's part of the problem?

Valdez: When we are no longer willing to commit to the creative purpose and have grown suspicious of critical thought, then the system has made perishable items of us all. Products of society "know the price of everything and the value of nothing."[2]

AD: What is "real" in your practice—your way of working, your medium, your social, professional, material, cultural, political relationships, your proximity to institutions? And what is sustainable? Do the two categories (real and sustainable) overlap, and to what extent?

Valdez: One must make the choice, every single day, to commit. Different artists commit to different motives. I am compelled to create work that functions beyond the equation of luxury and comfort. It is, at times, both terrifying and liberating. My commitment to this work is sustainable. Life and the world are not.

GC: Museums and cultural organizations once perceived as "pure" white boxes free of bias, are now being pushed to reckon with their own privilege and political baggage. As artists increasingly explore the meaning of "realness" in their work, I wonder how you negotiate the political context in which your work is inserted when it enters the museum.

Valdez: The real challenge, I believe, is to keep my work and all of its context entirely non-negotiable, inside and outside of the studio.

MW: The magician Karl Germain said that "conjuring is the only honest profession: a magician promises to deceive and does." And Picasso said, "We all know that Art is not truth. Art is a lie that makes us realize truth." In our current state, where there is no "truth," and "facts" have become a matter of opinion, how can artists wake us up from this unpleasant dream? How can you help us see the world and each other through a lens of hope, trust, and humanity?

Valdez: I offer my work as a report. I want to put it all down on record. To testify. I am caught in a stare-down with twenty-first-century America. I will not look away. All I want to do is to create images that enable others to see what I am seeing. This is my way of connecting. Bearing witness means that you, we, are willing to see things as they really are, even the things we would rather not see. One must be absolutely willing to confront the realities of the world, life, and death. This is what it means to be human. This is our responsibility. We will never begin to understand this time and place, understand each other or our own selves, until we are willing to open our eyes and confront the image in our mirror.

CG: How do you hold on to something so no one can take it away? Your beliefs? Your body? Your love? What tethers us here?

Valdez: Everything is temporary. Around age seven: early Sunday morning. One of the last times I jumped into bed with parents. Squeezed between them. Tired bodies. Warm, brown skin. Memorized their faces as they slept. So young and beautiful. Closed my eyes. Didn't want the sun to rise. "Remember this moment, this exact moment. Because someday it will be very different," I whispered. These memories will perish with me one day. Until then, I carry them with me—because they illuminate the darkness of accepting that nothing is permanent.

ES: Public health physicians distinguish between narrative compassion (where one or two or three people are at risk) and statistical compassion (where thousands or millions are at risk). We're fairly good at the first, and have many occasions to strengthen our capacity through daily acts of friendship and from reading literature. We're terrible at the second, and have almost no training in strengthening our feeble abilities in this region. To what extent can the medium you work in invite, or carry out, acts of narrative compassion and statistical compassion?

Valdez: This work reminds me on a daily basis that we are bound by similar patterns of history, experiences, and struggles for survival. Filtering the present through the past presents me with the difficult and private examination of my own tangled history—as a Mexican American in twenty-first-century America. I don't presume that painting can change the world. But, I stand firm in my belief that the artist can still provide critical moments of silence and clarity in times of immense distortion and chaos.

1 Gore Vidal, "The State of the Union," *The Nation*, September 13, 2004.
2 Oscar Wilde, *Lady Windermere's Fan*, 1892.

Dream Baby Dream, 2018
pp. 116–7

Dream Baby Dream (1–12), 2018 and _Requiem_ with Adriana Corral, 2016
pp. 118–9

Requiem, 2016–19
pp. 120–1

Procession for _Requiem_ with musicians (Miguel Torres II, Robert S. Casillas Jr., Aaron Daniel Salinas, Jon Wahl, Chris Handschuh and Vincent Valdez) and pallbearers (Richard Criddle, Patrick Fecher, Timothy Hartel, Ian Alden Russell, Brian Weisz, and Jon Rajkovich), 04.13.19
pp. 122–3

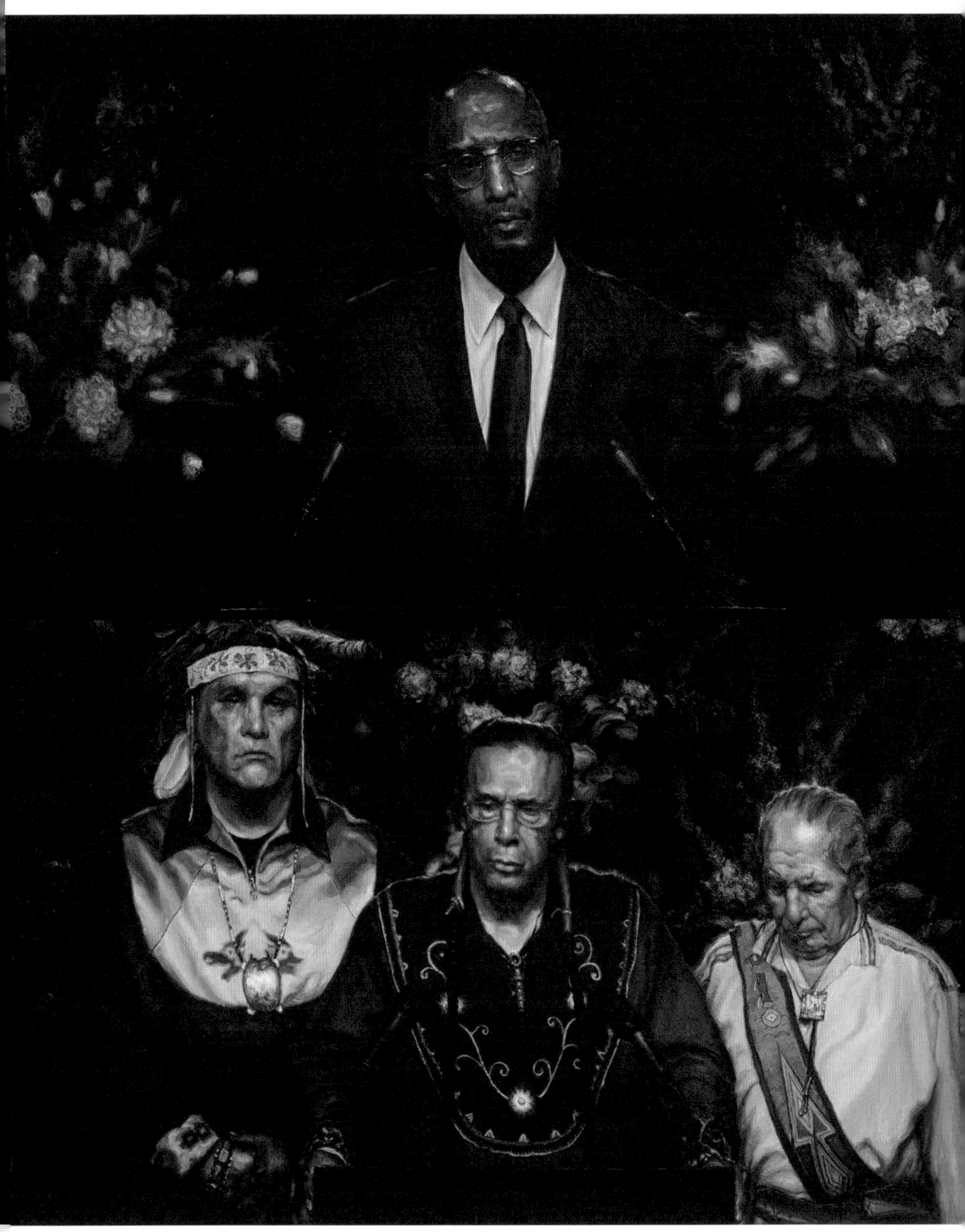

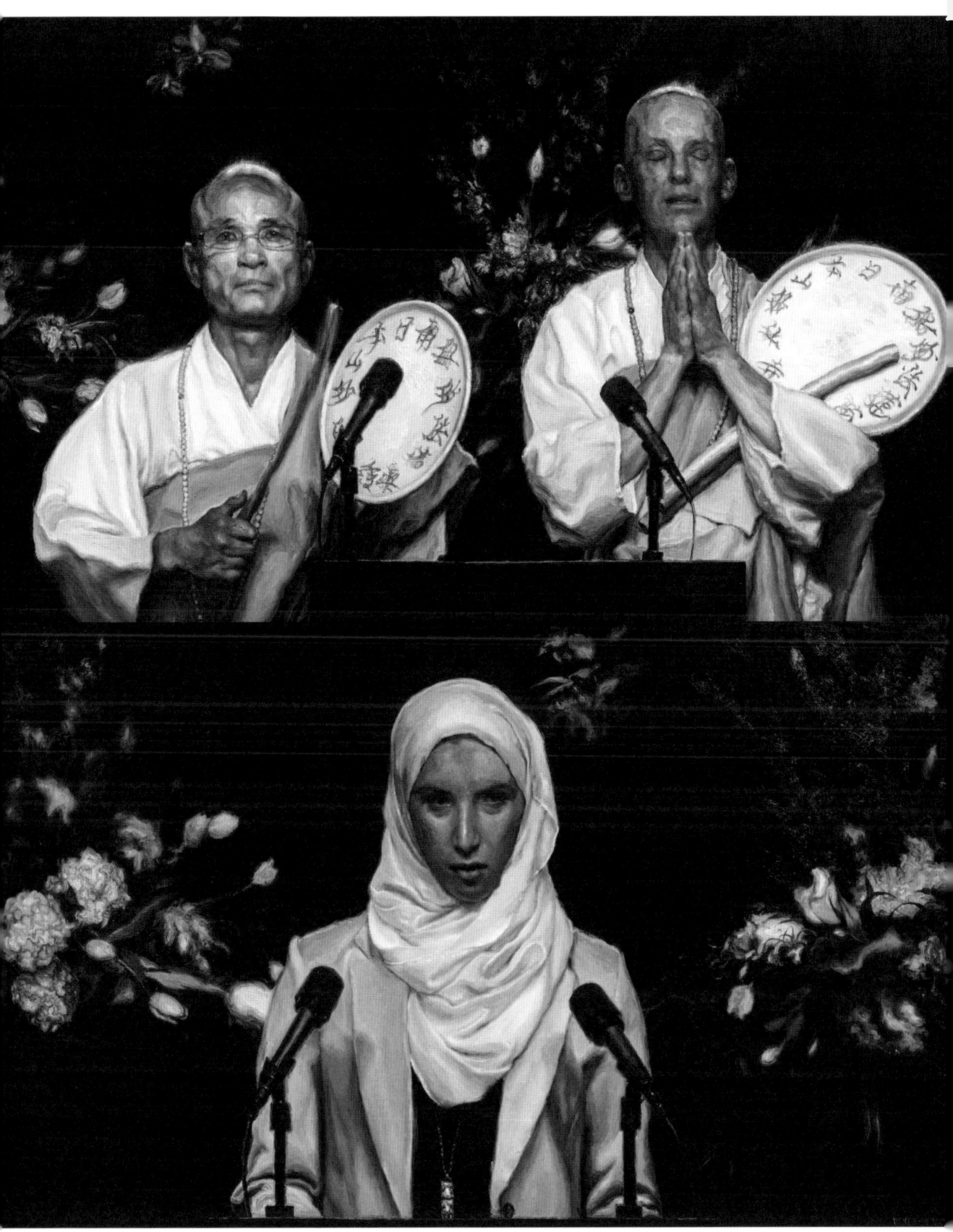

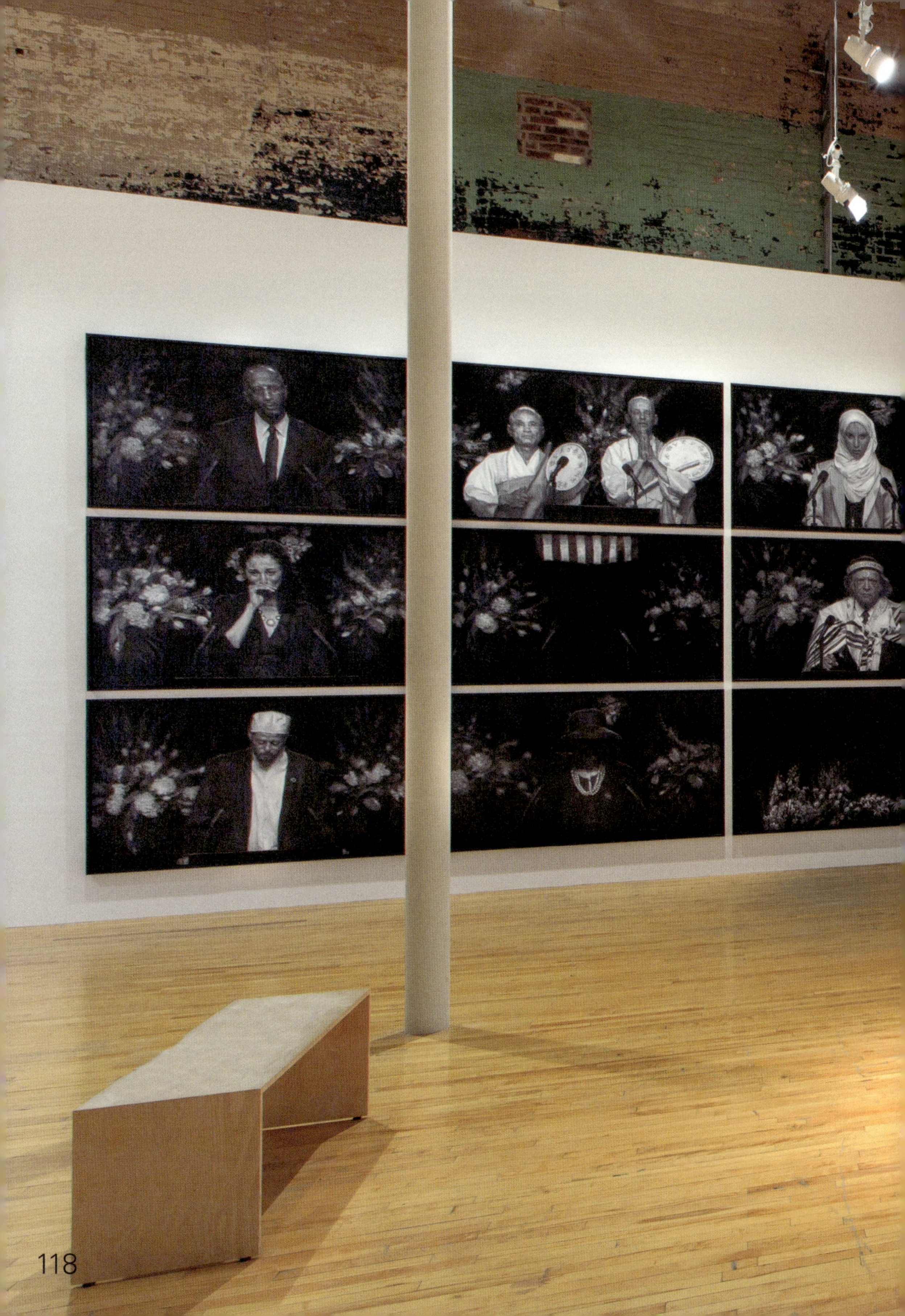

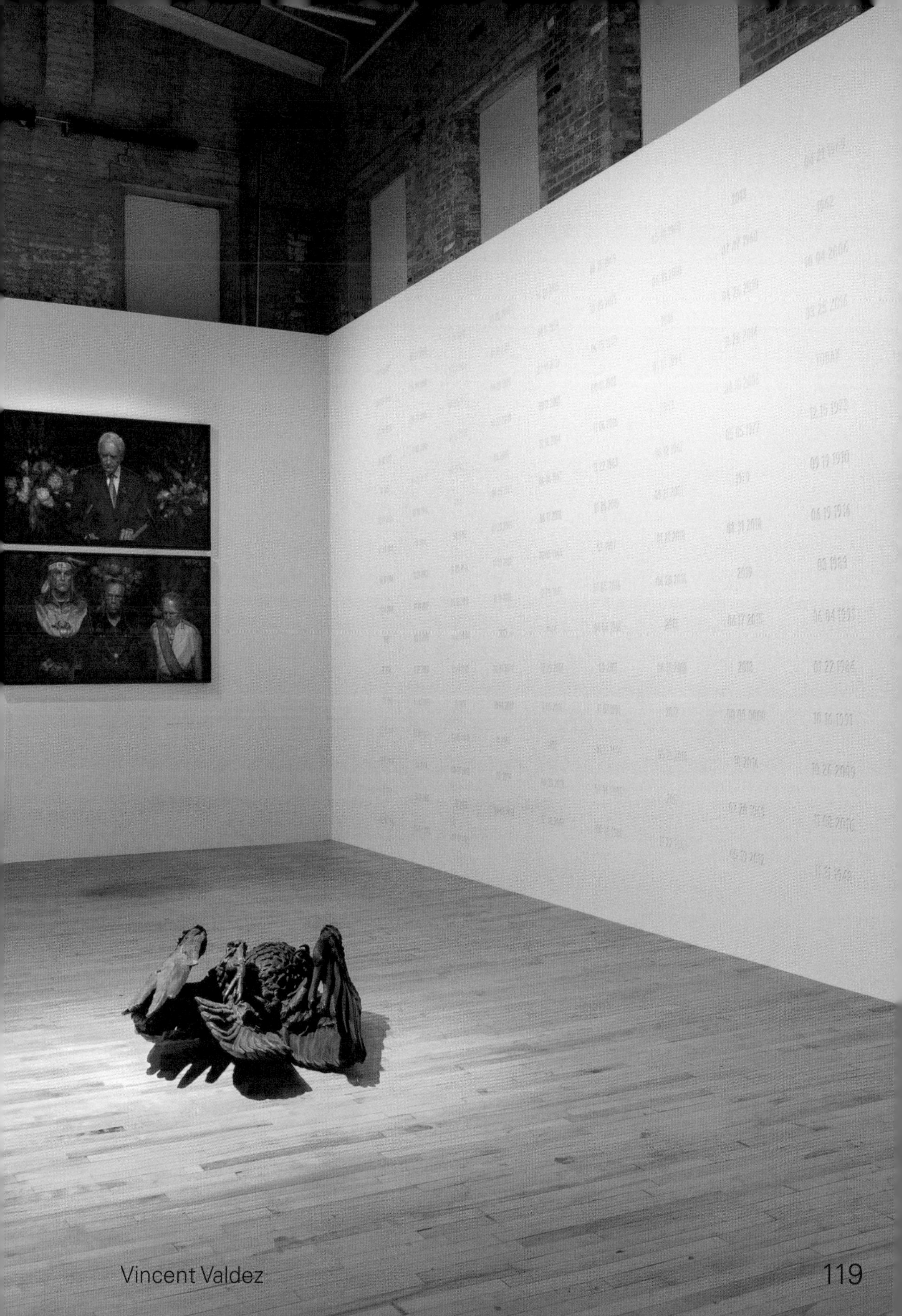

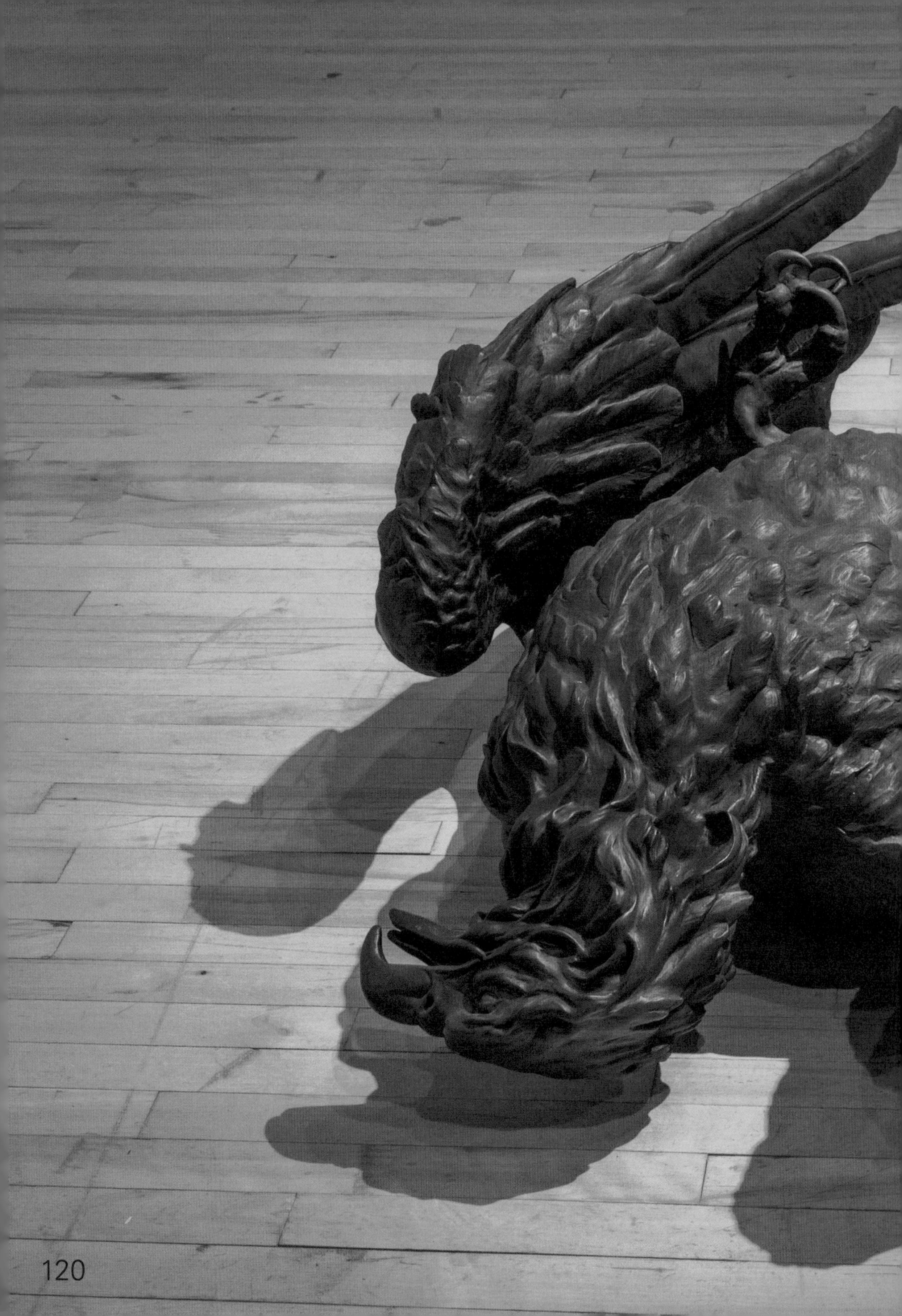

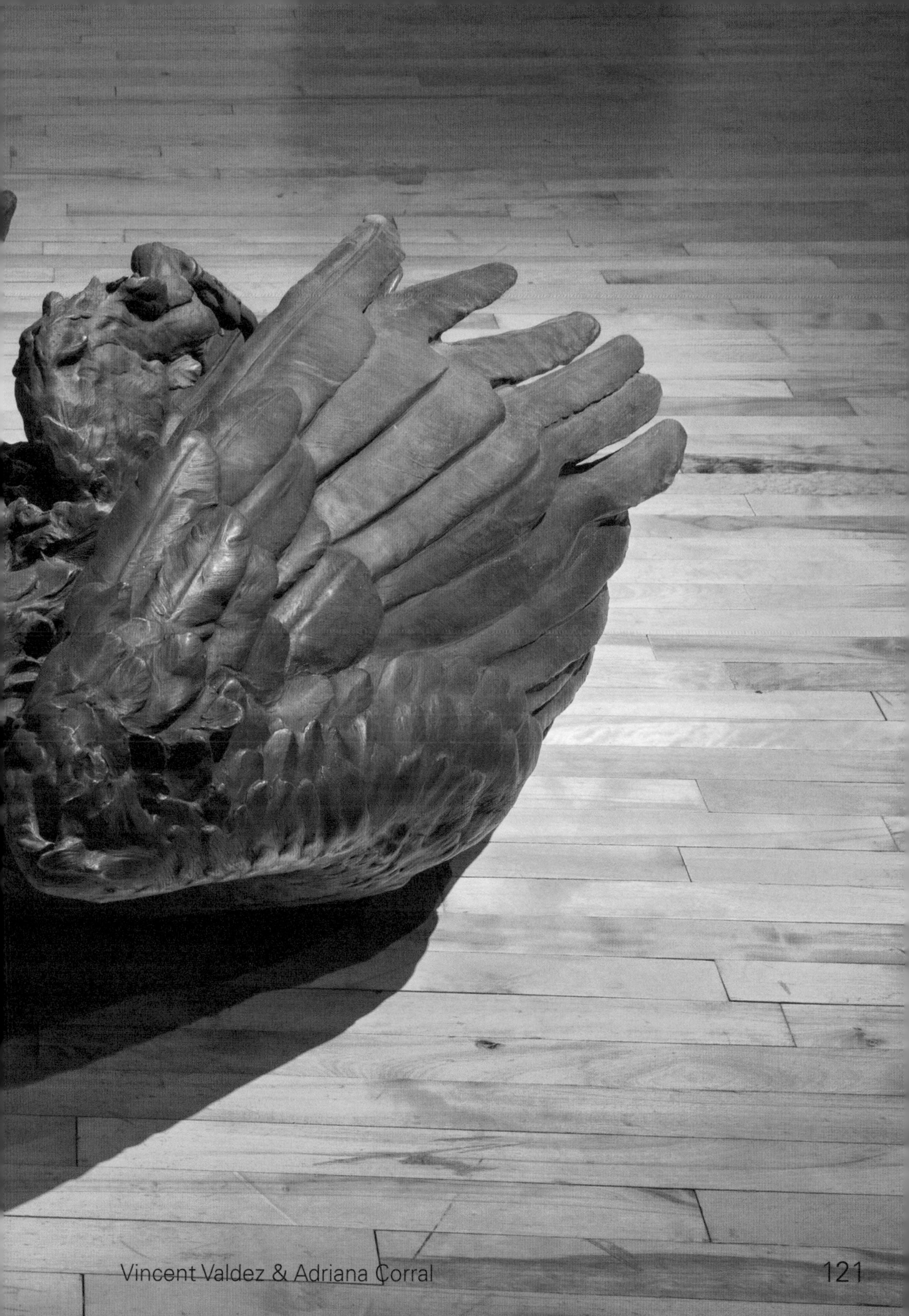

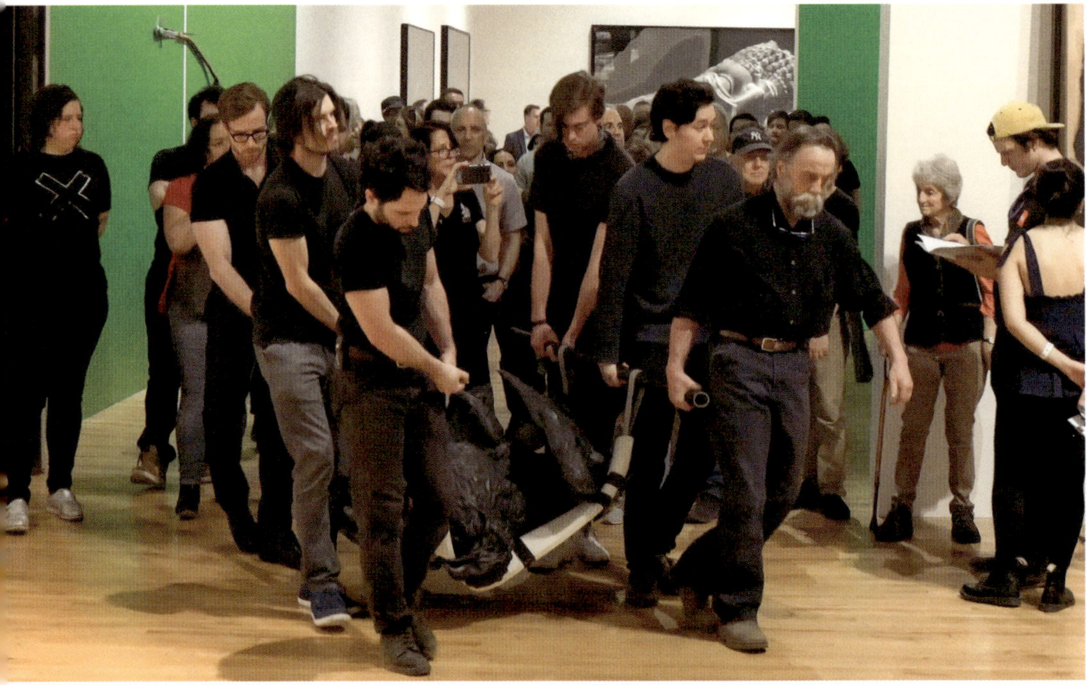

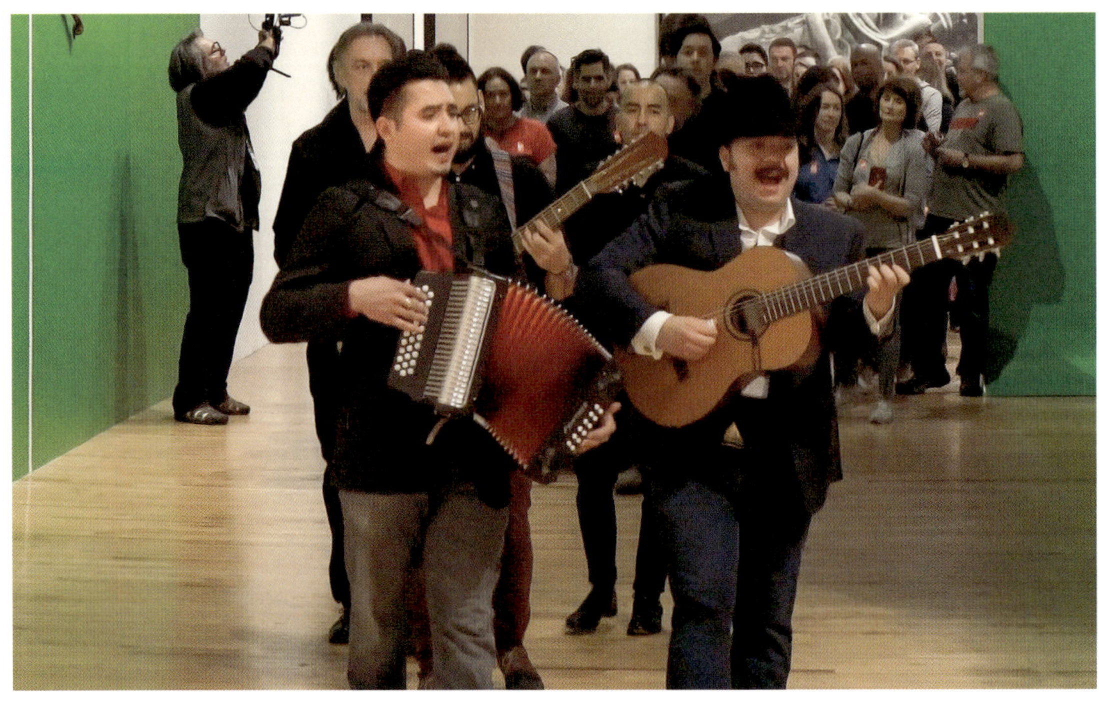

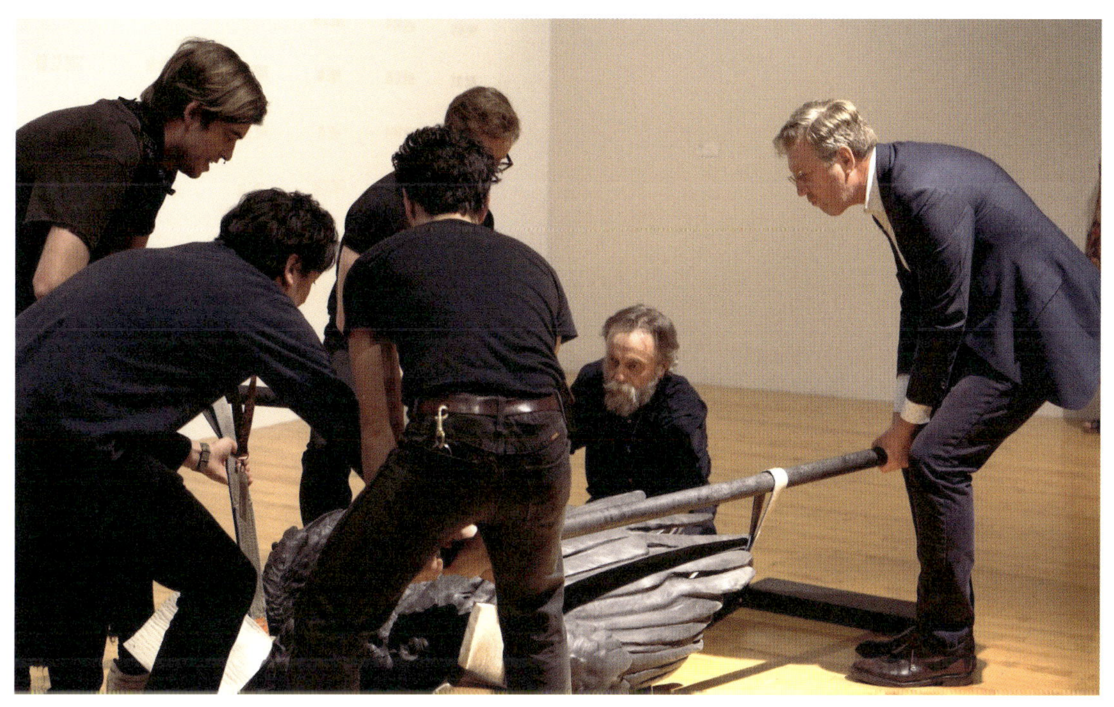

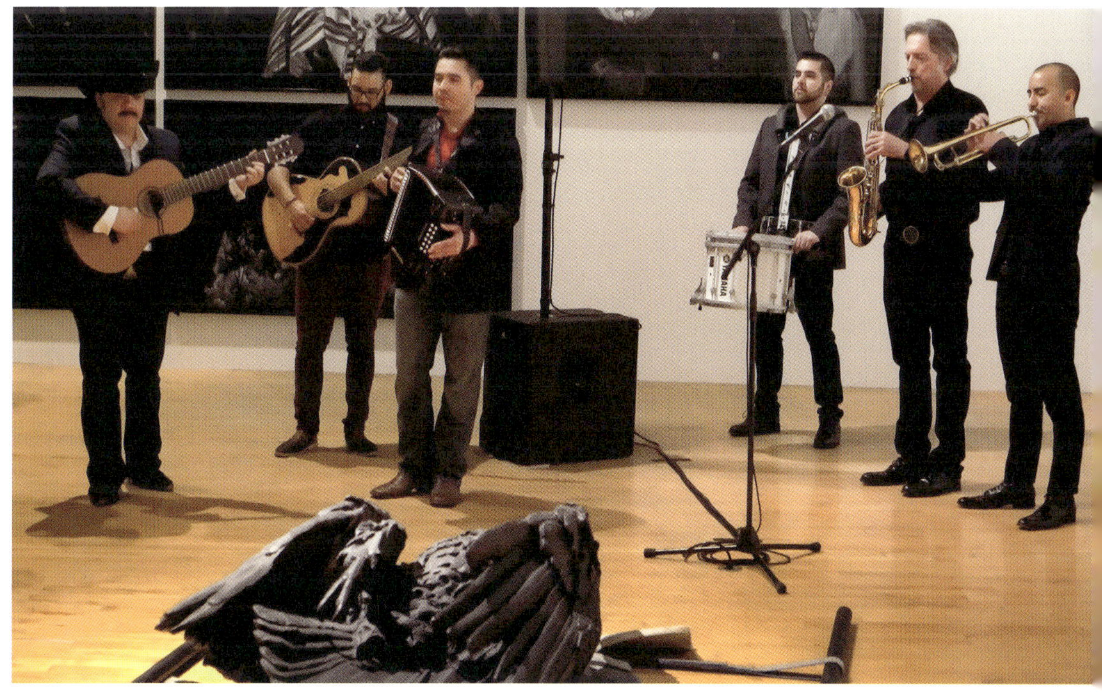
YAMAHA

Robert Longo

—

FM: When did the climate change? When did "this moment" become this moment?

Longo: After the Civil War.

AC: In an age where consumer capitalism constantly promotes the dream of expressing yourself, hasn't art become central to supporting and maintaining that power structure? However radical its messages are on the surface—isn't art underneath really constantly promoting the idea of self-expression and so promoting consumer capitalism? So maybe it's part of the problem?

Longo: Being an artist is not only a calling, it is also a profession. I'm fortunate to sell my work, to be able to pay my bills, and to feed myself. I don't take it for granted. I find it naive and frankly foolish to repudiate artists who make a living selling their work.

AD: What is "real" in your practice—your way of working, your medium, your social, professional, material, cultural, political relationships, your proximity to institutions? And what is sustainable? Do the two categories (real and sustainable) overlap, and to what extent?

Longo: To make something new is impossible. One can only aspire to make something real.

GC: Museums and cultural organizations once perceived as "pure" white boxes free of bias, are now being pushed to reckon with their own privilege and political baggage. As artists increasingly explore the meaning of "realness" in their work, I wonder how you negotiate the political context in which your work is inserted when it enters the museum.

Longo: Making art is an inherently political act. We, as artists, are responsible to report on the time in which we live. Although museums depend upon donations from the government and the wealthy, we cannot overlook their essential position in the world: helping to democratize art. Art is the most democratic form of narrative.

MW: The magician Karl Germain said that "conjuring is the only honest profession: a magician promises to deceive and does." And Picasso said, "We all know that Art is not truth. Art is a lie that makes us realize truth." In our current state, where there is no "truth," and "facts" have become a matter of opinion, how can artists wake us up from this unpleasant dream? How can you help us see the world and each other through a lens of hope, trust, and humanity?

Longo: Picasso also said, "What do you think an artist is? An imbecile who only has eyes if he's a painter, ears if he's a musician, or a lyre in every chamber of his heart if he's a poet—or even, if he's a boxer, only some muscles? Quite the contrary, he is at the same time a political being constantly alert to the horrifying, passionate or pleasing events in the world, shaping himself completely in their image.... No, painting is not made to decorate apartments. It's an offensive and defensive weapon against the enemy."[1]

CG: How do you hold on to something so no one can take it away? Your beliefs? Your body? Your love? What tethers us here?

Longo: I'm not a collector by nature, and I'm not concerned with owning things. Ownership, in a grander scale, is impossible. We all turn to dust.

ES: Public health physicians distinguish between narrative compassion (where one or two or three people are at risk) and statistical compassion (where thousands or millions are at risk). We're fairly good at the first, and have many occasions to strengthen our capacity through daily acts of friendship and from reading literature. We're terrible at the second, and have almost no training in strengthening our feeble abilities in this region. To what extent can the medium you work in invite, or carry out, acts of narrative compassion and statistical compassion?

Longo: In making my work I use images I've pulled from the image storm of the world. I seek to make powerful images with the most fragile medium, dust and paper, an attempt to slow down images, to provoke the viewer to consume their full power.

—

1 "Picasso n'est pas officier dans l'armée française," March 24, 1945, in *Les Lettres Françaises* [magazine published by the National Front], vol. V, p. 48.

***Untitled (Vietnam, 1968)*, 2017**
p. 125

***Untitled (Destroyed Head of Lamassu, Nineveh)*, 2016**
pp. 126–7

***Untitled (St. Louis Rams /Hands Up)*, 2016**
pp. 128–9

***Untitled (Nathan Bedford Forrest Statue Removal: Memphis, 2017)*, 2018**
pp. 130–1

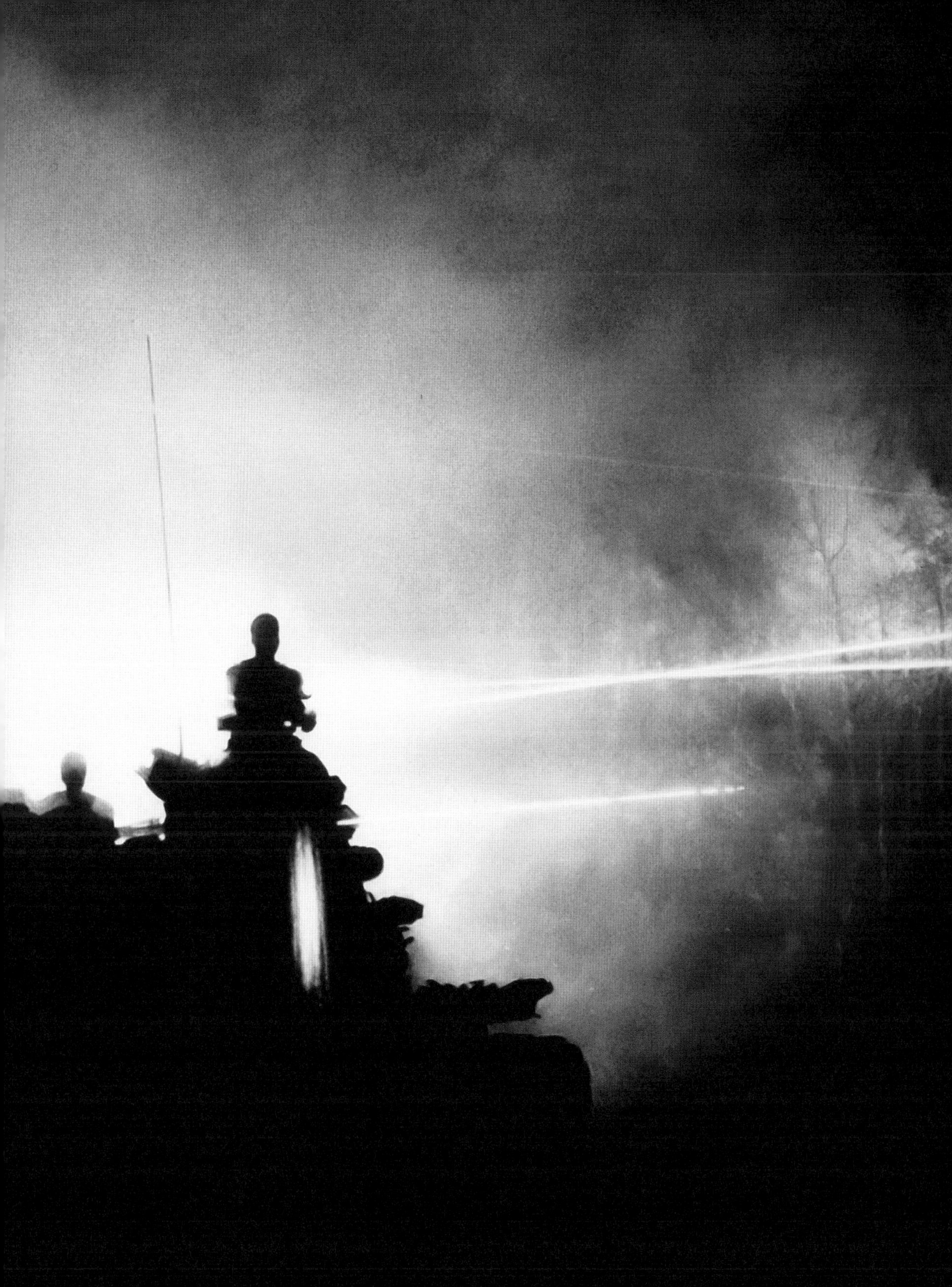

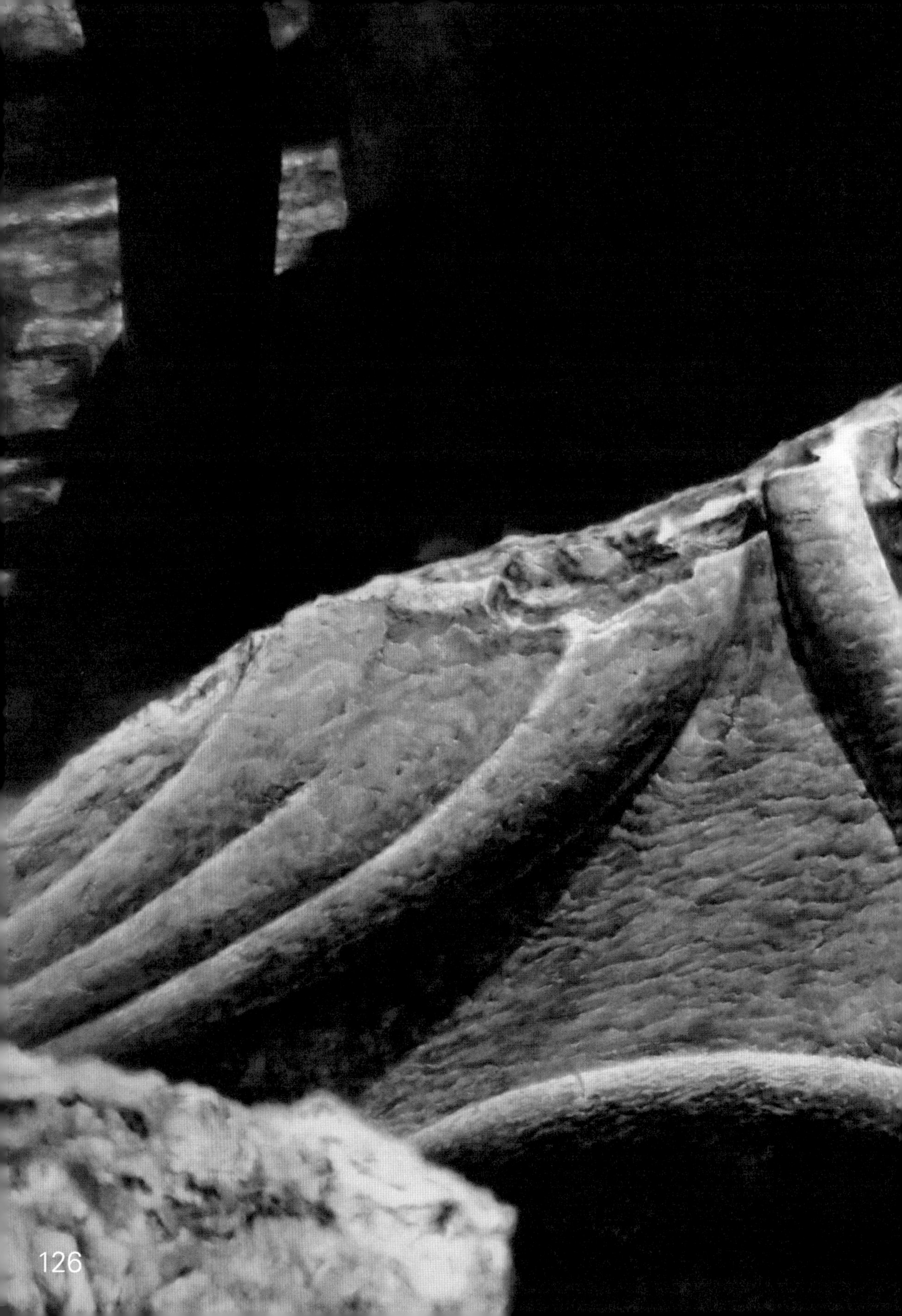

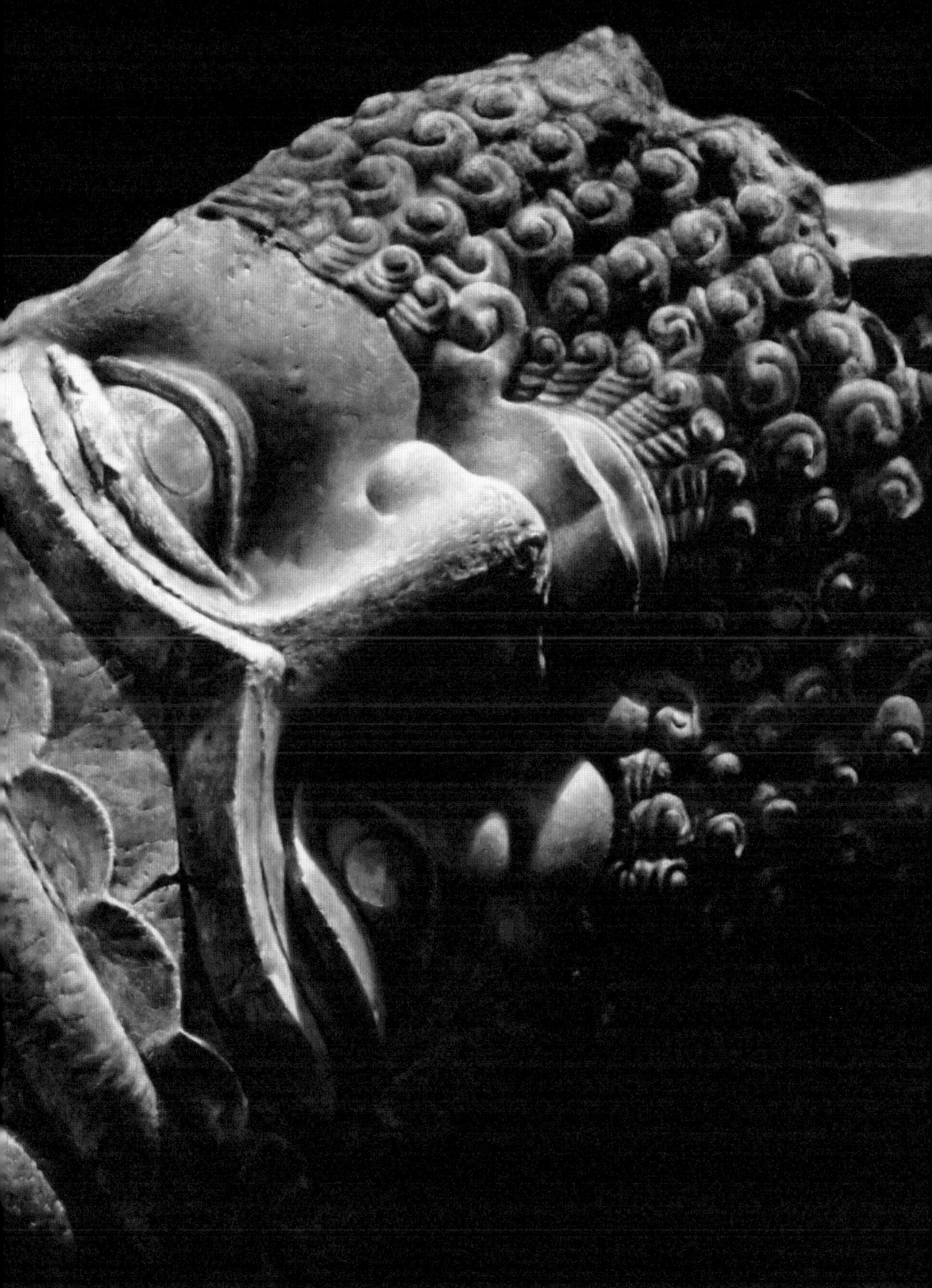

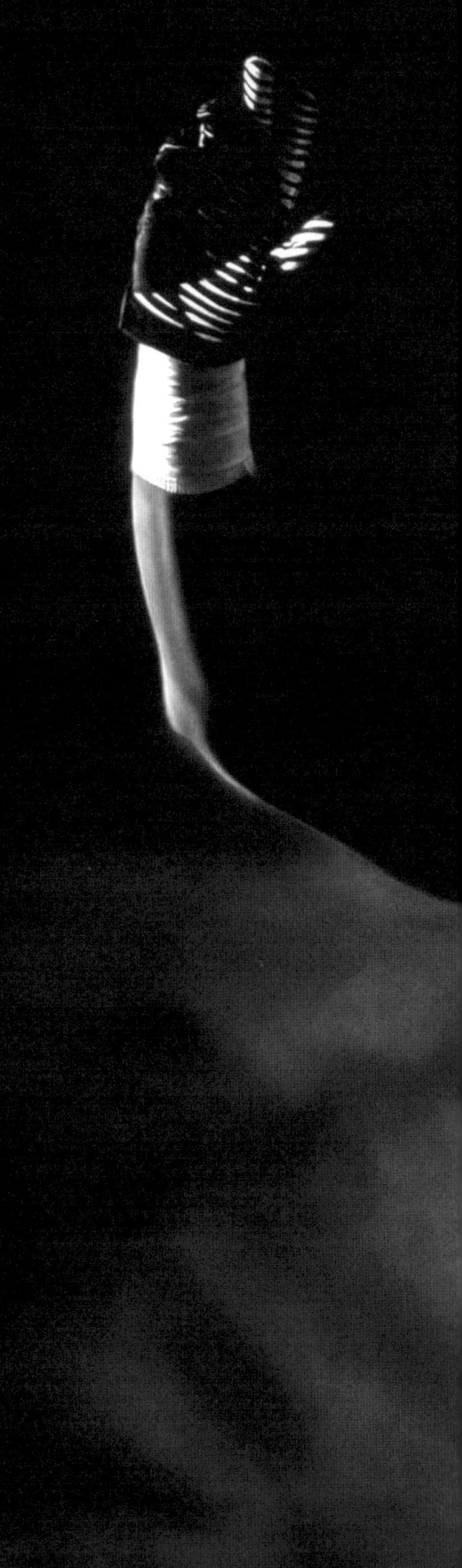

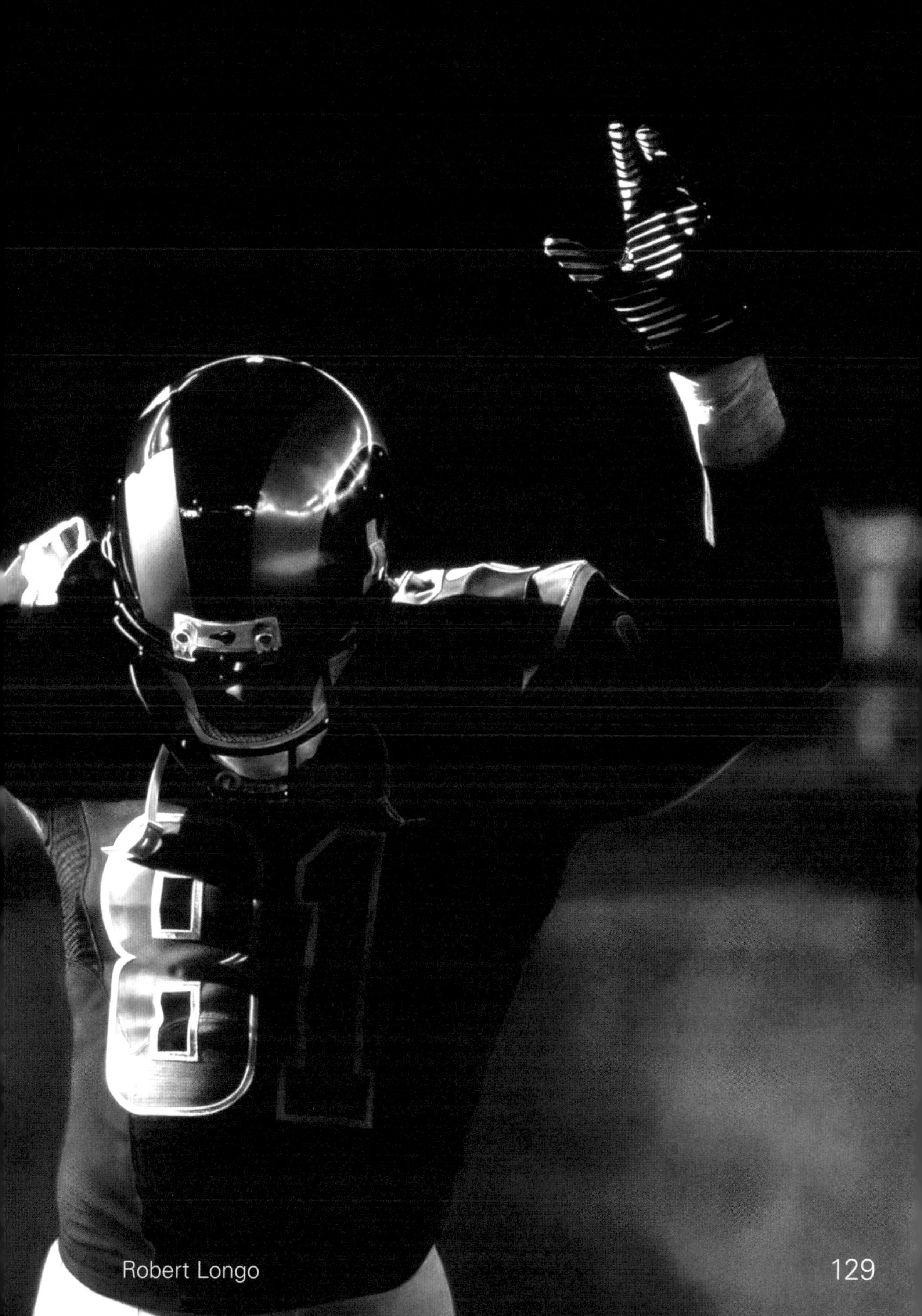

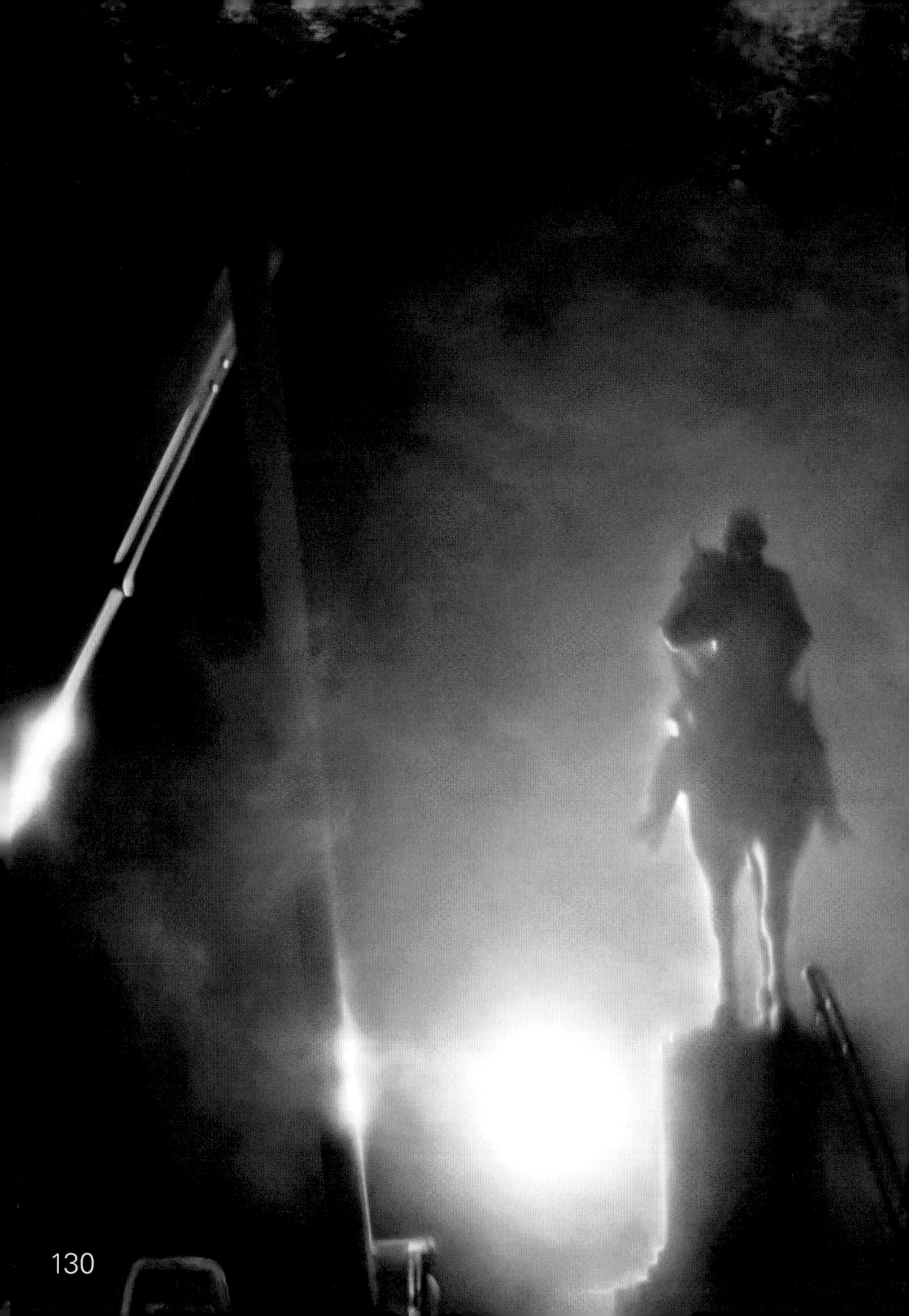

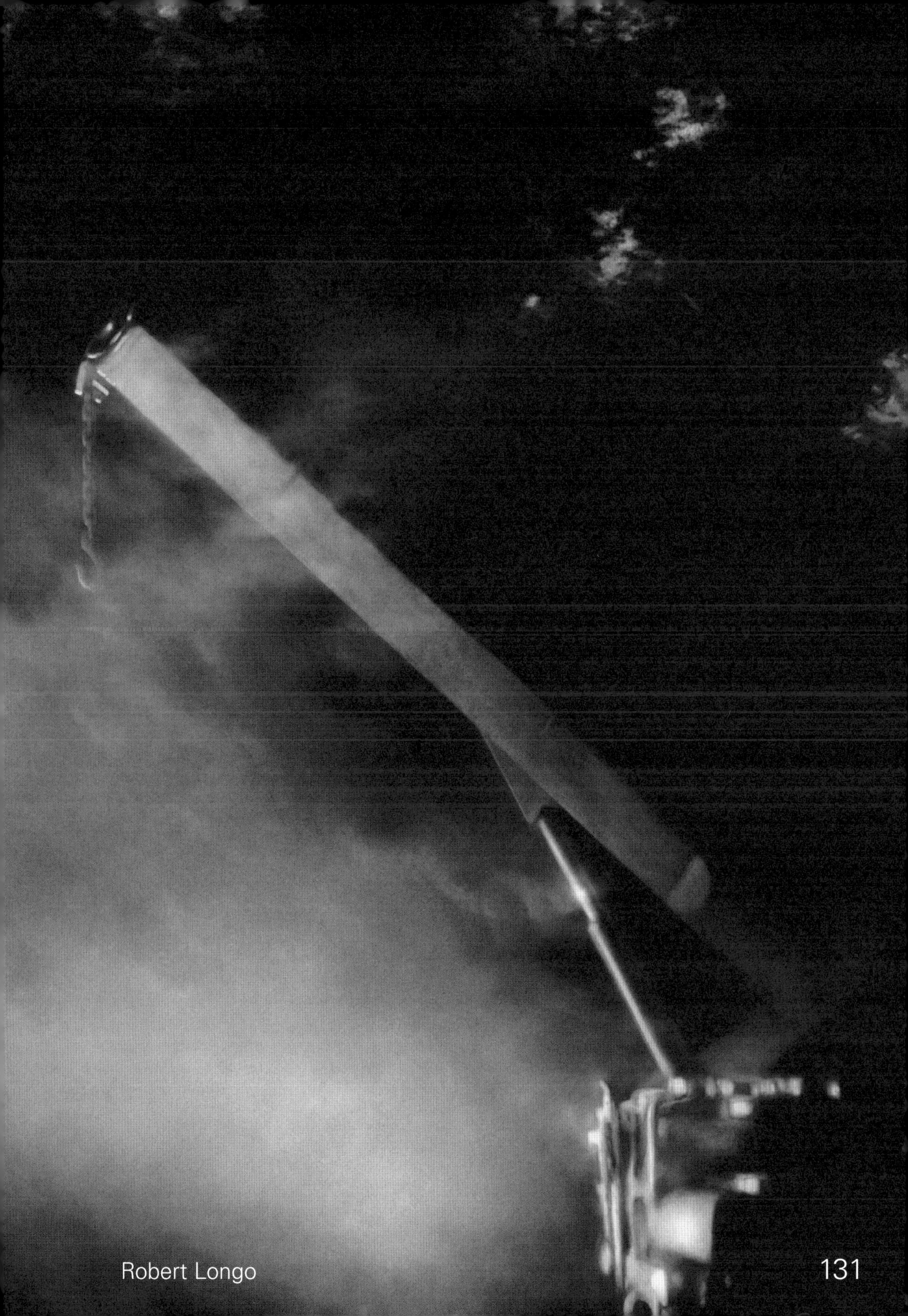

Titus Kaphar

—

FM: When did the climate change? When did "this moment" become this moment?

Kaphar: There is no moment, this is all a continuum. I think that we will forever find ourselves confronted by things we believe should have already been dealt with.

AC: In an age where consumer capitalism constantly promotes the dream of expressing yourself, hasn't art become central to supporting and maintaining that power structure? However radical its messages are on the surface—isn't art underneath really constantly promoting the idea of self-expression and so promoting consumer capitalism? So maybe it's part of the problem?

Kaphar: I—and every artist I have a relationship with—am first and foremost attempting to make something meaningful; first to the artist and then to the community that the work exists in. The market is the market.

AD: What is "real" in your practice—your way of working, your medium, your social, professional, material, cultural, political relationships, your proximity to institutions? And what is sustainable? Do the two categories (real and sustainable) overlap, and to what extent?

Kaphar: What is real ... it's all real. Or none of it is real. The pertinent questions are, "What do you value?" and "Do you live according to those values?"

GC: Museums and cultural organizations once perceived as "pure" white boxes free of bias, are now being pushed to reckon with their own privilege and political baggage. As artists increasingly explore the meaning of "realness" in their work, I wonder how you negotiate the political context in which your work is inserted when it enters the museum.

Kaphar: Museums have always been political spaces. The founders of these "pure" white boxes have always known that. I am not moved by this new profession of an obvious, historical fact. For those who care, we must be vigilant in pushing these institutions to speak to the politics of the communities that they exist in.

MW: The magician Karl Germain said that "conjuring is the only honest profession: a magician promises to deceive and does." And Picasso said, "We all know that Art is not truth. Art is a lie that makes us realize truth." In our current state, where there is no "truth," and "facts" have become a matter of opinion, how can artists wake us up from this unpleasant dream? How can you help us see the world and each other through a lens of hope, trust, and humanity?

Kaphar: That's not my job, and I do not accept that responsibility. The work that artists create might make you aware of painful things you never wanted to know. It might make you feel angry, and every now and then it will make you feel joy. An artist's responsibility is first and foremost to be honest to himself. I believe that if you don't prioritize that, it is virtually impossible to make work that has an impact on anyone else.

CG: How do you hold on to something so no one can take it away? Your beliefs? Your body? Your love? What tethers us here?

Kaphar: Family first; for some people that might not mean blood. We decide. We choose to stay. At some point, what you're holding onto might very well evaporate, and at that point it comes down to your strength of conviction.

ES: Public health physicians distinguish between narrative compassion (where one or two or three people are at risk) and statistical compassion (where thousands or millions are at risk). We're fairly good at the first, and have many occasions to strengthen our capacity through daily acts of friendship and from reading literature. We're terrible at the second, and have almost no training in strengthening our feeble abilities in this region. To what extent can the medium you work in invite, or carry out, acts of narrative compassion and statistical compassion?

Kaphar: That's never been something I sought out to do. My work always comes from a personal place, and yet there are those pieces that reverberate beyond expectation. In many cases, they have been shared, and re-shared. I don't know if we can know whether the work has the ability to resonate, until it does.

***Language of the Forgotten*, 2018**
p. 133

***A Pillow for Fragile Fictions*, 2016**
pp. 134–5

***Monumental Inversion: George Washington*, 2016**
pp. 136–7

***Seeing Through Time 2*, 2018**
p. 138

***Seeing Through Time 3*, 2019**
p. 139

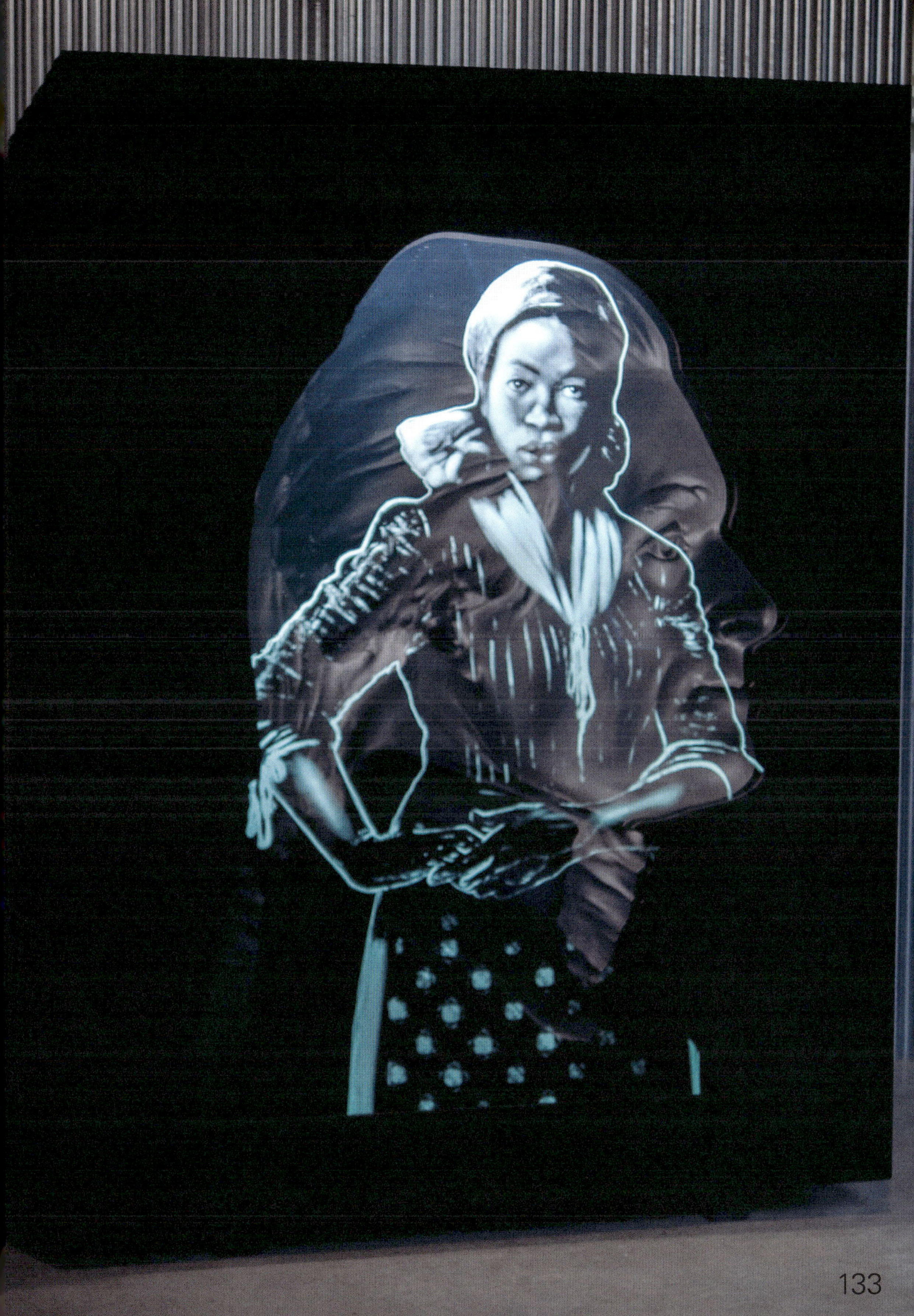

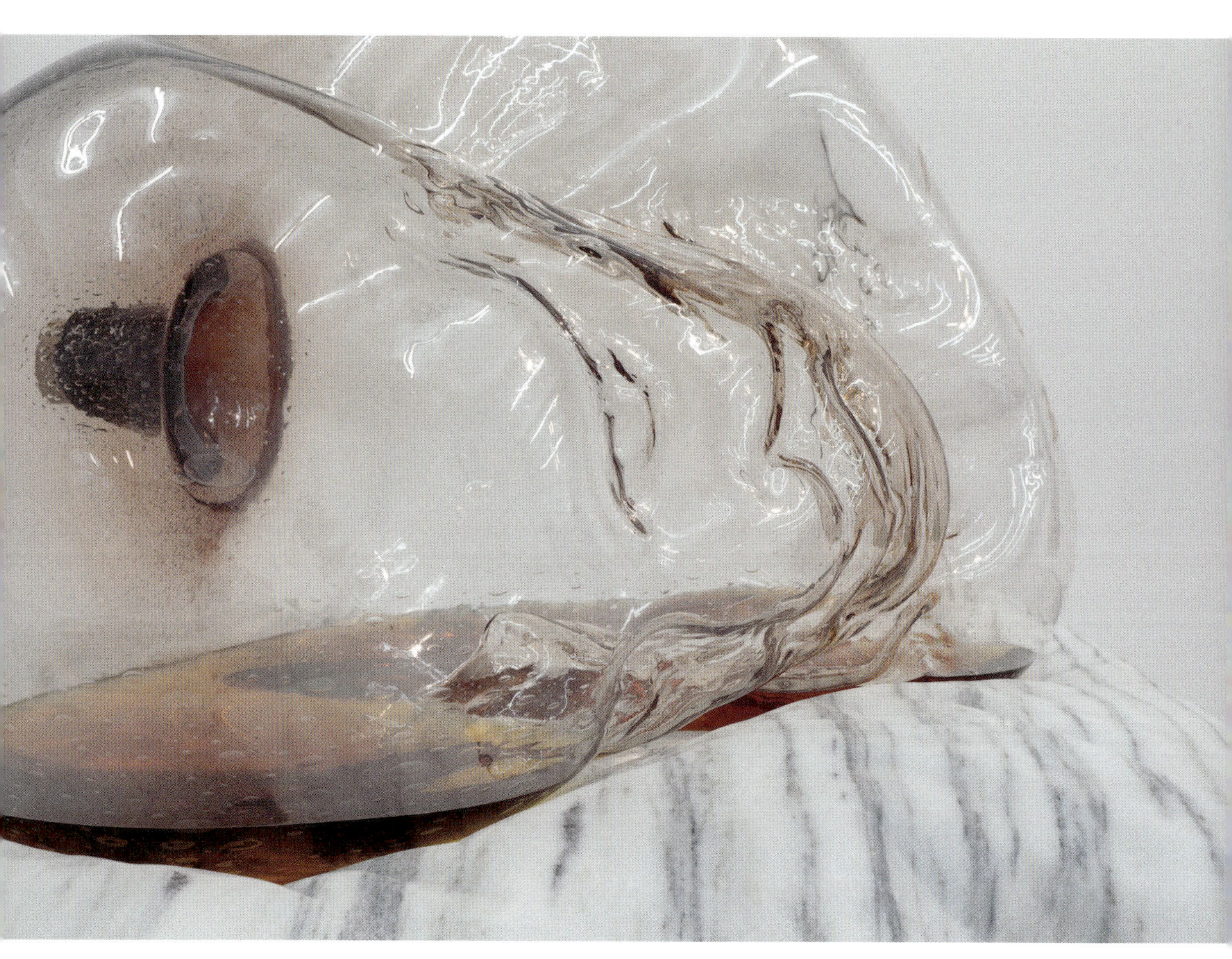

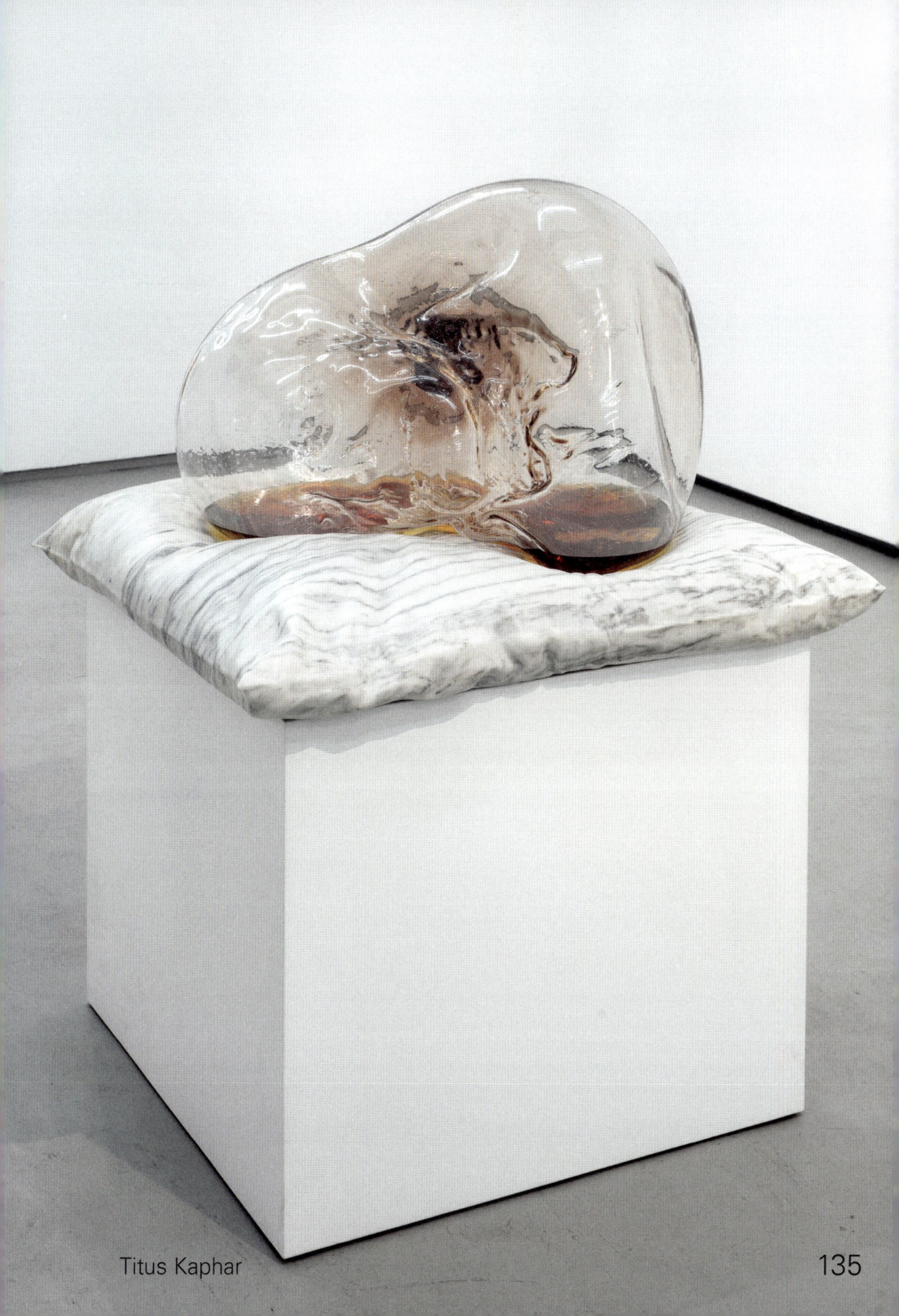

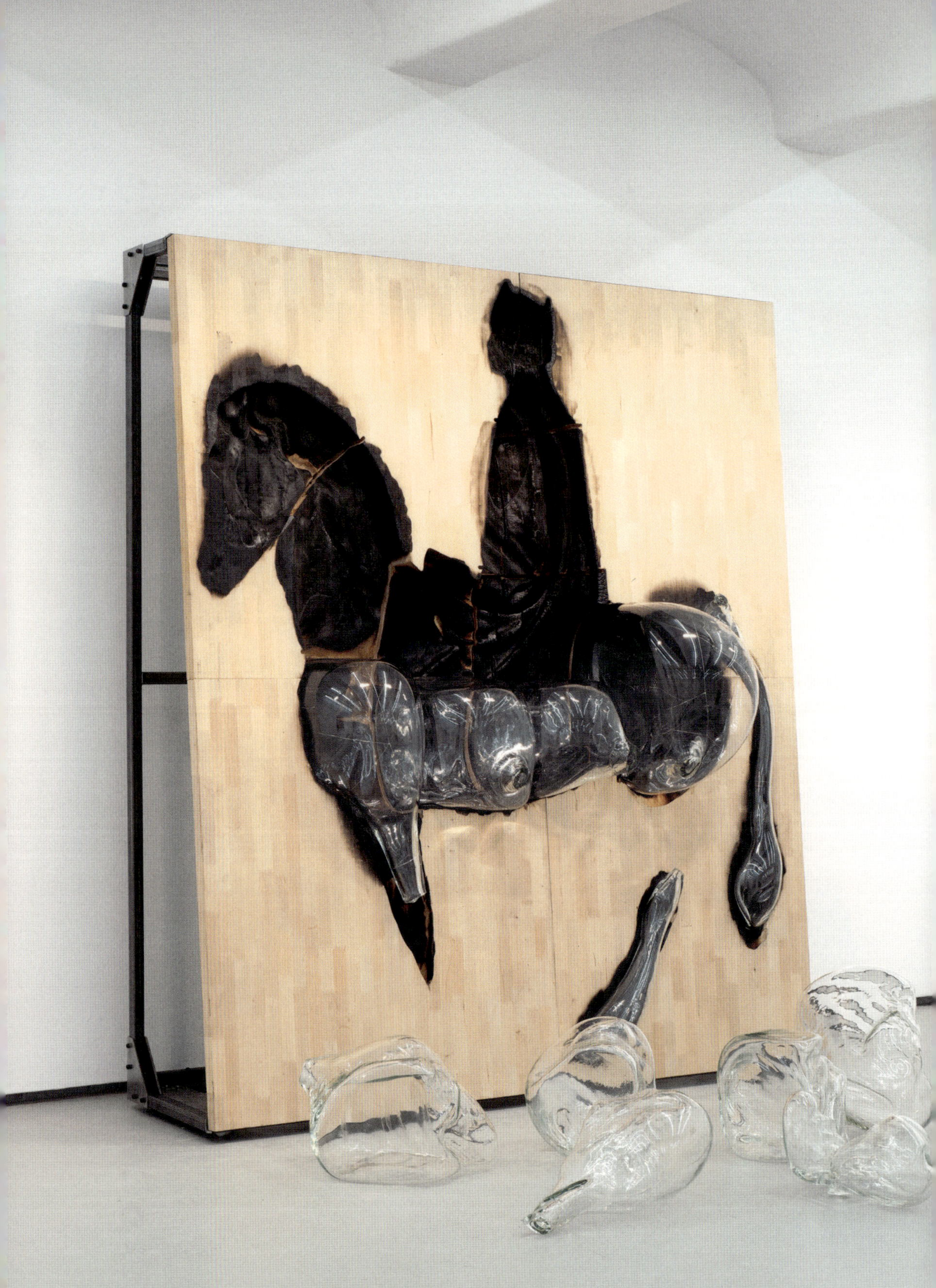

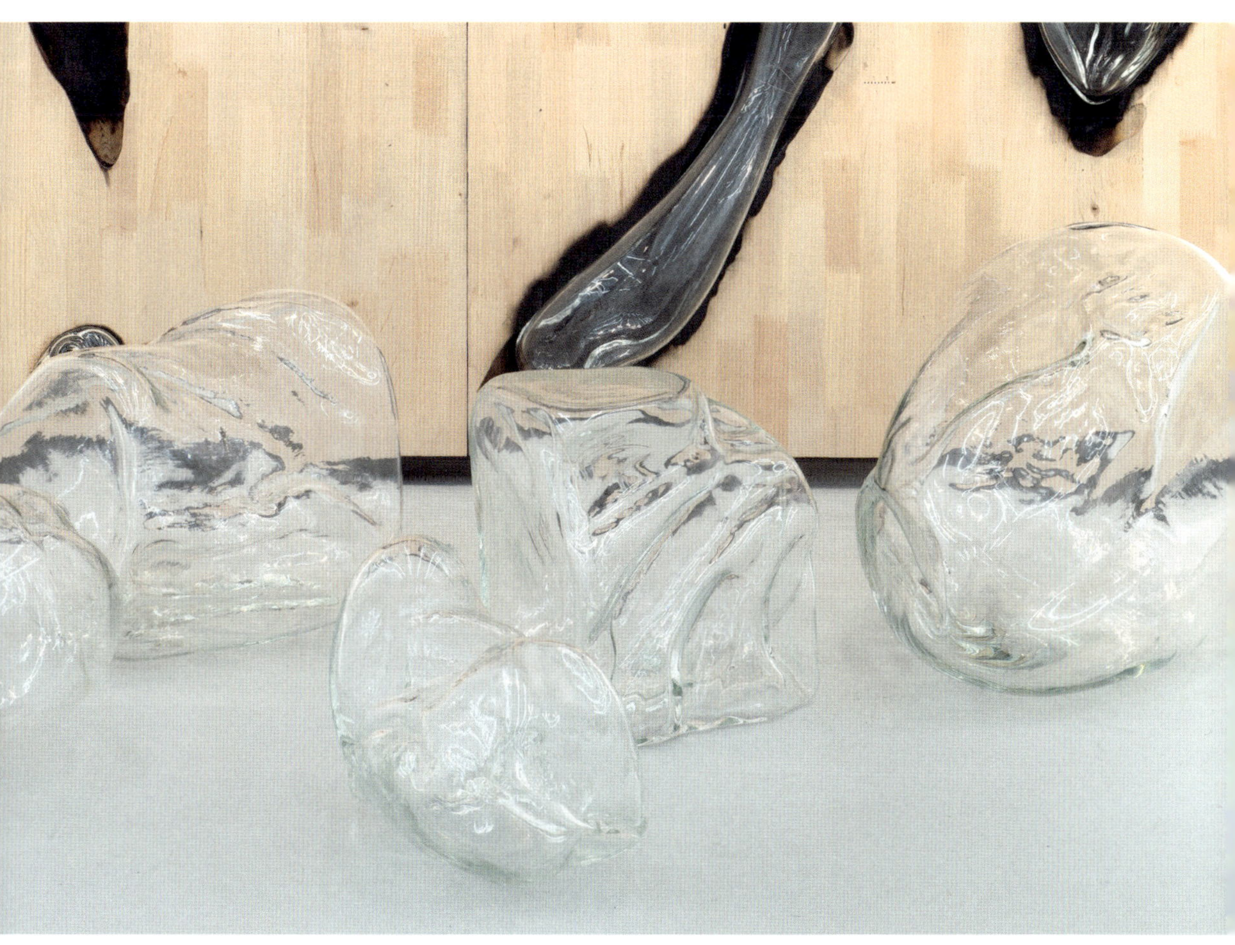

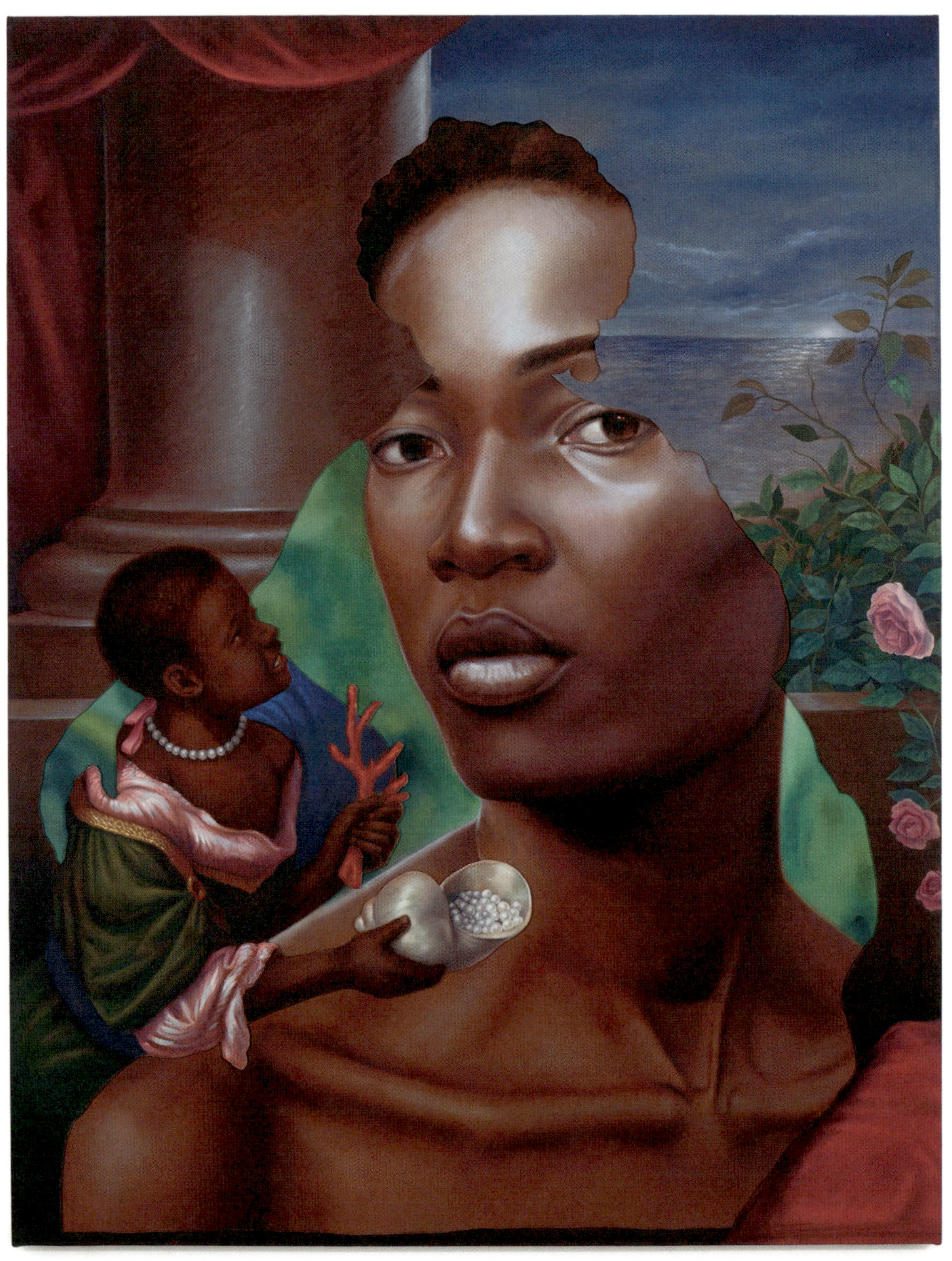

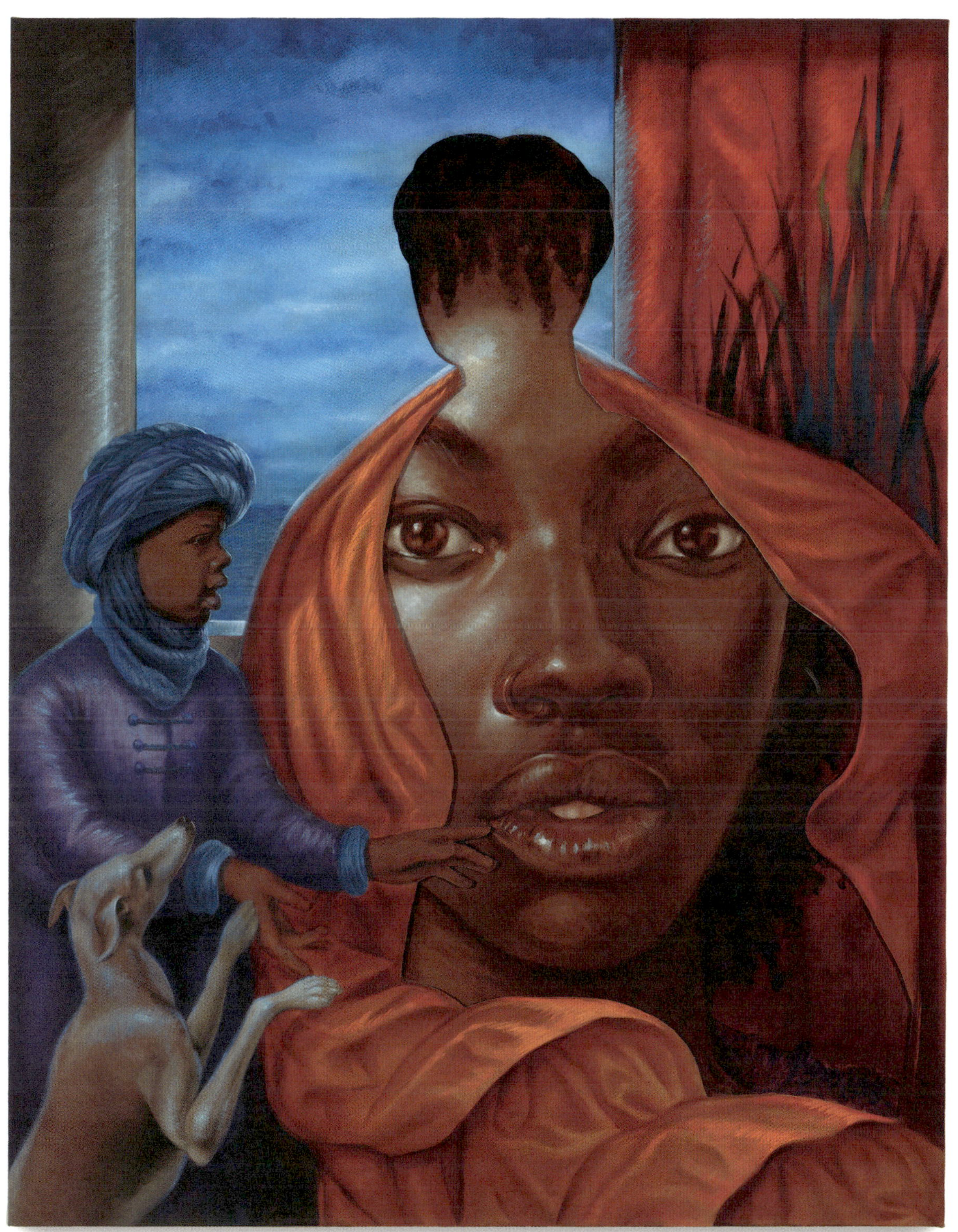

Hayv Kahraman

—

FM: When did the climate change? When did "this moment" become this moment?

Kahraman: As a refugee cum immigrant, I find it difficult to talk about the present without including the past. Memory assumes a critical role in defining this moment. This makes me question whose memory is being transmitted into the public sphere and which parts are highlighted. If memory is like the DNA of a society, then why do we have amnesia when it comes to certain people and their lived lives and deaths? This moment is riddled with blackouts that hide endless amounts of disposable lives with opaque white paint.

AC: In an age where consumer capitalism constantly promotes the dream of expressing yourself, hasn't art become central to supporting and maintaining that power structure? However radical its messages are on the surface—isn't art underneath really constantly promoting the idea of self-expression and so promoting consumer capitalism? So maybe it's part of the problem?

Kahraman: I'd like to console myself into thinking that I enact some sort of duck call in my work. A duck call is an object that imitates the sound of a duck in order to lure the attention of faraway ducks within the context of hunting. This process of mimicry is similar to the mechanisms I employ in my work. It's like learning the language of coloniality to then speak of decoloniality.

AD: What is "real" in your practice—your way of working, your medium, your social, professional, material, cultural, political relationships, your proximity to institutions? And what is sustainable? Do the two categories (real and sustainable) overlap, and to what extent?

Kahraman: When I fled to Sweden from Baghdad I had to learn to become a "Swede," erasing my identity as an Iraqi. I was good at hiding. I faked my way into creating a perception of a native Swede. I mastered the Swedish language. I bleached my hair and my skin and my tongue all in the efforts to fit in. This is one of the results of the darker side of modernity/coloniality. As I grew older, I started realizing that I was under the spell of coloniality and that I needed to break it. To this day I struggle with it, because I've come to realize that the spell is so deep that removing it would mean needing to remove my limbs. It is a scar I live with that reminds me of my time in captivity. It haunts my work, whether I choose to think about it or not. The trauma is what is real.

GC: Museums and cultural organizations once perceived as "pure" white boxes free of bias, are now being pushed to reckon with their own privilege and political baggage. As artists increasingly explore the meaning of "realness" in their work, I wonder how you negotiate the political context in which your work is inserted when it enters the museum.

Kahraman: It's easy for institutions/people to show and create vast imaginaries or illusions of who various artists are, in order to serve their own political interests. Sometimes I'm the female, war-torn Iraqi artist who paints nude women. I find these imaginaries interesting, because they reveal so much about the current state we are in; but they are also dangerous. Museums carry an incredible amount of authority, so being active in the dialogue around my work is essential. I tend to revert to subversion here and hope to expose these hierarchies.

MW: The magician Karl Germain said that "conjuring is the only honest profession: a magician promises to deceive and does." And Picasso said, "We all know that Art is not truth. Art is a lie that makes us realize truth." In our current state, where there is no "truth," and "facts" have become a matter of opinion, how can artists wake us up from this unpleasant dream? How can you help us see the world and each other through a lens of hope, trust, and humanity?

Kahraman: The question of humanity is urgent at this point in time, and the classification of who is actually human within the colonial framework is both political and hierarchal. Who is considered REAL or worthy of life and who is NOT REAL? If you are not fully European, or not heterosexual, or not white enough, etc., where does that put you within the scale of humanity? I have often felt dehumanized because of the color of my skin and the color of my hair and my accent and the fact that I am an Iraqi. I'm just one amongst many whom W. E. B. Du Bois called "problem people," and this is something that I navigate on a day-to-day basis. My answer to what we as artists can do is perhaps naive, but the only thing I know how to do is to speak louder, and if we were to speak louder then maybe we can inscribe our voices into history.

CG: How do you hold on to something so no one can take it away? Your beliefs? Your body? Your love? What tethers us here?

Kahraman: Frankly, I don't know how I feel about this. Perhaps it's too personal for me.

ES: Public health physicians distinguish between narrative compassion (where one or two or three people are at risk) and statistical compassion (where thousands or millions are at risk). We're fairly good at the first, and have many occasions to strengthen our capacity through daily acts of friendship and from reading literature. We're terrible at the second, and have almost no training in strengthening our feeble abilities in this region. To what extent can the medium you work in invite, or carry out, acts of narrative compassion and statistical compassion?

Kahraman: Compassion and/or empathy are ideas that I struggle with in my work. I don't think I aim to elicit empathy in my work. I think compassion or empathy can trigger ethical questions of humanity and emotions of pity, which I believe are not conducive to action. Dominick LaCapra discusses a "healthier" empathic reaction, which he defines as an empathic unsettlement that creates a distance between the witness and the narrator. So as a witness, you are not fully consumed by what you see or read; rather you understand that no matter what it is you are witnessing, you can never fully comprehend it, and it should not become your identity. This is an urgent concern for me, especially when painting, narrating, and expressing ideas that delve into immigration and migrant consciousness. How can I depict the suffering of distant others in a way that isn't reductive and does not perpetuate feelings of pity that turn into divisive hierarchies, creating a dangerous rhetoric of us and Other?

***Three Celebrities,* 2018**
p. 144

***Pussy Gold,* 2018**
p. 145

***The Appeal,* 2018**
pp. 146–7

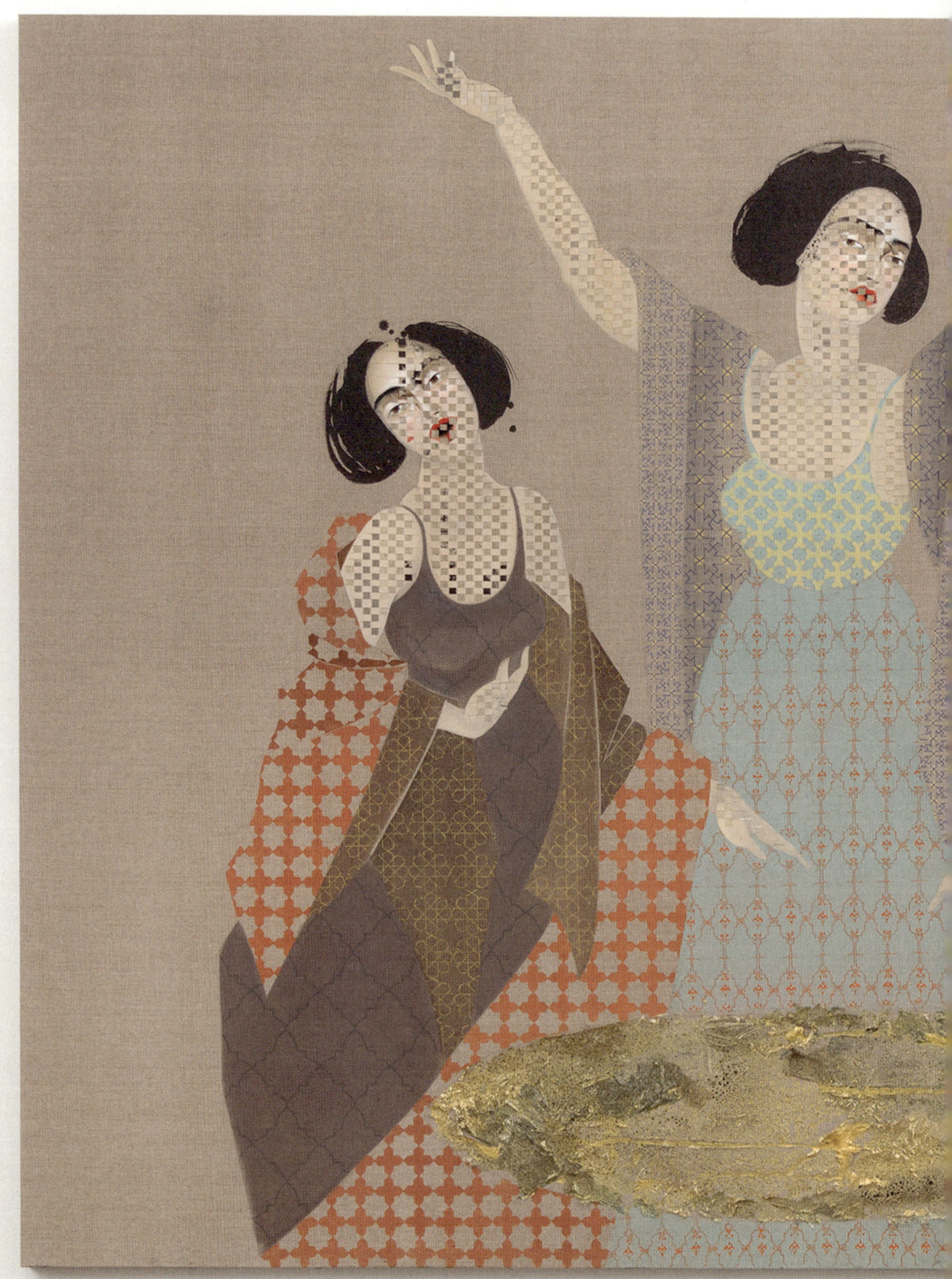

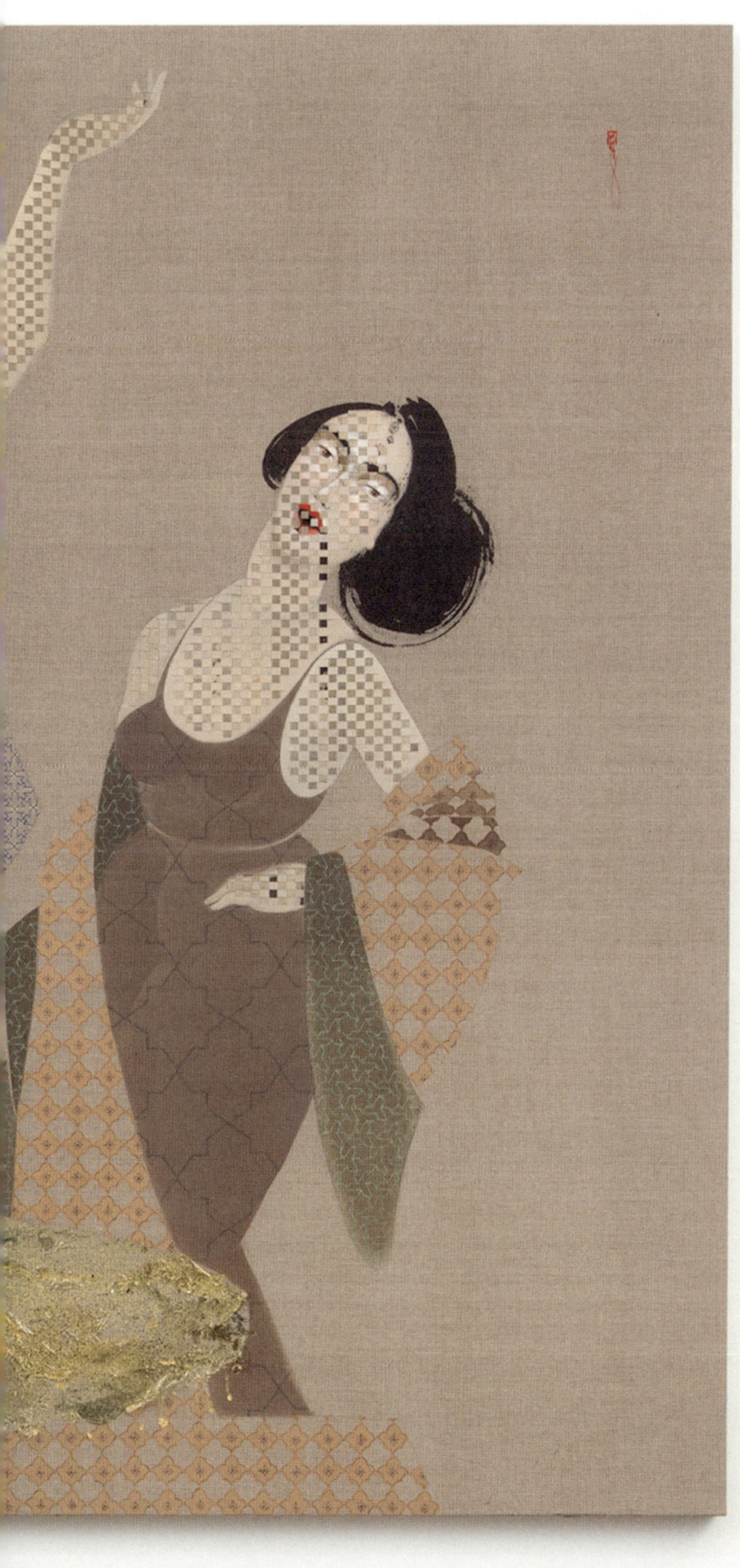

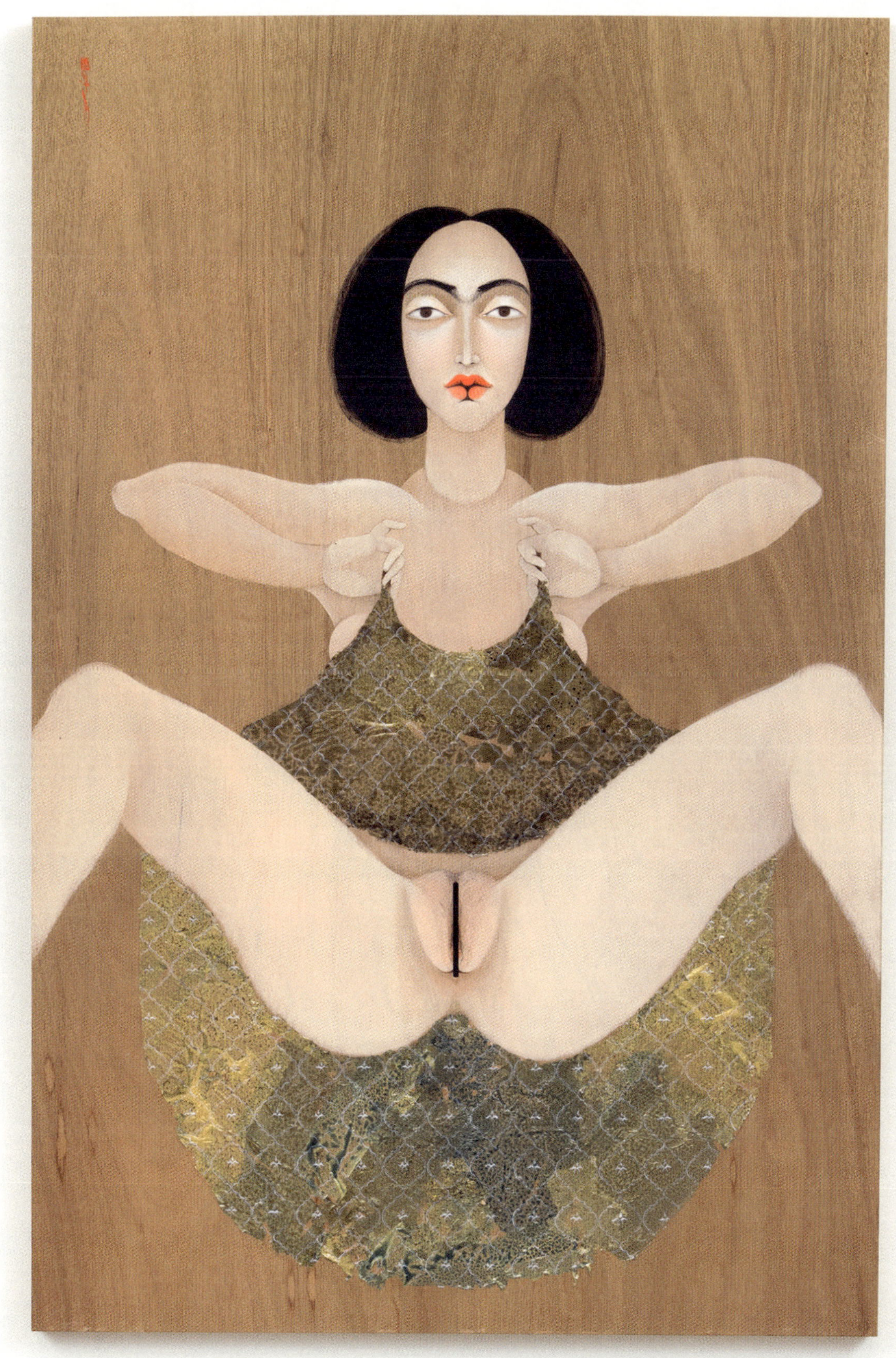

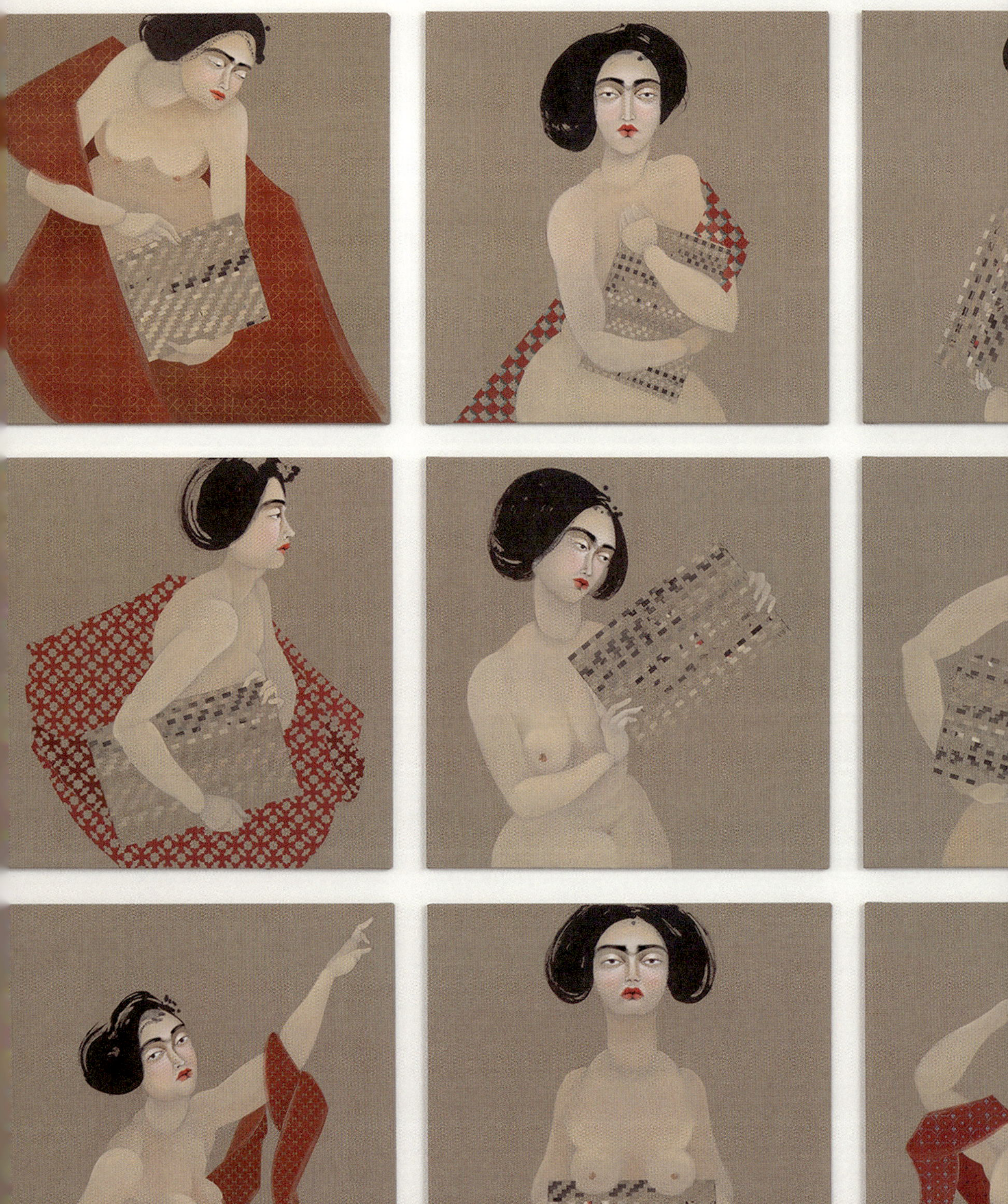

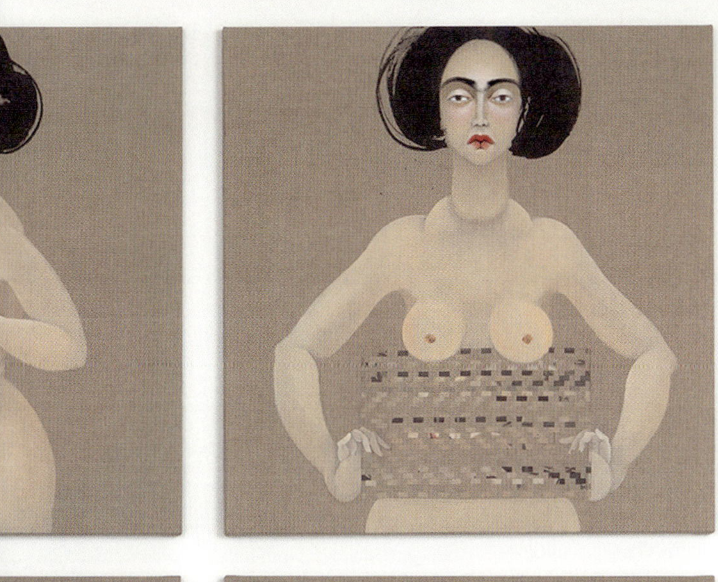
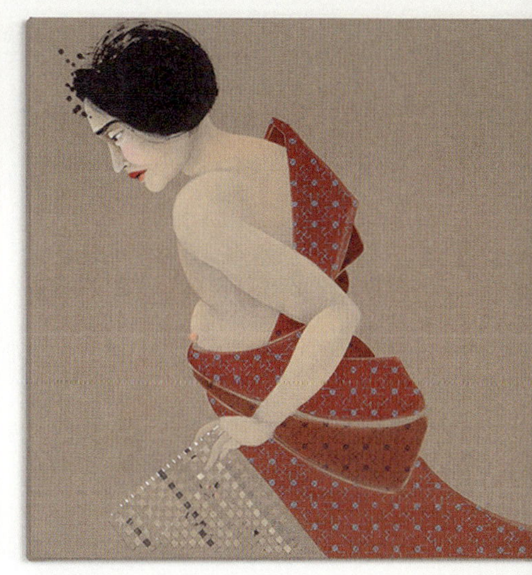
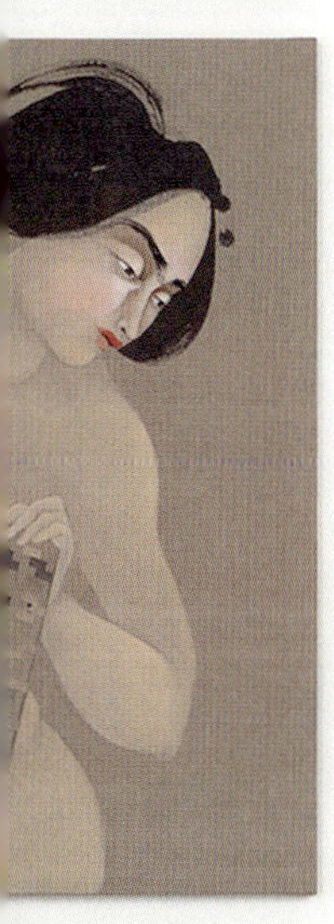
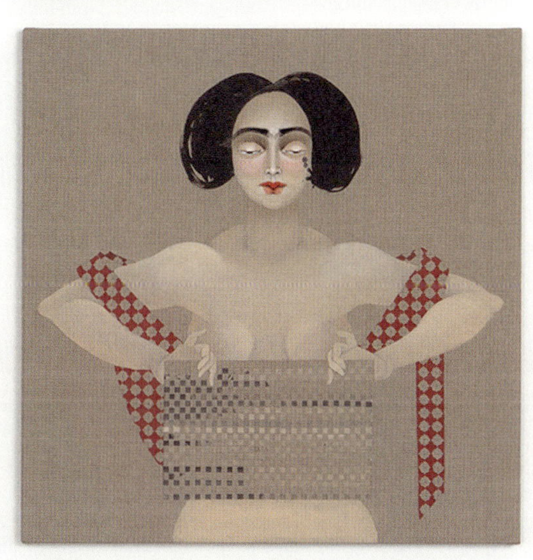
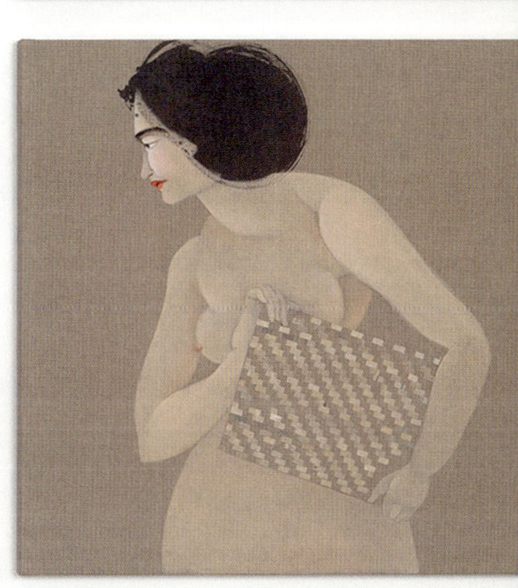

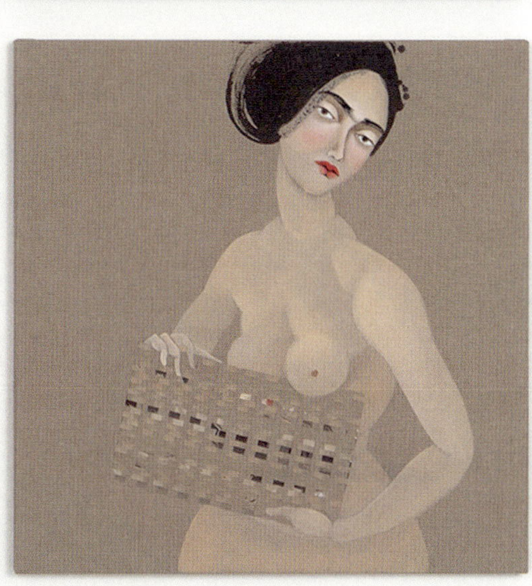
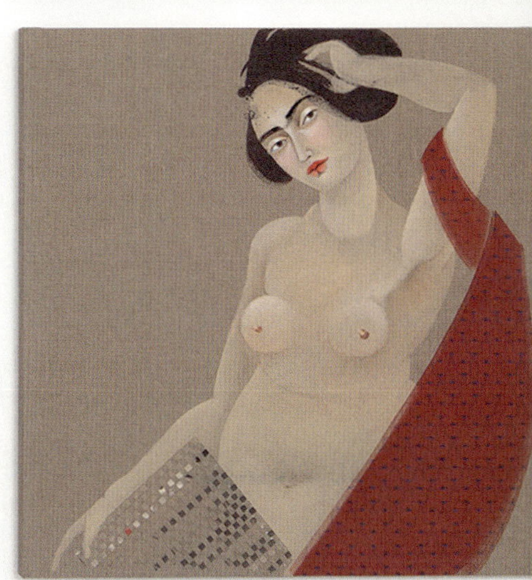

Reaching Guantánamo

—

Solmaz Sharif

Dear Salim,

Love, are you well? Do they you?
I worry so much. Lately, my hair , even
my skin . The doctors tell me it's .
I believe them. It shouldn't
. Please don't worry.
in the yard, and moths
have gotten to your mother's
, remember?
I have enclosed some —made this
batch just for you. Please eat well. Why
did you me to remarry? I told
and he couldn't it.
I would never .
Love, I'm singing that you loved,
remember, the line that went
" "? I'm holding
the just for you.

Yours,

Dear Salim,

Lightning across the sky all night, lighting up my .
But no rain. No .
When I get home, everything is
dust. One pair of
by the . One towel,
one , one
in the morning. Anyway, I couldn't ,
so I sat by the window watching
it streak and
thinking I must look like something
lit up and like this.

Yours,

Dear Salim,

At the store, they brought
already, bruised on the
but still juicy. I pitted sour
all day, the newspaper
went with their juice. I save you
jars of preserves for your return.
some plums, too. I haven't opened
a since they
you. Can't stand all those
, all those teeth. Or maybe
the , how they stain upholstery like
. I hope I don't make you me.
I hope they allow you some .

Yours,

Dear Salim,

said I need to
my tongue. It's getting sharp.
I told him to his own
business, to his own
wife. He didn't .
If he wasn't my
I would never
again. Sometimes, I write you
letters I don't send. I don't mean
to cause alarm. I just want the ones
you open to
like a hill of poppies.

Yours,

Dear Salim,

have made a nest
under our . And now
the nestlings always .
The of eggs has gone .
And rice. And tea. I don't know who
decides things.

Yours,

Dear Salim,

The neighbors got an apology
and a few thousand dollars.
They calculate based on
and
and age. The worth of a , of a human
. hands shook as she opened
. She took it out front
and ripped it . a little pile
and set fire to it right there, right in front of

says they'll send me
a check for . I would
! !
? Never.

Yours,

Dear Salim,

I read some Hikmet,
Human *Country.*
The wife sends letters to her
like I do. I don't read
now. He was like you.
I've the books,
all of them. Can't stomach their
. All
those spines lined up on my shelf. How you
would stand there, smelling the pages.
them. They all say
the same story
and none tell ours.

Section 3

Finding Hope in the Dark

IT WAS FOUR O'CLOCK IN THE MIDDLE OF AN AFTERNOON THAT NEVER HAPPENED, RIGHT IN THE MIDDLE OF A WEEK YOU COULDN'T FIND YOUR WAY TO IF YOU WERE THE BASTARD CHILD OF MARCO POLO AND SAINT CHRISTOPHER. THE SCENE IS AS FOLLOWS: ¶ LAVERNE IS SITTING BEHIND THE RECEPTION COUNTER. JIM IS FILLING OUT A SERVICE-COMPLETE FORM, LEANING ELBOW-WISE ON THE COUNTER LOOKING DOWN AT LAVERNE WHO IS TELLING HIM A STORY, SOMETHING YOU CAN'T HEAR BECAUSE YOU'RE NOT CLOSE ENOUGH, YOU DON'T KNOW THE PARTICULARS, THE PEOPLE IN QUESTION. BUT HE'S LAUGHING JUST A BIT. HE WORRIES THE PENCIL WITH HIS TEETH AND WRITES IN BLOCK CAPITALS. YOU MIGHT GET THE SENSE HE'S A SHITHEAD. I DON'T KNOW, YOU MIGHT LIKE HIM. ¶ THROUGH THE DOORWAY JUST BEHIND, JUST A LITTLE FURTHER IN, THERE'S THE THRESHOLD MOST DON'T CROSS. THE GOOD MAN STARTED THE BUSINESS, DESTO'S DISCOUNT PLUMBING, THIRTY DECADES AGO, OR SOMETHING LIKE THAT. HE'S ASLEEP IN HIS CHAIR AND THE DESK IS FULL OF THINGS THAT NEVER MOVE. THEY'VE BEEN STACKED THERE, ONE AT A TIME, BUT YOU CAN'T TELL THEM APART. NOT USING YOUR EYES. IT'S AN OLD MAN'S DESK, INDISSOLUBLE. IF YOU FOLLOW ME. ¶ THE STREET OUTSIDE THE DOOR IS THE KIND OF STREET WHERE YOU'D FIND A PLACE LIKE THAT. IF YOU WENT OUT THERE, YOU'D COME BACK IN, NO PROBLEM, MAYBE ASKING TO USE THE PHONE, OR THE BATHROOM, AND THEY'D TELL YOU TO GET LOST. LAVERNE ISN'T SHY ABOUT THAT KIND OF THING. ¶ NOW JIM IS TELLING LAVERNE SOMETHING. SHE IS SORT OF HIS MOTHER, A MOTHER-TYPE, NOT OLD ENOUGH FOR THAT, REALLY, BUT ALMOST. BILLY COMES OUT OF THE BACK ROOM, YOU CAN TELL HE'S BILLY BECAUSE THAT'S WHAT HIS SHIRT SAYS, SO JIM HAS TO START AGAIN. HE SAYS, AND THE CHECK COMES, IT WASN'T EVEN OUR CHECK. WE HADN'T ORDERED. FUCKING PLACE LIKE THAT. NOT CHEAP, YOU KNOW? WE SAT DOWN AND THEY BROUGHT US THE CHECK. SOMETHING SPARKED IN ME. I TURNED TO HER AND I WAS ABOUT TO SAY, I WANT A DIVORCE, AND RIGHT AT THAT MOMENT SHE TALKED OVER ME, YOU KNOW HOW SHE'S ALWAYS DOING IT. AND SHE SAYS, JIMMY, I'M NOT HAPPY. I SAID, BABY, I KNOW IT. I KNOW IT. AND SHE LOOKS AT ME LIKE EVERY LOVING THING, MUST HAVE BEEN THE FIRST TIME IN YEARS. THEN THE WAITER COMES WITH A BIRTHDAY CAKE, A KIND OF MISTAKE BUT MAYBE IT WASN'T. THEY'RE SINGING. ALL THE PEOPLE AT TABLES ARE TURNING AROUND. WE JUST CUT OUT. ¶ LAVERNE IS LOOKING AT BILLY LIKE IT'S HIS TURN TO SAY SOMETHING. BUT THAT'S NOT HIS STRENGTH, SO SHE LOOKS AT JIM AND SAYS WELL THERE WAS THAT TIME. WE THOUGHT MAYBE. I DON'T KNOW. YOU REMEMBER THAT TIME, THOUGH, RIGHT? ¶ YEAH IT WAS FRIDAY, HE SAYS. BILLY IS THINKING ABOUT IT TOO. HE'S HOLDING ONTO SOMETHING THAT LOOKS LIKE THE PETTY CASH BOX, MAYBE HE'S THINKING ABOUT LUNCH. FROM BEHIND THEM THERE'S A KIND OF COUGHING SOUND. IT ISN'T A SOUND THEY'VE HEARD, AND THEY ALL TURN. A CHAIR FALLS OVER. ¶ DESTO? DESTO? ¶ THE OLD MAN'S LAID OUT ON THE CARPET, LIKE SOMETHING FLEW IN THERE AND COULDN'T FIND THE WAY OUT. A REAL JOKE. THE THREE OF THEM, REGULAR PEOPLE, GOT A FLABBY OLD FAT ASS DEAD ON THE FLOOR LIKE IT'S THEIRS TO DO WITH AS THEY WILL. YOU EVER FEAST YOUR EYES ON SOMETHING LIKE THAT? THEY APPREHEND THE SITUATION IMMEDIATELY. LAVERNE LOOKS AT BILLY WHO LOOKS AT JIM WHO LOOKS AT LAVERNE. WHAT NOW? ¶ LAVERNE LOOKS AT HER FINGERNAILS. SHE'S TIRED OF THE CHAIR SHE SITS IN. I DON'T KNOW. WHY DO WE EVEN DO IT? YOU JUST TAKE A TICKET AND WAIT, TAKE ANOTHER TICKET AND WAIT,

USA Four O'Clock

—

Jesse Ball

It was four o'clock in the middle of an afternoon that never happened, right in the middle of a week you couldn't find your way to if you were the bastard child of Marco Polo and St. Christopher. The scene is as follows: ¶ Laverne is sitting behind the reception counter. Jim is filling out a service-complete form, leaned elbow-wise on the counter looking down at Laverne who is telling him a story, something you can't hear because you're not close enough, you don't know the particulars, the people in question. But he's laughing just a bit. He worries the pencil with his teeth and writes in block capitals. You might get the sense he's a shithead. I don't know, you might like him. ¶ Through the door way just beyond, just a little further in, there's the threshold most don't cross. The good man started the business, Desto's Discount Plumbing, thirty decades ago, or something like that. He's asleep in his chair and the desk is full of things that never move. They've been stacked there, one at a time, but you can't tell them apart, not using your eyes. It's an old man's old desk, indissoluble if you follow me. ¶ The street outside the door is the kind of street where you'd find a place like that. If you went out there, you'd come back in, no problem, maybe asking to use the phone, or the bathroom, and they'd tell you to get lost. Laverne isn't shy about that kind of thing. ¶ Now Jim is telling Laverne something. She is sort of his mother, a mother-type, not old enough for that, really, but almost. Billy comes out of the back room, you can tell he's Billy because that's what his shirt says, so Jim has to start again. He says, and the check comes, it wasn't even our check. We hadn't ordered. Fucking place like that. Not cheap, you know? We sat down and they brought us the check. Something sparked in me. I turned to her and I was about to say, I want a divorce, and right at that moment she talked over me, you know how she's always doing it, and she says, Jimmy, I'm not happy. I said, baby I know it. I know it. And she looks at me like every loving thing, must have been the first time in years. Then the waiter comes with a birthday cake, a kind of mistake but maybe it wasn't. They're singing. All the people at tables are turning around. We just cut out. ¶ Laverne is looking at Billy like it's his turn to say something, but that's not his strength, so she looks at Jim and says well there was that time. We thought maybe, I don't know. You remember that time, though, right? ¶ Yeah it was fishy, he says. Billy is thinking about it too. He's holding onto something that looks like the petty cash envelope, maybe he's thinking about lunch. From behind them there's a kind of coughing sound. It isn't a sound they've heard, and they all turn. A chair falls over. ¶ Desto? Desto? ¶ The old man's dead on the carpet, like something flew in there and couldn't find the way out. A real joke. The three of them, regular people, got an old fat ass dead on the floor like it's theirs to do with as they will. You ever feast your eyes on something like that? They apprehend the situation immediately. Laverne looks at Billy who looks at Jim who looks at Laverne. What now? ¶ Laverne looks at her fingernails. She's tired of the chair she sits in. I don't know. Why do I even do it? You just take a ticket and wait, take another ticket and wait, take another ticket and wait. It's garbage, just garbage. ¶ She walks over to the body, leans down, eases herself back and forth and climbs in like she's in the habit of doing that sort of thing. ¶ The old man stands right back up. He's chipper now. His eyes light up like Santa Claus. His paunch is overjoyed. His limbs flow at the edges of themselves. ¶ Well, boys, he says, let's hit the town, but first we got to find ourselves a new secretary. ¶ Jim just about shits himself there, and Billy's crying not like he's sad, but like someone asked him a question he can't answer. The question is: what is it? ¶ What is it? ¶ Desto passes the pair on his way to the door, slapping them both on the ass like an athlete would, maybe he's been waiting years to do it, who can say? ¶ Where you going? It's Jim. It's Jim, Desto, where are you going? Why don't you sit down for a minute. Let's just, let's just ... ¶ But the old man body is saying, I don't have the time to sit and talk with you. I've been doing everything wrong. I can't tell you the fucked up perspective I have at this moment. It's unstoppable. If I stepped in front of a bus, it wouldn't be too soon. My mind is crashing like a wing, like a wing into a glass window. Have you ever loved anyone, known anything? Anything at all? Even one thing, have you known it? ¶ Jim and Billy try to fathom what's being said. ¶ It isn't a string of numbers, says the old man mouth, because there aren't any numbers unless they tell you there are. Just take off all your hats one by one, and then find something to strangle yourself with. Slit your throat. Take a pharmacy worth of pills and hold on like an anchor until no help comes ... I can tell you, boys, it's all better from here on in. ¶ Out the door it goes. The door slaps shut and they can hear the horrible noise of a truck encountering that fleshy rotundity in some final way. From the wreck of the body there's just laughter, laughter rising. ¶ Now I'm the truck, says Laverne. Now I'm the trees. Now I'm a fucking idea of a bird. Later, chumps!

TAKE ANOTHER TICKET AND WAIT. IT'S GARBAGE, JUST GARBAGE. ¶ SHE WALKS OVER TO THE BODY, LEANS DOWN, EASES HERSELF BACK AND FORTH AND CLIMBS IN LIKE SHE'S IN THE HABIT OF DOING THAT SORT OF THING. ¶ THE OLD MAN STANDS RIGHT BACK UP. HE'S CHIPPER NOW. HIS EYES LIGHT UP LIKE SANTA CLAUS. HIS PAUNCH IS OVERSIZED. HIS LIMBS FLOW AT THE EDGES OF THEMSELVES. ¶ WELL, BOYS, HE SAYS, LET'S HIT THE TOWN! BUT FIRST WE GOT TO FIND OURSELF A NEW SECRETARY. ¶ JIM JUST ABOUT SHITS HIMSELF THERE, AND BILLY'S CRYING NOT LIKE HE'S SAD, JUST LIKE SOMEONE ASKED HIM A QUESTION HE CAN'T ANSWER. THE QUESTION IS: WHAT IS IT?. ¶ WHAT IS IT?. ¶ DESTO PASSES THE PAIR ON HIS WAY TO THE DOOR, SLAPPING THEM BOTH ON THE ASS LIKE AN ATHLETE WOULD, MAYBE HE'S BEEN WAITING YEARS TO DO IT, WHO CAN SAY?. ¶ WHERE ARE YOU GOING?, IT'S JIM. IT'S JIM, DESTO, WHERE ARE YOU GOING?. WHY DON'T YOU SIT DOWN FOR A MINUTE?. LET'S JUST, LET'S JUST... ¶ BUT THE OLD MAN BODY IS SAYING, I DON'T HAVE THE TIME TO SIT AND TALK WITH YOU. I'VE BEEN DOING EVERYTHING WRONG. I CAN'T TELL YOU THE FUCKED UP PERSPECTIVE I HAVE AT THIS MOMENT. IT'S UNSTOPPABLE. IF I STEPPED IN FRONT OF A BUS, IT WOULDN'T BE TOO SOON. MY MIND IS CRASHING LIKE A WING, LIKE A WING INTO A GLASS WINDOW. HAVE YOU EVER LOVED ANYONE, KNOWN ANYTHING?. ANYTHING AT ALL?. EVEN ONE THING, HAVE YOU KNOWN IT?. ¶ JIM AND BILLY TRY TO FATHOM WHAT'S BEING SAID. ¶ IT ISN'T A STRING OF NUMBERS, SAYS THE OLD MAN MOUTH, BECAUSE THERE AREN'T ANY NUMBERS UNLESS THEY TELL YOU THERE ARE. JUST TAKE OFF ALL YOUR HATS, ONE BY ONE, AND THEN FIND SOMETHING TO STRANGLE YOURSELF WITH. SLIT YOUR THROAT. TAKE A PHARMACY WORTH OF PILLS AND HOLD ON LIKE AN ANCHOR UNTIL NO HELP COMES... I CAN TELL YOU, BOYS, IT'S ALL BETTER FROM HERE ON IN. ¶ OUT THE DOOR IT GOES. THE DOOR SLAPS SHUT AND THEY CAN HEAR THE HORRIBLE NOISE OF A TRUCK ENCOUNTERING THAT FLESHY RETUNOITY IN SOME FINAL WAY. FROM THE WRECK OF THE BODY THERE'S JUST LAUGHTER, LAUGHTER RISING. ¶ NOW I'M THE TRUCK, SAYS LAVERNE. NOW I'M THE TIRES. NOW I'M A FUCKING IDEA OF A BIRD. LATER, CHUMPS!

How I Got Over

—

Saul Williams

Lift me up
so I can
tell them

how you came
to cut the ropes

that had blossomed
like the strangest fruit

descending
from my hopes.

And when I
thought my neck
would crane

to see
what level eyes
could not

I felt the ground
beneath my feet
and listened.

Subharmonic symphony
swelling from beneath.

Mastery over mystery.

Worlds beyond belief.

Karma of
the buffalo.

Innocence
was lost.
Suffering was
the death
of me.

Freedom
had a cost.

How I got over.

I had betrayed
him with a kiss
is how they told it.

Convinced myself
to trust each soul
encountered.

Believed my honesty
could only reap truth.

Destroyed the fear
which kept me
from my calling.

Absolved myself
from history's
dangling
noose.

Yet still
rivers
to cross,
mountains
to climb.

Weapons
worn by
passing soldiers
sang to me.

Angry women
kissed and licked
their names
into me.

Forty days
if decades
were knights.

Whole cavalries
fought youth.

Time is a
privatized prison.

Beauty manipulated.

Timeless standard
of give and take

and all
that love
would give.

Forgiven
for freedom.

To be abandoned by

time.

To be loved.

To be love.

Joey Fauerso

—

FM: When did the climate change? When did "this moment" become this moment?

Fauerso: During hot dry weather, fire ant colonies move deeper into the ground, forgoing mounds and entering the nest via hidden tunnels. It is easy to forget something exists when it's hidden. In hindsight, the election of Barack Obama created the path to Donald Trump's presidency. Like a fire ant colony after a rain, the fringe communities of white nationalism began to make themselves visible. Trump was the foot that kicked the mound, allowing the ants to spill out.

AC: In an age where consumer capitalism constantly promotes the dream of expressing yourself, hasn't art become central to supporting and maintaining that power structure? However radical its messages are on the surface—isn't art underneath really constantly promoting the idea of self-expression and so promoting consumer capitalism? So maybe it's part of the problem?

Fauerso: Archeologists recently discovered a 40,000-year-old drawing of a bull in a cave in Borneo. Art has always been central to being human; it has always been part of the problem. When art fails to transcend self-expression, it is like telling someone about your dreams and expecting them to be interested. However, when art reveals a shared condition—a physical manifestation of what Yuval Harari calls the "inter-subjective"—it becomes central to how we tell our stories and locate ourselves in space and time. A world without art is a bleak place. I'm reminded of this every time I sit in a doctor's office, forced to stare at a giclée print of brushy rectangles and fall leaves.

AD: What is "real" in your practice—your way of working, your medium, your social, professional, material, cultural, political relationships, your proximity to institutions? And what is sustainable? Do the two categories (real and sustainable) overlap, and to what extent?

Fauerso: For a long time, I thought that to be taken seriously as an artist, particularly as a woman artist, I had to keep my creative work and my family life separate. But in 2014, when I was thirty-eight and my children were three and five, I was diagnosed with breast cancer. Confronted with so much uncertainty and fear, I witnessed how, almost by necessity, everything began to mix. As my children and their ways of thinking entered the studio, I became more aware of the poignancy and poetry of our everyday life. My art became more vulnerable, more truthful to my experience, and I think more interesting. I have continued this open-door policy, letting the spheres of my life overlap, and keeping my work closer to the bone.

GC: Museums and cultural organizations once perceived as "pure" white boxes free of bias, are now being pushed to reckon with their own privilege and political baggage. As artists increasingly explore the meaning of "realness" in their work, I wonder how you negotiate the political context in which your work is inserted when it enters the museum.

Fauerso: Rebecca Solnit writes, "Every woman who appears wrestles with the forces that would have her disappear. She struggles with the forces that would tell her story for her. Or write her out of the story, the genealogy, the rights of man, the rule of law. The ability to tell your story, in words or images, is already a victory, already a revolt."[1] In this time and place, dominated by the forces of white nationalism and a president who mocks and denigrates women and people of color, the museum's role to make the underrepresented visible and heard has never been more important. There's no neutral place for art. Whether it is a commercial gallery, a museum, a university, or a public space, there are always conditions that constrain and define meaning. But one thing that I find encouraging is the role museums are increasingly taking in re-canonizing and de-colonializing the history of art. I loved walking into *America is Hard to See* at the Whitney Museum and seeing Lee Krasner's epic painting *The Seasons* (1957) front and center.

MW: The magician Karl Germain said that "conjuring is the only honest profession: a magician promises to deceive and does." And Picasso said, "We all know that Art is not truth. Art is a lie that makes us realize truth." In our current state, where there is no "truth," and "facts" have become a matter of opinion, how can artists wake us up from this unpleasant dream? How can you help us see the world and each other through a lens of hope, trust, and humanity?

Fauerso: I keep thinking of Marie Howe's poem, "After the Movie." She writes: "Simone Weil says that when you really love you are able to look at someone you want to eat and not eat them."[2]

This makes me think about the limits and expressions of love in totally new ways. That is how art is able to wake us up—by complicating our assumptions of how thing are, how things go, and presenting new and completely unexpected ways to engage with the world.

CG: How do you hold on to something so no one can take it away? Your beliefs? Your body? Your love? What tethers us here?

Fauerso: I don't think there is anything that can't be taken away and won't be taken away. That may sound harsh, but a lot of life is about learning to let go. I grew up in a Transcendental Meditation community, who call this ability to let go "transcendence." I try to hold on to the things that make life beautiful and bearable—humor, empathy, love, and imagination.

ES: Public health physicians distinguish between narrative compassion (where one or two or three people are at risk) and statistical compassion (where thousands or millions are at risk). We're fairly good at the first, and have many occasions to strengthen our capacity through daily acts of friendship and from reading literature. We're terrible at the second, and have almost no training in strengthening our feeble abilities in this region. To what extent can the medium you work in invite, or carry out, acts of narrative compassion and statistical compassion?

Fauerso: After Hurricane Harvey, I traveled to Rockport, Texas, to help my mom clean up the damage to our family home. It was devastating; much of the town was destroyed. One thing contributing to the chaos was the huge accumulation of donated clothes, bedding, and stuffed animals piled in parking lots and at the sides of roads—unprotected, unsorted, wet, and molding. The piles of donated items represented thousands of people trying to help without a larger understanding of the situation or the implications of their actions. How do we help in the right ways? Art presents new ways of looking at old problems, and can make the invisible visible, both complicating and clarifying our assumptions about the ways things are and should be done.

—

1 Rebecca Solnit, "Grandmother Spider," from *Men Explain Things To Me*, 2014.
2 Marie Howe, *The Kingdom of of Ordinary Time*, 2008.

***You Destroy Every Special Thing I Make,* 2017–19**

pp. 162–7

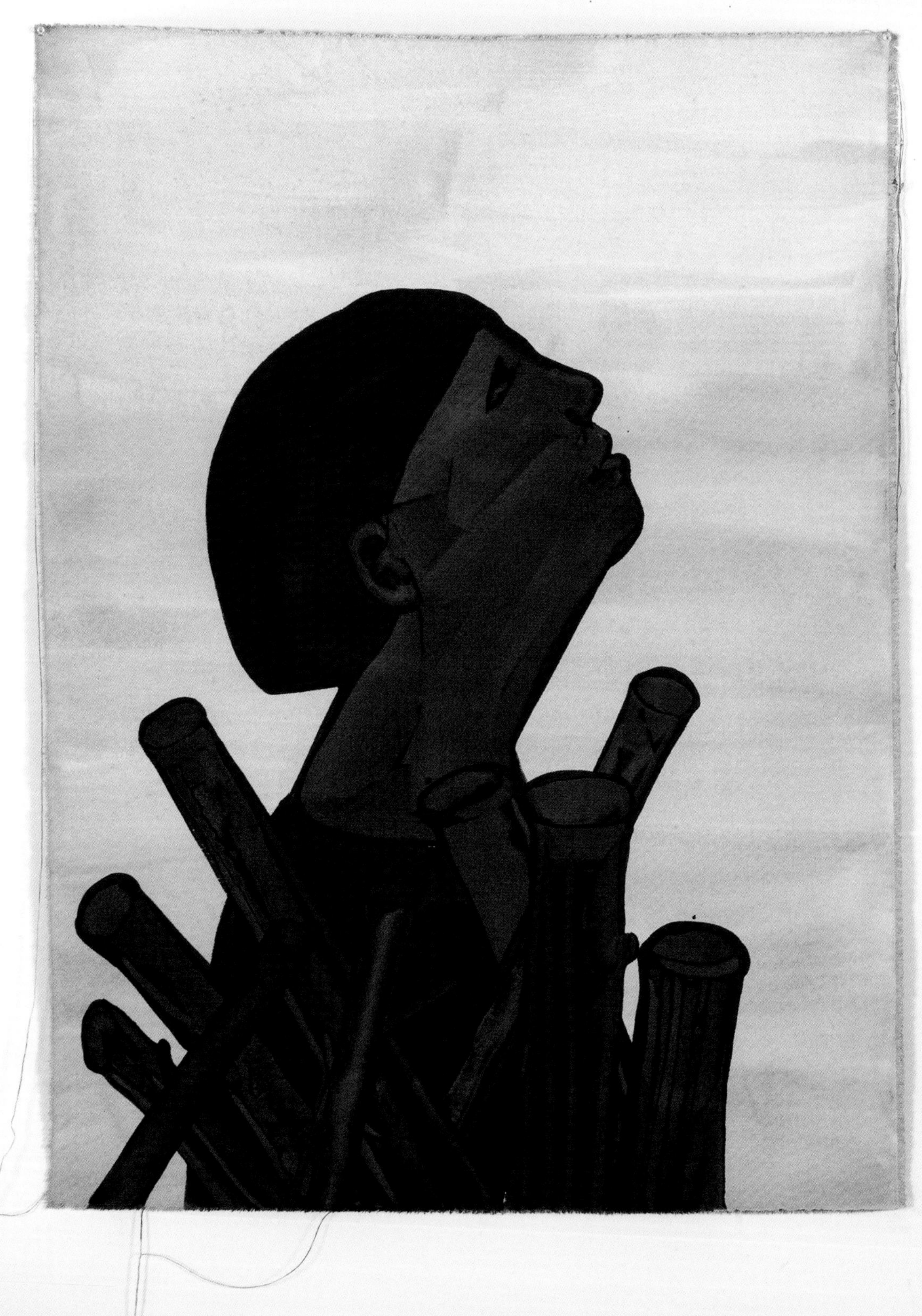

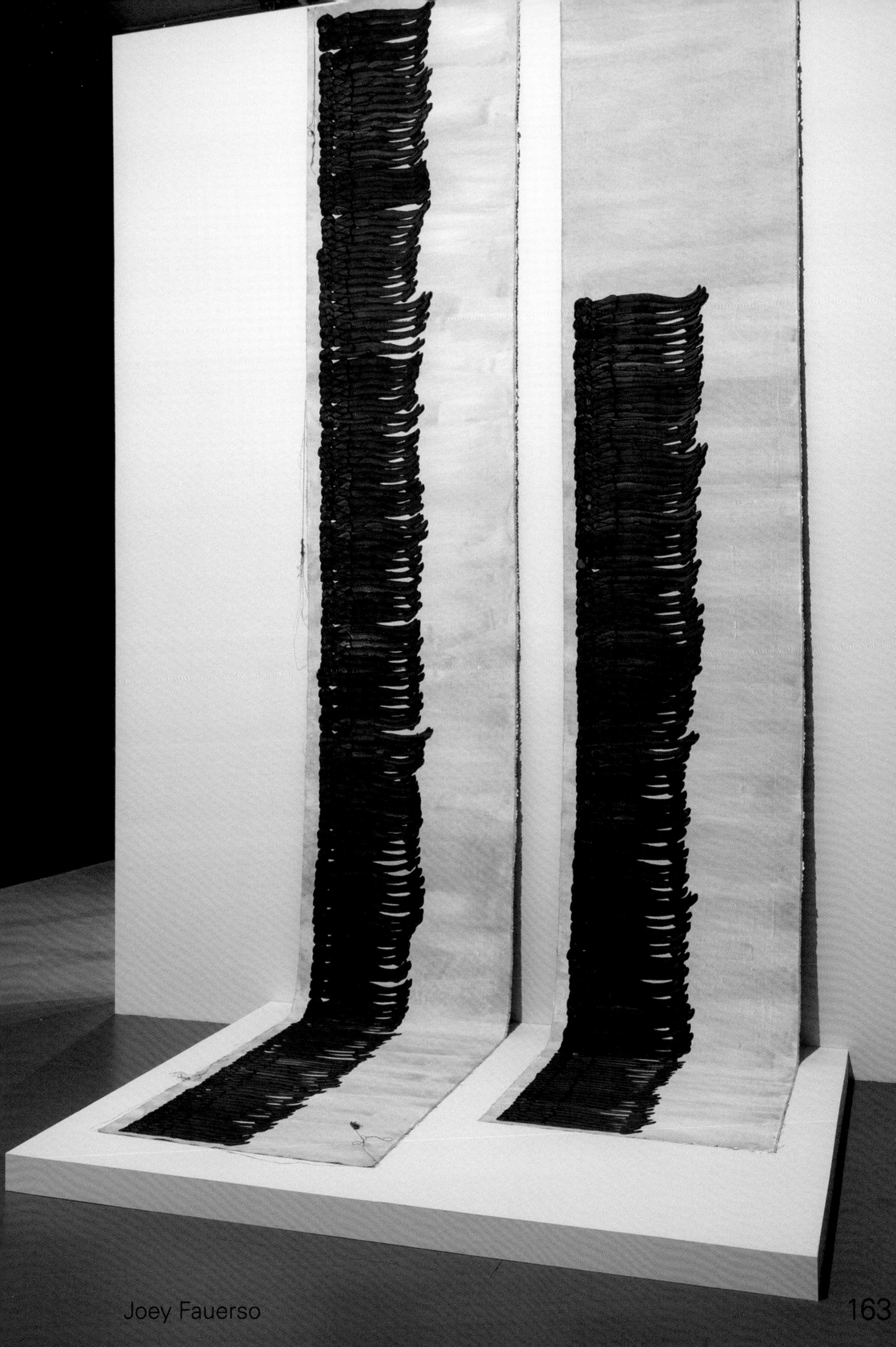

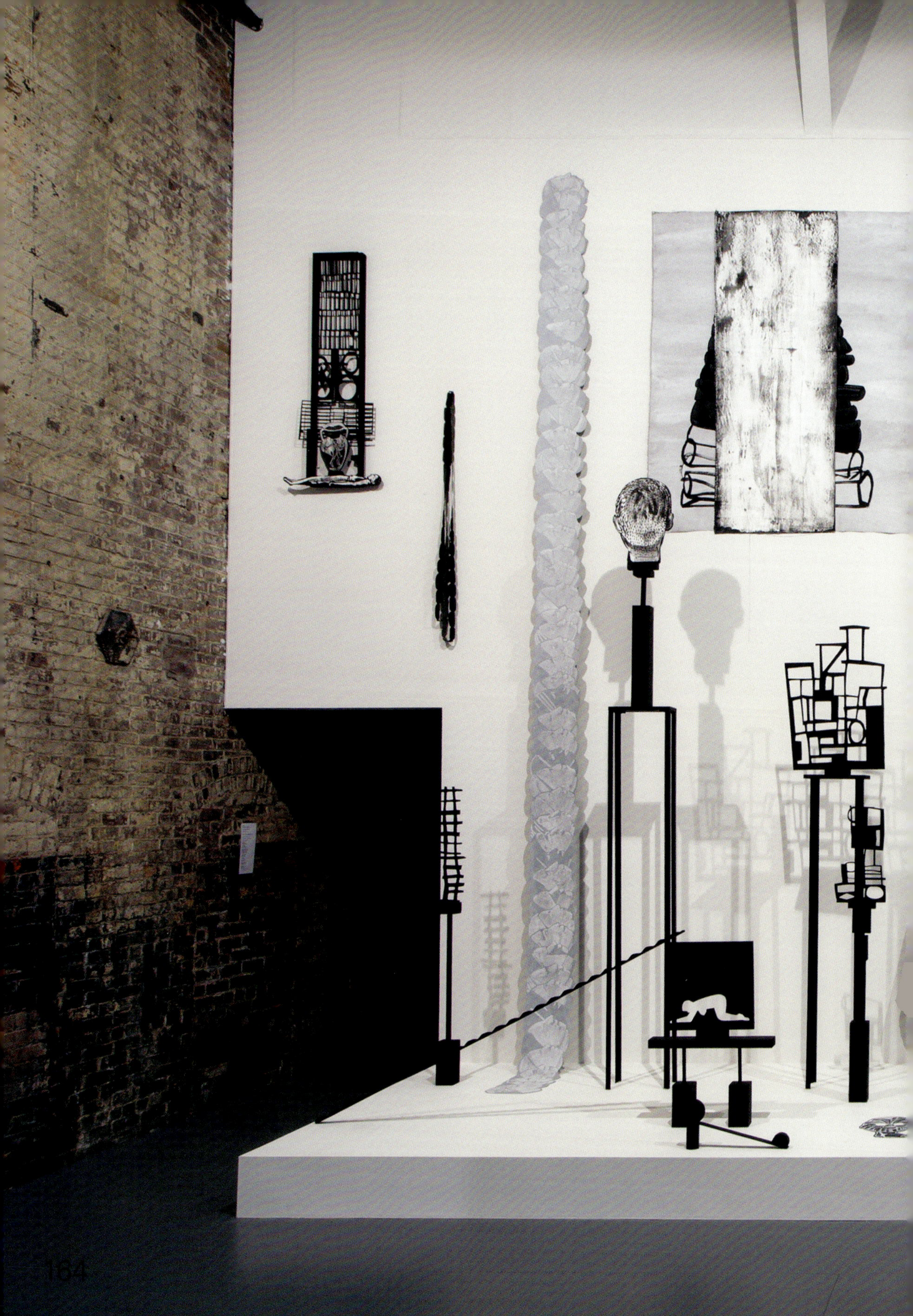

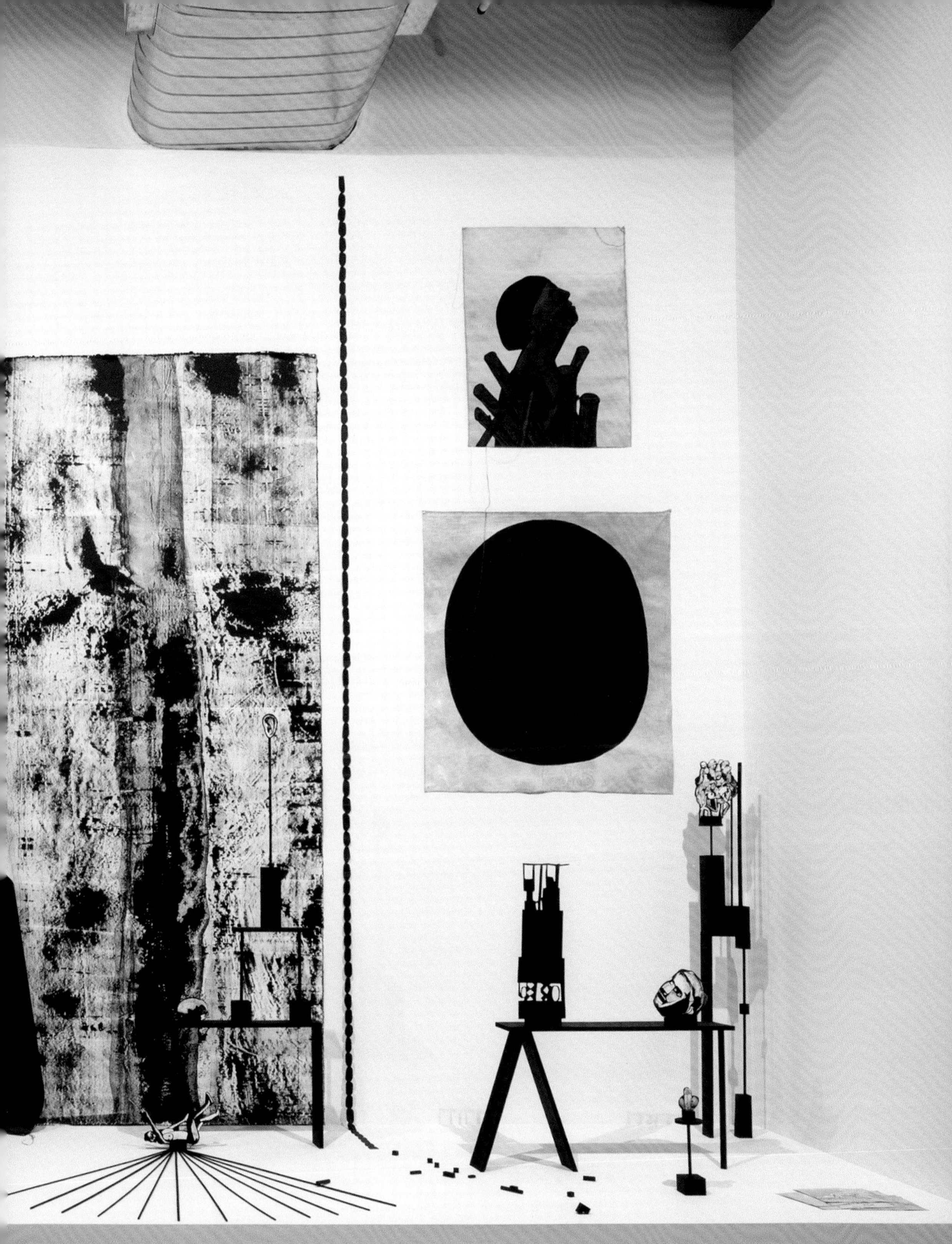

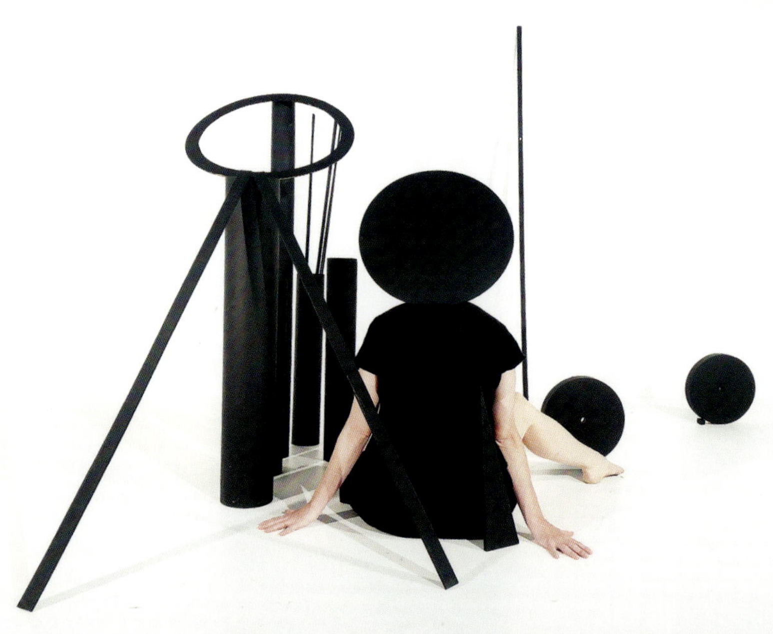

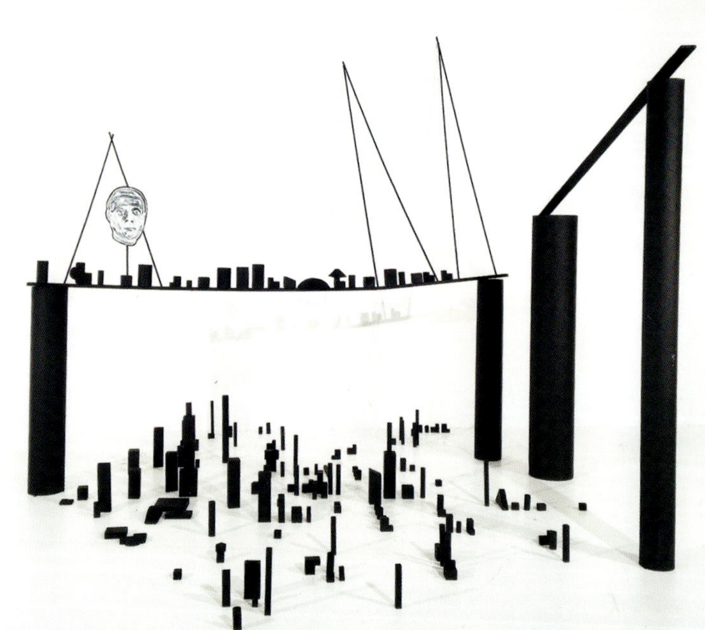

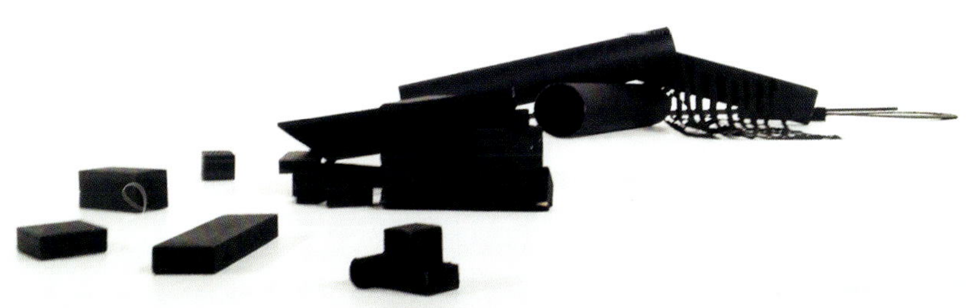

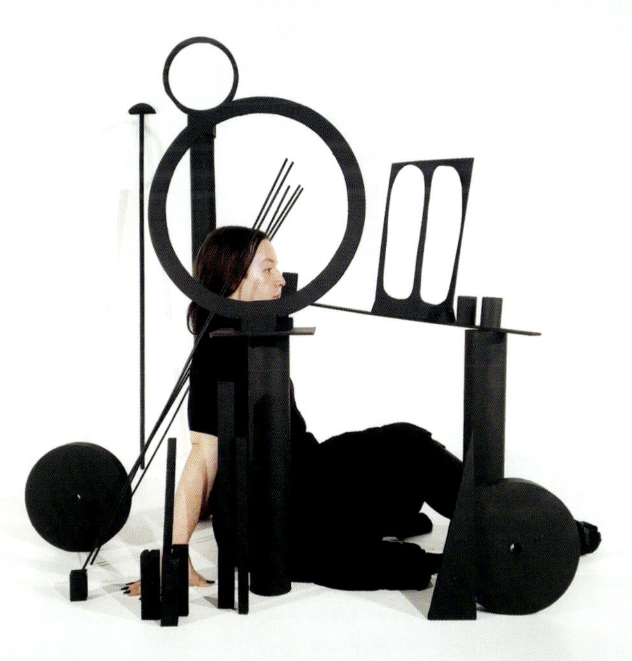

Keith Sklar

—

FM: When did the climate change? When did "this moment" become this moment?

Sklar: When Fox News metastasized into the dominant information source for much of our nation.

When Dick Cheney was born and his unformed heart escaped and rolled down the drain like mortified beads of mercury.

When social media took off, using algorithms that sharpened the alienated to organize their victimhood, buy guns, troll women, dismiss facts, share lies and hate and rage.

When "scump" amplified existing racist paranoia by challenging Obama's birth certificate and millions of white men and women seemed fine with the Republican Party promoting Jim Crow as Justice Department head.

When my first-generation, Jewish aunt said, "Why can't they speak English!" at two condo gardeners speaking Spanish, despite growing up in a home where her parents mainly spoke Hungarian.

When empathy was replaced with a crowd-gasm of violence, racism, and bullying.

AC: In an age where consumer capitalism constantly promotes the dream of expressing yourself, hasn't art become central to supporting and maintaining that power structure? However radical its messages are on the surface—isn't art underneath really constantly promoting the idea of self-expression and so promoting consumer capitalism? So maybe it's part of the problem?

Sklar: The tens of thousands of years of global human expression predate consumer capitalism by tens of thousands of years.

The tension between imagined autonomous self-expression and naïf tool has been discussed for generations. Solution or problem? The answer is, Yes. I view binary constructs as mostly arbitrary and exclusionary, because eventually somebody or something I care about gets screwed. I see social change as a spectrum hanging by a thread, weaving empathy and laundering complicity. Organic apples and oranges with sour grapes at their core. Monsanto sucks. Through this bee's eyes lens, I can view art as helping create a mixed-metaphor, plural world where people across histories and identities are empowered to live their open selves.

AD: What is "real" in your practice—your way of working, your medium, your social, professional, material, cultural, political relationships, your proximity to institutions? And what is sustainable? Do the two categories (real and sustainable) overlap, and to what extent?

Sklar: My inability to follow a standard course is real. I move forward in retrospect. I build with stabs in the dark, what-the-hells, and shifts in indecision. The head apparently not caring what the hand is doing, until of course it does. This approach is real to me.

Perhaps nothing sustains. If we as a species survive, what might sustain us is the drive for interconnection, the shared between, the symbiosis of viewer, artist, artwork, curator, and institutions. Family and community sustain me, they are real. My need for distance from my cynicism and paranoia is as real as the death-cult direction of our nation and our world.

GC: Museums and cultural organizations once perceived as "pure" white boxes free of bias, are now being pushed to reckon with their own privilege and political baggage. As artists increasingly explore the meaning of "realness" in their work, I wonder how you negotiate the political context in which your work is inserted when it enters the museum.

Sklar: I remain epoxied to unearned privilege. Bald, hip glasses, another white, US born, upper-middle class, hetero male. I kept the mistrust, but threw out the victimhood. I make art for galleries and museums. It's a clear contradiction, but I recognize the privilege and oxymorons poured into the concrete foundations of art. No one thought to bring a level. Fuck the equity threatening, white-brite museum space. Except damn, my works look best on white. A quiet little lebensraum, assuming the surrounding wall space as their own. Like the worst of John Wayne and Robert Moses, manspreading others further away. Yet maybe art acts as disruption in the signal, and at its most effective, collaborates with the viewer to soothe, jolt, or knit connections between previously unconnected areas of the brain. Like a bridge between beaten to a pulp, the comfort of the couch, the play of light on a surface, and the sweat on the skin.

MW: The magician Karl Germain said that "conjuring is the only honest profession: a magician promises to deceive and does." And Picasso said, "We all know that Art is not truth. Art is a lie that makes us realize truth." In our current state, where there is no "truth," and "facts" have become a matter of opinion, how can artists wake us up from this unpleasant dream? How can you help us see the world and each other through a lens of hope, trust, and humanity?

Sklar: I am scared for real about our brutal cultural and political willingness to discard facts, data, ethics, decency, the future, and simple observable science. I don't believe that artists can wake us up from this dream. In a time when angry authoritarians are normalized, I choose to believe that my work conjures viewers to survive lies and act in more ethical ways.

CG: How do you hold on to something so no one can take it away? Your beliefs? Your body? Your love? What tethers us here?

Sklar: My body can be taken away at any time. By a virus, a pollutant, a bullet, an authoritarian, an accident, a change in climate, a car. We are tragically and powerfully fragile creatures. It is this fragility of memory, social connection, of life itself, that requires us to strive for hope, fight for meaning, and even act with empathy and compassion. Conscious or not, our brevity on this plane tethers us to each other and to this life. Though it's a frayed, wobbling tether. The kind where the director keeps focusing on closeups of the rope unraveling thread by thread, as the eyes of the hero and the hot-babe genius scientist with no agency meet, until the rope is down to a single thread. The hero mushes his mouth on hers because she's been waiting and she's thirty years younger and they're going to die. But they don't.

ES: Public health physicians distinguish between narrative compassion (where one or two or three people are at risk) and statistical compassion (where thousands or millions are at risk). We're fairly good at the first, and have many occasions to strengthen our capacity through daily acts of friendship and from reading literature. We're terrible at the second, and have almost no training in strengthening our feeble abilities in this region. To what extent can the medium you work in invite, or carry out, acts of narrative compassion and statistical compassion?

Sklar: My work models the acts of a person trying to understand and respond to overwhelming forces beyond one's control. While there are few big solutions in the work, I would hope in each piece there is compassion. And a sense that we are all in this together; even in isolation, even in our loss, we still somehow move onward. Resistant and stumbling. The parable of the blind leading the sighted leading the deaf leading the lame. The key word is leading.

***Pool*, 2019**
p. 170

***Stand*, 2019**
p. 171

***Sitting Down for a Drink with my Shadow*, 2019**
pp. 172–3

***Gilt*, 2019**
pp. 174–5

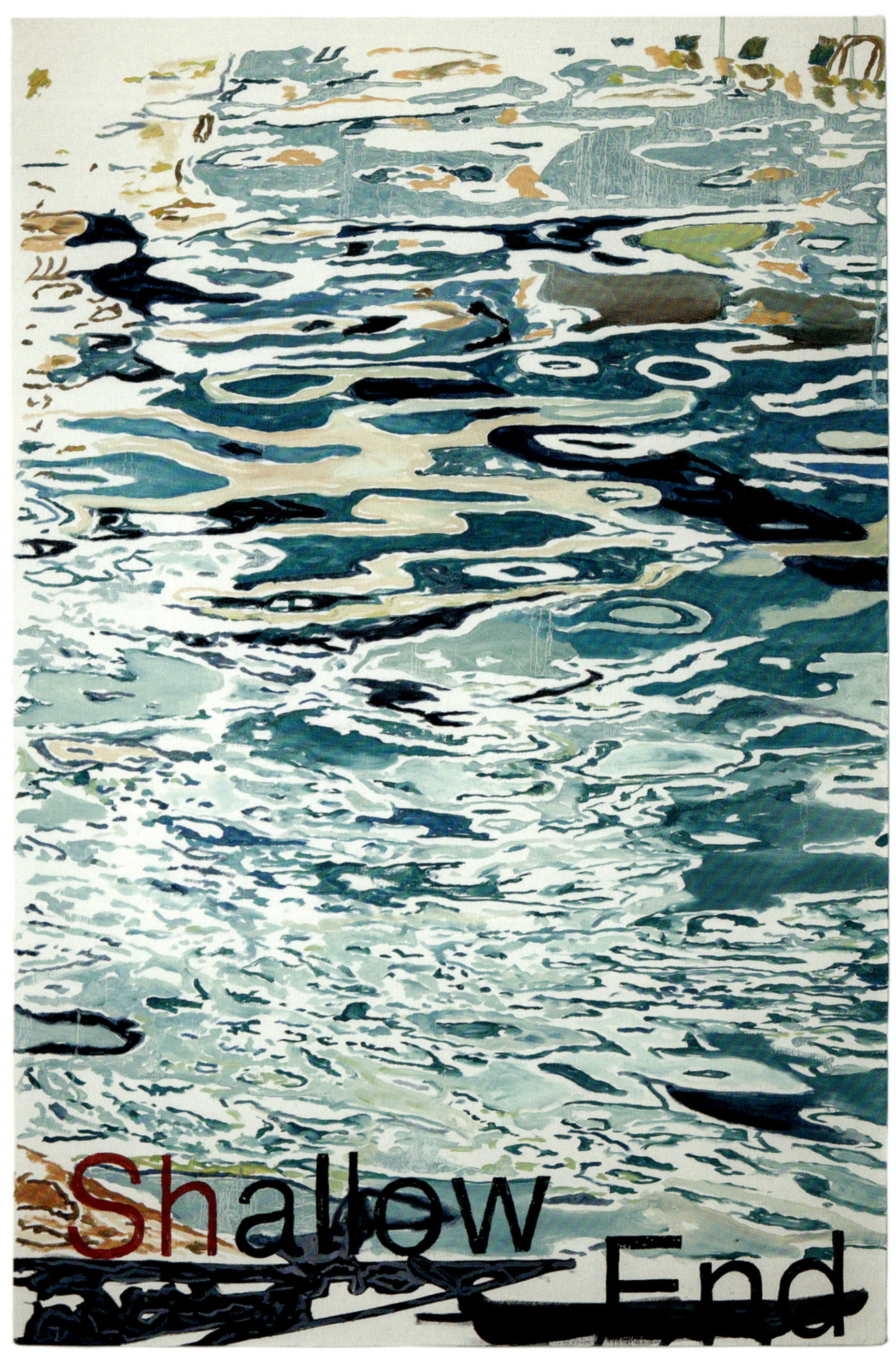
Shallow
End

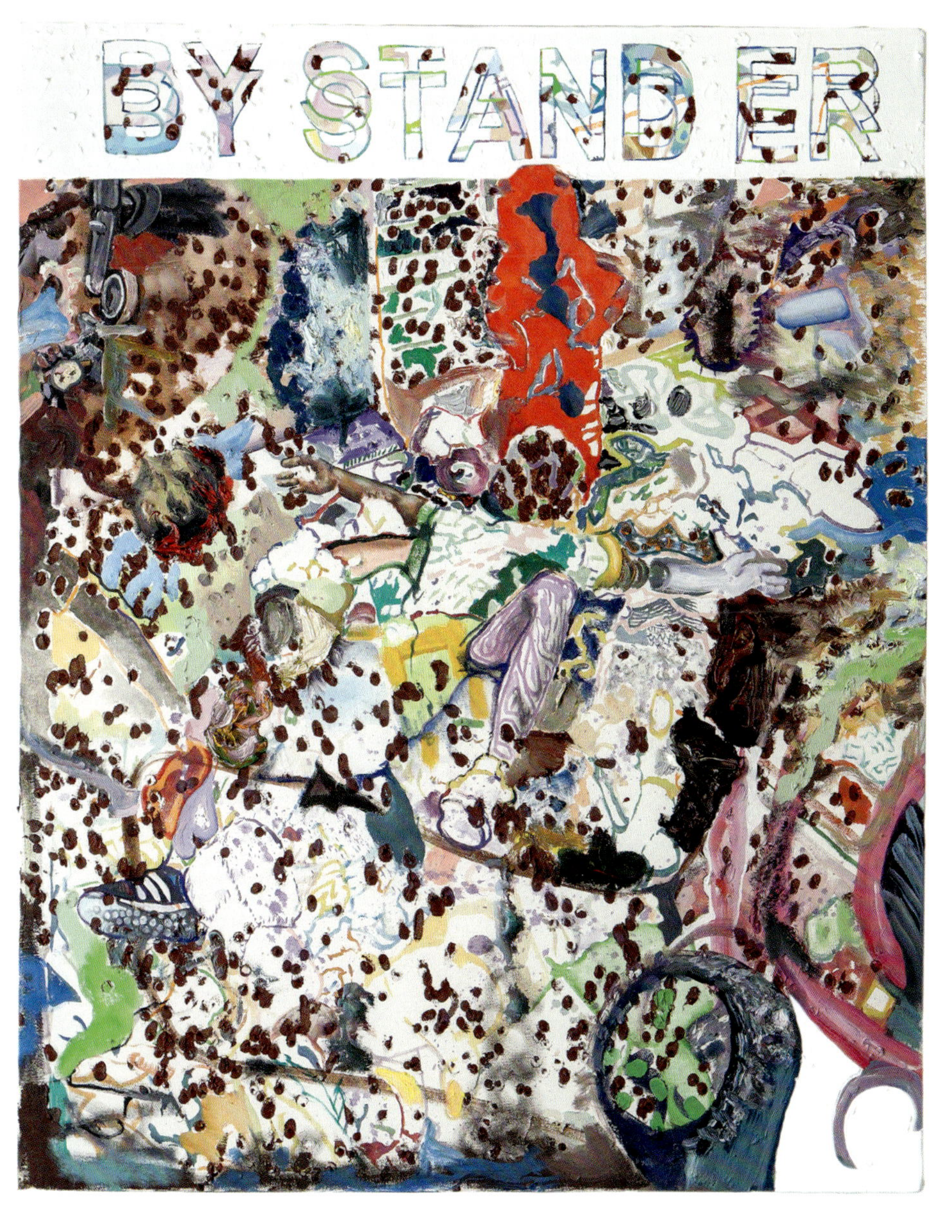
BY STAND ER

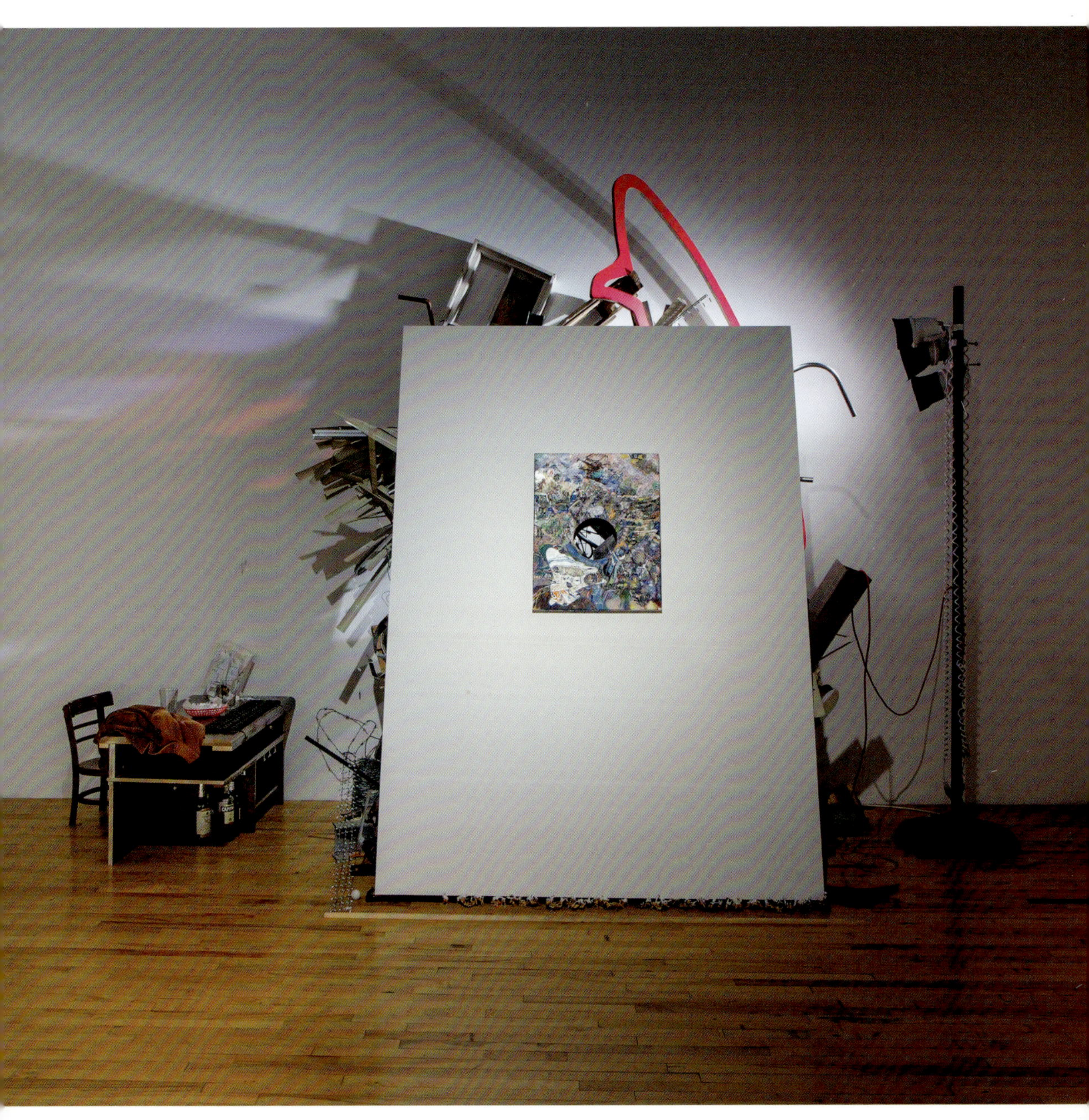

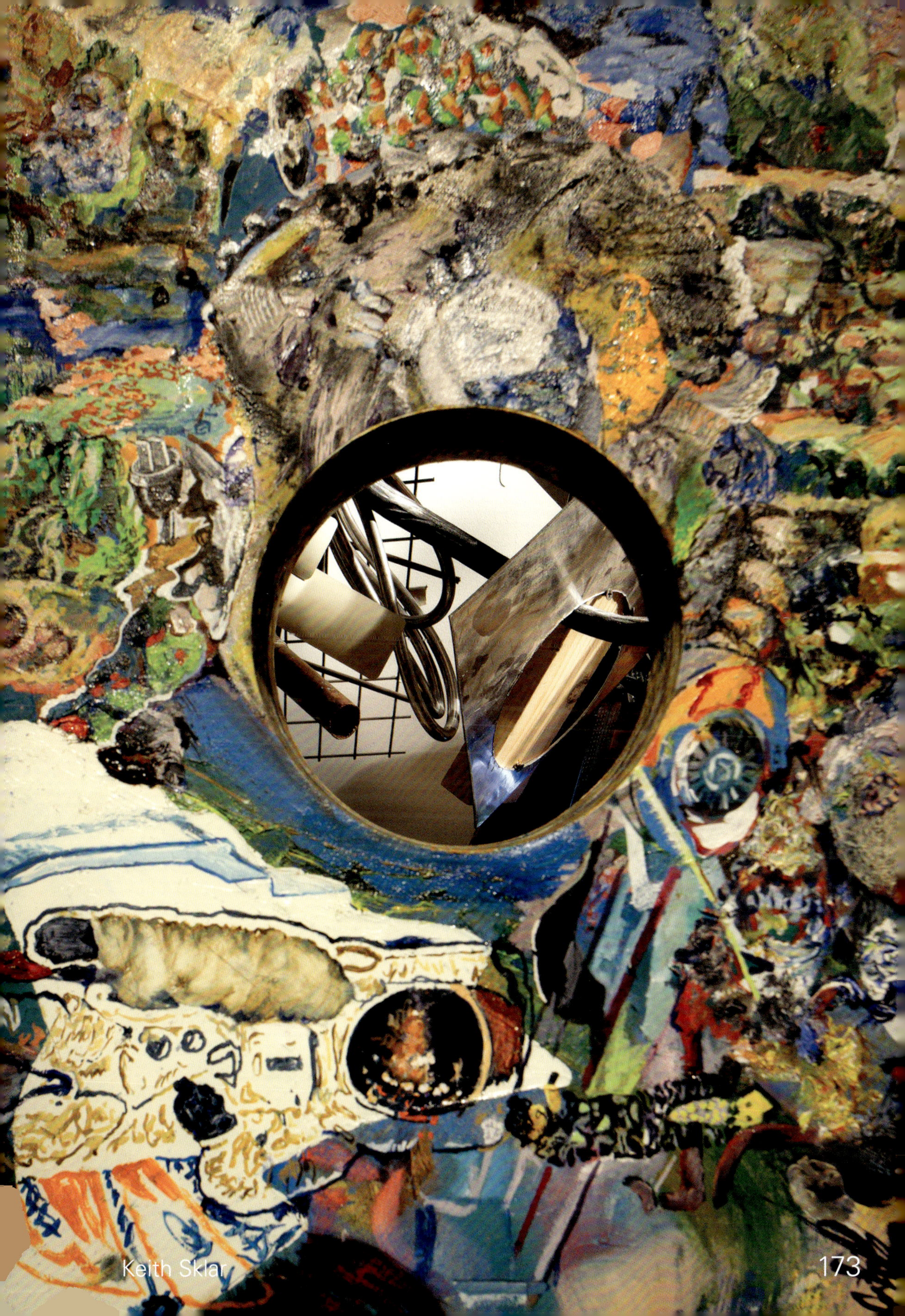
Keith Sklar

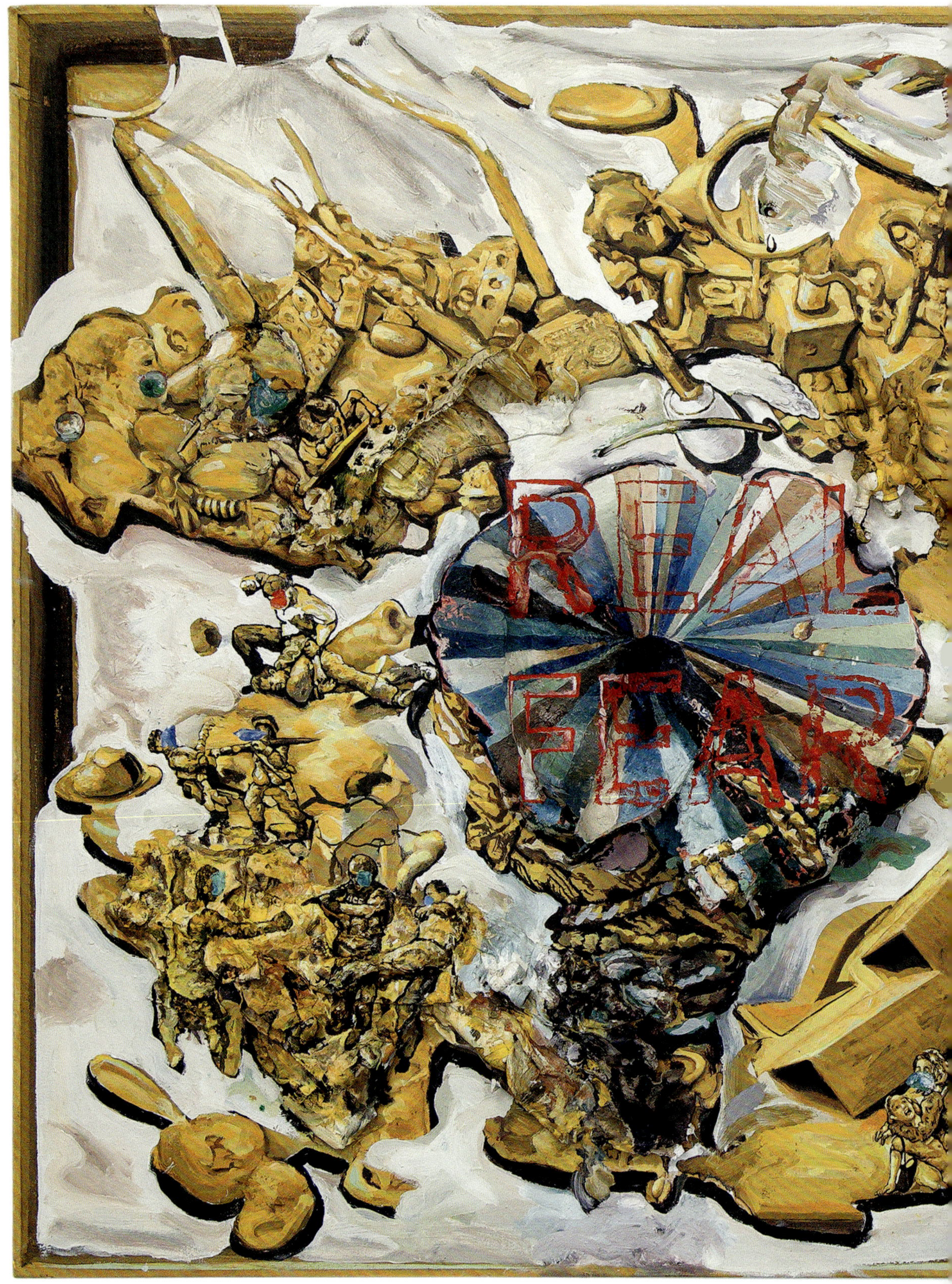
REAL
FEAR

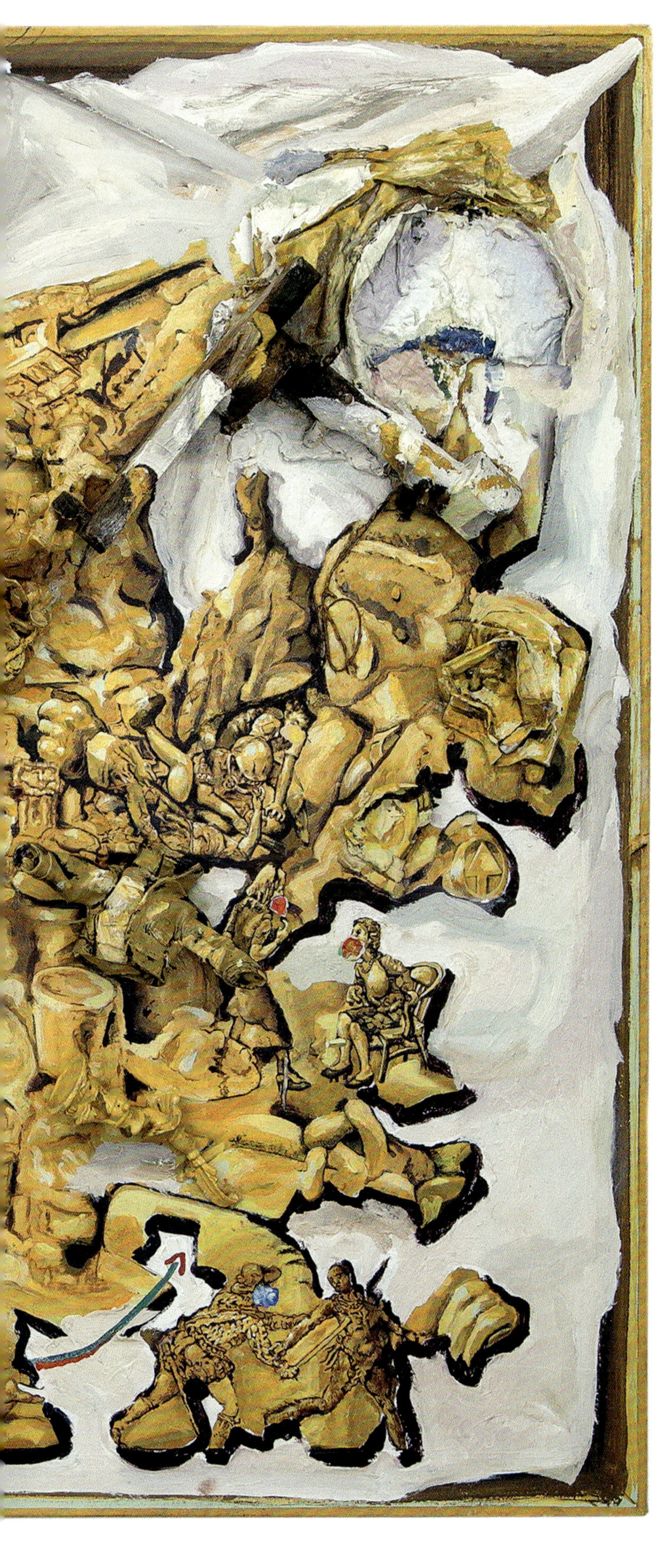

Allison Schulnik

—

FM: When did the climate change? When did "this moment" become this moment?

Schulnik: I am not really sure. Things seem to swing back and forth. One movement reacts to another. It would be easy to say the election of Trump changed everything. However, so much goes into that. The question should be, what the fuck do we do now? We can start by paying attention, learning from history, giving, and voting.

AC: In an age where consumer capitalism constantly promotes the dream of expressing yourself, hasn't art become central to supporting and maintaining that power structure? However radical its messages are on the surface—isn't art underneath really constantly promoting the idea of self-expression and so promoting consumer capitalism? So maybe it's part of the problem?

Schulnik: Maybe and often yes. Really though, besides basic survival needs, love and self-expression may be the root of human experience and worth. Creating true and real things, with integrity and heart, without compromise or thought about the consumer or capital is the only radical expression. We don't really have a choice but to try and not be the problem. Art can take root in any gut and spread. Art is like a parasite. Some help their host, others kill.

AD: What is "real" in your practice—your way of working, your medium, your social, professional, material, cultural, political relationships, your proximity to institutions? And what is sustainable? Do the two categories (real and sustainable) overlap, and to what extent?

Schulnik: I can't make something other than what I make. I don't know if I can separate from my work, in the same way that I could not imagine separating from my arm. My heart is real, and my material is tactile. I don't know that anything is sustainable.

GC: Museums and cultural organizations once perceived as "pure" white boxes free of bias, are now being pushed to reckon with their own privilege and political baggage. As artists increasingly explore the meaning of "realness" in their work, I wonder how you negotiate the political context in which your work is inserted when it enters the museum.

Schulnik: I understand showing work in the world immediately puts it in a political context. It's not something I think about in the studio, although I am aware of what I am, and what I might be seen as. I just try to make honest work. It is the work of a forty-year-old woman, first-time mother. I negotiate fantasy in my work, at the same time honesty and truth, but really just let it be what it is naturally.

MW: The magician Karl Germain said that "conjuring is the only honest profession: a magician promises to deceive and does." And Picasso said, "We all know that Art is not truth. Art is a lie that makes us realize truth." In our current state, where there is no "truth," and "facts" have become a matter of opinion, how can artists wake us up from this unpleasant dream? How can you help us see the world and each other through a lens of hope, trust, and humanity?

Schulnik: By being hopeful, trusting and humane. By having integrity and honesty in every gesture. By narrowing in on passions and discarding the bullshit.

CG: How do you hold on to something so no one can take it away? Your beliefs? Your body? Your love? What tethers us here?

Schulnik: You cannot hold onto anything for the sole purpose of not letting anyone take it away. That never works. You can only hold onto things by loving them truly. No one can ever take away your beliefs and your love, really. Nothing tethers us here. We are only floating free in space, with only love and ideas to give.

ES: Public health physicians distinguish between narrative compassion (where one or two or three people are at risk) and statistical compassion (where thousands or millions are at risk). We're fairly good at the first, and have many occasions to strengthen our capacity through daily acts of friendship and from reading literature. We're terrible at the second, and have almost no training in strengthening our feeble abilities in this region. To what extent can the medium you work in invite, or carry out, acts of narrative compassion and statistical compassion?

Schulnik: All we can do is try. If an artist can create something honest, put it in the world, make someone feel something real and electrifying, and possibly stir their heart just by expressing the same feeling that person feels, assuring them they are not alone, then I think that is something.

***Moth*, 2019**

pp. 177–183

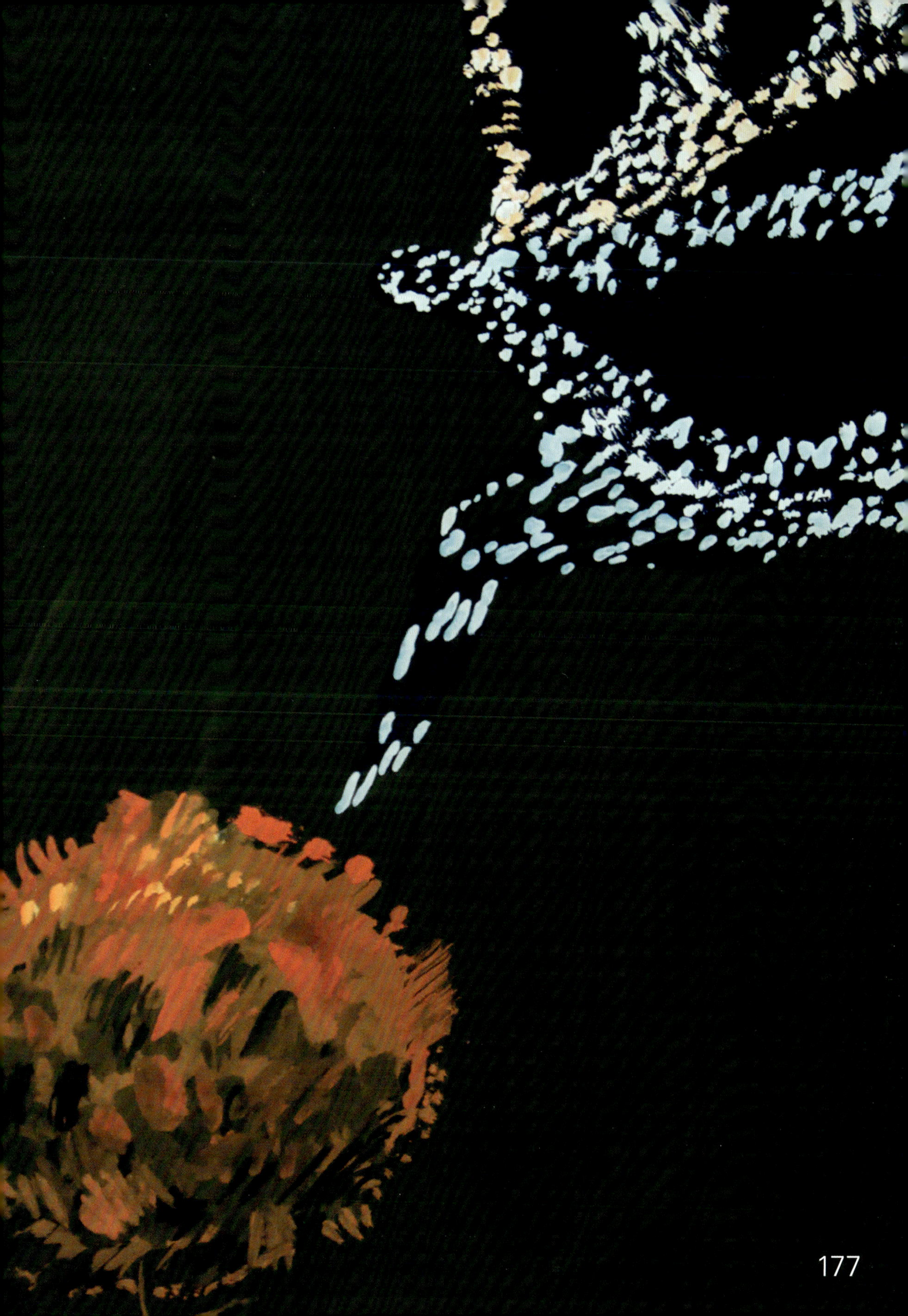

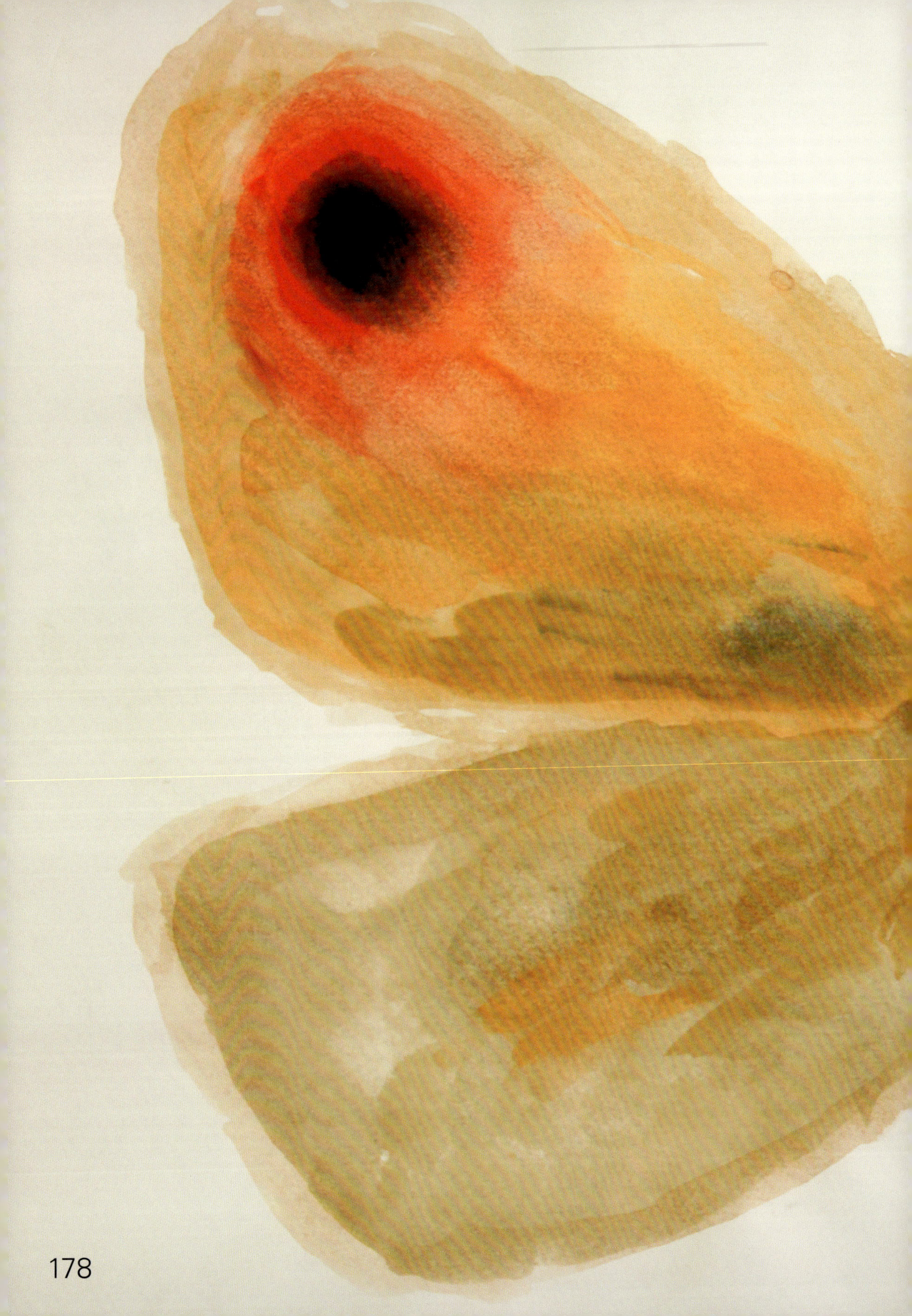

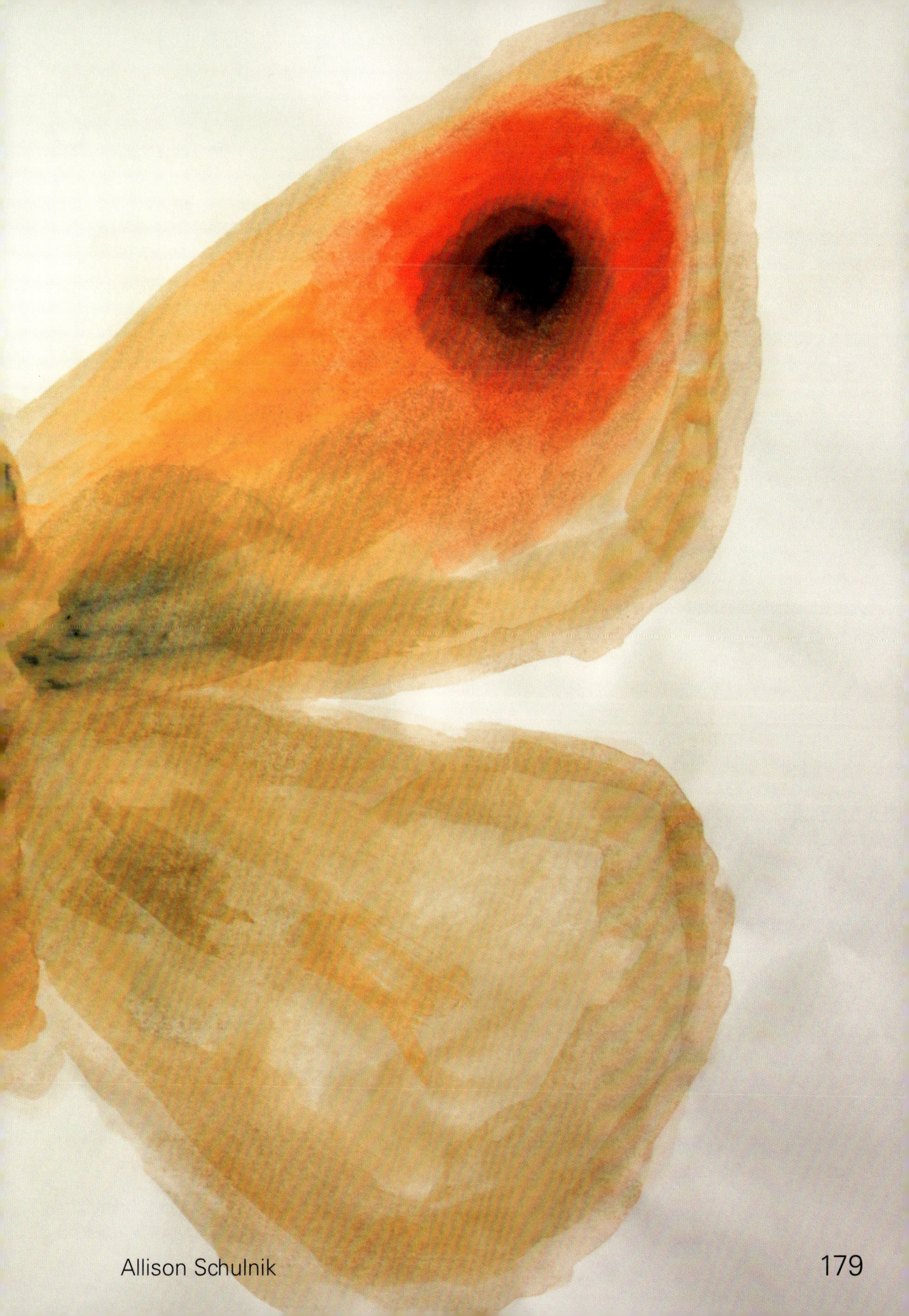

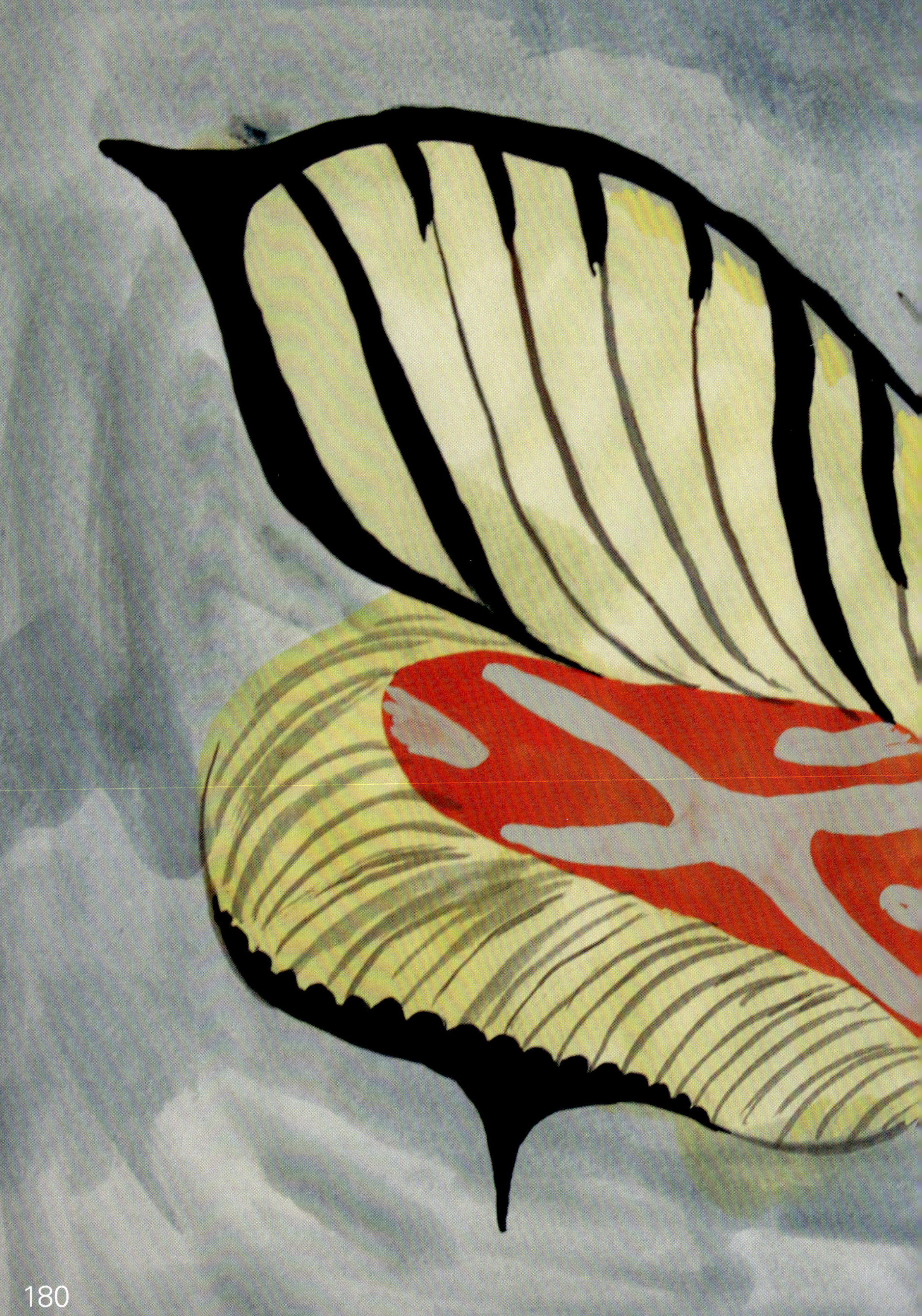

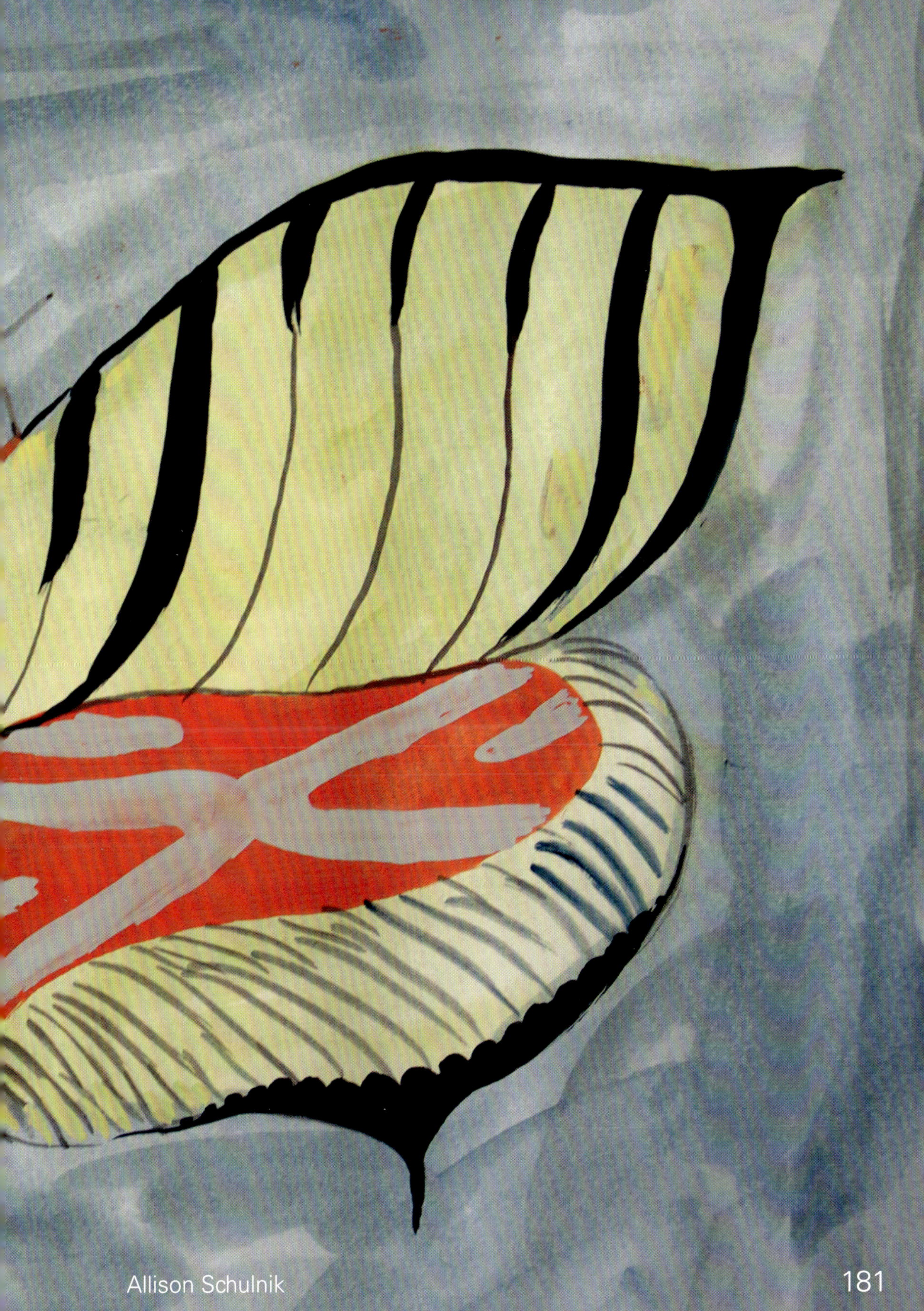

Allison Schulnik

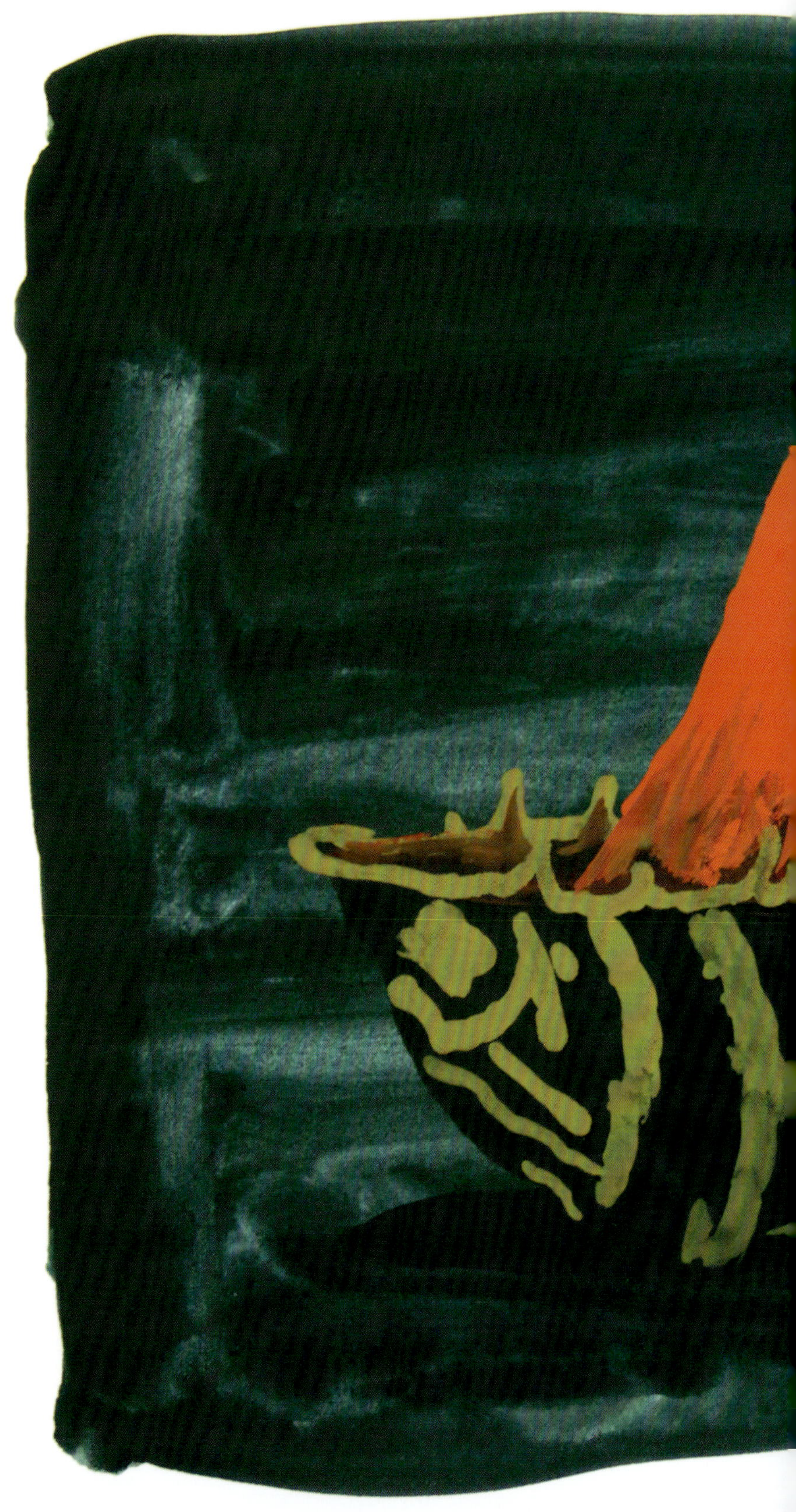

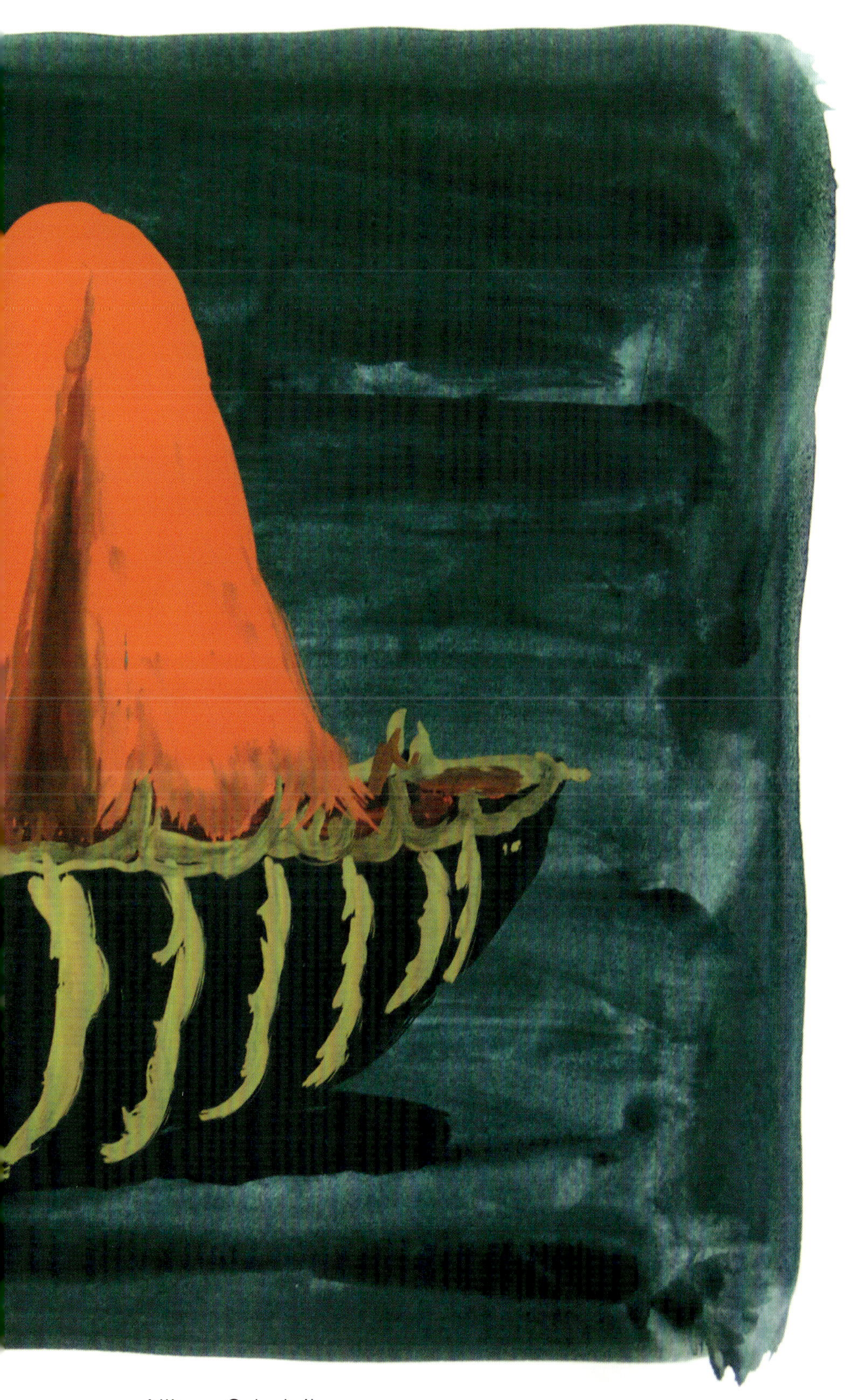

Christopher Mir

—

FM: When did the climate change? When did "this moment" become this moment?

Mir: September 11, 2001.

AC: In an age where consumer capitalism constantly promotes the dream of expressing yourself, hasn't art become central to supporting and maintaining that power structure? However radical its messages are on the surface—isn't art underneath really constantly promoting the idea of self-expression and so promoting consumer capitalism? So maybe it's part of the problem?

Mir: I am not personally promoting the idea of self-expression. I just express myself and take advantage of accidents.

AD: What is "real" in your practice—your way of working, your medium, your social, professional, material, cultural, political relationships, your proximity to institutions? And what is sustainable? Do the two categories (real and sustainable) overlap, and to what extent?

Mir: I think all of it is real. It feels objectively real. And it appears to be sustainable. The realness of paintings (or cultural artifacts) is self-evident. They are physical objects in space and time.

The social, professional, cultural, political, and institutional relationships are real in the sense that they involve interactions with friends, colleagues, peers, constituents, and staff. And there are observable outcomes like conversations, shows, publications, reviews, collaborations, etc.

GC: Museums and cultural organizations once perceived as "pure" white boxes free of bias, are now being pushed to reckon with their own privilege and political baggage. As artists increasingly explore the meaning of "realness" in their work, I wonder how you negotiate the political context in which your work is inserted when it enters the museum.

Mir: I would describe myself as a far-left secular humanist. Inclusivity is the only viable moral position. That's how I approach the political context, and that is the intention I put into my work.

MW: The magician Karl Germain said that "conjuring is the only honest profession: a magician promises to deceive and does." And Picasso said, "We all know that Art is not truth. Art is a lie that makes us realize truth." In our current state, where there is no "truth," and "facts" have become a matter of opinion, how can artists wake us up from this unpleasant dream? How can you help us see the world and each other through a lens of hope, trust, and humanity?

Mir: I think artists give us hope when they make work that is uncompromising in its subjectivity. It points the way to the numinous and the transcendent. It's like an electric current in every cell of your body.

CG: How do you hold on to something so no one can take it away? Your beliefs? Your body? Your love? What tethers us here?

Mir: I wish I knew. Maybe AI will save us!

ES: Public health physicians distinguish between narrative compassion (where one or two or three people are at risk) and statistical compassion (where thousands or millions are at risk). We're fairly good at the first, and have many occasions to strengthen our capacity through daily acts of friendship and from reading literature. We're terrible at the second, and have almost no training in strengthening our feeble abilities in this region. To what extent can the medium you work in invite, or carry out, acts of narrative compassion and statistical compassion?

Mir: I am not sure art can address statistical compassion. I do want the work to connect with people I don't know and may never meet, but that's not really the same thing, obviously.

There is a Buddhist meditation/visualization called Metta that works beautifully.

***Broken Model*, 2018**
p. 185

***Candle*, 2018**
p. 186

***Disco Grid*, 2018**
p. 187

***Fight*, 2018**
p. 188

***Flowers*, 2018**
p. 189

***Ghost Ship*, 2018**
p. 190

***Teeth*, 2018**
p. 191

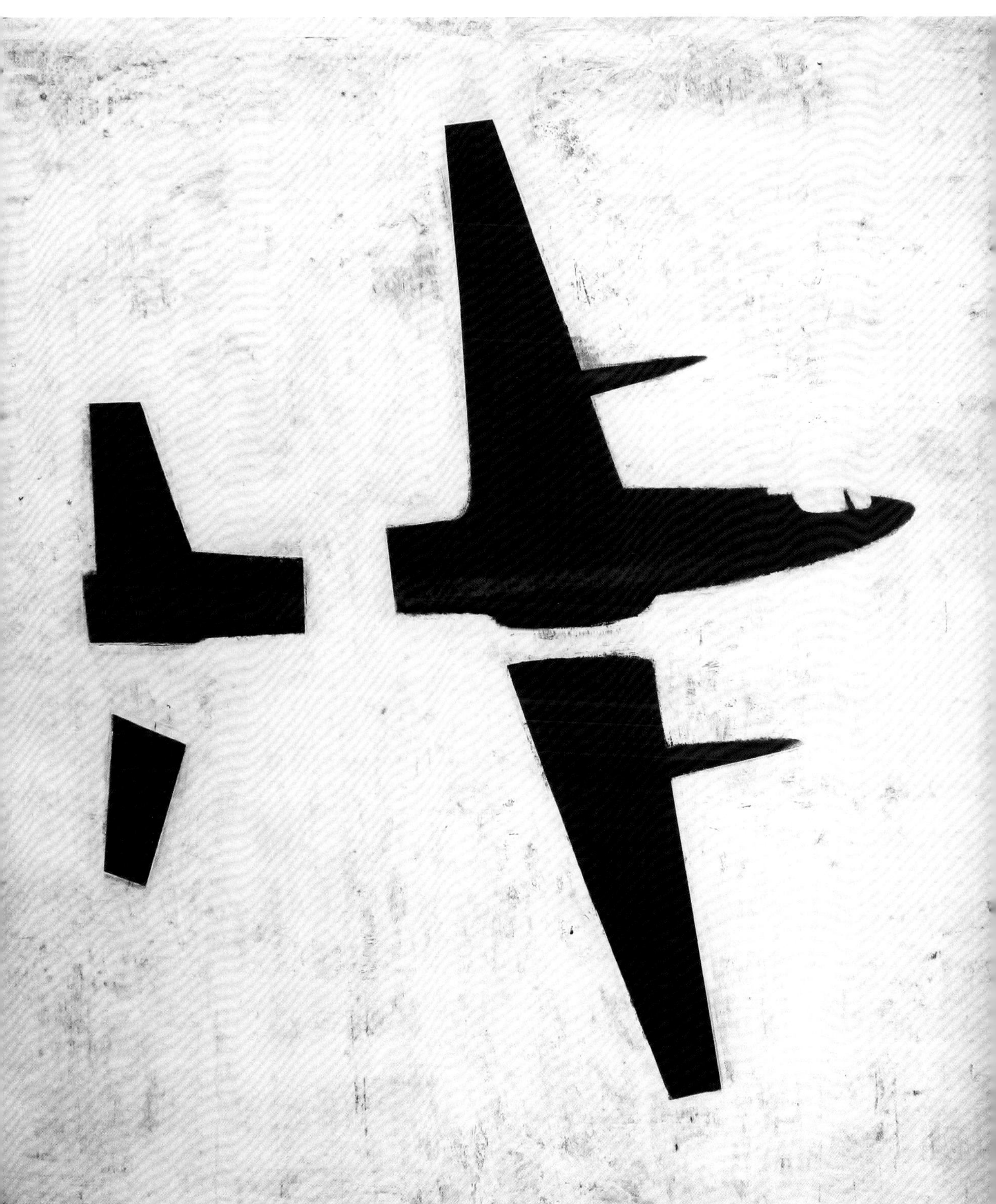

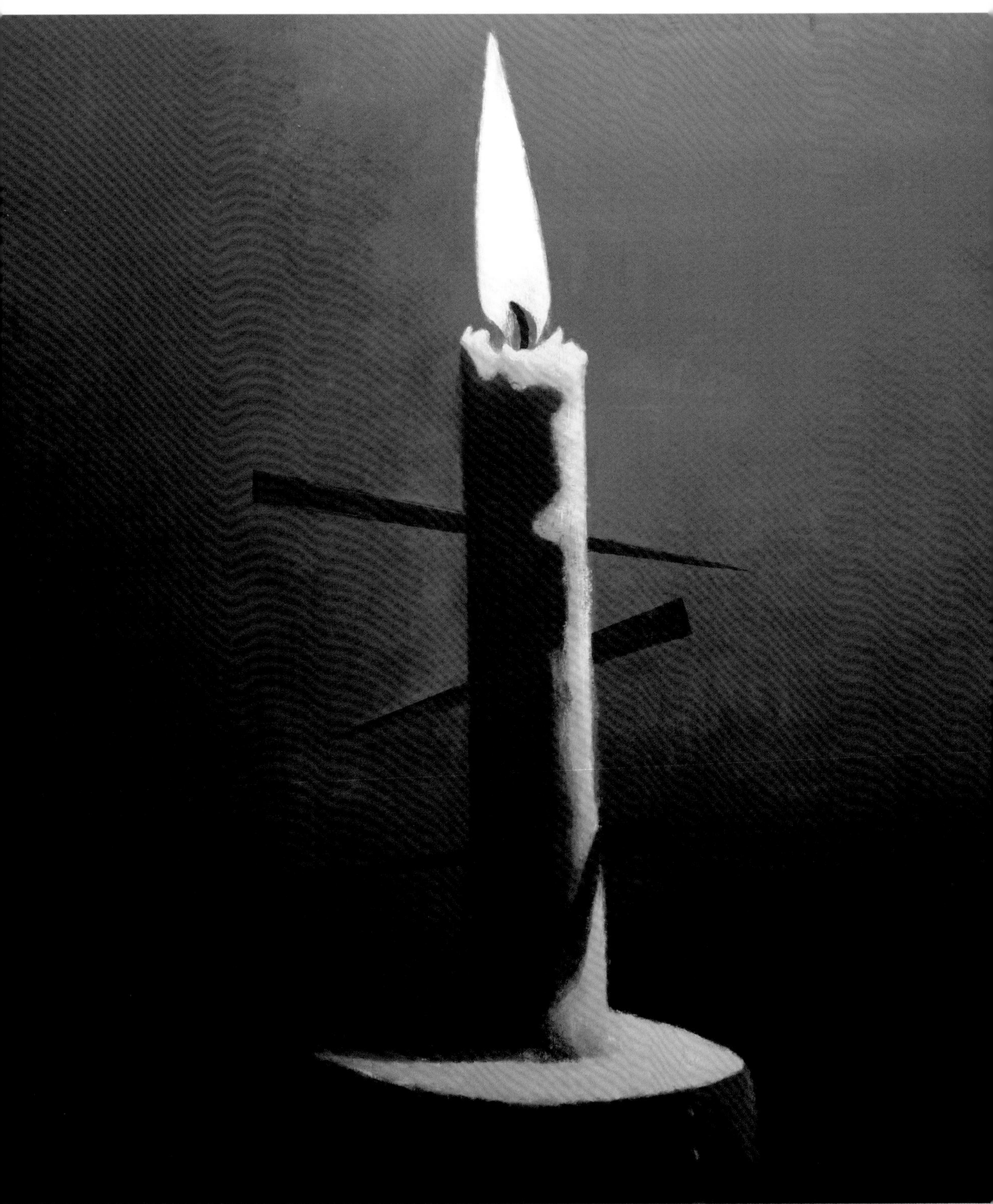

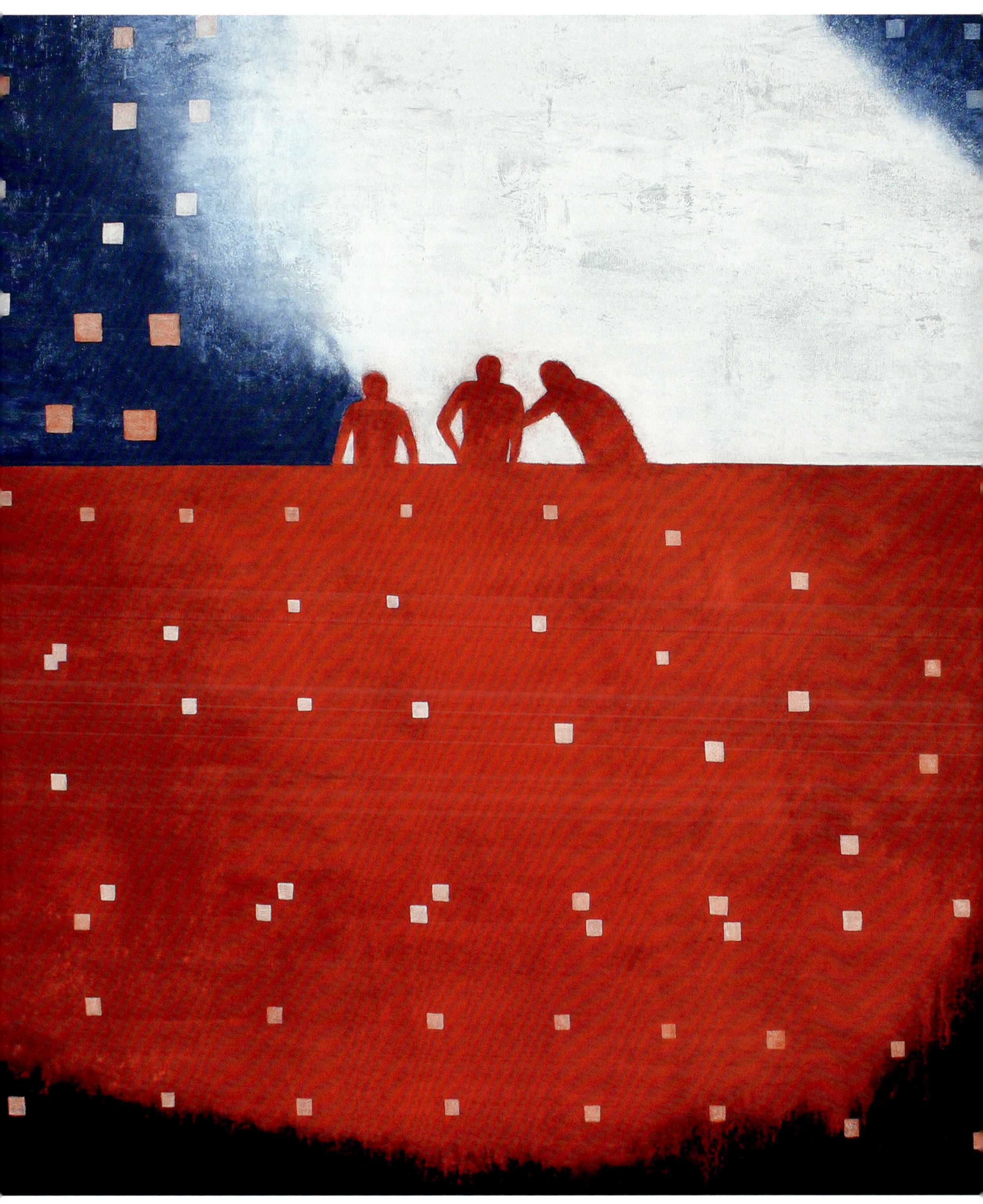

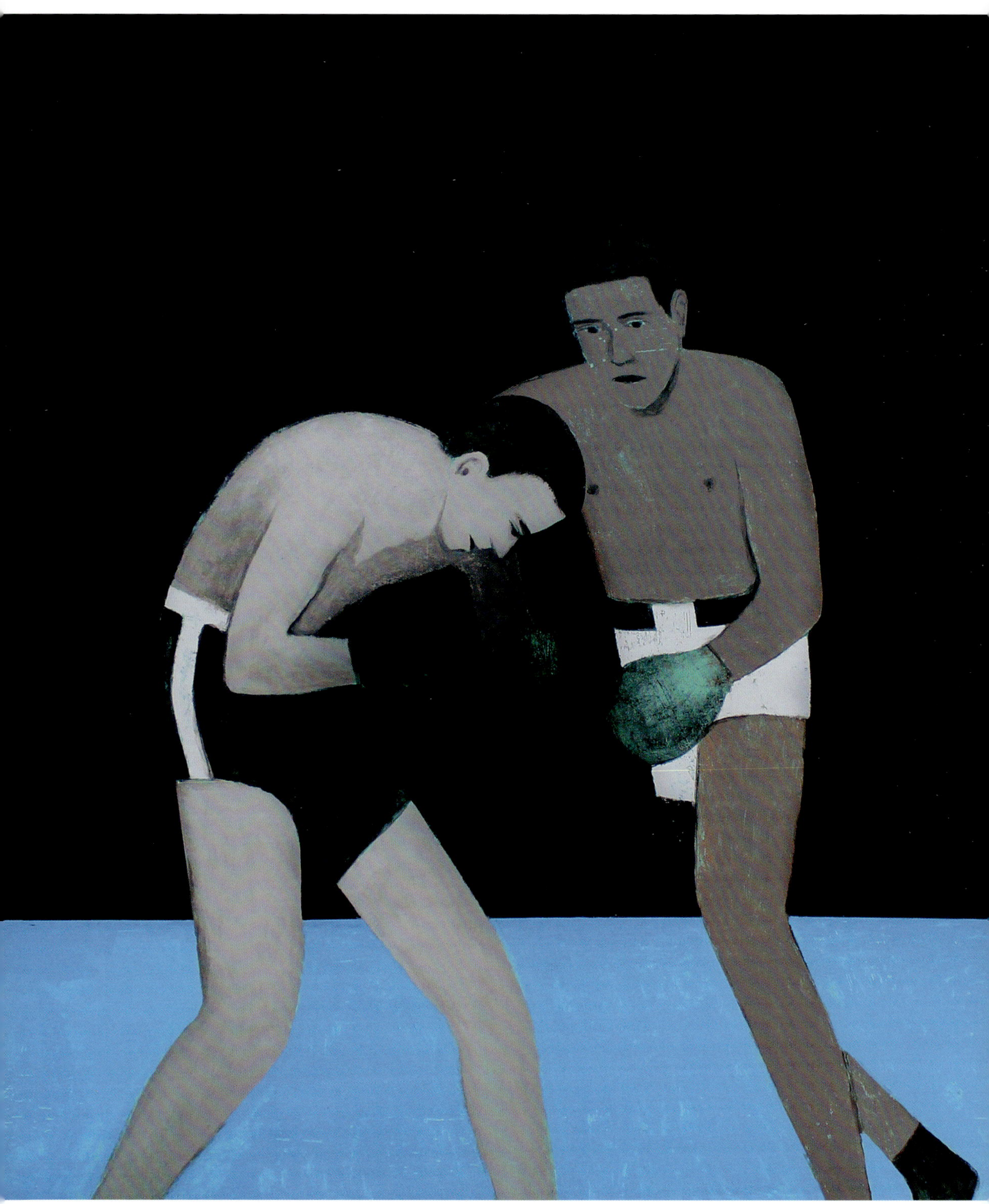

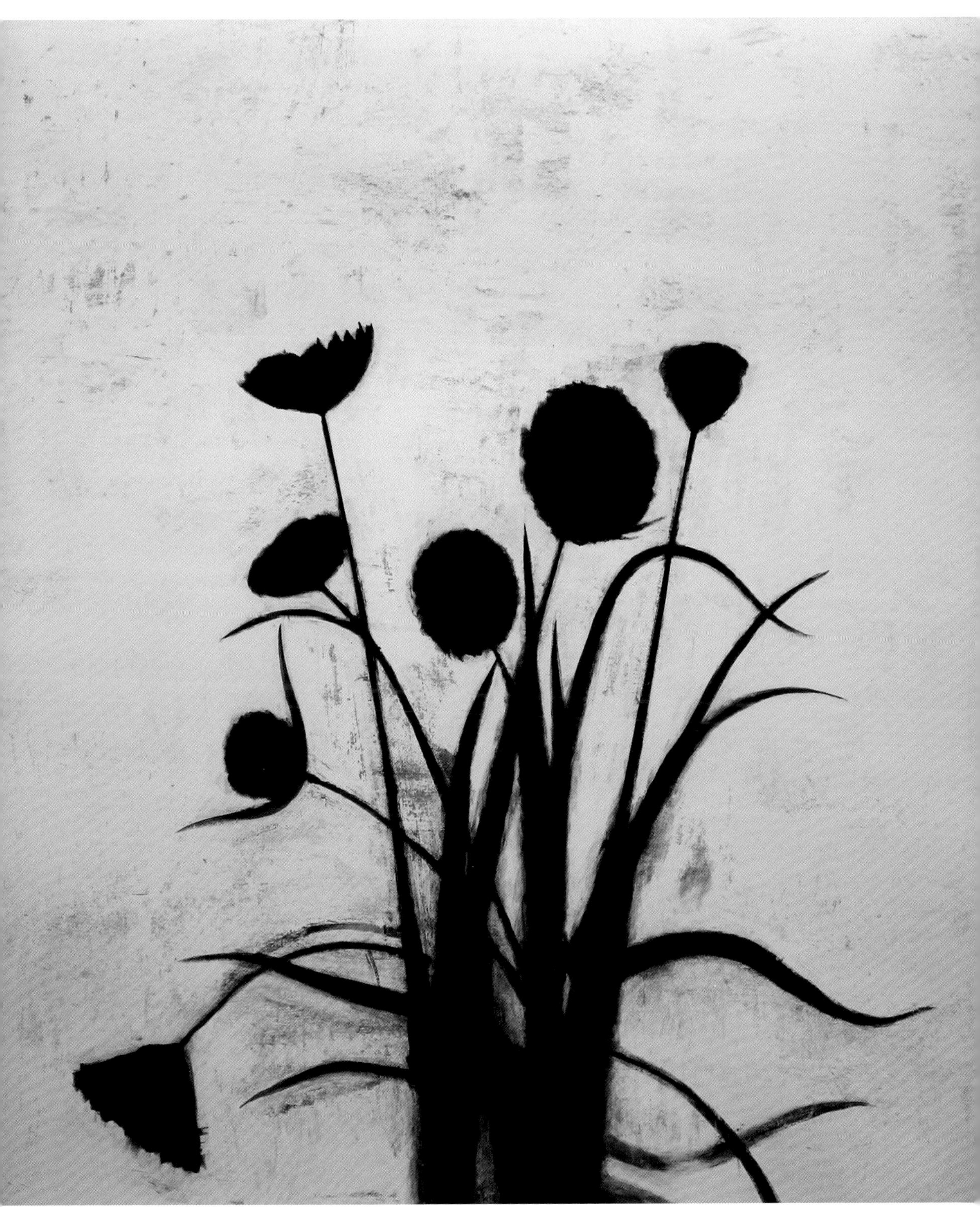

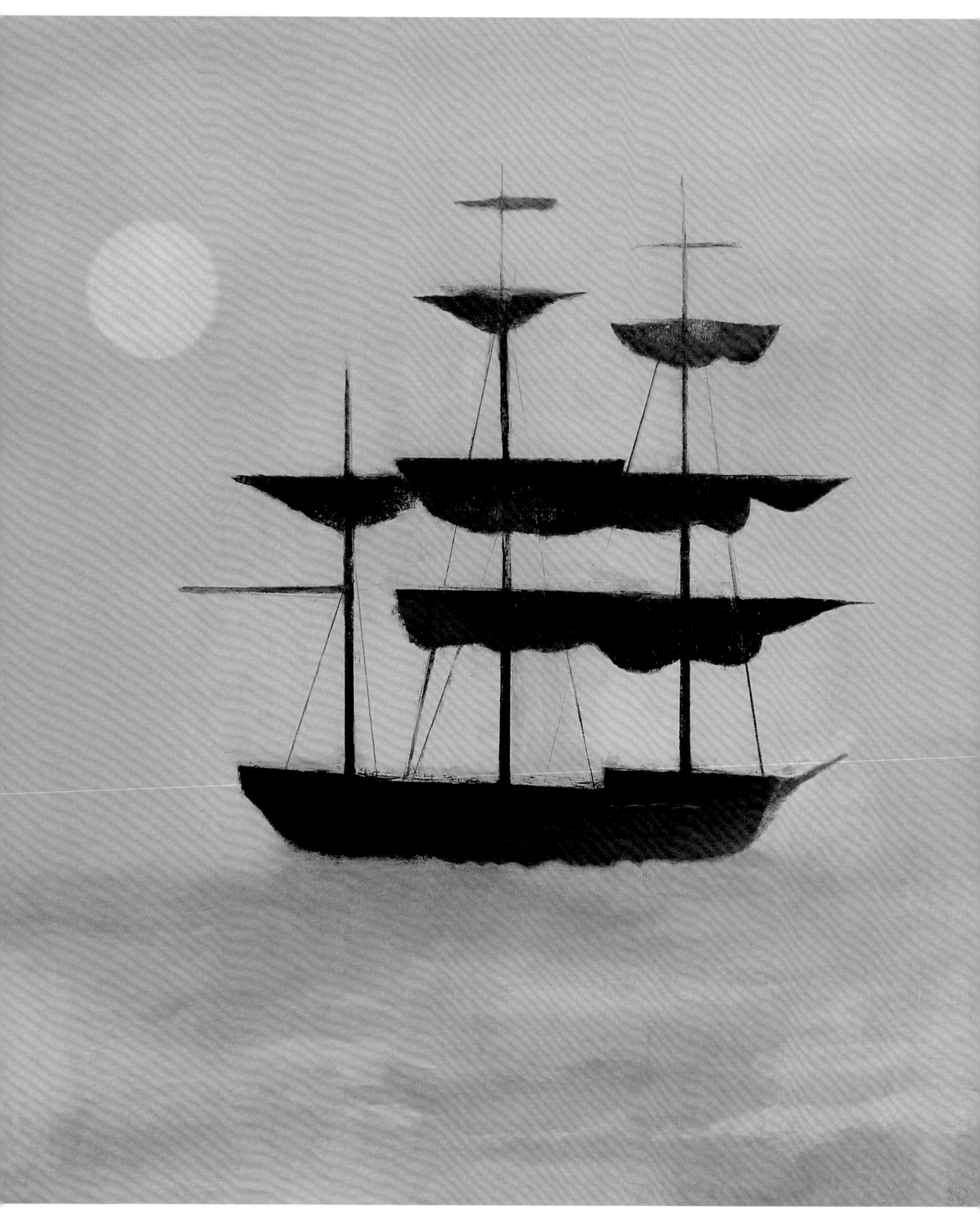

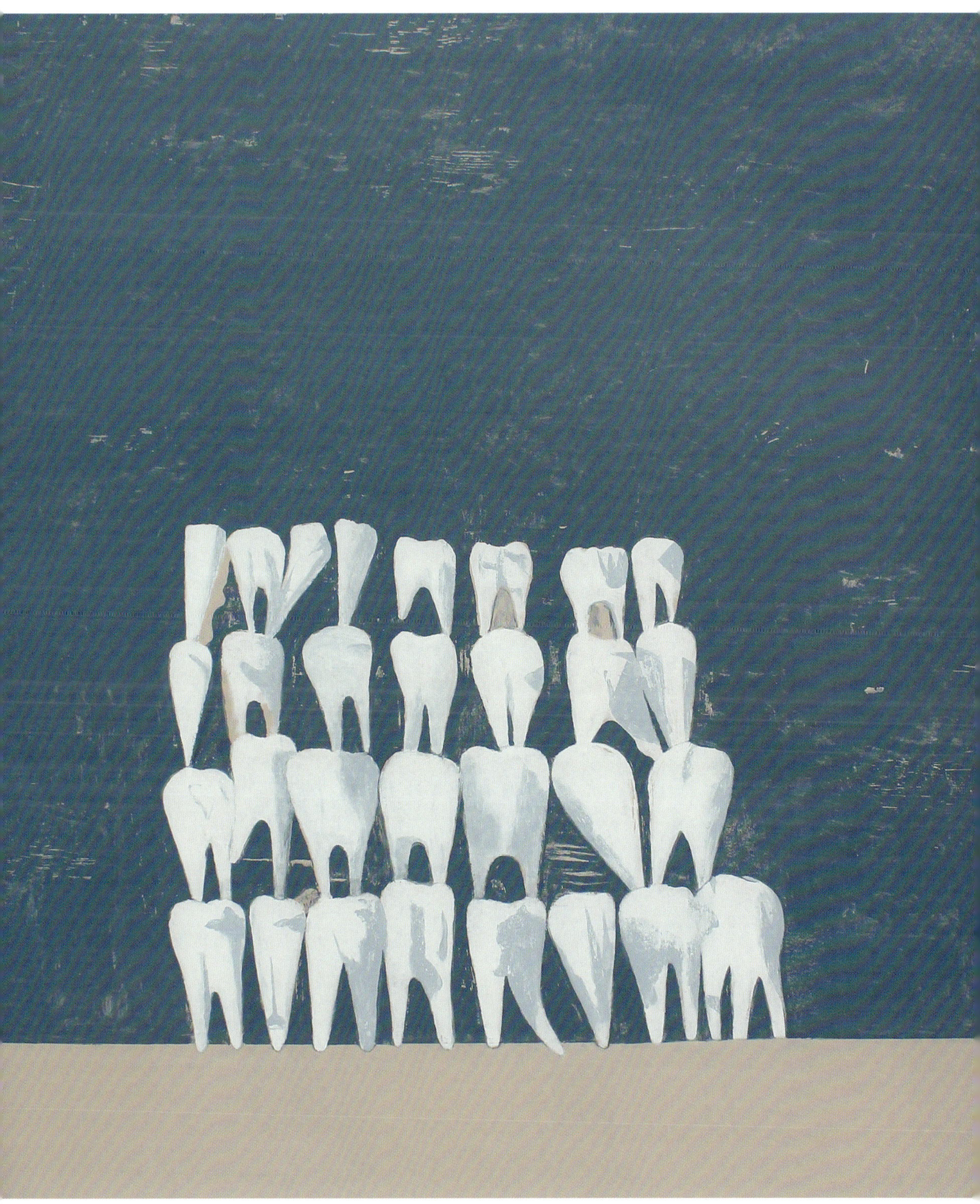

Jeffrey Gibson

—

FM: When did the climate change? When did "this moment" become this moment?

Gibson: "This moment" has been in the making for centuries and I think long before recorded history. The root of this moment is human nature. It takes a tremendous amount of energy to be compassionate, patient, to listen intently, to speak thoughtfully, and unfortunately it can be easier to react emotionally, to try and sabotage the other, to silence the other, to rid the other, in hopes of establishing one's own agenda.

AC: In an age where consumer capitalism constantly promotes the dream of expressing yourself, hasn't art become central to supporting and maintaining that power structure? However radical its messages are on the surface—isn't art underneath really constantly promoting the idea of self-expression and so promoting consumer capitalism? So maybe it's part of the problem?

Gibson: I don't agree entirely. There are many artists who are expressing themselves and their views, but remain unknown to the public. It sounds like you are referring to the commercial art world. The art world shares many other and different concerns than individual artists. There are moments in an artist's career that are less commercial than others and I believe really good artists struggle with trying to not do what you are suggesting and try to maintain a practice that is not entirely product oriented and commercial.

AD: What is "real" in your practice—your way of working, your medium, your social, professional, material, cultural, political relationships, your proximity to institutions? And what is sustainable? Do the two categories (real and sustainable) overlap, and to what extent?

Gibson: What is "real," or perceived to be real, is often personal. When that moment moves on, there is a performance of what is/was considered "real." The performance is not sustainable. For me, real and sustainable can overlap. It's a challenge, but ultimately, I think that acknowledging the real, present, and complicated environment that surrounds us allows an artist to continue to transform over time. There is nothing not "real" in my practice.

GC: Museums and cultural organizations once perceived as "pure" white boxes free of bias, are now being pushed to reckon with their own privilege and political baggage. As artists increasingly explore the meaning of "realness" in their work, I wonder how you negotiate the political context in which your work is inserted when it enters the museum.

Gibson: The idea that museums and cultural institutions are free of bias ceased to exist for me, personally, very early on. I did not see people like myself represented very often, or the representations of Indigenous people were included with a narrow focus. It became important for me to insert myself into the context of museums in hopes that younger generations could see some version of themselves represented, to open things up a bit. Now, I realize that once you are represented in an institutional context, there are many things beyond your control. I have to do my best to manage that representation, to maintain my voice, even if public response is out of my control.

MW: The magician Karl Germain said that "conjuring is the only honest profession: a magician promises to deceive and does." And Picasso said, "We all know that Art is not truth. Art is a lie that makes us realize truth." In our current state, where there is no "truth," and "facts" have become a matter of opinion, how can artists wake us up from this unpleasant dream? How can you help us see the world and each other through a lens of hope, trust, and humanity?

Gibson: Everyone should try to help each other wake up, not just artists. We need to create physical, psychological, and philosophical spaces for people to develop themselves without the threat of being taken advantage of. A strong artwork can do this by allowing a viewer to engage with any number of experiences and ideas, provided the viewer feels welcomed and included, not spoken down to and intimidated. Artists should take into consideration who they are speaking to, and do so in ways that support those audiences. Both artists and the general public do not consider the relationship between the medium and the message enough.

CG: How do you hold on to something so no one can take it away? Your beliefs? Your body? Your love? What tethers us here?

Gibson: As much as I'd love to think that there is a way to hold on to something so no one could take it away, I know this is an impossibility and would cause a continuous state of anxiety for me and those around me. We all have to work hard for equality, safety, humanity, and justice and fight for it at every level in the face of inequality, danger, inhumanity, the unjust, and apathy. Losing these things has the ability to silence and erase anyone. When we recognize that someone is traumatized and suffering we need to step out of our comfort zones and offer help.

ES: Public health physicians distinguish between narrative compassion (where one or two or three people are at risk) and statistical compassion (where thousands or millions are at risk). We're fairly good at the first, and have many occasions to strengthen our capacity through daily acts of friendship and from reading literature. We're terrible at the second, and have almost no training in strengthening our feeble abilities in this region. To what extent can the medium you work in invite, or carry out, acts of narrative compassion and statistical compassion?

Gibson: I allow for a great deal of subjectivity in my work in hopes that it will speak specifically to others who may have a shared background. I return to my goal of representation of the "other" and using my own subjectivity to create spaces for other peoples' "other." It is important for people to feel that they are not invisible, or silenced. I hope that my inclusion in a public and cultural context will have impact beyond a small number of people. I now see that there are many more Indigenous artists and curators working in similar ways. I see us as a community that extends each other's communities beyond established borders.

***SPEAK TO ME SO THAT I CAN UNDERSTAND*, 2018**
p. 194–5

***Clown Witness*, 2018**
pp. 196

***PEOPLE LIKE US*, 2018**
p. 197

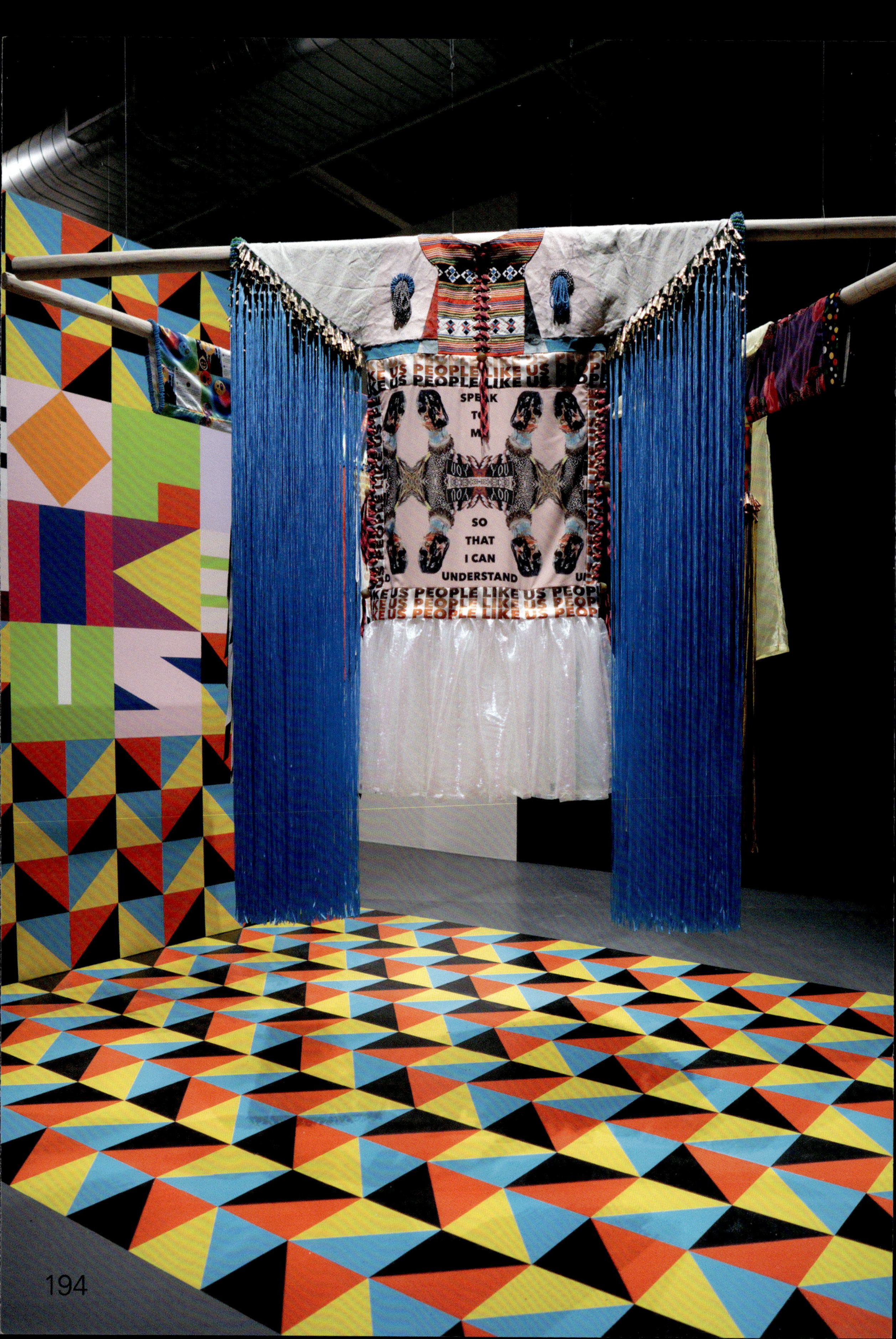
US PEOPLE LIKE US
US PEOPLE LIKE US
SO
THAT
I CAN
UNDERSTAND
US PEOPLE LIKE US
US PEOPLE LIKE US

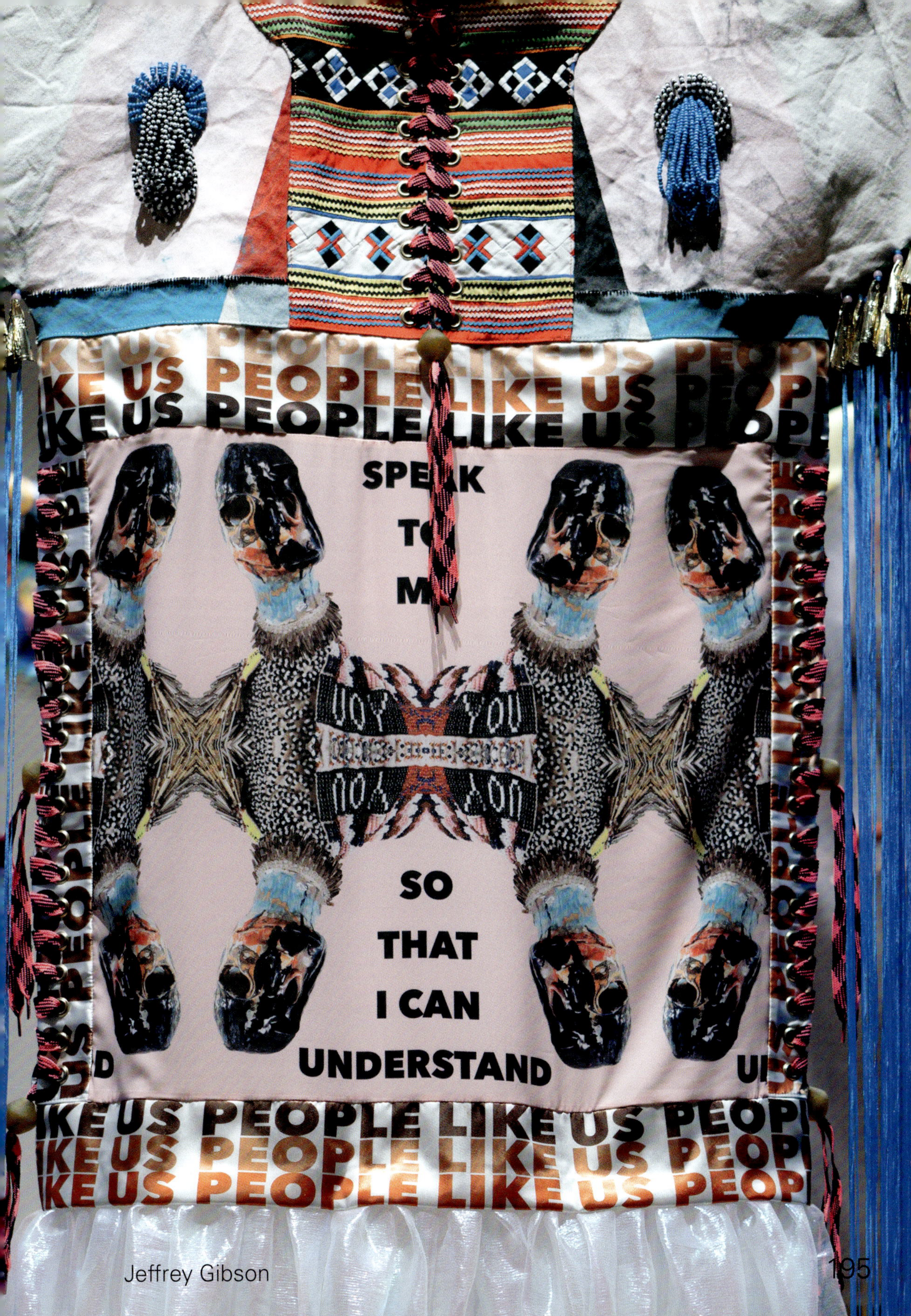
SPEAK
TO
ME
SO
THAT
I CAN
UNDERSTAND

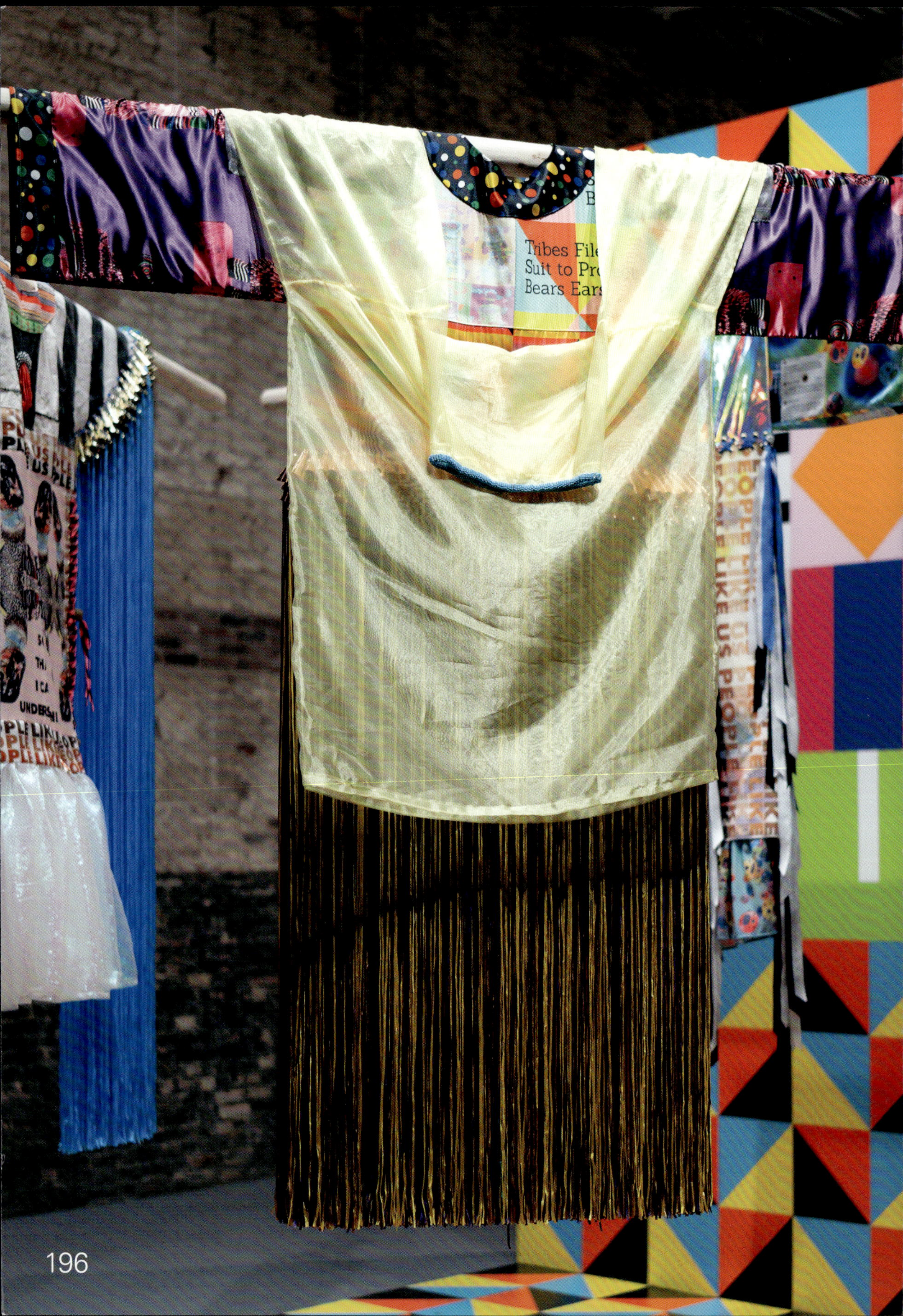
Tribes File
Suit to Pr
Bears Ear

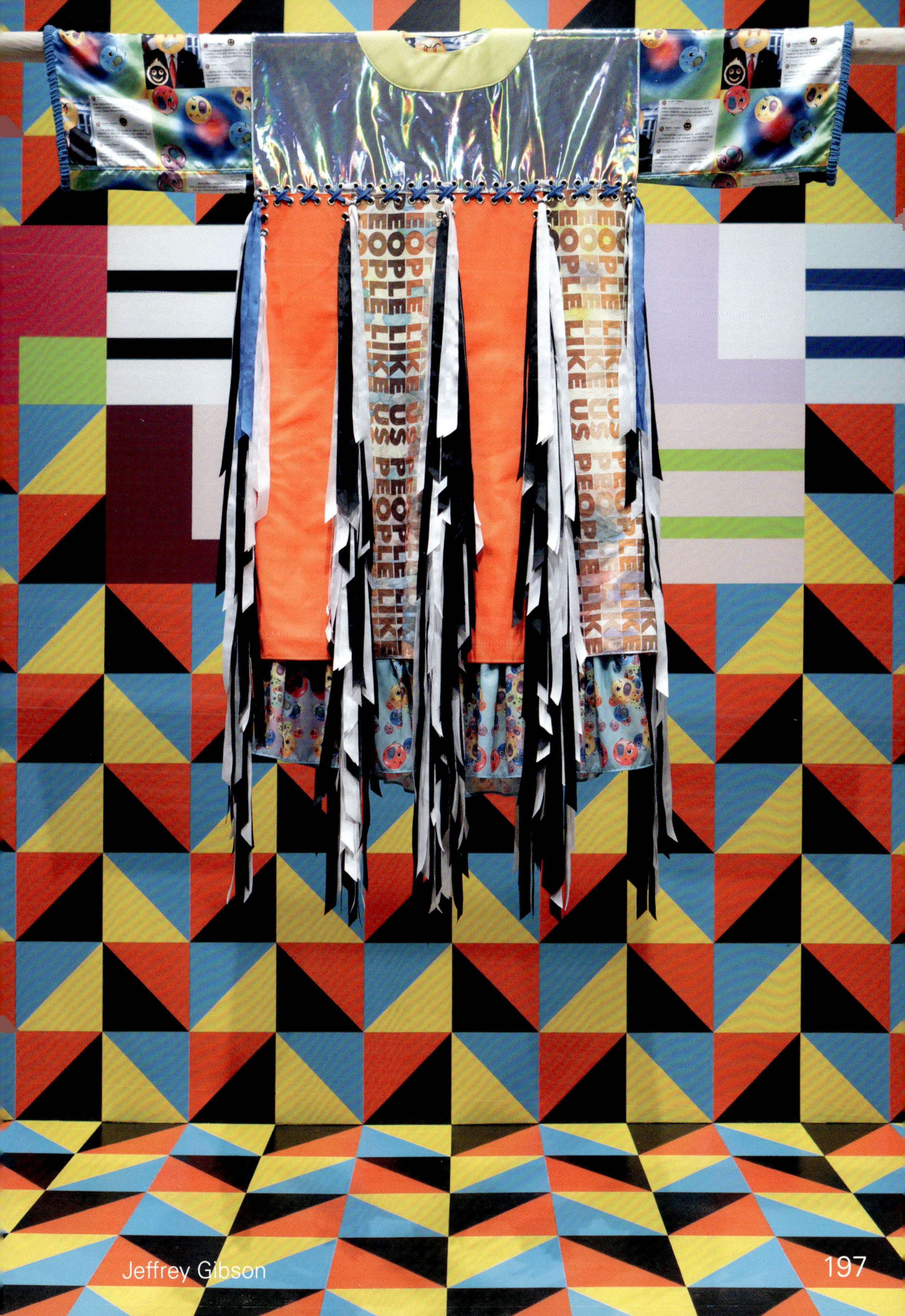
PEOPLE LIKE US PEOPLE LIKE
PEOPLE LIKE US PEOPLE LIKE

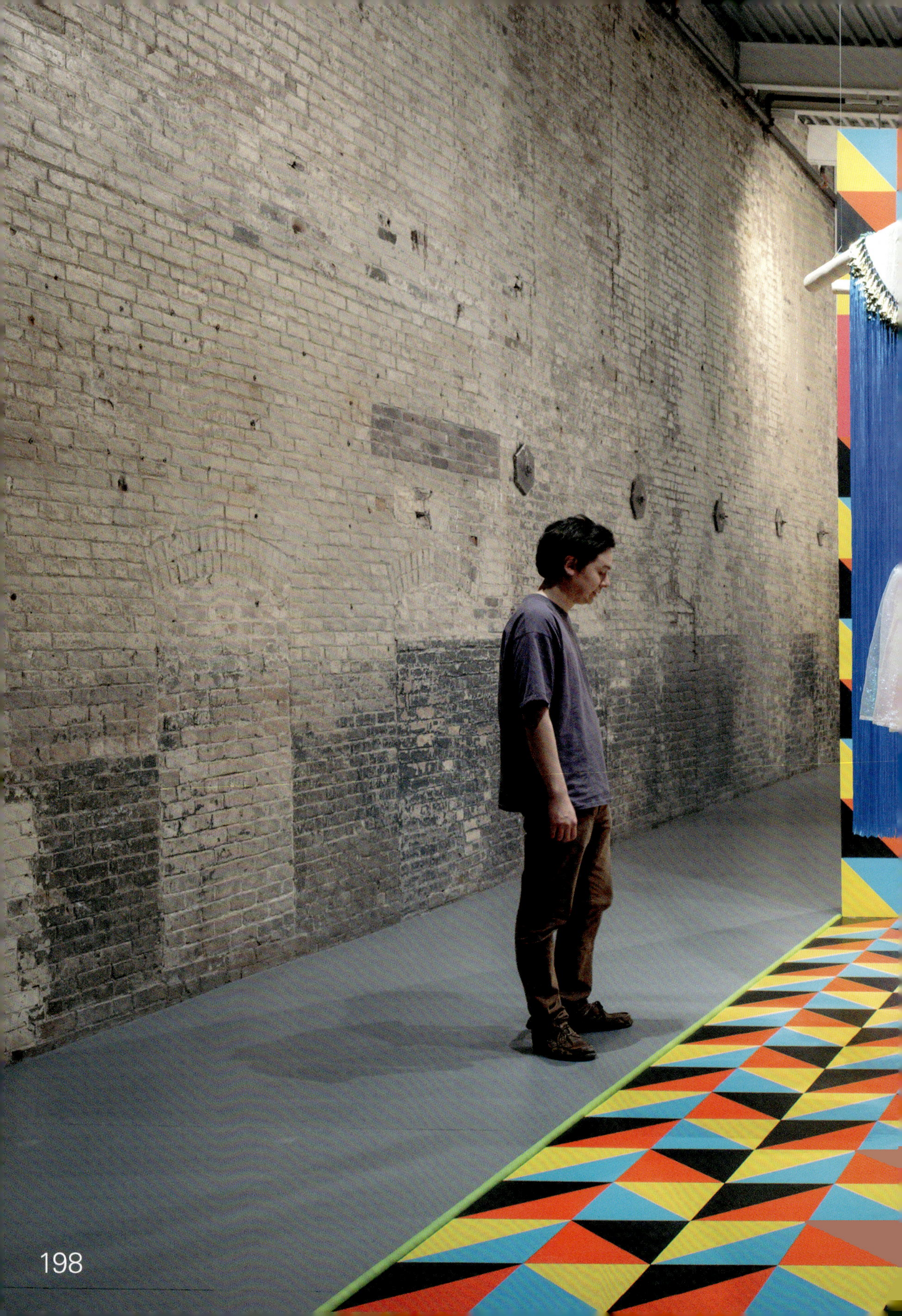

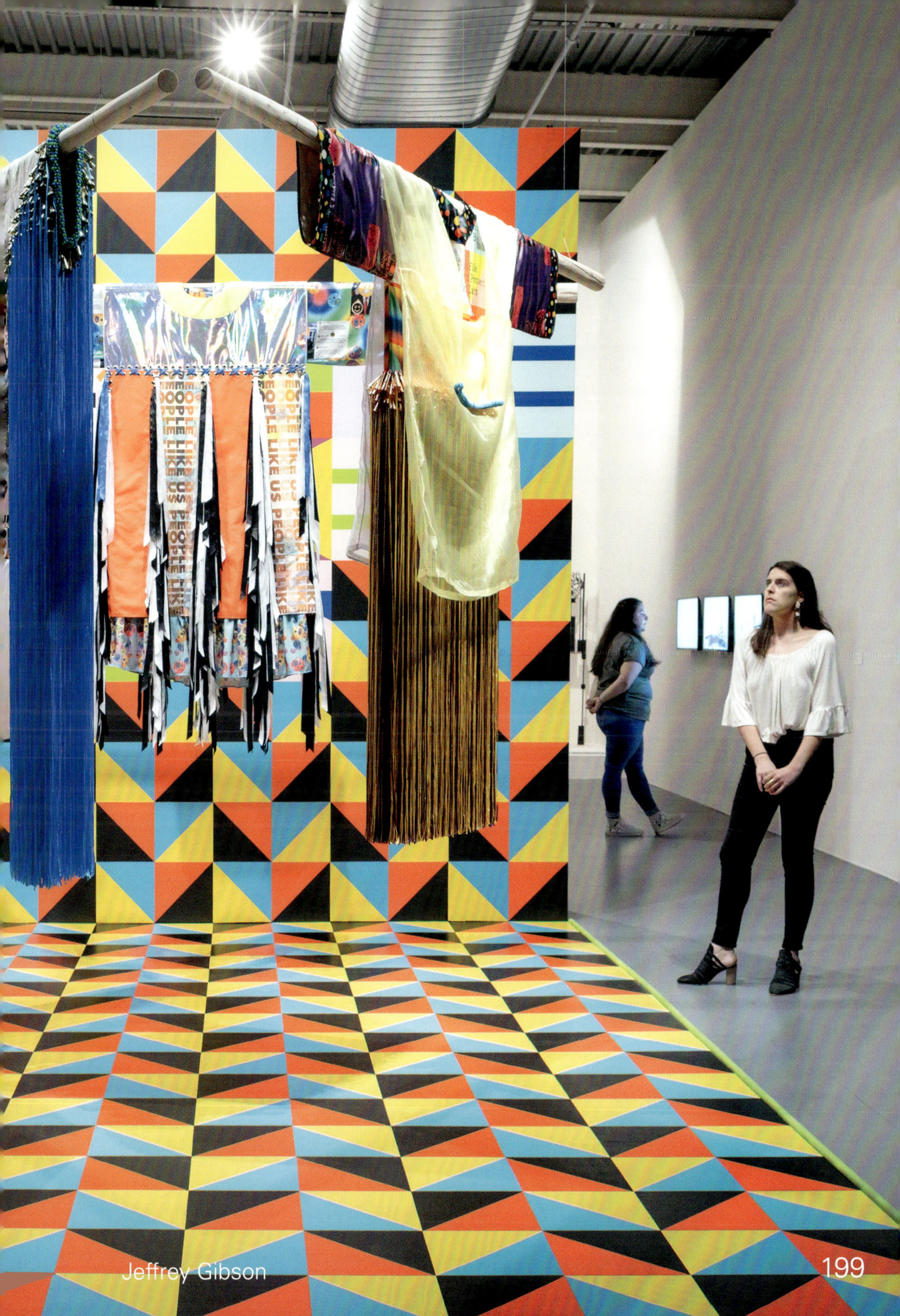
PEOPLE LIKE US PEOPLE LIKE

Jennifer Karady

—

FM: When did the climate change? When did "this moment" become this moment?

Karady: In 2002, the Iraq war was sold to the American public on the basis of a falsehood—that Saddam Hussein possessed weapons of mass destruction and was developing nuclear weapons. This mainstream deployment of what we now call "fake news" resulted in the destabilization of the region, over a million deaths, the flight of refugees, and over a trillion American taxpayer dollars spent.

AC: In an age where consumer capitalism constantly promotes the dream of expressing yourself, hasn't art become central to supporting and maintaining that power structure? However radical its messages are on the surface—isn't art underneath really constantly promoting the idea of self-expression and so promoting consumer capitalism? So maybe it's part of the problem?

Karady: Art as a commodity remains relatively marginal and is rarely part of the broader conversation: it exists as an elite cultural phenomenon. Some of the best art undermines the commodification of self-expression and power. My project, *Soldiers' Stories from Iraq and Afghanistan*, focuses on the aftermath of two wars fought in the name of capitalism and seeks to illuminate the lingering challenges that 2.8 million returning veterans face in becoming civilians again.

AD: What is "real" in your practice—your way of working, your medium, your social, professional, material, cultural, political relationships, your proximity to institutions? And what is sustainable? Do the two categories (real and sustainable) overlap, and to what extent?

Karady: In *Soldiers' Stories*, I collaborate with veterans to create staged narrative photographs that reveal how their experiences of war infiltrate their daily civilian lives. By interviewing people over time and engaging them in the interpretation of their stories, a real, often lasting relationship develops. Even though the photograph is a meticulously choreographed scene, there is an experiential aspect to the photo shoot. The process is intended to be helpful for the veteran. He/she enacts a pose or action from his/her chosen memory, in uniform, within a safe space, often in his/her everyday environment, surrounded by family and friends.

To maintain the truthfulness of the staged moment and the authenticity of the veteran subject's participation, there is no digital alteration. My images are shot on film, have a tangible, physical presence and function beyond the exhibition space, particularly as objects in the veterans' homes that invite conversation.

GC: Museums and cultural organizations once perceived as "pure" white boxes free of bias, are now being pushed to reckon with their own privilege and political baggage. As artists increasingly explore the meaning of "realness" in their work, I wonder how you negotiate the political context in which your work is inserted when it enters the museum.

Karady: *Soldiers' Stories* was conceived to speak to a wide audience of both civilians and veterans. This project aims to create opportunities for dialogue and understanding between these audiences. The work activates non-traditional, diverse audiences to interact with traditional art spaces that are situated in areas with a significant veterans' community.

I remain optimistic that this project can open people's minds by challenging assumptions and expectations; by encouraging people to empathize and care about a war that often feels distant and far away; and by helping them better understand both the conditions of these particular conflicts and their hidden costs here at home.

MW: The magician Karl Germain said that "conjuring is the only honest profession: a magician promises to deceive and does." And Picasso said, "We all know that Art is not truth. Art is a lie that makes us realize truth." In our current state, where there is no "truth," and "facts" have become a matter of opinion, how can artists wake us up from this unpleasant dream? How can you help us see the world and each other through a lens of hope, trust, and humanity?

Karady: I am interested in revealing an interior/internal, emotional truth through the fictional space of my staged photographs. The collision or collapse of the soldier's world and the civilian world enables the viewer to glimpse a fragment of what is going on in the soldier's mind, evoking the psychology of life after war, and the challenges, both large and small, that adjustment to the home front entails. The photographs reveal something invisible and unconscious—how it can feel to live in two different realities at once and how the past can infiltrate the present—whether in the form of a flashback, a memory, a dream or an instinct. A psychiatrist at the National Center for PTSD wrote to me that "the pictures seemed more true than true stories or literal pictures ever could."

CG: How do you hold on to something so no one can take it away? Your beliefs? Your body? Your love? What tethers us here?

Karady: Human relationships ground us and our shared vulnerabilities in this world. The stories we tell, about ourselves and others, represent our beliefs and connect us to others who might identify directly or be moved enough to empathize.

ES: Public health physicians distinguish between narrative compassion (where one or two or three people are at risk) and statistical compassion (where thousands or millions are at risk). We're fairly good at the first, and have many occasions to strengthen our capacity through daily acts of friendship and from reading literature. We're terrible at the second, and have almost no training in strengthening our feeble abilities in this region. To what extent can the medium you work in invite, or carry out, acts of narrative compassion and statistical compassion?

Karady: During my initial research to develop *Soldiers' Stories, I read Odysseus in America* (2002) by Dr. Jonathan Shay, a VA psychiatrist, who calls for artists to participate in "the circle of communalization," a social process essential to the healing of individual veterans. He writes, "It is impossible to overstate the importance of the arts in creating supportive social movements that permit trauma to have voice and the voice to be heard, believed and remembered." I still believe this is at the heart of my work.

The careful, collaborative process of working with each veteran to make a photograph takes between one month and four months, and is in itself, an act of narrative compassion. When presented, the photographs and the stories attest to a personal connection forged between subject and photographer that is rooted in mutual respect, trust, and empathy. The larger project, which as of 2018 consists of twenty-one photographs, asks viewers to extrapolate compassion for the individuals in the photographs to a generational group of millions, going beyond faceless statistics. I do think about the individual stories as archetypes—each is one example of many others like it.

Former Staff Sergeant Andrew Davis, 75th Ranger Regiment, U.S. Army, veteran of Operation Iraqi Freedom and Operation Enduring Freedom, with wife, Jodie, and Iraq war veterans and friends Tom and Andy; Saratoga Springs, NY, October 2009

p. 202

Former Specialist Shelby Webster, 24th Transportation Company, 541st Maintenance Battalion, U.S. Army, veteran of Operation Iraqi Freedom, with children, Riley, Dillin and Sidnie, brother Delshay, and uncle Derek; Omaha Natlon Reservation, NE, October 2010

p. 203

Former Specialist Lucero Morales, 25th Transportation Company, 25th Infantry Division, U.S. Army, veteran of Operation Iraqi Freedom, with children Emma and Nicolas; Azusa, CA, June 2015

pp. 204–5

Staff Sergeant Kyle Winjum, Explosive Ordnance Disposal Technician, U.S. Marine Corps, veteran of Operation Enduring Freedom and Operation Iraqi Freedom, with fellow Marines; Twentynine Palms, CA, April 2014

p. 206

Former Specialist Brittny Gillespie, 139th Military Police Company, 16th MP Brigade, U.S. Army, veteran of Operation Iraqi Freedom, with Volunteers of America-Los Angeles Battle Buddy Elizabeth Saucedo and friend Corey; Los Angeles, CA, February 2014

p. 207

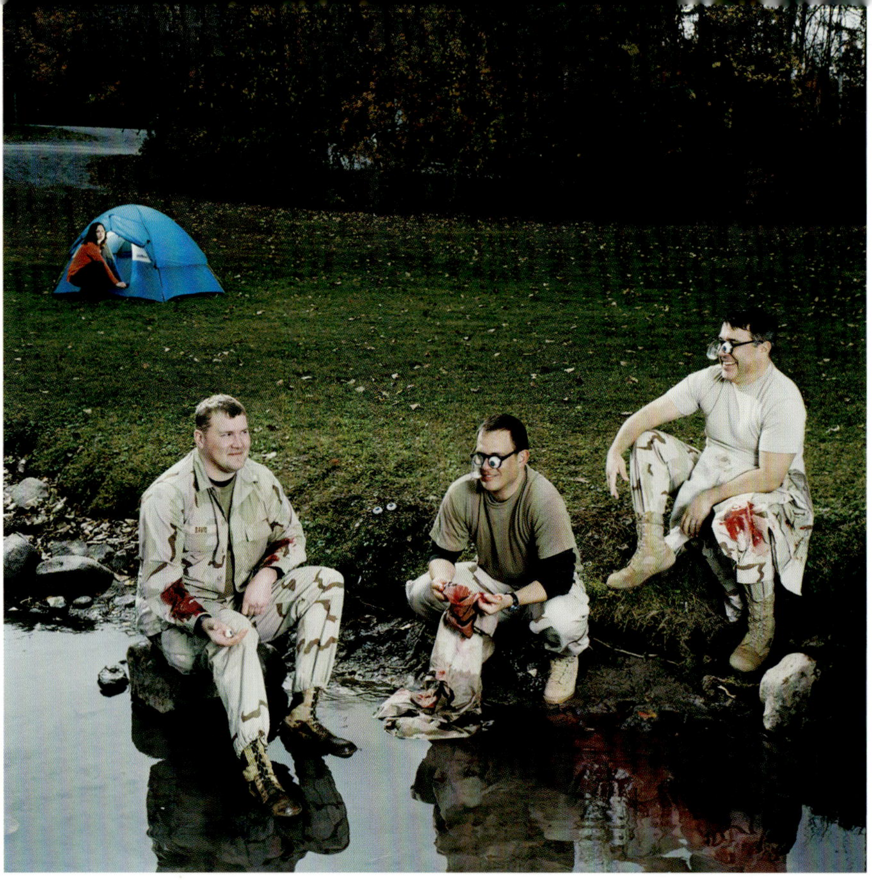

At the beginning of the war, my mortar section and a company of rangers were sent to Haditha. There is a hydroelectric dam about nine kilometers long on the Euphrates River that was rumored to be laced with explosives. If it blew, it would flood the Euphrates floodplain, keeping us out of Baghdad. It was supposed to be a two-hour mission, and we ended up in a thirteen-day firefight. // It was about day five when Jeremy, one of my mortar gun-leaders, was hit. It was the middle of the day and hot as hell. There was a wall on the front of the top of the dam and a wall in the back. We were on the backside, and we started making shelters to protect us from the harsh sun. We placed our rain ponchos on the wall of the dam, secured them with rocks and stretched them to the ground, creating a little tent. I told my soldiers constantly: "Don't fucking stand up, you're a silhouette, you're on top of this dam, they can see everything you're doing, right?" But since the artillery hadn't hit anywhere close to us in a few days no one thought that anything was going to happen. // Jeremy and I were literally sharing a poncho, and one of the rocks holding it in place fell down. Jeremy stood up to fix it, we heard a whistle, and he was laid out. His eye was just kind of dangling and it was the craziest thing I've ever seen. I quickly called for the medic. In the meantime we stopped the bleeding as much as we could, put his eye in his head, and covered his head. The medic came down, and I started gathering my men to move once the medic took over. The last thing I remember was looking at Jeremy and seeing the medic, and he went like that [makes gesture of sliding hand across throat], and I just thought, "Holy fuck, all these guys were best friends." I wasn't even worried about me anymore. // After that, I told my soldiers to get down to the water and clean the blood off their clothes. They had their buddy's blood on them, and we weren't getting new clothes anytime soon. You can't be wandering around with your friend's blood because it ruins morale. We started joking about it, making eyesight jokes, which sounds morbid to your average person, but it's the only way to get through it. Looking back, things like that were just sick, but everyone laughed at the time. It gave new meaning to the fight; everyone got more careful. I always think about all of us sitting in a circle with our helmets and Kevlar on, and it was hot and there was blood everywhere, and just making jokes. It was so primitive and so sick but it was what helped get everybody back to normal. // I was an avid backpacker and camper before I went into the military. I was an Eagle Scout, I was always camping, and I won't set foot under a tent now. When I think about it, I honestly don't know if what happened on that dam is the reason, but I won't anymore. My wife has probably asked me a hundred times to go camping. I don't even like sleeping away from my base—I mean, my house.

While Andy Davis's friend and colleague Jeremy survived his injuries, he is blind in both eyes and sustained some brain damage. Andy ran for the Minnesota House of Representatives in 2006 and narrowly lost the election. He is the cofounder of a nonprofit that assists student veterans on campus based at the University of Minnesota. At the time of the photograph, Andy worked for the New York State Division of Veterans' Affairs in Albany, NY. This text was transcribed and edited from interviews conducted by Jennifer Karady in July 2009.

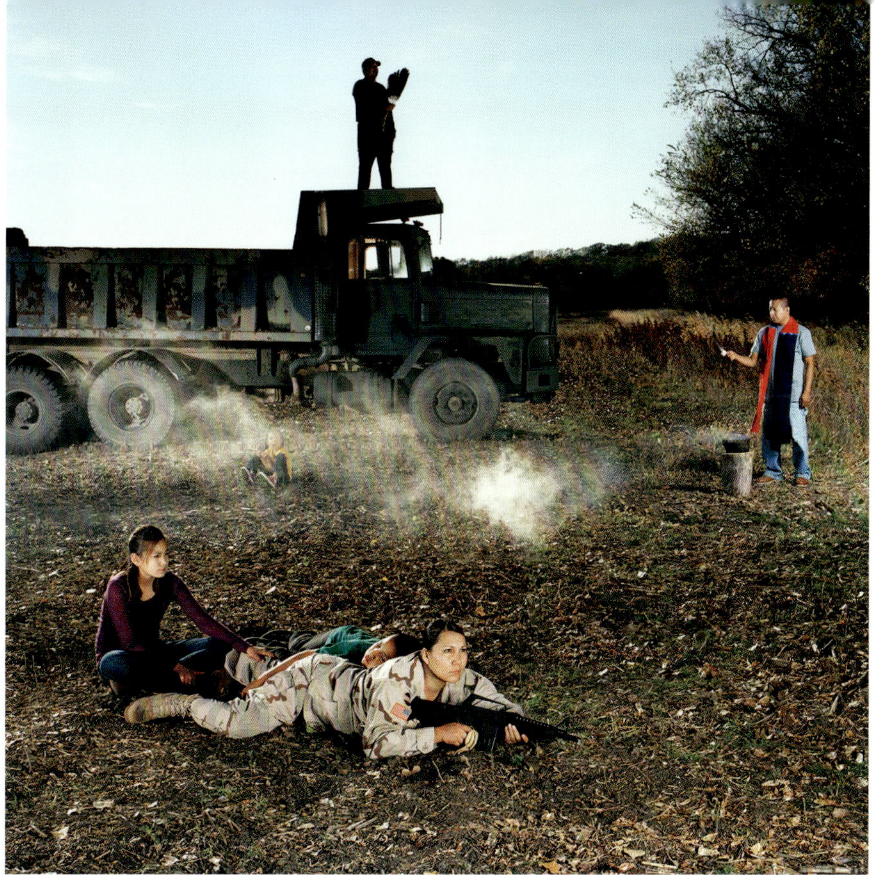

I was 20 years old when I joined the Army. I was a single mom and I had two babies that I left—a two-year-old and a three-year-old. When I found out that I was deploying, I remember crying on the phone to my dad, "I don't want to go." I didn't join just to join. I joined the military thinking I would give my kids a better life. // I drove a PLS [palletized load system truck]. We transported all sorts of supplies from Kuwait into Iraq when there was nothing there. Whatever they needed, we hauled. The funny thing about it is that we weren't armored. We only had flak vests and our little M16s. // When we convoyed into Iraq for the first time, it was probably two o'clock in the morning. I remember being so tired and seeing explosions and thinking, "Wow, this is like the movies. This isn't happening." Then we started getting attacked. We had a big convoy of about 20 trucks. We stopped and my squad leader, Sergeant Jackson, jumped out and said, "Be ready, lock and load!" At that point I thought, "How am I going to shoot and drive?" I remember shaking and almost freezing up. And my TC [passenger and vehicle commander], Gabe, said, "It's OK, Web. It's OK. I've been through this already." He was trying to reassure me because I was terrified. // They had us line up all the trucks in four rows. Sergeant Jackson told us to get out of our trucks just in case. So we were in the sand, lying in the prone position just waiting. Then we hear gunfire and I remember thinking, "What am I going to do, I'm a girl." I lay there crying to myself, "God, please, I don't want to die. I want to go home to my kids." I was so scared. It was so hard. // I'm Native American and I believe in my culture. I believe in my Omaha ways. I said a little prayer to myself asking God to protect me and to watch over my babies if something were to happen to me. This feeling came over me and, I don't know if it was my subconscious or what, but I heard a voice that said, "It's going to be alright." I recognized that voice as my Grandpa Danny's voice. I was 10 when he passed, but I remember him—he was a good grandpa and always protective. // In this moment I also smelled cedar and we pray with cedar. When I smelled it, I took a deep breath and I smelled and smelled. I thought, "What the heck?" I looked around and asked Gabe, "Do you smell that?" He said, "No, I don't smell nothing." I could still see and hear tracer rounds and explosions and could feel the ground shake. But a feeling of calmness had come over me and I thought, "I can do this." When I called home and told my Dad that I smelled cedar, he cried. He said, "Well, we've been praying for you. We've been having meetings for you." // My Dad had my kids while I was gone. It seemed like during those two years I saw my kids probably one or two times. My kids are ten and eleven years old now and I had another baby after I got back. My youngest is now five years old and totally different compared to my older kids who have separation anxiety—they always have to know where I am. My youngest is more independent; she's her own kind of person. But the older two are always looking for me, asking, "Where's Mom?" And I say, "I'm right here."

At the time of the photograph, Shelby Webster was working as a probation officer at the Omaha Tribal Court. This text was transcribed and edited from interviews conducted by Jennifer Karady in August and October 2010.

I deployed to Iraq as a specialist with a transportation company. We provided security for other military convoys. One of the incidents that I have most in my head was on a day when all of the roads were black, which means that you're not able to go outside the wire to deliver anything unless it's necessary like water, food or ammunition. We were escorting a National Guard company on a road that people usually didn't take because it was dangerous. // We left around 4 am and we took a wrong turn, because of course we didn't know where we were going. So we went through the front of the camp when we were supposed to go through the back and we passed through this town, Najaf, where they have one of Iraq's holiest mosques. That morning, they had brought down two Marine helicopters, so everyone was on their toes. I was the TC [passenger and vehicle commander] in the first gun truck, and my friend was the driver and we had our gunner on the back. Normally when you went through a town it was full of people. But there was no one. I remember relaying the message, "There's something wrong here, keep your eyes open, be aware." As our last gun truck is coming into the town, we start hearing bullets flying everywhere. And I can see them. I can remember every detail, every scent. I can remember the faces that I saw—the Iraqis, everyone. I can tell you what they were wearing. I can remember their positions, where they were peeking from, the guns they were using. I remember seeing an RPG [rocket-propelled grenade] that went just inches from our window—the driver saw it too. We looked at each other thinking we're going to die and just kept shooting. We were issued seven magazines each and I don't even remember switching our magazines that fast. When we finally got out of the danger zone and pulled into the camp, there was no one behind us. So we radioed back—it turns out that one of the drivers had been killed and the TC crashed the truck. // It was a very hard day and it wasn't even over yet because after we drove into the camp, they blew up a fuel tank and we were hit for the rest of the night. We were stuck there for three days. We couldn't leave because we didn't have enough people so they called in the Marines to rescue us. // When I came back, I got married right away, we got pregnant, and then I got out of the Army a few months after I had my son. I was a stay-at-home mom and home schooled our kids. I'm Mexican so we always have to keep our house clean—laundry's made, food is ready, all of that good stuff. My ex-husband, he's in the military, but I was never part of anything with him, military-wise. I kind of felt like if I didn't see it, I didn't talk about it, it didn't happen. I suppressed all that. // I just started recently going to the VA and I told the therapist that all that I have trouble with now are balloons and Pillsbury cans. She asked what was wrong with balloons and Pillsbury cans. "Well they pop!" Let's say I'm making biscuits and gravy in the morning—it was one of my ex-husband's favorite breakfasts. My heart will start to race because I just know that I'm going to open that Pillsbury can any time now. I'll start doing everything else, making the gravy and sausage. Opening the can will be the last thing I do. I carefully peel a little piece of the wrapper, my hands start getting all sweaty, my heart starts to race. I'm clenching my eyes because I know it can pop in my hands because it has happened before. But I peel a little piece off of the can, and I throw it—it can land on the floor, it can land wherever—and I just run. And I scream. Then I hear the pop and I think, "It wasn't even that loud. Why do I make such a big deal of it?" I fight with myself, but I still can't open a Pillsbury can without having that fear. I tell myself, "You're at home, you're cooking. It's not dangerous." It's something so small yet it kind of triggers something so big from back then.

At the time of the photograph, Lucero Morales was studying history at Citrus College in Glendora, CA. This text was transcribed and edited from interviews conducted by Jennifer Karady in January 2014 and May 2015.

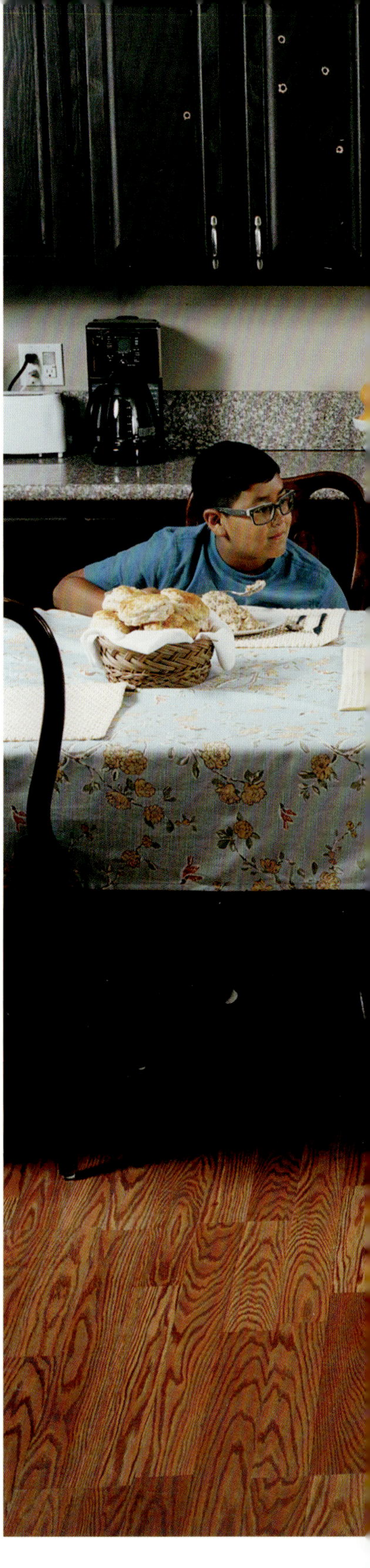

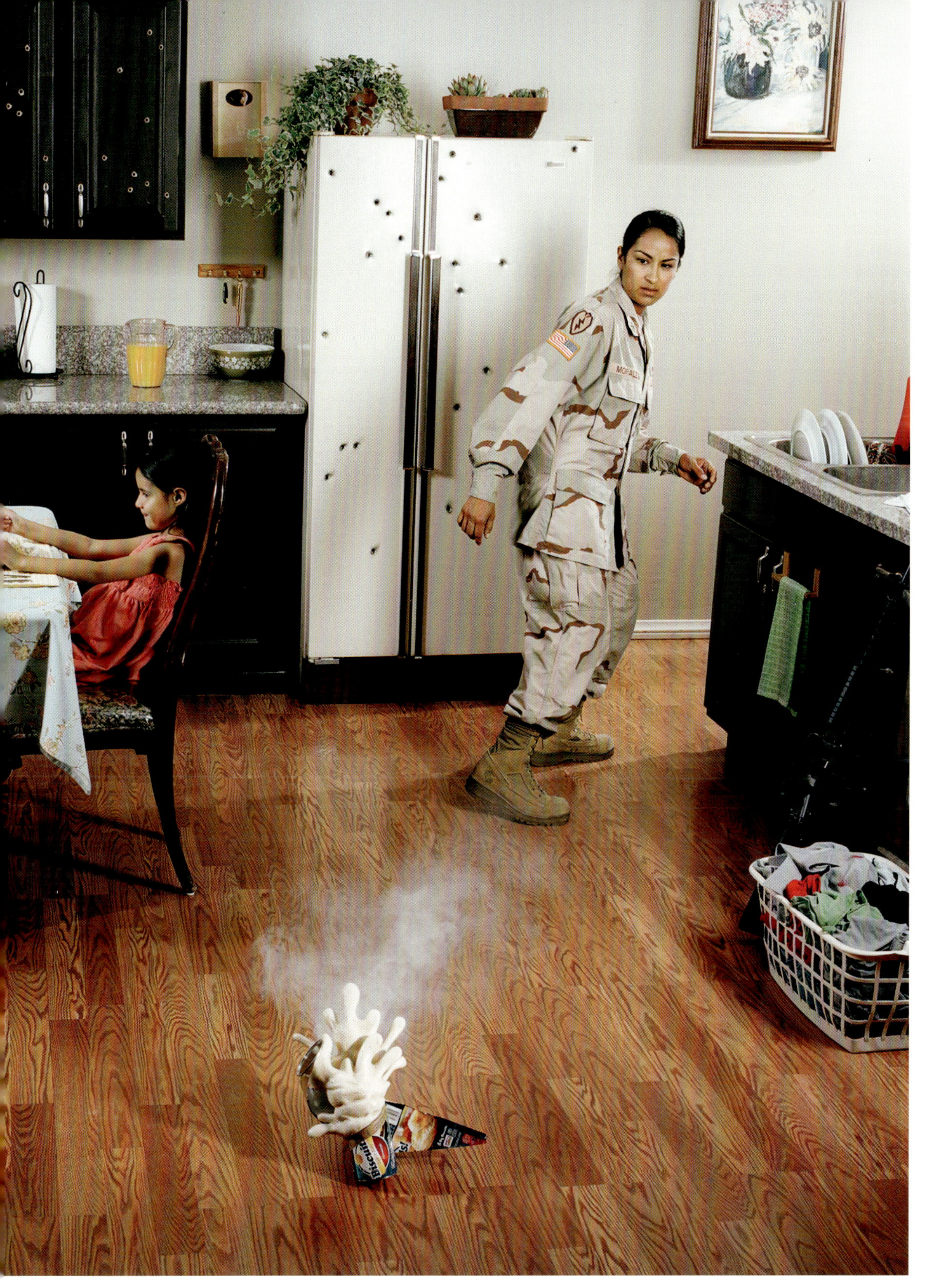

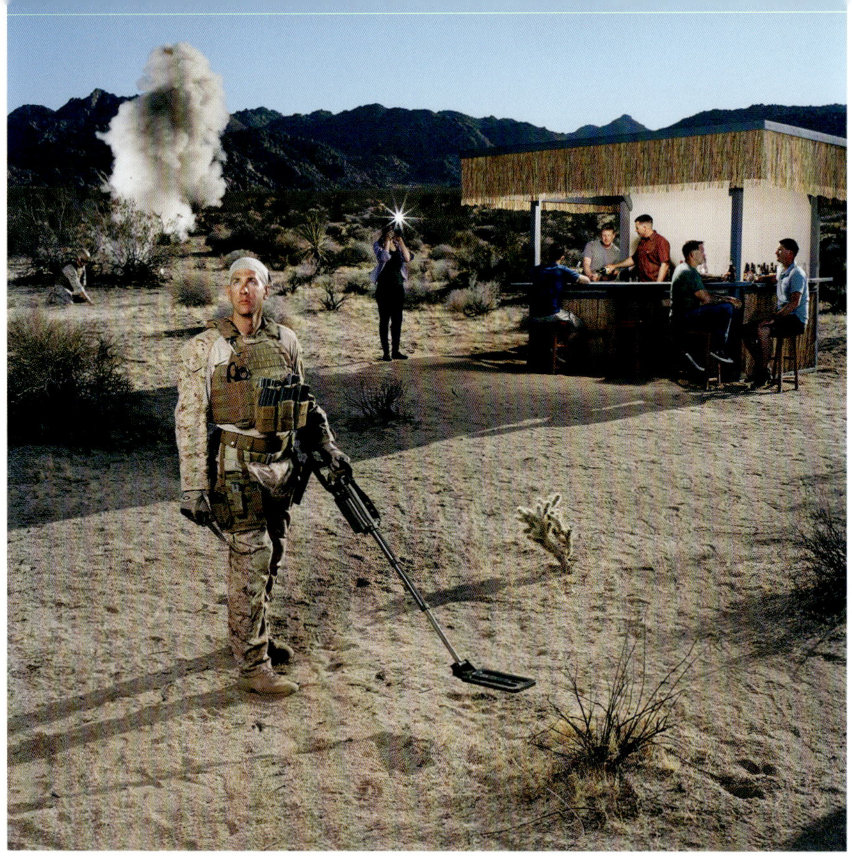

During my deployment in Afghanistan, we got information from one of our sources that there were improvised explosive devices [IED] set on a hilltop, so we went out looking for IEDs. We found two around eight o'clock that morning and set them off. We pretty much woke up the whole town because it was early. In our search, we went up the hill sweeping with our metal detectors. // My team leader, Jeremy, was in a little low area between a couple of trees. I was watching him investigate an area—he was kneeling down probably within five meters from it when it went off. Time slowed down when I saw the explosion. I saw the fireball and the blast wave come out and push the trees and the dust and the dirt out and I also watched it suck itself back in, creating a mushroom cloud. I saw the fragmentation flying up in the air, and it was white and it was red and it was orange and it turned yellow. It goes up white-hot and as it's coming down, it's cooling down. I was watching it change colors. It was a very intense experience for a brief moment but it seemed like forever. // I looked up and down at both of my arms and thought, "OK, I don't see any holes, I don't see any blood, I feel OK." I looked at my legs and did the same thing. Then I started getting up and yelled for Jeremy to make sure that he was OK. I heard him and I knew that he was at least coherent. Our third team member, Matt, was on the other side of the hill and he was OK too. // We all regrouped in our little safe area. My right ear was ringing, as was everybody else's. We calmed ourselves a little bit, we all smoked cigarettes. We replaced the batteries on our counter-measures equipment and we went back in. We had to do an investigation. I was scared shitless going back again. I was thinking, "What the fuck!?" My whole body was shaking as I was sweeping. But I kept calm enough to know, "This is part of the job. This is what we're doing. And this one's already gone off so it can't be too bad." // It was almost a year later—I was out in a bar with a bunch of my friends. People were taking pictures and one photograph flash caught my eye in the same manner that that IED had gone off. And I lost it. I was freaking out. I was wondering where my friends were. "Where am I? What am I doing? Is everybody OK?" I walked around the bar searching for my friends and picking them out. "OK, there's my friend—he's safe. There's my friend—he's safe. There's my friend—he's safe. There's his girlfriend—she's safe." I knew physically I was still in a bar but mentally and emotionally, I was back in Afghanistan. I saw the camera flash and my brain instantly saw that explosion flash, and it went back to seeing everything. // After that, I talked with my friend because he's been in some past experiences and he suggested that I go to see his therapist. I went the very next day. I'm glad that I did because the therapist I saw really helped me. // That's the only experience I've had with more or less being blown up so far. I hope it doesn't happen again, but I'm still on the job. I mean, there's still always the potential and possibility whether we have to go back to Iraq or Afghanistan or wherever else in the world.

At the time of the photograph, Kyle Winjum was an active duty Marine who was stationed at Twentynine Palms Marine Corps Air Ground Combat Center. He deployed to Kuwait in 2015 from Camp Pendleton and as of 2017, was promoted to Gunnery Sergeant in a deployable unit. This text was transcribed and edited from interviews conducted by Jennifer Karady in March 2014.

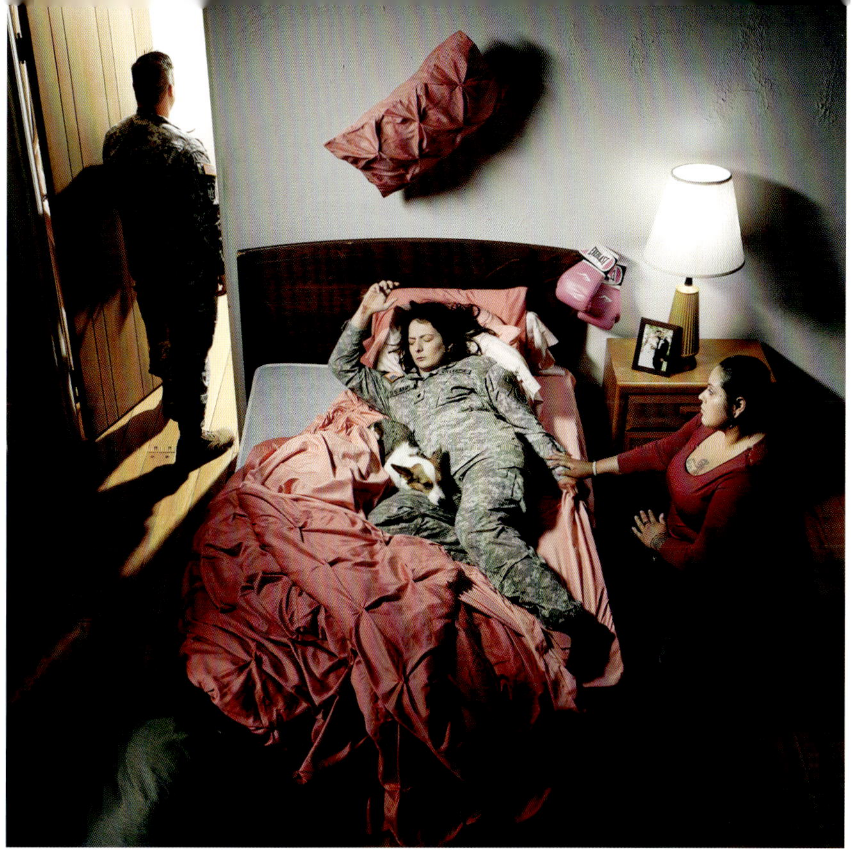

I served four years in the U.S. Army as a diesel mechanic. I deployed to Iraq from 2009-2010 where I also acted as a military police officer. // The biggest issue that I had was actually right before we deployed to Iraq. I was still new to the unit and didn't know a lot of people, so they invited me out. I thought, "OK, cool." We went out, had a good time, got back to the barracks, and one of the guys said, "Well, I'll walk you to your room." I grew up with all guys. That was normal for me. That's just what they do. They help you out and make sure you're safe. We have PINs on our doors, keypads to get in. I went in and closed my door and about five or ten minutes later I heard my door open. He had watched me put my PIN in. I was half-asleep already, a little bit drunk. He snuck into my room—my roommate wasn't home. I couldn't fight him off. He was probably about twice my size. I was in the shower for like three hours afterwards. By the time I went to talk to the NCO [non-commissioned officer], the guy was already spreading rumors that it was consensual. // The NCO kind of just looked at me funny, like it was a joke or something. I said, "I want to report a rape." And he said, "That's not what I've been hearing, and it's not that big of a deal, anyway. We're getting ready to deploy, we've got training to do. I don't have time to deal with this. No one would believe you anyway." It was pretty much a slap in the face. // When I deployed, we were all in one small compound, and I was with this guy for twelve months straight every day. It made it really hard to deal with the men in general. I had really bad panic attacks for a while. When I got home, I had night terrors really bad. I would wake up screaming, flailing around. I dreamt that someone was on top of me holding my throat, and I'd wake up freaking out, sweating and screaming, like I couldn't breathe. It's not as bad now, but I'd wake up and my knuckles would be all busted, bruised up. I'd be scratched up from hitting the headboard. Luckily at the time I was doing a lot of fight training, so they thought it was from me training and not from me punching my wall in my sleep. // At night I have my dog, Bella, so she helps. Any little noise or anything, she wakes me up. Honestly, I don't know, between her and my friend Liz, that's the only thing that's kept me from losing my shit altogether. When I got back from Iraq, Liz and I got really close. She was really good to talk to because she had a similar situation happen to her while we were deployed. // I got married when I got home. He knew about what happened. It's still scary when your wife's in bed next to you flailing around, or she starts crying for some random reason. I didn't think that I was good enough to get married. I didn't feel that it was fair, because I was still edgy, nervous and couldn't be 100 percent trusting. That ended up being a downfall, really, of my marriage.

At the time of the photograph, Brittny Gillespie was studying biology at Citrus College in Glendora, CA. She credited the help of Volunteers of America-Los Angeles, an organization that provides essential services to traumatized veterans. This text was transcribed and edited from interviews conducted by Jennifer Karady in January 2014. This photograph, funded by Getty Images, was used in a media campaign for VOA-LA that was designed by Fraser Communications.

Personal Effects (excerpts)

—

Solmaz Sharif

> Like guns and cars, cameras
> are fantasy-machines whose use is addictive.
> —Susan Sontag

I place a photograph of my uncle on my computer desktop, which means I learn to ignore it. He stands by a tank, helmet tilting to his right, bootlaces tightened as if stitching together a wound. Alive the hand brings up a cigarette we won't see him taste. Last night I smoked one on the steps outside my barn apartment. A promise I broke myself. He promised himself he wouldn't and did. I smell my fingers and I am smelling his. Hands of smoke and gunpowder. Hands that promised they wouldn't, but did.

How could she say
the things she does not
know. A poison

tipped arrow, she told
classmates at recess,
to the neck, hollow whistle

of it launched
from a blowgun
cutting the air between them.

According to most
definitions, I have never
been at war.

According to mine,
most of my life
spent there. Anthrax

in salt and pepper shakers,
patrol car windshields
with crosshairs painted over them,

some badge holding
my father's pocket contents
up to him and asking

where the cash is from.
The war in Iraq, I read,
is over now.

The last wheels gathering
into themselves
as they lift off

the sad tarmac. I say
begin. I say *end*
and you are to believe

this is what happens
I say *chew 40 times*
before swallowing, slime,

and you go home to mother,
press a dog tag to your temple,
press a gun to that,

the tag flowering
into your skull. Thank God
for all-weather floor mats

and the slope of my personal driveway
and beer cans that change
color to let me know

they are cold enough.
The full-sized cab
smelling of iron and Axe body spray.

In 2003, a man held a fistful
of blood and brains to a PBS camera
and yelled

is this the freedom
they want for us? It was from his friend's
head. They were marching

as they figured Americans do.
Between them, hardly three horsepower
and still we shot him.

We say the war is over, but still
the woman leans across
the passenger seat

my son, my son.
I wasn't there
so I can't know, can I?

His mother's bed.
A grief we don't attempt to CONSOLE.

I killed him she'll tell me
years later. Fuck

CELESTIAL GUIDANCE.

I killed him she'll say
in the midst of CIVIL AFFAIRS

he surprises, he arrives,
eyes taped shut, torso held together
by black thread, fridge-cold—

            grief is a CLOSED AREA
      CLUTTERed with his fork against the plate
and other forgotten musics.

The enlarged ID photo above her mantel
means I can know Amoo,
my dear COLLATERAL DAMAGE,

as only a state or a school might do,

each photo is an absence,
a thing gone, namely
a moment, sometimes cities,
a tour boat balanced
on a two-story home
miles from shore

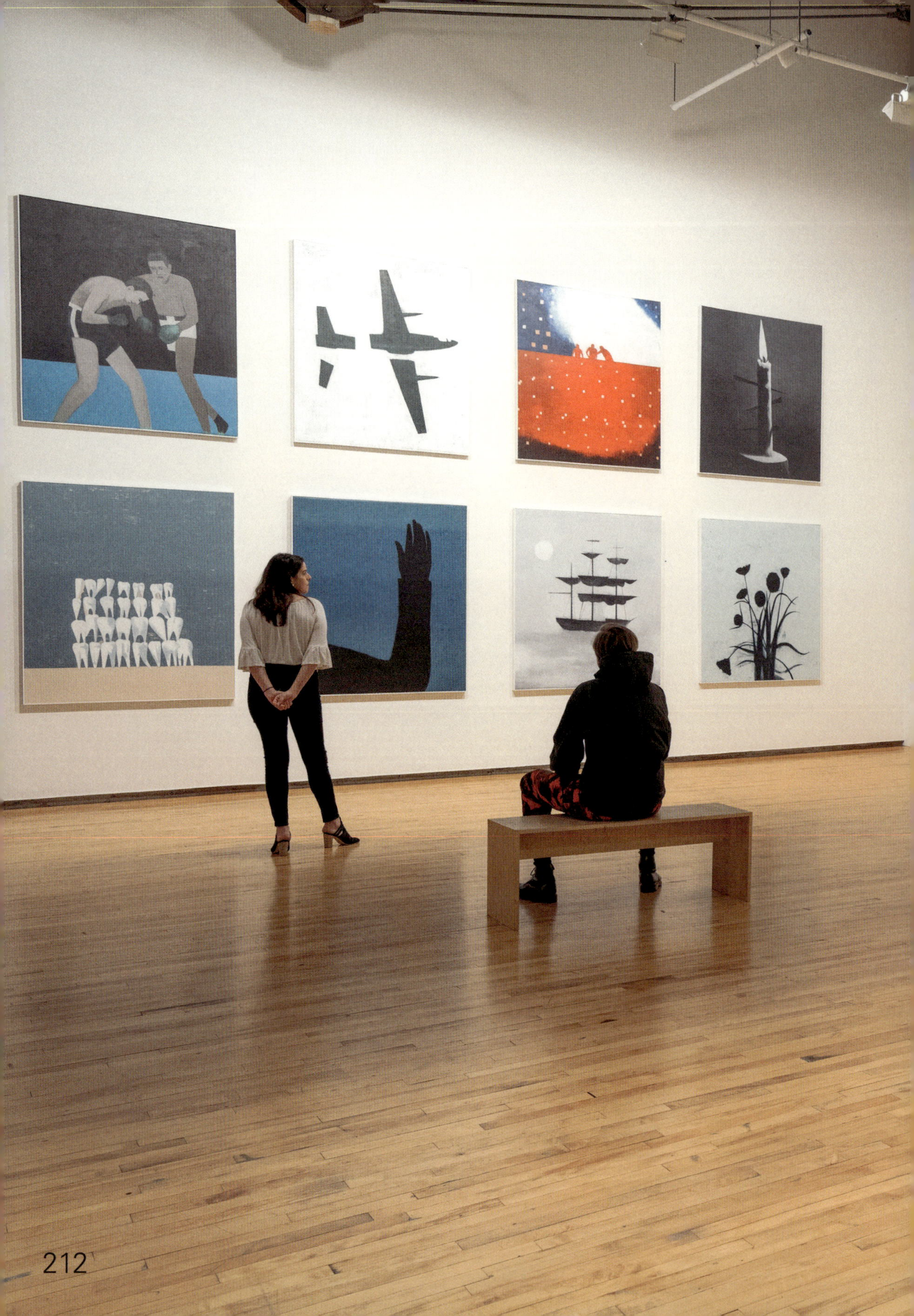

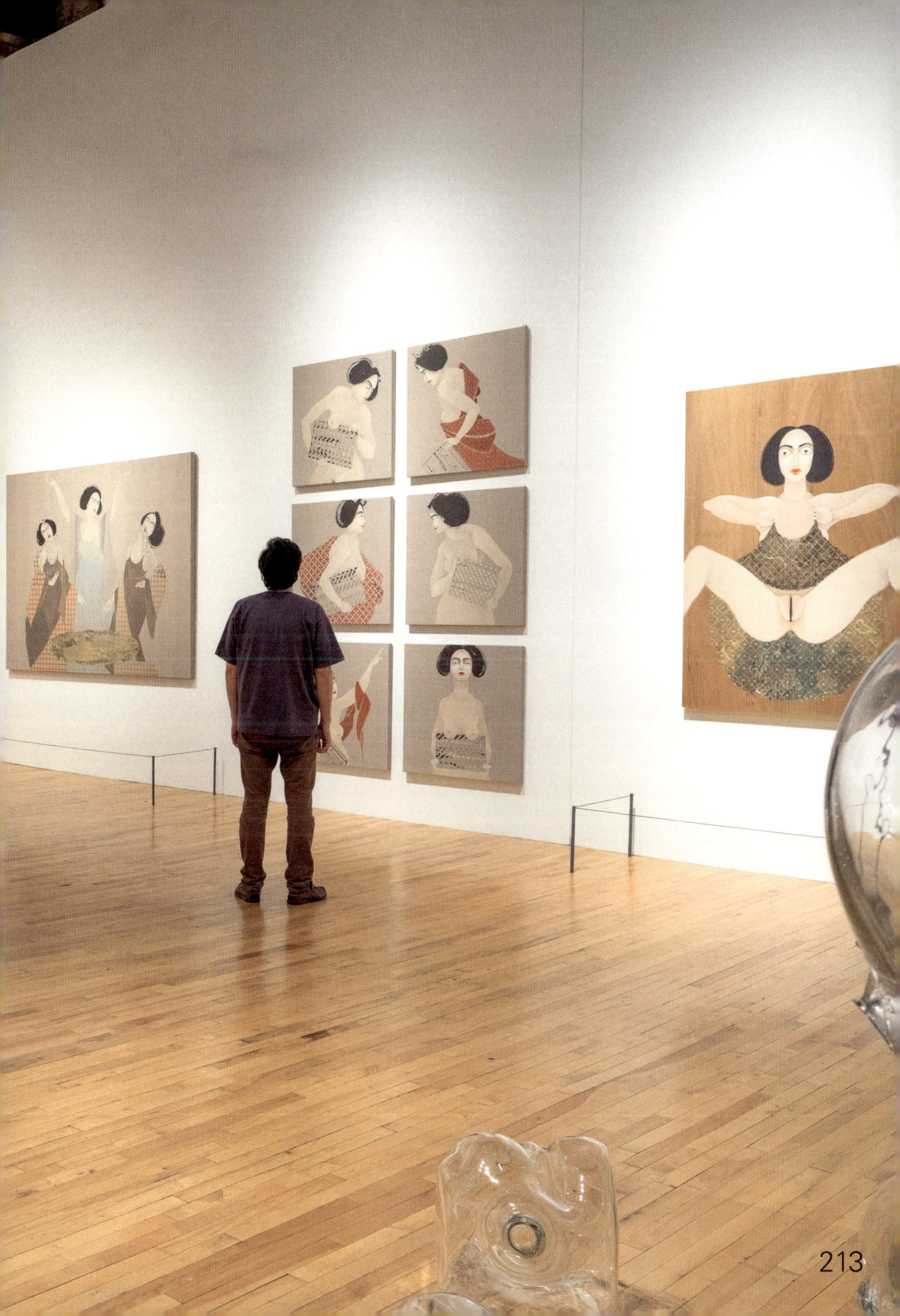

Artist Biographies

Anthony Aziz (b. Lunenburg, MA) and **Sammy Cucher** (b. Lima, Peru) have been living and working together since 1991. They are pioneers in the field of digital imaging and post-photography, using diverse media to explore the issues of our time. The duo has exhibited at the 1995 Venice Biennale (representing Venezuela); the Los Angeles County Museum of Art; the Herzliya Museum of Contemporary Art, Israel; the New Museum of Contemporary Art, New York; the Indianapolis Museum of Art; the Museo Nacional Centro de Arte Reina Sofía, Madrid, Spain; and the San Francisco Museum of Modern Art. They are on the Fine Arts faculty at Parsons School of Design, New York, and are based in Brooklyn, NY.

Cassils (b. Canada; resides in Los Angeles, CA), who was listed by the *Huffington Post* as "one of ten transgender artists who are changing the landscape of contemporary art," has achieved international recognition for a rigorous engagement with the body as a form of social sculpture. Featuring a series of bodies transformed by strict physical training regimes, Cassils's artworks offer shared experiences for contemplating histories of violence, representation, struggle, and survival. Bashing through gendered binaries, Cassils performs transgender not as a crossing from one sex to another, but rather as a continual process of becoming, a form of embodiment that works in a space of indeterminacy, spasm, and slipperiness. It is with sweat, blood, and sinew that Cassils constructs a visual critique around ideologies and histories.

Adriana Corral's installations, performances, and sculptures embody universal themes of loss, human rights violations, memory, and erased historical narratives. Her practice is rigorous and research based, often driving her to work directly within archives. Experts ranging from historians, librarians, anthropologists, writers, journalists, gender scholars, human rights attorneys, and victims' families provide Corral with vital data that aids in the conception of her works. Corral received her MFA from The University of Texas at Austin and completed her BFA at The University of Texas at El Paso. She was invited to attend the 106th session of the Working Group on Enforced and Involuntary Disappearances at the United Nations in Geneva, Switzerland (2015) and was selected for the Joan Mitchell Foundation Emerging Artist Grant (2016). Corral attended the McDowell Residency (2014), Künstlerhaus Bethanien Residency in Berlin, Germany (2016), the International Artist-in-Residence at Artpace (2016), is a fellow at Black Cube, a Nomadic Art Museum (2017), an artist research fellow at the Archives of American Art and History at the Smithsonian Institution (2018), and an Artist-in-Residence at the Joan Mitchell Center (2018).

Joey Fauerso is an artist and associate professor of art at Texas State University. Her work takes the form of painting, drawing, installation, performance, and video, and draws from her children and domestic life as a way to speak to broader collective experiences. Her work has been exhibited nationally and internationally with recent shows at The Drawing Center, New York; Artpace, San Antonio, TX; the David Shelton Gallery, Houston, TX; and the Museo de Arte Moderno, Medellín, Colombia. Fauerso has been the recipient of numerous grants and residencies, including the two-year Open Sessions program at The Drawing Center and a residency at Kunstlerhaus Bethanien, Berlin, in 2017. She lives with her husband, artist Riley Robinson, and their two sons, Brendan and Paul, in San Antonio.

Jeffrey Gibson grew up in the United States, Germany, Korea, and England. A member of the Mississippi Band of Choctaw Indians, he is half Cherokee. This unique combination of global cultural influences converges in his multidisciplinary practice. Gibson's works are in the permanent collections of the Whitney Museum of American Art, New York; the Museum of Fine Arts, Boston, MA; the Smithsonian; the National Gallery of Canada, Ottawa, ON; and Crystal Bridges Museum of American Art, Bentonville, AR. Solo exhibitions include the Denver Art Museum, CO; the Ruth and Elmer Wellin Museum, Clinton, NY; the Savannah College of Art and Design Museum of Art, GA; The Institute of Contemporary Art, Boston, MA; and the Cornell Fine Arts Museum, Winter Park, FL. He lives and works in Hudson, NY.

Hayv Kahraman's work grapples with the concept of migrant consciousness, including memory, gender, and assimilation processes inflicted by the darker side of modernity/coloniality. The body/ies in her paintings are instruments of mediation, in which various attempts to delink from the myths of western modernity are enacted. Solo exhibitions include *Acts of Reparation*, Contemporary Art Museum (CAM), St. Louis, MO; *Hayv Kahraman*, Pomona College of Art Project 52, CA; *Audible Inaudible*, Joslyn Art Museum, Omaha, NE; *Sound Wounds*, Asian Art Museum, San Francisco; *Gendering memories of Iraq: A Collective Performance*, staged in multiple institutions such as Victoria and Albert Museum, London; CAM St, Louis; Birmingham Museum of Art, AL; and The Nelson-Atkins Museum of Art, Kansas City, MO. She lives and works in Los Angeles, CA.

Jennifer Karady works with American veterans returning from Iraq and Afghanistan to create staged narrative photographs that depict their individual stories and reveal their adjustment to civilian life. After an extensive interview process, Karady collaborates with the veteran to restage a chosen moment from war within a safe space, often in their everyday environment, surrounded by family, friends, and community members. Her solo exhibitions include the Palm Springs Art Museum, CA; the University of Michigan, Ann Arbor; CEPA Gallery, Buffalo, NY; Momenta Art, Brooklyn, NY; SF Camerawork, San Francisco; and White Columns, New York. Public collections include San Francisco Museum of Modern Art; the Albright-Knox Art Gallery, Buffalo, NY; Palm Springs Art Museum, CA; Smith College Museum of Art, Northampton, MA; and the Harn Museum of Art, Gainesville, FL. Karady's numerous residencies and awards include the Witt Residency at the University of Michigan, Yaddo, MacDowell, The Headlands, Getty

Creative Images Grant, and grants from the Compton Foundation for courageous storytelling. She lives and works in Brooklyn, NY.

Titus Kaphar explores the history of representation by transforming its styles and mediums with formal innovations that emphasize the physicality and dimensionality of the canvas and materials themselves. Recent awards and recognition include a 2018 MacArthur Fellowship and 2018 Art for Justice Fund Grant; recent solo exhibitions include *Impressions of liberty*, Princeton University, NJ; *Unseen: Our past in a new light*, The National Portrait Gallery, Washington, DC; Titus Kaphar: *Selections from Asphalt and Chalk*, MoMA PS1, Long Island City, NY; and *The Vesper Project*, which traveled throughout the United States, 2013–17. His work is in the collections of The Museum of Modern Art and The Studio Museum in Harlem, both New York; and the Seattle Art Museum, among others. Kaphar resides in New Haven, CT.

Robert Longo makes monumental charcoal drawings that address the psychology and anxiety of what it means to be human. He has had retrospectives at the Hamburger Kunstverein, Berlin, Germany; the Menil Collection, Houston, TX; the Los Angeles County Museum of Art; the Museum of Contemporary Art, Chicago; and the Isetan Museum of Art, Tokyo, Japan. His work has also been exhibited at Documenta 8; the 2004 Whitney Biennial; and the 47th Venice Biennale. Longo resides in New York and is represented by Metro Pictures, New York; Galerie Hans Mayer, Düsseldorf; and Galerie Thaddaeus Ropac, Paris.

Christopher Mir's paintings explore the slippages between consciousness and dream states. Solo exhibitions include RARE Gallery, New York; Galería Senda, Barcelona, Spain; Galerie Schuster, Berlin, Germany; the Wadsworth Atheneum Museum of Art, Hartford, CT; and TMproject, Geneva, Switzerland. Group exhibitions include The Aldrich Contemporary Art Museum, Ridgefield, CT; the deCordova Sculpture Park and Museum, Lincoln, MA; and Bellwether, New York. His work is in the collections of Yale University Art Gallery; Susan and Michael Hort; Jeff Bezos, Beth Rudin DeWoody; Simon Watson; and Pamela Auchincloss. He lives and works in Hamden, CT.

MPA is an artist that currently lives in Twentynine Palms, CA.

Wangechi Mutu uses her training in sculpture and anthropology to draw out contradictions of female and cultural identity, referencing colonialism and cultural trauma, environmental destruction and fashion through a feminist eye. Her recent solo exhibitions include *A Promise to Communicate*, The Institute of Contemporary Art, Boston, MA; *Wangechi Mutu*, Austin Contemporary, TX; *20 Years / 20 Shows: Wangechi Mutu*, SITE Santa Fe, NM; Musée D'art Contemporain de Montréal, Canada; the Museum of Contemporary Art, Sydney, Australia; and *A Fantastic Journey*, Nasher Museum of Art at Duke University, Durham, NC, which traveled to Brooklyn Museum of Art, NY, among others. In 2017, she was part of *Performa17*. Mutu, who works between New York and Nairobi, Kenya, is represented by Gladstone Gallery, New York; Susanne Vielmetter, Los Angeles; and Victoria Miro, London.

Allison Schulnik uses painting, ceramics, and handmade traditional animation to choreograph her subjects in compositions that embody a spirit of the macabre, a Shakespearean comedy/tragedy of love, death, and farce. Her works were compared to "the comic-grotesque visionary James Ensor" by *The New York Times*. Solo exhibitions include the Wadsworth Atheneum Museum of Art, Hartford, CT; Laguna Art Museum, Laguna Beach, CA; Oklahoma City Museum of Art; Nerman Museum of Contemporary Art, Overland Park, KS; ZieherSmith, New York; and Galería Javier López & Fer Francés, Madrid, Spain. Schulnik has been making animated films since she was seventeen; they have been included in internationally renowned festivals and museums, including the Hammer Museum, Los Angeles; Los Angeles County Museum of Art; Annecy International Animated Film Festival, France; and Animafest Zagreb, Croatia. She received "Best Experimental Animation" at the Ottawa International Animation Festival and Special Jury Prize at SXSW Film, Austin, TX. Schulnik's work is in the permanent collections of over a dozen institutions, including Los Angeles County Museum of Art and Museum des Beaux Arts, Montreal, Canada. She lives and works in Sky Valley, CA.

Keith Sklar's drawings and paintings are densely packed with cultural references, absurdist humor, and pathos. His works have been shown at the Los Angeles County Museum of Art; San Francisco Museum of Modern Art; and Scottsdale Museum of Contemporary Art, AZ. Solo exhibitions include P·P·O·W, New York; Rosamund Felsen Gallery, Santa Monica, CA; and Dorsch Gallery, Miami, FL. Sklar has received a Robert Rauschenberg Foundation Residency, a California Arts Council Fellowship in Visual Arts, and multiple Artist-in-Communities Grants. An artist and art educator, he lives and works in Chicago, IL.

Robert Taplin's sculptures in the series *History of Punch* track the intersection of alienation and creativity by setting the ancient trickster figure of Punch loose in our contemporary world. Solo exhibitions include the Pennsylvania Academy of the Fine Arts, Philadelphia; Grounds For Sculpture, Hamilton, NJ; The Aldrich Contemporary Art Museum, Ridgefield, CT; the Zilkha Gallery, Wesleyan University, Middletown, CT; Smack Mellon, Brooklyn, NY; the Salt Lake Art Center, UT; and Winston Wachter Fine Art, New York. Taplin has made commissions for the New York Metropolitan Transportation Authority and the State of Connecticut, and received grants from the John Simon Guggenheim Foundation, the National Endowment for the Arts, and the Connecticut Commission on the Arts. He lives and works near New Haven, CT, and is represented by Winston Wachter Fine Art, New York.

Vincent Valdez is recognized for his monumental portrayals of the contemporary figure. His drawn and painted subjects remark on a universal struggle within various socio-political arenas and eras. He states, "My aim is to incite public remembrance and to impede distorted realities that I witness, like the social amnesia that surrounds me." Born in 1977 in San Antonio, TX, Valdez received a full scholarship to study at the Rhode Island School of Design and earned his BFA in 2000. A recipient of the Joan Mitchell Foundation Grant for Painters and Sculptors (2016), as well as residencies at the Skowhegan School of Painting (2005), the Vermont Studio Center (2011), and the Kunstlerhaus Bethania Berlin Residency (2014), Valdez currently lives and works in Houston, TX. Exhibitions and collections include: The Ford Foundation, New York; Los Angeles County Museum of Art; the Blanton Museum of Art, Austin, TX; The Museum of Fine Arts, Houston; the Smithsonian Museum of American Art and the National Portrait Gallery, Washington, DC; among others. He is represented by David Shelton Gallery, Houston, and Matthew Brown Gallery, Los Angeles, CA.

Writer Biographies

Jesse Ball is an American novelist and poet. His works are distinguished by the use of a spare style and have been compared to those of Jorge Luis Borges and Italo Calvino. He won the 2008 Plimpton Prize and was longlisted for the National Book Award. He has been a fellow of the NEA, Creative Capital, and Guggenheim Foundation. His novels include *Samedi the Deafness* (2007); *The Way Through Doors* (2009); *The Curfew* (2011); *Silence Once Begun* (2014); *A Cure for Suicide* (2015); *How to Set a Fire and Why* (2016); and *Census* (2018). Ball is based in Chicago and on the faculty at the School of the Art Institute of Chicago.

Andy Campbell is an assistant professor of Critical Studies at the USC-Roski School of Art and Design. He is the author of two forthcoming books, *Queer X Design: 50 Years of Signs, Symbols, Banners, Logos and Graphic Art of LGBTQ* (Black Dog and Leventhal) and *Bound Together: Leather, Sex, Archives, and Contemporary Art* (Manchester University Press). As a working critic, his writing has appeared in *Artforum*, *Aperture*, *GLQ*, *caa.reviews*, *Art Papers*, and others. Born and raised in Austin, TX, he now lives in Los Angeles, CA.

Gonzalo Casals explores cultural production as a vehicle to foster empowerment, social capital, civic participation, and community development. He has worked at El Museo del Barrio, Friends of The High Line, and now at the Leslie-Lohman Museum for Gay and Lesbian Art, exemplifying a generation of cultural workers who are redefining the civic role of cultural organizations and their relationship with communities, neighborhoods, and cities.

Adam Curtis is a British documentary filmmaker whose works explore areas of sociology, psychology, philosophy, and political history. His films include *The Cost of Treachery* (1984); *The Century of the Self* (2002); *Bitter Lake* (2015); and *HyperNormalisation* (2016).

Aruna D'Souza writes about modern and contemporary art, intersectional feminisms and other forms of politics, and how museums shape our views of each other and the world. Her work appears regularly in 4Columns.org and has been published in *The Wall Street Journal*, *CNN.com*, *Art News*, *Garage*, *Bookforum*, *Momus*, *Art in America*, and *Art Practical*, among others. Her book, *Whitewalling: Art, Race, and Protest in 3 Acts*, was published in 2018.

Catherine Gund, the founder and director of Aubin Pictures, is an Emmy-nominated producer, director, writer, and activist. Her work focuses on strategic and sustainable social transformation, arts and culture, HIV/AIDS and reproductive health, and the environment. Her films include *Chavela*; *Dispatches From Cleveland*; *American Rhapsody* (in progress); *Born to Fly: Elizabeth Streb vs. Gravity*; *What's On Your Plate?*; *A Touch of Greatness; Motherland Afghanistan*; *Making Grace*; *On Hostile Ground*; and *Hallelujah! Ron Athey: A Story of Deliverance*.

Denise Markonish is the senior curator and managing director of exhibitions at MASS MoCA. Her exhibitions include *Trenton Doyle Hancock, Mind of the Mound: Critical Mass*; *Nick Cave: Until*; *Explode Every Day: An Inquiry into the Phenomena of Wonder*; *Teresita Fernández: As Above So Below*; *Oh, Canada*; *Nari Ward: Sub Mirage Lignum*; *These Days: Elegies for Modern Times*; and *Badlands: New Horizons in Landscape*. She edited the books *Teresita Fernández: Wayfinding* (DelMonico/Prestel) and *Wonder: 50 Years of RISD Glass*, and co-edited *Sol LeWitt: 100 Views* (Yale University Press). Markonish has taught at Williams College and the Rhode Island School of Design.

Fred Moten is the author of *In the Break: The Aesthetics of the Black Radical Tradition* (2003); *Hughson's Tavern* (2009); *The Feel Trio* (2014), a poetry finalist for the National Book Award and Los Angeles Times Book Prize and winner of the California Book Award for poetry; *The Little Edges* (2015), a finalist for the Kingsley Tufts Poetry Award; *A Poetics of the Undercommons* (2016); and a three-volume collection of essays, *consent not to be a single being* (2017–18). Moten is co-author, with Stefano Harney, of *The Undercommons: Fugitive Planning and Black Study* (2013). In 2016 he was awarded a Guggenheim Fellowship and the Stephen E. Henderson Award for Outstanding Achievement in Poetry by the African American Literature and Culture Society.

Rebecca Rickman is an independent producer who conceives programs and events for a wide variety of cultural institutions in the United States and Europe. Trained as a classical musician, she worked for the Los Angeles Philharmonic, the Netherlands Opera, and the Institute of Contemporary Art in Boston. Based in Los Angeles, she has most recently produced a trilogy of large-scale multidisciplinary programs for the Library Foundation of Los Angeles and the Los Angeles Public Library that viewed classic texts (*Moby-Dick*, the *Odyssey*, and the *Oxford English Dictionary*) through a contemporary Southern California lens. Under the rubric of "Ideamachine," she also programs conferences, lectures, and multi-media performance events and writes catalogue essays and exhibition labels.

Elaine Scarry is an American essayist and professor of English and American Literature and Language at Harvard University. Her books include *Naming Thy Name* (2016); *Thermonuclear Monarchy* (2014); *Thinking in an Emergency* (2011); *On Beauty and Being Just* (1999); *The Body in Pain* (1985, a National Book Critics Circle Award Finalist); and others. She has appeared on the Anderson Cooper 360° Radio Program, the Today Show, NPR, and Fox News, among others. She is the winner of the 2000 Truman Capote Award, and, in 2005, *Foreign Policy* and *Prospect* magazine named her one of the world's one hundred leading intellectuals.

Solmaz Sharif was born in Istanbul to Iranian parents and is a poet whose work has appeared in *The New Republic, Poetry, The Kenyon Review*, and *Granta*. The work of Sharif, the former managing director of the Asian American Writers' Workshop, has been recognized with a "Discovery"/ *Boston Review* Poetry Prize, Rona Jaffe Foundation Writers' Award, and an NEA fellowship. She recently received a 2016 Lannan Literary Fellowship and the Holmes National Poetry Prize from Princeton University. A former Stegner Fellow, she is currently a lecturer at Stanford University. Her first poetry collection, *LOOK*, published by Graywolf Press in 2016, was a finalist for the National Book Award.

Michael Weber is a magician, mentalist, and inventor. Weber and his co-conspirator Ricky Jay founded the consulting company Deceptive Practices, which provides "Arcane Knowledge On a Need-To-Know Basis" to film, theater, and television. He has worked with writers and directors ranging from Errol Morris, Wes Craven, and Martin Scorsese to George Wolfe, David Mamet, and Robert Zemeckis. Examples of Weber's work can be seen in dozens of plays and feature films, including *Forest Gump, Angels in America, The Parent Trap, The Illusionist, Top Dog Underdog, The Prestige, The Year of Magical Thinking*, and *Ocean's 13*.

Saul Williams is an American rapper, singer-songwriter, musician, slam poet, writer, and actor. His work has been published in *The New York Times, Esquire, Bomb Magazine*, and *African Voices*, and he has released collections of poetry including *She* (1999); *Said the Shotgun to the Head* (2003); *The Dead Emcee Scrolls* (2006); and *US (a.)* (2015). His debut album, *Amethyst Rock Star*, released in 2001, was executive produced by Rick Rubin. Other releases include *Saul Williams* (2004); *The Inevitable Rise and Liberation of Niggy Tardust* (2007); *Volcanic Sunlight* (2011); and *MartyrLoserKing* (2016). Williams has performed in over thirty countries and read in over three hundred universities, with invitations that have spanned the White House, Sydney Opera House, Lincoln Center, the Louvre, the Getty Center, Queen Elizabeth Hall, and countless villages, townships, community centers, and prisons across the world.

Exhibition Checklist

All dimensions h x w x d unless otherwise noted

Aziz + Cucher
You're Welcome, and I'm Sorry, 2019
HD multi-channel video installation with sound, dimensions variable
Courtesy of Gazelli Art House, London

Choreography consultant: Asli Bulbul
Performers: Asli Bulbul, Pedro Osorio, Kayvon Pourazar, Sophie Bortolussi, Diana Lopez, Mickey Mahar, Darrin Wright
Costumes: Beto Guedes
Videography: James Pickett, Brigitte Lustenberger
Additional videography: Dana Melaver, Kendall Finley-Jacob, Meagan Sundlie
Sound design/composition: Jonathan Zalben
3D graphic assistance: Nicholas Herrera
2D graphic assistance: Isobel Chiang & Xingman Cheng

Made possible with generous support from Alida and Christopher Latham, Gazelli Art House, London, Parsons School of Design, New York
Special thanks to Carin Kuoni, Daniel Greenfield-Campoverde, and The New School

Cassils
Inextinguishable Fire, 2015
Single channel video with sound
Total running time: 14 minutes
Performance & Director: Cassils
Producer: Nicole Ettinger
First assistant director: Buzz Hughes
Set PAs: Cristy Michel & Robbie Ettinger
Production coordinator: Valeria Lopez
Craft services: Cristy Michel
Director of photography: Alison Kelly
First assistant camera: Ryan Guzdzial
Second assistant camera: Will Zignego
Phantom tech: Enrique del Rio
Set photographers: Graham Tallman & Clover Leary
Stunt coordinator: Mark Chadwick
Safeties: Jim Churchman & Ben Hoffman
Pyrotechnician: Frank Ceglia
Key grip: Athit Naik
Dolly grip: Nick Bodkin
Grip/electric: Sam Philips & Preston Wood
Sound mixer: A. Tad Chamberlain
Boom operator: John Carchietta
Sound designer (post): Kadet Kuhne
Editor (post): Nick Tamburri
Gaffer: Dean Hayasaka
Costume designer: Franc Fernandez
Transport: Kandoo Films
Set medic: Set Medics LA
Fire safety officer: Los Angeles County Fire Department
Supported by Canada Council for the Arts and MU Eindhoven

Fourteen Encapsulated Breaths, 2017
Hand-blown glass, each unique
Various sizes, approx. 4 to 16 in.
Courtesy of the artist and Ronald Feldman Gallery, New York

Adriana Corral
Requiem, 2019
Site-specific installation, dates hand-carved into drywall
Dimensions variable
Courtesy of the artist

Joey Fauerso
You Destroy Every Special Thing I Make, 2017–19
Wood, canvas, video
Dimensions variable
Courtesy of the artist and David Shelton Gallery, Houston, TX

Jeffrey Gibson
Clown Witness, 2018
Polyester organza, glass beads, printed polyester, printed cotton, canvas, nylon, tipi poles, deer hide
80 x 85 x 25 in.; tipi pole 125 in.

PEOPLE LIKE US, 2018
Vinyl, neoprene, printed polyester, glass beads, brass grommets, nylon, printed cotton, acrylic paint, tipi poles, deer hide
100 x 67 x 15 in.; tipi pole 125 in.

Speak to Me So That I Can Understand, 2018
Acrylic paint, canvas, vintage Seminole patchwork, plastic beads, glass beads, nylon, printed polyester, metal jingles, tipi poles, deer hide
85 x 70 x 15 in.; tipi pole 130 in.
Courtesy of the artist

Hayv Kahraman
Pussy Gold, 2018
Oil on wood
72 x 48 in.
Collection of Dalal Ani Arnold and Zack Arnold, New York

The Appeal, 2018
Oil on linen
6 canvases, 35 x 35 in. each
Courtesy of the artist, Vielmetter Los Angeles, Jack Shainman Gallery, NY, and Third Line Gallery, Dubai

Three Celebrities, 2018
Oil on linen
72 x 96 in.
Collection of Carol and David Kaplan, Los Angeles, CA

Titus Kaphar
A Pillow for Fragile Fictions, 2016
Blown glass with molasses, rum, lime, tamarind on a marble base
Glass 19.5 x 28 x 19 in.; pillow 6 x 37 x 32.5 in.
Collection of Alexandra and Ted Shor, Hamden, CT

Language of the Forgotten, 2018
Charred white oak, high-density urethane, glass, and LED lights
90 x 68 x 52 in.

Monumental Inversion: George Washington, 2016
Blown glass, wood, and steel
99.25 x 88.75 x 32 in.
Edition 1 of 3
Courtesy of the artist

Seeing Through Time 2, 2018
72 x 92 x 1.5 in.
Oil on canvas
Collection of Reginald and Aliya Brown, Newtown, PA

Seeing Through Time 3, 2019
Oil on canvas
60 x 48 x 1.5 in.
Collection of Ellen and Steve Susman, Houston, TX

Jennifer Karady
Former Staff Sergeant Andrew Davis, 75th Ranger Regiment, U.S. Army, veteran of Operation Iraqi Freedom and Operation Enduring Freedom, with wife, Jodie, and Iraq war veterans and friends Tom and Andy; Saratoga Springs, NY

Former Specialist Shelby Webster, 24th Transportation Company, 541st Maintenance Battalion, U.S. Army, veteran of Operation Iraqi Freedom, with children, Riley, Dillin and Sidnie, brother Delshay, and uncle Derek; Omaha Nation Reservation, NE

Former Specialist Brittny Gillespie, 139th Military Police Company, 16th MP Brigade, U.S. Army, veteran of Operation Iraqi Freedom, with Volunteers of America-Los Angeles Battle Buddy Elizabeth Saucedo and friend Corey; Los Angeles, CA

Staff Sergeant Kyle Winjum, Explosive Ordnance Disposal

Technician, U.S. Marine Corps, veteran of Operation Enduring Freedom and Operation Iraqi Freedom, with fellow Marines; Twentynine Palms, CA

Former Lance Corporal West Chase, U.S. Marine Corps, Combat Service Support Company 113, I Marine Expeditionary Force, veteran of Operation Iraqi Freedom and Operation Enduring Freedom, with fiancée, Emily Peden; Ann Arbor, MI

Former Specialist Lucero Morales, 25th Transportation Company, 25th Infantry Division, U.S. Army, veteran of Operation Iraqi Freedom, with children Emma and Nicolas; Azusa, CA

Chromogenic color prints on Fujiflex mounted on Plexiglas
50 x 50 x 2 in.

Courtesy of the artist

Robert Longo
Untitled (St. Louis Rams / Hands Up), 2016
Charcoal on mounted paper
66 x 121 x 4 in.

Untitled (Destroyed Head of Lamassu, Nineveh), 2016
Charcoal on mounted paper
93.75 x 145.25 x 5.125 in.

Untitled (Vietnam, 1968), 2017
Charcoal on mounted paper
87.125 x 127.125 x 4 in.

Untitled (Nathan Bedford Forrest Statue Removal: Memphis, 2017), 2018
Charcoal on mounted paper
77.125 x 124.125 in.

Courtesy of the artist and Metro Pictures, New York

Chris Mir
Broken Model
Candle
Disco Grid
Fight
Flowers
Ghost Ship
Short History of the Shadow
Teeth
All acrylic on canvas, 2018
60 x 53 in.

Courtesy of the artist

MPA
1, 2, 3, For, 2019
Installation between four walls

Copper Conductor with Brad Dilger
Wood, plastic, metal, copper, motors

1
Latex paint, plaster wall pieces, lapis lazuli

2: Alpha and Omega
Tutu, aluminum satellite dishes, latex paint, powdered pigment

3: Meeting of Sword and Wand
Latex paint, mesquite wood, steel, tape, sequins, lapis lazuli

Center
Ammonolite

Courtesy of the artist

Wangechi Mutu
Mwotaji The Dreamer, 2016
Polished bronze, hand-carved Carrara marble, steel base
Bronze head: 10 x 13 x 5.5 in.
Stone base: 19.75 x 15.75 x 3 in.
Steel base: 38 x 19.75 x 15.75 in.
Co-published by Carolina Nitsch + Elisabeth Ross Wingate
Courtesy of the artist

Mary & Magda, 2018
Variegated leather (pigskin), dyed and painted by hand, hand stitched and assembled with cotton thread, synthetic fiber fill, and sand weights, in two parts; on welded steel bed with blackened wax finish

Each 45 in. length, 18–36 in. circumference
Steel bed: 60 x 38 x 18 in.
Edition of 5 variants, with 3 AP
Co-published by Carolina Nitsch + Elisabeth Ross Wingate
Courtesy of the artist and Carolina Nitsch + Elisabeth Ross Wingate.

One Cut, 2018
Bronze
24 x 15 x 4 in.
Courtesy of the artist and Gladstone Gallery, New York, and Brussels

Allison Schulnik
Moth, 2019
Gouache on paper, hand-painted, animated video
Running time: 4 minutes
Courtesy of the artist

Keith Sklar
Inversion, 2015
Digital print on paper
Edition 1 of 5
72 x 48 in.

All the Answers I Could Ever Know, 2019
Oil on canvas
30 x 24 in.

Blunderbuss, 2019
Oil on canvas
16 x 20 in.

Core Value, 2019
Oil on canvas
28 x 22 in.

Declaration, 2019
Oil on canvas
22 x 28 in.

Feat, 2019
Oil on canvas
40 x 30 in.

Gilt, 2019
Oil on canvas and mixed media
50 x 39 x 5 in.

Pool, 2019
Oil on canvas
24 x 36 in.

Sitting Down for a Drink with my Shadow, 2019
Mixed media installation
Dimensions variable

So Fa, 2019
Oil on canvas
121 x 66 in.

Stand, 2019
Oil on canvas
24 x 30 in.

Swell, 2019
Oil on canvas
28 x 34.5 in.

Courtesy of the artist

Robert Taplin
Punch Stopped at the Border, 2005 (enlarged 2019)
Cast resin
33 x 42 x 36 in.

Punch Makes a Public Confession, 2012 (enlarged 2014)
Milled foam, wood, gypsum, steel
106.5 x 64 x 44.5 in.

Punch Does a Magic Trick, 2010 (enlarged 2018)
Cast resin
32 x 48 x 23.5 in.

Young Punch Scratches His Burro's Ears, 2007 (enlarged 2018)
Cast resin
26.5 x 25 x 12 in.

Courtesy of the artist

Vincent Valdez
Dream Baby Dream (1–12), 2018
Oil on paper
42 x 72 in. each
Courtesy of the artist and David Shelton Gallery, Houston, TX
Number 3 in the collection of Ellen Sussman, Houston, TX

Vincent Valdez & Adriana Corral
Requiem, 2016–19
42 x 60 x 24 in.
Bronze and ash
Courtesy of the artists and David Shelton Gallery, Houston, TX

Acknowledgments

Thank you to MASS MoCA's unflappable, unparalleled visual arts team (Richard Criddle, Chris Nelson, Megan Tamás, Tavish Costello, Dig Divine, Anna Rafalowiski, Brian Weisz, Caitlin Tucker-Melvin, Brad Dilger, Allie Foradas, and Kathryn Pruett)—you truly make the dreams of artists and curators come true and everything that ends up in our galleries bears your proud stamp upon it; director Joe Thompson, for believing in the power of what art can do for society; the performing arts team, for always being great co-conspirators (Sue Killam, Addie MacDonald, Matt Palmieri, Meghan Labbee, John Tibbetts, Taylor Doyle, Rachel Chanoff, Olli Chanoff, and Diane Eber); our crack marketing team (Jodi Joseph, Hannah Fiske, Patrick Fecher, and Kaelan Burkett); our dedicated graphic designers (Jenny Wright, Taylor Smaldone, and Amy Chen); our amazing education team (Laura Thompson, Amanda Tobin, and Emily Ross); our buildings and grounds crew, for making everything look so good (Joe Bordeau, Mike Kurpiel, and Dave Tatro); and our interns Mary-Elisabeth Moore and Lindsey Howard.

Many thanks to those who made this book possible: Brett Yasko for his always stellar design; L. Jane Calverley and Paulette Wein for their copy editing and proofreading skills; the team at Prestel (Mary DelMonico, Karen Farquhar, and Katie Hands); the contributors: Solmaz Sharif, Saul Williams, Andy Campbell, Rebecca Rickman, Jesse Ball, Fred Moten, Adam Curtis, Aruna D'Souza, Gonzalo Casals, Michael Weber, Cat Gund, and Elaine Scarry; and the following individuals, for making connections: Glenn Kaino, Matthew Spellberg, Teresita Fernández, Lily Cox-Richard, Sanford Biggers, Lars Jan, Margaret Wertheim, Jen Bervin, and Laurie Anderson. Special thanks to the Metabolic Studio (especially Lauren Bon, Tristan Duke, and Rich Nielson) for giving me the space and inspiration to write.

Thank you to the lenders to the exhibition—the artists, Carol and David Kaplan, Dalal Ani and Zack Arnold, Alexandra and Ted Shor, Reginald and Aliya Brown, Ronald Feldman Gallery, David Shelton Gallery, Susanne Vielmetter Gallery, Metro Pictures Gallery, Carolina Nitsch+Elisabeth Ross Wingate, and Gladstone Gallery. And, of course, we express our sincere appreciation to the funders, with principal exhibition support provided by the Artist's Resource Trust, a fund of the Berkshire Taconic Community Foundation; lead support from Christopher and Alida Latham; contributing support from Bridget Rigas; and additional support from Caroline Cunningham and Donald Young. Generous funding for the exhibition catalog comes from the Elizabeth Firestone Graham Foundation. All programming at MASS MoCA is made possible in part by the Barr Foundation, Horace W. Goldsmith Foundation, and Mass Cultural Council.

Lastly, my thanks to the sixteen artists whose work is on view in this exhibition for a year's worth of conversations about what art can accomplish in our fraught political climate. It has been inspiring to build this show with all of you—and it gives me hope.

For Murray.

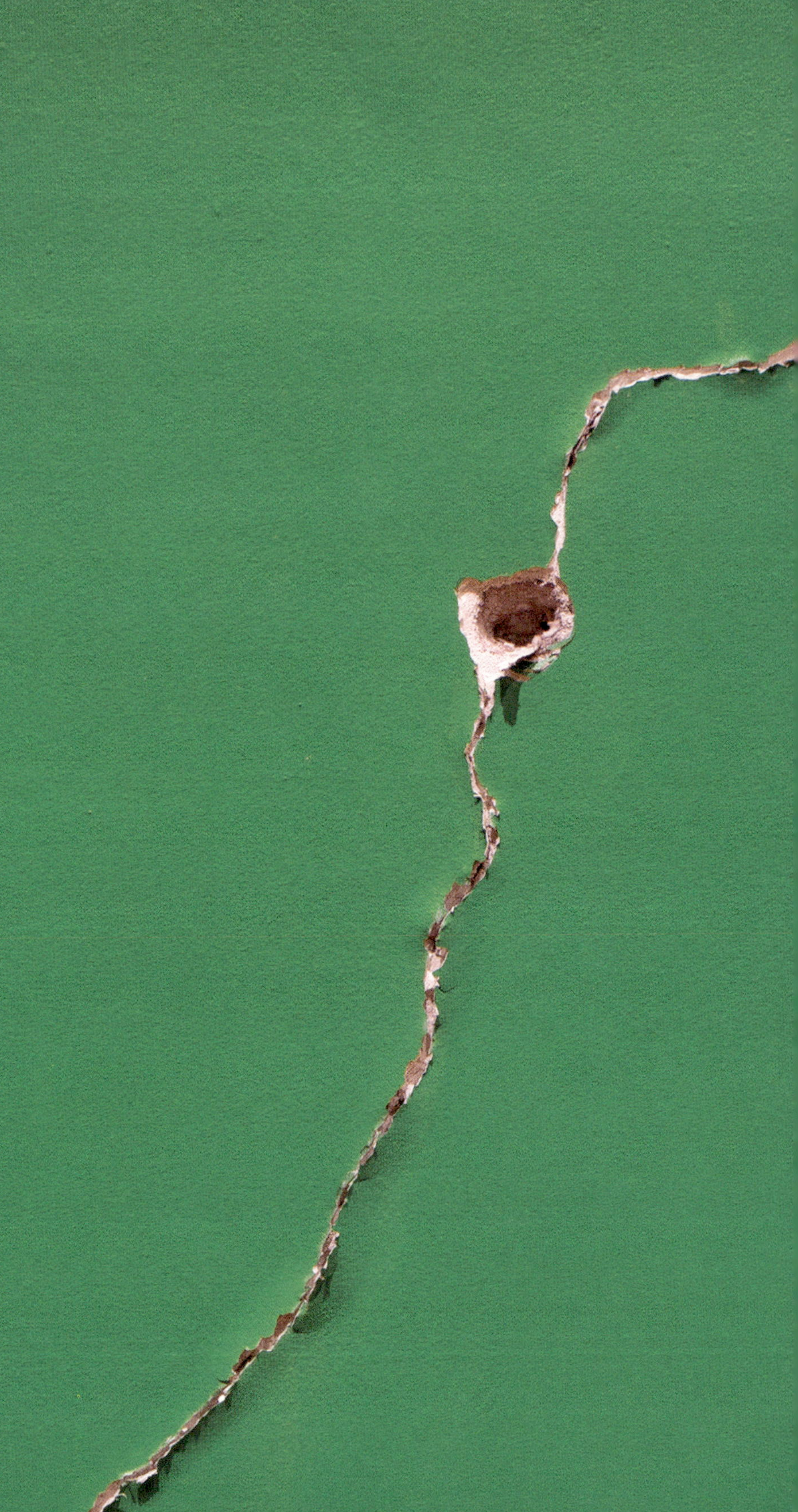

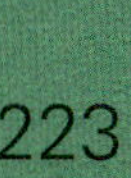
223

Published on the occasion of
Suffering from Realness
Curated by Denise Markonish
April 13, 2019–February 2, 2020

MASS MoCA
1040 MASS MoCA Way
North Adams, MA 01247
413.662.2111
massmoca.org

Principal exhibition support is provided by the Artist's Resource Trust (A.R.T.) Fund, a fund of Berkshire Taconic Community Foundation, with lead support from Christopher and Alida Latham, contributing support from Bridget Rigas, and additional support from Caroline Cunningham and Donald Young. Generous funding for the exhibition catalog comes from the Elizabeth Firestone Graham Foundation. Programming at MASS MoCA is made possible in part by the Barr Foundation, Horace W. Goldsmith Foundation, and Mass Cultural Council.

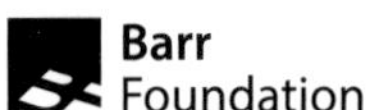

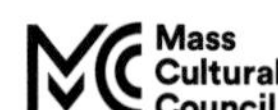

Published by MASS MoCA
and DelMonico Books • Prestel

DelMonico Books, an imprint of Prestel Publishing, a member of Verlagsgruppe Random House GmbH

Prestel Verlag
Neumarkter Strasse 28
81673 Munich

Prestel Publishing Ltd.
14-17 Wells Street
London W1T 3PD

Prestel Publishing
900 Broadway, Suite 603
New York, NY 10003

prestel.com

Editor: Denise Markonish

Copy editing: L. Jane Calverley
Proofreading: Paulette Wein

Installation photography:
Kaelan Burkett, Davis Dashiell

Design: Brett Yasko

Printed and bound in Turkey
by Ofset Yapımevi

ISBN 978-3-7913-5819-2

Library of Congress Control Number: 2019930166
A CIP catalogue record for this book is available from the British Library.

Cover: Vincent Valdez, *Requiem I*, 2014 oil on canvas 136 x 85 in. Courtesy of the artist and David Shelton Gallery, Houston, TX

pp. 222–3: MPA, *1, 2, 3, For*, 2019 (detail)

Photo Credits: pp. 2–3; 50–1; 80–1; 90–1; 108–9; 112–13; 122-23; 194–9; 212–4 photos: Kaelan Burkett; p. 10 photo: Denise Markonish; p. 16 Grosz: Photolithograph. Composition (irreg.): 11.5625 x 17 in.; sheet 15.4375 x 19 in. Publisher: Malik-Verlag, Berlin. Printer: Hermann Birkholz, Berlin. Edition: 125 (Edition A: 20 signed, on Strathmore "japan" paper, issued in half-parchment bound portfolio, numbered 1–20; Edition B: 40, signed, on heavy Bütten paper, issued in half-silk bound portfolio, numbered 21–60; Edition C: 65 on lighter Bütten paper, issued in half-linen bound portfolio, numbered 61–125 [this ex.] Abby Aldrich Rockefeller Fund The Museum of Modern Art, New York, NY, U.S.A. © 2019 Estate of George Grosz / Licensed by VAGA and Artist Rights Society (ARS), NY Digital Image © The Museum of Modern Art / Licensed by SCALA / Art Resource, NY; Dix: Etching. Sheet 12, Inv. Karsch 81. © 2019 Artists Rights Society (ARS), New York / VG Bild-Kunst, Bonn photo: bpk Bildagentur / Kupferstichkabinett, Berlin / Jörg P. Anders / Art Resource, NY; Kollowitz: Abby Aldrich Rockefeller Fund. (1655.1940.4), The Museum of Modern Art, Digital Image © The Museum of Modern Art / Licensed by Scala / Art Resource, NY; p. 17 Golub: Presented by the American Fund for the Tate Gallery, courtesy of Ulrich and Harriet Meyer (Building the Tate Collection) 2012 © 2019 The Nancy Spero and Leon Golub Foundation for the Arts / Licensed by VAGA at Artists Rights Society (ARS), NY, © Tate, London 2019; Spero: Institute for Contemporary Art, Boston, Gift of Barbara Lee Collection of Art by Women. Licensed by VAGA, New York © 2019 The Nancy Spero and Leon Golub Foundation for the Arts; p. 18 Art Gallery of South Australia; p. 23 Brancusi: Bronze, 6.30 x 9.84 x 7.09 in. Inv. AM 1374S. Musée National d'Art Moderne, Paris, photo: Adam Rzepka, © Succession Brancusi–All rights reserved (ARS) 2019, © CNAC/MNSAM/Dist. RMN-Grand Palais / Art Resource, NY; p. 28 photo: Eileen Travell. © Metropolitan Museum of Art, New York; p. 29 Permanent Collection, Blanton Museum of Art, University of Texas at Austin; p. 30 photo courtesy of Adriana Corral and Black Cube; p. 33 Fauerso: Courtesy of the artist and David Shelton Gallery, Schulnik photo: Robert Wedemeyer, Goya: Museo del Prado, Madrid; p. 40 Image courtesy of SPARC Archives sparcinla.org; p. 43 © Zoe Leonard Courtesy the artist, Galerie Gisela Capitain, Cologne and Hauser & Wirth; p. 45 Stiftung Bauhaus Dessau (I 677 G) / © (Brandt, Marianne (geb. Liebe)) VG Bild-Kunst, Bonn [Jahr]; p. 46 installation photo: EPW Studio/ Maris Hutchinson, © Felix Gonzalez-Torres, Courtesy of The Felix Gonzalez-Torres Foundation; pp. 56–7 Courtesy the artist and Ronald Feldman Gallery, New York, photo: Cassils and Robin Black; pp. 58–60 Installation shots from the exhibition *Solutions*, Station Museum of Contemporary Art, Houston, TX, photo: Alejandro Santiago, Image courtesy of the artist and Ronald Feldman Gallery; pp. 68–9 photos: David Regen; pp. 114–5 photos: Peter Molick courtesy of David Shelton Gallery; pp. 120–1 Peter Molick; p. 133 Billy Simms; pp. 142–3; 145; 146–7 photos: Jeff McLane; pp. 162; 166–7 photos: Jason Reed; pp. 172–3; 174–5 photos: Lane Cameron. MASS MoCA installation photos: pp. 72–7; 82–3; 118–21; 163–5; 172–3, 222–3 photos: Davis Dashiell.